Story of My Life
Philip Meadows Taylor

INTRODUCTION BY DENNIS WALDER

CW01507076

PLUTO PRESS

First published 1878 by William Blackwood & Sons
This edition published 1989 by Zwan Publications
11-21 Northdown Street, London N1 9BN

Introduction copyright © Dennis Walder 1989

Printed and bound in the United Kingdom by
Billing & Sons Ltd, Worcester

British Library Cataloguing in Publication Data

Taylor, Philip Meadows
  Story of my life.
  1. Taylor, Philip Meadows   Biography
  2. Authors, English   19th century   Biography
  I. Title   II. Taylor, A.M.
  954.03'1'0924   PR5549.T36Z/

  ISBN 1-85305-090-3

Story of My Life

INTRODUCTION

DENNIS WALDER

In 1839 a young English officer on his first home leave from India suddenly found himself famous. His first novel, *Confessions of a Thug*, an account of the life of an Indian 'thug' or strangler, had just been published, and it was an immediate success. Even before its appearance, the young Queen Victoria had directed publisher Richard Bentley to send sheets to her as they were revised by the author. Within months of publication a second edition was called for. Flattering reviews were followed by a commission to write another novel as the forerunner of a series of works on Indian subjects. Literary London, in particular Lady Blessington's circle at Gore House (which included Louis Napoleon, Count D'Orsay, Daniel Maclise, Bulwer Lytton and Charles Dickens), opened its arms to the unknown writer. Lady Morgan, he later recalled in his autobiography, 'was insatiable about Indian stories, and I had to invent or improvise when memory failed me' (p. 110). Yet, as *The Story of My Life* also reveals, nobody could have been more concerned to provide the plain truth about the country and the people he loved, nor was there anyone quite so well suited in personality and circumstance to do so, than Philip Meadows Taylor.

Philip Meadows Taylor (1808–76) is best known to posterity, in so far as he is known at all, as the author of *Confessions of a Thug*, which established his reputation as a writer with unique insight into the life and culture of the peoples of India. Despite its sensational subject matter – the life story of a devotee of the hereditary cult of strangler–robbers which had preyed upon travellers all over India for generations, supposedly under the patronage of the Hindu goddess Kali – the *Confessions* was a sober, largely factual and at times sympathetic account, 'not published to gratify a morbid taste in any one for tales of horror and of crime', as the author insisted in the Introduction, but to make the public 'more conversant with the subject' and help stamp out the thugs. This twin motive, to inform the audience at home and to make it more aware of its responsibilities towards the 'improvement' of Indian society, runs throughout Meadows Taylor's work, which may fairly be said to reveal just how humane and enlightened Imperial rule could sometimes be, and so often was not. One of the last of the simple adventurers to go out to India, Meadows Taylor was unusual, too, in being employed neither by the Crown nor the East

India Company, but by a 'native prince', the Nizam of Hyderabad. This impaired his chances of promotion and distinction, but it enabled him to gain an intimate understanding of the impact upon the local population of British rule, and the feelings of the Indians themselves. Indeed, it will be no surprise to the reader of this autobiography to learn that since his death his memory has been kept alive by Indian rather than British commentators. G.S. Mansukhani, author of the only book-length study of Taylor's life and work, described him as 'first and last, a friend of India, who not only interpreted Indian life, history and thought to the European world but did his best to raise the Indian character in the estimation of the English people and promoted a sense of fellowship and understanding between the East and the West'. There is still a street in Aurangabad called Captain Meadows Taylor Street. [1]

The Story of My Life, which was completed in 1874, was first published by Blackwood's in 1877, in two volumes edited by his daughter Alice, and with a preface by his old friend and second cousin Henry Reeve (1813–95). It is a transparently truthful, modest and engaging personal history, written 'about the people among whom I lived, and whom I love and shall always love to the last' (p. 463). It is hard to find any comparable document among the vast outpouring of memoirs and reminiscences generated by the British in India, almost all of which concentrate upon the view from the verandah, in so far as they look beyond the over-heated intensities of Anglo-Indian life at all. Benevolent and sincere, Meadows Taylor's own personality rarely obtrudes. Where its presence may be felt, it is that of a decent, hardworking, Christian gentleman, concerned above all to fulfil the trust placed in him by those around him. The last word of his autobiography is 'duty' (p. 464). His is not one of the great names, such as Wellesley, Outram (who was his friend) or Lawrence; neither do his life and opinion overshadow those of the people he deals with. Culled from a voluminous correspondence to members of his family, particularly his father, the autobiography retains the freshness, even naivety, of first impressions, while adding the perspective of 36 years – apart from one spell of leave home – spent in the subcontinent. The narrator of *The Story of My Life* is throughout absorbed in the day-to-day affairs of an Indian state yet, also, because of his position as an outsider, privileged but often insecure and lonely, forced to view his little corner of the Empire with exceptional clarity and objectivity.

Meadows Taylor tries to show the Indian community he knew from within; and if he is bound to express some at least of the typical prejudice of the time, such as that the Indian states were irrevocably corrupt and could only be brought to good order through British intervention, he nevertheless shows little of the racist ideology with allowed other whites to ignore or belittle the Indian people with whom they came into contact – an ideology which became dominant after the bloody rising of 1857-8. The independence of his position, under neither Company nor Crown – although he was ultimately responsible to the British Resident – as well as his intimate closeness to those he observed – his wife Mary was granddaughter of a begum of Oudh – gave him an opportunity of thoroughly understanding Indian life which few Britons could have enjoyed, and virtually nobody else has written about. As *The Times* obituarist acknowledged, he 'acquired a knowledge of the languages and people of Southern India which has seldom been equalled. He studied the laws, the geology, the antiquities of the country; he was alternately Judge, engineer, artist, and man of letters ...'[2]

After *Confessions of a Thug*, he wrote five more novels, all with major Indian characters and settings, and with a background of turning-points in Indian history. He was also *The Times* correspondent in India, 1840–53. He published sketches and descriptive accounts of the architecture and topography of southern India. He wrote and lectured widely on the art, music, literature and history of the country. And he managed, without any previous training or experience, to become a successful army officer, surveyor, administrator and ultimately effective ruler 'over 36,000 square miles of area, and a population of upwards of five millions of a most industrious and intelligent people, not only without a single complaint against my rule, but, as I think and hope, with a place in their affections and respect, gained by no other means than by exercising simple courtesy and justice to all' (p. 446). The usual emphasis upon the military and economic power which enabled a tiny minority of Europeans to rule a country of many millions tends to obscure the importance of this moral power. But 'moral power' is an ambivalent notion: later it was to feed that ideology according to which the subject races instinctively accepted Imperialist rule as they recognised the supposed moral superiority of their rulers. This was not what should be taken from Meadows Taylor, whose respect for the Indians he met was always sincere and unforced. He intended his autobiography to teach future rulers and administrators the value of simple virtue: as Reeve put it in his preface to the first volume edition, it was designed to enforce the lesson that 'ability, happiness and success' in the great work of ruling India 'depend very much upon the estimate they form of the native character, and on the respect and regard they show to the natives in the several ranks of society'. Aware of the dark side of Indian life, he resisted easy condemnation – whether of the 'horrible profession' of thuggee, or of the laxness and despotism of certain Indian princes – preferring instead to shed light upon the common humanity and culture he perceived. His was the liberal view, in the best sense, according to which progress would inevitably follow knowledge; but it was a view which was tied to a situation doomed to disappear and so it, too, was doomed. What is important is the assumption implicit throughout, that the British could not 'improve' the Indians, unless they first 'improved' themselves. Their authority ultimately derived from virtue, not power; and so they were to be judged.

Philip Meadows Taylor was born in Liverpool on 25 September 1808, the first of five sons, only three of whom survived to old age. His father, who bore the same name, was a merchant who married Jane, daughter of Bertram Mitford of

Mitford Castle in Northumberland. His grandfather, the Reverend Philip Taylor of Old Court, Harold's Cross, in the county of Dublin, was grandson of John Taylor of Norwich, the Dissenting divine. His great-great-grandfather married into the Meadows family, from one of whom, Sir Philip Meadows (a well-known figure at the time of the Restoration), like other members of his family, he derived his first two names – although 'Philip' seems to have been dropped from early on. Meadows Taylor could thus, as he says, claim descent from two of the ancient families of England, one Puritan and one Royalist: a pedigree which, however, seems not to have helped much when, in 1815, his father's affairs became 'involved'.

Illness made him a 'querulous and weak' child, who was sent to the care of relatives in Ireland to recuperate. He called himself 'King Pippin' and was initially somewhat demanding. Apart from the 'rudiments of English and Latin', his schooling was negligible, and had something of the quality of Dotheboys Hall: at Mr Barrons's near Prescot, for example,

> at stated seasons, especially in spring, we were all gathered together in the dining-hall, where the old lady stood at the end of the room at a small table, on which was a large bowl of that most horrible compound, brimstone and treacle. The scene rises vividly before me, as we all stood with our hands behind our backs, opened our mouths and received each our spoonfull, swallowed it down as best we could – and had to lick the spoon clean too! (p. 6)

His father's affairs becoming more involved, the family shifted to Ireland, and the young boy found himself at Dr Hutton's day school in Dublin, where the discipline was, once again, severe. His mother's 'religious teachings' now became 'more earnest and constant than before', which had a shaping impact upon his character, leading to 'the feelings which I have all my life experienced of love and humble devotion to our glorious Church' (p. 9).

His father's straitened circumstances soon led to removal from school, however, and Taylor was sent back to Liverpool at the age of 14 or 15, to a hard and uncongenial clerkship at Messrs Yates Brothers & Co., West India merchants. The steady determination which was to mark his career now begins to show itself; as does his novelistic eye – one day, he was drawn in to a revivalist church meeting by overhearing distressing cries of 'Save me!', 'The devil has me!', 'Go away, Satan', and the like,

> with prayers so profane and shocking that I dare not write them down. Sometimes one got up, man or woman, and gave his or her experience of sins and crimes, horrible to hear, but which, nevertheless, fascinated me. I know not how long I stayed, but a girl sat down by me at last and whispered, 'Come and kiss me, you beautiful boy – come away.' I gained the door, and fled rapidly in the darkness up the street. (p. 11)

The intrigues of his fellow clerks at Messrs Yates made Taylor so wretched that he gave up his indentures. Meanwhile his father had become acquainted with a Mr Baxter, Bombay merchant, who proposed good terms for the boy. The result was that, to improve his health and career at once, he was sent out to India. He left Greenwich on the *Upton Castle* on 15 April 1824, aged 15. Father and son, who seem to have been equally credulous, believed that he should return in no time rich and prosperous, and a partner in the firm.

Fortunately for Taylor, his mother's cousin William Newnham was at the time Chief Secretary to the Government in Bombay, so that when he arrived to find Baxter's 'house' was no more than a retail shop in a poor way of business, alternative employment was found for him: a commission in the Nizam's Army, obtained through the aid of Sir Charles Metcalfe, then Resident at Hyderabad. Thus, on 18 November 1824, Lieutenant Meadows Taylor, of the 6th Infantry of his Highness the Nizam's Service, left Bombay to begin a military career. He was just 16.

Appointments to the East India Company's Service, Civil or Military, were made by the Court of Directors in England, and Meadows Taylor was never in the running for that privilege. Unlike the youngsters (many of them of similar age) he saw on arrival in Bombay with 'nothing to do but to learn the Hindostanee and Persian languages, and ride about in palankeens, with a score of black fellows at their heels' (p. 18), he was always to be excluded from the security of Company service, his position dependent upon the vagaries of British dealings with the Indian States. Yet, at the same time, his personal qualities, including a soon-to-be-discovered gift for acquiring the local languages, were to stand him in good stead; so, too, was his sympathetic and courteous manner with the local people. Withing a year, he had learned 'to speak Hindostanee like a gentleman', noting at the same time that 'our people unintentionally insult a native gentleman by speaking to him as they would to their servants' (p. 32).

Newnham had assured Mrs Taylor that the Nizam's service held out good prospects for appointment in civil administration, but things were not quite so straightforward. This was partly because of the origin and nature of the Nizam's Army. It is familiar fact that the remarkable growth of British power during the eighteenth century coincided with, if it was not indeed a major result of, the decline of the Moghuls, and the fragmentation of their empire. One aspect of this fragmentation was the departure of Asaf Jah, Nizam-ul-mulk (or governor of the empire) from Delhi to his Deccan provinces, to become in 1724 a ruler virtually independent from Hyderabad, of a state the size of Spain. Asaf Jah established a new dynasty, which was to rule the major part of southern India as the Nizam of Hyderabad down to 1948.

The connection of Hyderabad State with the British Government dates from a treaty of 1766, with Nizam Ali, who ruled until 1803. To ensure the security of the state against the French and the brilliant Tipu Sultan, Lord Wellesley instituted the 'subsidiary treaty', a device by which the nizams bound themselves to accept a force for which they had to pay but which would be under the control of a British Resident. This meant freedom from Indian conquest at the price of subjection to the British. Thus, territorial acquisitions in the wars against Tipu were ceded to the British in 1800 to pay for the cost of the Nizam's Army: and again, in 1853, the districts known as Berar, as specified in a minute to the Resident from Meadows Taylor (p. 265), were ceded in perpetuity to the British to 'settle' the costs of what thereby became the Hyderabad Contingent, auxiliary to the Government of India.

When Meadows Taylor joined the Nizam's Army, it was officered from two sources: by members of the Company's armies of Bengal, Madras and Bombay; and by 'local' officers appointed by the Resident – including an uneven mixture of retired Royal Navy and Army officers, military adventurers, and the sons of officers of the King's or Company's armies of mixed British and Indian blood, offspring of the fairly frequent and often permanent liaisons between the Europeans and local women at that time. Taylor evidently enjoyed himself in his new profession, which involved him in big game hunting, putting down rebels, and an education in military surveying. From early on, he began associating 'with native gentlemen, and observing their manners and customs, modes of speech and conversation' (p. 37), and although such contacts were much more common during the earlier decades of the century, it is clear that Taylor preferred the company of local notables to his own society, obsessed as that was with 'high play' (p. 38). Such a preference may seem surprising to those who know only the familiar European perspective upon that time and place. But the Court at Hyderabad, always in much less contact with western ways than Delhi, continued for many years to reflect a rich indigenous culture, including a considerable literature, and the local gentry with whom Taylor communed exercised long-established forms of careful politeness derived from the traditions of the Moghul Court. There is a photograph of Taylor dressed as an Indian gentleman, smoking a hookah, and looking quite at home. Soon his proficiency in the local languages, familiarity with local custom and hardworking, upright way of life attracted the favourable notice of the Resident, who appointed him Superintendent of Bazars at Bolarum and, not long after, Assistant Superintendent of Police for the south-western districts. By the age of 18, then, he was effectively in charge of policing an area of some ten thousand to twelve thousand square miles, including a population of more than a million.

The young Taylor's abilities in his role are revealed in a characteristic episode, concerning corrupt flour-sellers in Tuljapur. They had been mixing sand with their product to make it go further. Taylor called the sellers and asked them each to weigh out a seer (two pounds) of flour. Then he ordered them to eat it themselves.

They saw that I was in earnest, and offered to pay any fine I imposed. 'Not so,' I returned; 'you have made many eat your flour, why should you object to eat it yourselves?' (p. 45)

Some tried to eat, but soon spat out the half-moistened flour, much to the amusement of the bystanders. The flour-sellers sought Taylor's pardon, and swore never to give bad flour again. It was as Superintendent of Police that he first came across evidence of the horrors of thuggee, without knowing the meaning of the strangled bodies unearthed by the roadside. But before he could investigate further (to his lifelong regret), his civil appointment came to an abrupt end, as a result of a characteristic reversal of policy in the dealings between the British and the Indian States.

In 1829 the old Nizam, Sikander Jah, who had ruled since 1803, died and was replaced by Nazir-ud-Dowlah. At the instigation of his Chief Minister, Chandu Lal, the new Nizam demanded the withdrawal of the 'feringhees', who were 'interfering in his country' (p. 56). Lord William Bentinck, then Governor-General, although a convinced radical reformer who had already suppressed suttee (the burning of widows on the funeral pyres of their husbands), and was to ensure the later suppression of thuggee, was in favour of non-intervention and offered to withdraw the European officers from employment in the Nizam's civil administration, and even to agree to the abolition of his Army on payment of 20 lakhs in its place – a huge sum. The result was that Taylor and others were recalled and the Nizam appointed his own civilian officers, who farmed out revenue to the highest bidder – with predictably corrupt results. The Nizam retained his Army, however, being proud of it and sensing its importance for his security; and Taylor was posted again to his regiment, which he served until he went on leave in 1837, being its adjutant from 1830. His continuing success as an officer in the Nizam's Army, in which role he always preferred moral persuasion to force of arms, was testified to by an affectionate sobriquet given to him by his sepoys, 'Bolo Mahadeo Baba Ki Jey!' ('Victory to the son of Mahadeo', a local deity), which followed him through his career, and, on one occasion, probably saved his life. This was at the turbulent time of the Mutiny, when Taylor had been instructed to go to Berar and 'hold on by your eyelids' (p. 367). With only four men he was attempting to cross the Godavari when a group of Muslims set up the ominous 'Deen! Deen!' (call to arms); but before they could act, an elderly man set up the 'the old cry', which many then joined, drowning out the threats and protecting Taylor until the arrival of an escort sent by 'an old friend of mine, the Talookdar of Umber' (pp. 373–4).

Meanwhile in 1832 Taylor married Mary Palmer, daughter and eldest child of William Palmer (1780–1867), the son of General William Palmer, once military secretary to Warren Hastings and afterwards Resident at three of the Indian states. William Palmer the elder's second wife was a begum of the ruling family of Oudh, who lived on after her husband's death in 1816 as an honoured guest in her son's household until her own death in 1828. When Taylor was sent to police the south-western districts it was she, 'the Begum Sahib', who 'blessed me, and tied a rupee in a silk handkerchief round my arm, praying the saints to have me in their holy keeping' (pp. 39–40).

William Palmer the younger, after an English education, had come to

Hyderabad towards the end of his father's period as Resident there. After some 14 years in the Nizam's Army, he founded a banking and mercantile firm which, for several years, financed the state to an extent which led eventually to crisis and enforced bankruptcy. The ins and outs of the Palmer affair divided loyalties in England and India, as Taylor's remarks indicate. If we presume he was likely to support his father-in-law, it does look as if he was not alone in doing so. Palmer's case was that the money he had advanced to the Nizam at a very high rate of interest was found from Indian capitalists at rates very little below what he charged, and that it financed the Nizam's treaty obligations at a crucial period of the Maratha wars. However, Sir Charles Metcalfe, the Resident, felt the Nizam was being plundered, and he was also opposed to the enormous political influence of the Palmer firm. He prohibited Chandu Lal from settling one large claim the firm held against the Nizam's Government, so ensuring its collapse. The root of the problem, again, was the anomalous position of the Nizam's Army, which was eating up one-third of the state's finances by the time of the settlement of 1853.

Meadows Taylor probably made the acquaintance of the Palmer household on his arrival at Aurangabad. Certainly he was a constant visitor from 1826. Palmer's residence was palatial, and accommodated intrigue on a palatial scale; no better introduction, perhaps, to local politics and history. Palmer was a fascinating and powerful figure, and may well have had a decisive influence upon Taylor's decision to marry his daughter. In any case, Meadows Taylor was deeply attached to his wife, who bore him two sons (both died in infancy) and two daughters, Alice and Amy, during the next few years – years marked by bouts of malaria, and the beginning of Taylor's literary career. Stationed with his regiment in Hingolee, Taylor had offered to help in the campaign led by Captain (later Sir) William Sleeman in collecting evidence against the thugs, and the confessions of one 'approver' (informer) in particular caught his imagination. In 1833 he sent home to his father an article on thuggee, which was shown to Bulwer Lytton, who sent word that 'had he possessed any local knowledge of India or its people, he would write a romance on the subject' (p. 73). Three years later Taylor began the *Confessions*, having reached the rank of Captain in the Nizam's force. Long periods of convalescence and the encouragement and criticism of his father-in-law helped him complete the book in 1837. He took the manuscript with him on what was to be his first and only furlough, begun in November that same year after a doctor's warning that it was his last chance for good health. (Members of the Nizam's Army were not normally permitted furlough abroad, unlike officers of the Crown or Company.)

After an adventurous voyage, the Taylors arrived in England in 1839. Captain Taylor surprised his relations by having 'the manners of a gentleman' and no 'traces of contact with the savage tribes of India', a view which made him the more determined to show that 'the people among whom I had been living were highly civilised, and in many ways resembled ourselves' (p. 105). The immediate success of *Confessions of a Thug*, which had been placed by his cousin

Sarah Austin with publisher Richard Bentley, did not entirely serve the author's announced aims, on account of its horrific material. But Taylor had introduced a new realism into the depiction of Indian life and culture, especially when he followed his first book with the (less successful) *Tippoo Sultaun: A Tale of the Mysore War* a year later. Some successful articles on Indian subjects led to a commission to 'correspond' with *The Times*, a position probably obtained for him by Henry Reeve, who was a principal leader writer during the years Taylor wrote for the newspaper, and who generally backed Taylor's views in what he wrote (pp. 294–5).[3] This brought about a remarkable degree of influence for an otherwise minor and relatively obscure official.

One of the issues upon which Taylor exerted his influence was education. Where he might have been expected to support the 'orientalists', who wanted to continue the earlier policy of patronising Persian, Arabic and Sanscrit studies, Taylor instead vigorously advocated Bentinck's reformist view that English and the vernacular should be encouraged, although he could never have agreed with Macauley's famous Minute of 1835 in support of the change – which argued that 'a single shelf of a good European library is worth the whole native literature of India and Arabia'. On the contrary, Taylor's advocacy represented the modernising aspirations of all those who, like the Brahmin Ram Mohun Roy (1777–1833), saw the replacement of Persian by English in official use as the key to the long-term improvement of India, without wishing in any sense to denigrate the worth of the classical Indian literatures nor to dislodge the vernaculars. During his long spell with *The Times*, Taylor was opposed to official policy on more than one occasion; the annexation of Sind he considered 'a blot' on Indian history (pp. 217–20). Nor could he accept Dalhousie's policy of territorial acquisition by annexation (p. 294).

In 1841, soon after his return to the regiment, and a tumultuous welcome, Taylor was selected by the new Resident, General Fraser, to become Political Agent in Shorapur, a feudatory state under the suzerainty of the Nizam's Government, during the minority of the Raja. There, indeed, he founded a school, amongst other works of enlightened reform (see p. 279). The finances of the principality improved dramatically under Taylor's management, as did almost every other department of the administration. The whole fascinating story, covering some 12 years of Taylor's career and 150 pages of narrative, provides one of the most vivid and richly enjoyable sections of *The Story of My Life*. Perhaps only a novelist could have done justice to characters like the widow Rani, 'a very Messalina' (p. 102) and her accomplice, the official Regent, Pid Naik, as they intrigued to undermine the authority of the boy Raja and his English protector. Certainly Taylor's account of how peace and prosperity came to a community riddled with corruption, as a result of the exercise of a combination of tact, zeal, sheer good sense and humanity, is more gripping than anything else he wrote. Typically, he managed to keep the unruly Beydurs (who made up a large proportion of the population of Shorapur) in peace by, for example, reminding an assembly of the heads of the clans that it was difficult for him to exert himself so much now that his wife was dead, which touched them deeply, so that 'they crowded around me, placing their hands on my feet and neck, and earnestly exclaiming, "They would never *vex her spirit* by causing me pain or anxiety" ' (p. 177). By appealing to the best in those over whom he held power, Taylor made a success of an almost impossible job.

Yet it has to be said that his behaviour was that of the paternalist: benign and sympathetic, always doing his best for the fatherless boy whose charge he had, only rarely able to obtain a glimpse of just why it might be that the Rani and Pid Naik should have been driven to extremes in their frustrated struggles for power. Pid Naik ended a hopeless drunk, the Rani died of 'dissolution' – but before she did so, she took leave of Taylor: reminding him of what she once told him about the young Raja,

> 'Ah,' she continued, 'he is the last – the last of his race! He will lose all his ancestors ever gained; and all the pains you have taken with him, and all the money you have saved for him will be poured like water into the sea; and you will be grieved – sorely, sorely grieved! But I shall not see it, for I am dying, my friend, dying fast now. Will you forgive me all that I have done to you? I am a mean old woman. You are going one way, and I am going another; we shall never meet again.'
>
> I bent over her as she lay upon her bed, and touched her hand with my lips. She could not speak; but smiled, waved her hand gently, and I left her. (pp. 265-6)

In its simple pathos, historic overtones and prophetic intimations (the young Raja later shot himself after a futile attempt to join the rebellion in 1858, pp. 408–11), this can stand beside any of the great death-bed scenes of the nineteenth century.

Mary Taylor had died suddenly in 1844, after a short illness. Her husband was bereft: 'I tried humbly to bow to the will of God; but I had lost in her not only my loving and beloved wife, but my steady, true friend, my comfort and my happiness' (pp. 170-1). These words are the more forceful in that Meadows Taylor refers so rarely to his intimate feelings, or to his family – and from then on, it is 'my little State' (p. 181) that concerns him most (his daughters had been sent to England). Nine years later he admits that 'Since my great sorrow I had led a cheerless, lonely life' (p. 281). It has been suggested that Taylor subsequently relished a well-stocked harem, in the manner of many of his fellow exiles, who compensated for their isolation by following the ways of Indian gentlemen but with a more than Indian excess.[4] Not only does this seem out of key with Taylor's nature and principles, for all his profound involvement in Indian culture, but there is clear evidence to the contrary in a letter to Reeve, frankly denying the possibility in terms which are unambiguous:

No, I have no zenana. Carry and you are wrong, and I am glad of it. I have had a struggle with myself about it, but have hitherto kept free and hope to do so. I say I have had a struggle and you may believe it for here chastity in women is, I hear, rare, and I had offers enow. They have ceased now, being refused, and the women, I believe, feel I am not to be tempted. Verily and truly I am alone...[5]

Hard work sustained, although it also wearied him through many years. If his private life was essentially lonely, he none the less enjoyed the company of local people:

The palace children often came to see me, and loved to hold their dolls' feasts among my flowers with their playmates. Native friends would come up in the evenings, and a game of chess with one or other often followed ...
My books were my constant delight, and with these and my telescope, a fine Dollond, I had always plenty of occupation ... I could not go on with literary work, as at the day's close, my brain was generally wearied out ... but I felt I was gaining more and more real knowledge of native life and character, under circumstances that fall to the lot of very few Englishmen, and that hereafter, if life were spared, I might turn my experience to good account. (p. 281)

But before he restarted his literary career, a 'new phase' of his life in India began.
'In 1853', as Meadows Taylor remarked in his *Student's Manual of the History of India* (1870: p. 695), 'the affair of Hyderabad came to a crisis.' The Nizam had been carrying on the affairs of state himself in a desultory, unsuccessful way through an agent, Suraj-ul-mulk, whom he finally appointed his Chief Minister, but whose attempts at reform were largely dissipated by intrigues. Debts had mounted to an intolerable level, and the cession of territory to the British seemed the only way out, as the Nizam reluctantly agreed. The districts of Berar, Nuldrug and Raichore were finally assigned to British management, the Nizam retaining sovereign rights, after the Governor-General, Lord Dalhousie, had consulted with Meadows Taylor amongst others; and payment for the Nizam's Army, the major drain upon the State's finances, was correspondingly reduced. The brilliant Salar Jung, later knighted for his services, became the Nizam's new minister, following the death of Suraj-ul-mulk. Taylor was given charge of the Nuldrug district where, after the expulsion of Arab rebels, he settled down to survey work and irrigation schemes. He was now, as he says, no longer responsible to the Nizam, but to the Company; yet still only as an 'uncovenanted outsider', and so not appointable to Hyderabad, where he could have had 'home and friends for my children' (p. 320). He continued to work 12 to 16 hours a day, carrying out those improvements which he felt would best serve the country. Despite his disagreement with Dalhousie's annexation of Oudh, which he considered an incentive to the outbreak of rebellion in 1857,

Taylor fully believed in and supported the Governor-General's remarkable modernisation programme – which brought the telegraph, railways, roads, large irrigation projects and much else to the subcontinent.

In 1857, Taylor's promotion to the Deputy-Commissionership of North Berar, which he was to hold 'by his eyelids', helped prevent any very serious out-break of rebellion in the province: no mean feat in the absence of armed force, and a remarkable testimony to the trust he inspired. Although the rebellion or Mutiny is sometimes thought of as predominantly an affair of Bengal and the north it seems from Taylor's own account of the threatening letters and rumours, the fears and suspicions he encountered, that 'a general uprising of the people' was a real possibility (p. 335). The other side of his benevolent and respectful disposition towards the Indian people was, as with so many even of the virtuous Europeans, temporarily all too visible. According to the letters home he himself quotes in his autobiography, the rising made him regret the 'utter inability of these people to rule themselves', the futility of 'the promo-tion of natives to offices of trust and confidence' and, worse still, it made him feel that here was proof that 'civilisation of mind, which most of us thought had made progress' was only 'skin-deep' after all (p. 350).[6] As the generalis-ing, racial imperatives take over, Taylor loses his earlier sympathetic, imaginative responsiveness to the individuals he has worked and lived with. But this was a temporary aberration, as all the novels which were to come make us realise – including, for instance, *Seeta* (1872), which took the 'struggle' of 1857–8 as its setting, and which reveals a more objective perspective. It may generally have been true that, as Victor Kiernan has observed, the bitterness 'that India had always felt was now felt on both sides, and the gulf had become impassable':[7] but Taylor slips out of the general condemnation implicit in this, once the heat and trauma of the moment are past.

So I believe; although it could also be argued that, with the abolition of the Company and the transfer of authority from that now anomolous body to the Crown in 1858, followed by the declaration of 1876, by which the Queen became Empress of India, British feelings of security and prestige were so enhanced that it was safe, once again, to be sympathetic. But that sympathy was essen-tially long-distance, the view of an aloof (at best) minority, certain of their right to govern 'the niggers' – a term which began to appear in the 1850s, and con-tinued to flourish thereafter, despite the attempts of 'old hands' such as Taylor to point out that respect and understanding were the qualities which were most desirable in India's alien rulers.

Taylor's autobiography was an attempt, late and probably futile, to counteract the increasingly dominant ideology of race. Broken by hard work and ill-health, he himself was finally obliged to leave for home in 1860, still hoping that the new treaty which restored two of the ceded districts, Nuldrug and Raichore to the Nizam, and which marked the assumption of control by Sir Salar Jung, would somehow enable him still to find a useful role in the state of Hyderabad (pp. 435–6, 455). His extraordinary popularity among ordinary people, the farmers and traders, was touchingly demonstrated to him before he left by excited crowds; and the feelings of the local aristocracy, officials and rulers, by fulsome addresses. The Queen appointed him a Companion of the Order of the Star of India in 1869, but nothing more came to him in the way of honours at home – indeed, the designation 'Colonel', which appears on the title-page of his autobiography, was not a promotion he ever actually achieved, and appears to have been a usage common among the old officers of the Nizam's Service, who felt they deserved better than they got from Her Majesty's Government. As his daughter tells in her concluding chapter, the old and dying man was invited back to Hyderabad (by Salar Jung) for a last visit, during which he was told how 'the women sang ballads to his honour as they ground their corn, and related stories of him to their children' (p. 467). On the voyage home with Alice, Taylor finally succumbed, on 13 May 1876, and was buried where he died, in Mentone.

Two years after his return to the family home at Harold's Cross, Dublin, in 1860, Taylor had recuperated sufficiently to contemplate returning to the literary career he had been planning for nearly 20 years, since the publication of his second novel, *Tippoo Sultaun*. Encouraged by his old friend, the novelist Frances Cashel Hoey (1830-1908), he decided to take up again a story that had begun to germinate all those years ago, and in 1863 *Tara, a Mahratta Tale*, appeared. It was 'loudly praised' by *The Times* and the usual quarterlies (p. 457) and was, indeed, to prove the best of Taylor's Indian 'historical romances'. Set at the time of the rise of Maratha power against the Mughal empire in the seventeenth century, it recounts the adventures of the Maratha widow Tara, who is carried off by the villainous Moro Trimmul, then rescued by Fazil, the son of Afzul Khan, at the desecration of the temple at Tuljapur – one of Taylor's favourite places (p. 43) – only to be recaptured after the treacherous murder of Afzul. To preserve her honour she declares herself suttee, but is then saved just in time by Fazil, who marries her after executing Moro Trimmul.

These are the bare bones of an exciting narrative, played out against the struggle of the Marathas to establish themselves as an independent power in the Deccan. As Bhupal Singh has remarked, the novel 'displays a wonderful knowledge of the domestic life of Hindus and Mohammedans', although the final marriage of the Hindu Tara to the Muslim gallant who saves her is perhaps a little improbable.[8] Even less likely, however, is the marriage of the devout Hindu widow heroine of *Seeta*, to Cyril Brandon, 'the Collector of Noorpoor', an alliance which Meadows Taylor's contemporaries among the Anglo-Indian community regarded as 'doubtful and dangerous'.[9] Again, this is evidence of how far he was moving against the tide of European opinion, in India if not at home. Taylor came from an earlier phase of the 'raj' and, as his autobiography makes clear, he had no hesitation about racial or religious mixing himself, in so far as that was acceptable to the local communities within which he lived.

His refusal to consider remarrying clearly had nothing to do with racism, and everything to do with the memory of his wife. It is important to notice not only that he cared to present an accurate and sympathetic account of Indian history and culture in his fiction, but that he was also especially interested in creating memorable (if idealised) female characters, whose eventual unions symbolise a hoped-for coming together of the varied races and religions. It is difficult to resist speculating about how far his own, tragically short-lived, marriage to Mary Palmer (herself the product of a 'mixed' marriage) lies behind these heroines; but we know too little about her to say more than that there evidently was a connection.

In a recent attempt to do some justice to the neglected writers who preceded Kipling, B.J. Moore-Gilbert plays down the significance of this 'mixed marriage' theme in Meadows Taylor, on the grounds that Taylor stresses the 'un-Indian' aspects of Seeta's appearance, for example.[10] But this is to undervalue the weight of what Taylor knew (as his autobiography shows) he was opposing by the 1870s, as well as the virulence of Anglo-Indian opinion by this time. It is also to forget that, for all their superiority as novelists over Taylor, Kipling and his English successors were by comparison unable to visualise without patronising the behaviour of ordinary Indian men and (especially) women, relying, sometimes, in E. M. Forster's case, on ventriloquism, where Taylor could simply depict what he had seen and heard over decades of close, often intimate, contact. Taylor never criticises what is simply alien. Nevertheless, his idealism does sometimes strain credibility, a strain which becomes more evident in the novels which succeeded *Tara* – *Ralph Darnell* (1865), the aforementioned *Seeta*, and his last and weakest novel, *A Noble Queen: A Romance of Indian History*, which appeared in the Indian *Overland Mail* before posthumous publication in volume form (1878).

An admirer of Sir Walter Scott, Taylor planned *Tara*, *Ralph Darnell* and *Seeta* as a trilogy, illustrating significant moments in Indian history, just as Scott's first three novels were intended to illustrate three key episodes in Scottish history. Scott also wrote an Indian tale, *The Surgeon's Daughter* (1827), which was as unreal as all other fictions set in India before *Confessions of a Thug* with the possible exception of Hockley's *Pandurang Hari* (1826). Like Scott, Taylor kept his historical personages for minor roles, and the broad sweep of history for background. But he lacks Scott's humour and complexity; and, despite his remarkable knowledge of Indian history, is unable always to be accurate or persuasive – indeed, he was so taken with the Hindu astrologers' prediction that certain turning-points in Indian history would occur at exact intervals of 100 years, that he used these predicted moments as the basis for his trilogy, despite the distortions involved. As he confessed in a defensive Introduction to the first edition of *Seeta*, it was the power of 'the weird prediction' upon 'the native mind' in 1857 which swayed his own belief in it. Thus *Tara* takes 1657 and the sack of the temple at Tuljapur as the moment when the Marathas rose to power; *Ralph Darnell* takes 1757 and the battle of Plassey as the key moment when the foundation of the British Empire in India was laid; and *Seeta* takes the Revolt of 1857, 'a combination to regain what had been lost', as its moment – leading to the expulsion of the Company, as Taylor says, but not, of course the British, as the prediction foretold.

Yet if Taylor's grasp of history is shaky, one reason is that he had become imbued with contemporary Indian ways of thinking. As his Indian commentators themselves have observed, he was not only quite exceptional in his insight into the ways of thinking of those he met and whom he embodied in his novels, but their dialogue, the descriptions of everything from weddings to meals, his own language (his letters are replete with Anglicised Indianisms), above all the pervading interest in fatalism, suggest just how much he took on the character of those he depicted. In Edward Said's brilliant analysis of *Orientalism* (1978), it is suggested that one of the effects upon Europeans in Asia is to lead them, in defence of their own identity, to exaggerate the traits which appear to make them who they are.[11] What is remarkable about Meadows Taylor (whom Said does not mention), is that something much more complex appears to have happened: not only do the stereotypical early and mid Victorian values of self-help, duty, improvement and Christian idealism find strong, although hardly exaggerated representation in Taylor's most personal writing, the 'story' of his life; but the reverse, too, happens, and his mind reveals an 'Indian' cast: as when he comes to believe in the old astrologer of Tuljapur, whose predictions about his own life were after all 'spoken truly' (p. 463). In a telling early incident at Hyderabad city, he goes to a grand fancy ball as a nobleman of the Nizam's Court, and 'As I spoke Hindostanee fluently, and could assume all the native manners, nobody found me out' (p. 232). Perhaps any well-informed linguist and actor might have done the same, and yet retain a sense of his own identity and, indeed, superiority, as Richard Burton's famous visit to Mecca in disguise in 1853 suggests. But Burton was exceptional; and Taylor's integrity towards the people he knew and loved as individuals and as different communities (his was not the 'universal love' of sentimental liberalism) is finely shown by his public response (in *The Times of India*) to a Brahmin who picked him up upon some inaccuracies of caste observance and custom in his novels: 'Now, why do not you, or some one of your friends, take up the subject of novels or tales, and instruct *us* on the subject of your people? If you wrote in Marathi, or Gujerati, you would have a vast audience. If in English, we – if the work were simply and truthfully written – would welcome the author warmly'; what is needed, he continued, was 'writing that will move the hearts of the people, and become the foundation of a national literature of fiction, healthy, pure, and instructive to future generations' (p. 469). An apt and a prophetic conclusion to *The Story of My Life*.

Notes

1. G.S. Mansukhani, *Philip Meadows Taylor: A Critical Study*, Bombay, 1951, p.4. See also G.S. Amur, 'Meadows Taylor and the Three Cultures', in *The Image of India in Western Creative Writing*, eds Naik, M.K., Desai, S.K. and Kallapur, S.T., London, 1971, pp. 1-12; and Rehana Shah, 'Meadows Taylor on Aspects of Indian Culture', *Indian P.E.N.*, vol. 46, May-June 1984, pp. 8-11.
2. *The Times*, 'Col. Meadows Taylor', 8 May 1876.
3. See Sir Patrick Cadell (ed.), *The Letters of Philip Meadows Taylor to Henry Reeve*, Oxford, 1947: Introduction, pp. xxii-xxiii. This is an invaluable complementary source to the *Life*, covering the period 1840-9.
4. See D. Kincaid, *British Social Life in India, 1608-1937*, London, 1938, p. 160.
5. Letter 13 May 1847, in Cadell, *Letters*, pp. 269-70.
6. Taylor's *Letters ... Written during the Indian Rebellion* were privately published in 1857.
7. V.G. Kiernan, *The Lords of Human Kind: European Attitudes towards the Outside World in the Imperial Age*, Harmondsworth, 1972, p. 49.
8. B.Singh, *A Survey of Anglo-Indian Fiction*, London, 1934, p. 52.
9. *Calcutta Review* (1873), quoted in Singh, ibid., p. 50.
10. B.J. Moore-Gilbert, *Kipling and 'Orientalism'*, London and Sydney, 1986, p. 52.
11. See Edward W. Said, *Orientalism*, Harmondsworth, 1985 ed, p. 3.

THE STORY OF MY LIFE

BY THE LATE

COLONEL MEADOWS TAYLOR

AUTHOR OF 'CONFESSIONS OF A THUG,'
'TARA : A MAHRATTA TALE,' ETC.

EDITED BY

HIS DAUGHTER

WITH A PREFACE BY HENRY REEVE

PREFACE.

For several years before his death, the writer of these Memoirs had been urged by his friends to leave on record some account of his adventurous and useful life. The materials at hand were authentic and abundant; for, not only was he possessed of an excellent memory and great powers of retaining and narrating numerous and compli- cated details with entire accuracy, but during the forty years he spent in India, he carried on a copious corre- spondence with his father and other members of his family, and a great portion of these voluminous letters has been not only preserved, but carefully transcribed in England. I venture, therefore, to say that nothing is related in these volumes upon vague recollection or traditional evidence, but every incident is told as it happened.

Although it was not the fate of Meadows Taylor to rise to a high rank in the civil or military administration of India, and he cannot lay claim to the distinction and fame which belong to the illustrious founders and servants of the British Empire in the East, there were circumstances in his career not less remarkable than in the lives of greater men. He was one of the last of those who went

out to India as simple adventurers—to use the term in no
disparaging sense, for Clive and Dupleix were no more—
and who achieved whatever success he had in life solely
by his own energy and perseverance, independent of the
patronage of the great Company or the authority of the
Crown. A lad of fifteen, after a few years spent at a
second-rate school, and a few months in the drudgery of a
Liverpool merchant's counting-house, is sent to Bombay
upon a vague and fallacious promise of mercantile employment. It was long before the days of Indian examinations and Competition Wallahs. Arrived at Bombay, the house of business he was to enter proved to
be no better than a shop, and its chief an embarrassed
tradesman. By the influence and assistance of a kins-
man, a commission was obtained for the misfortune-stricken
boy in the Nizam's military contingent. Thus only he
started in life. But the stress of circumstances and
the tenacity of his own character had already taught
him the all-important lesson of self-reliance and independence. Already, on the voyage, he had commenced the
study of Eastern languages, to which he applied himself
with extreme assiduity in his new position, perceiving
that until a man has mastered the language of a country,
he can know little of its inhabitants, and may remain for
ever a stranger to the intelligence and the hearts of those
over whom he exercises authority. His perfect acquaintance with the languages of Southern India, Teloogoo, and
Mahratta, as well as Hindoostanee, was no doubt the
foundation of his extraordinary influence over the natives
of the country, and of his insight into their motives and
character. It was also the first step to his advancement
in his profession. At seventeen he was employed as

interpreter on courts-martial, and recommended for much higher duty by the Resident; and at eighteen he found himself Assistant Police Superintendent of a district comprising a population of a million souls. Nor were the duties of that office light. They involved not only direct authority over the ordinary relations of society, but the active pursuit of bands of dacoits, Thugs, and robbers, who infested a half-civilised territory. Occasionally, military expeditions were necessary to reduce some lawless chief of higher degree to obedience. The head of the police was, in short, the representative of law and order in a wild country. These duties, at this early age, Meadows Taylor performed, and with such success as to merit the notice of the sagacious old Minister of the Nizam, Chundoo Lall, and the approval of the Resident.

It would be superfluous in this preface to notice the details of his advancement in life, which are more fully related by himself in the following pages. But I may venture to point out one or two considerations on which the simplicity and modesty of his own nature forbade him to dwell. By mere perseverance and industry, he carried on the work of self-education through life, with very remarkable results; and this, chiefly, at military stations in the interior of the Deccan, with no advantages of books or European society. Having mastered the native languages, he soon found that the government of an Indian district and population means that English intelligence, integrity, and foresight are to supply all that is wanting in these respects to a less civilised people; and he applied himself to make good from such resources as he possessed all these deficiencies. Thus he taught himself the art, and even invented a new method, of land-surveying, be-

cause the revenue settlement of the country depends upon
it ; and without augmenting the burdens of the people, he
largely increased the revenue of the State in several districts.   He taught himself engineering, because the construction of roads, tanks, and buildings was an essential
part of the improvement of the country.   He acquired a
considerable knowledge of law, both Hindoo, Mohammedan, and English, because he had to administer justice to
the people ; and he framed for himself a simple code and
rules of procedure applicable to a country where there
were no courts of law and no written laws at all.   He
studied geology and botany, because he observed the
direct bearing of these sciences on the productiveness of
the soil.   He brought to the knowledge of Europe the
curious antiquities of Southern India, so nearly allied in
form to some of the remains of Ireland, Cornwall, and
France.   He beguiled his leisure hours with painting and
music, in which he had, I know not how, acquired considerable proficiency ; and he cultivated literature with
no mean success, as is proved by the series of novels
beginning with the 'Confessions of a Thug,' in which the
manners and superstitions of India are portrayed with
wonderful fidelity, and by the 'Manual of Indian History,' which is the most complete summary in existence
of the annals of that country.   His various literary productions, which have stood the test of time, and still
exercise a fascinating power over the reader, are not so
much works of imagination as living pictures of the men
and women amongst whom he dwelt.   There is hardly a
character in these volumes that was not drawn from some
real person, whom he had seen and known in his various
expeditions or in the repression of crime.   And he

acquired, as if by nature, an extraordinary force and flexi-
bility of style, which brings the native of India, with his
peculiar forms of language, his superstitions, his virtues,
and his crimes, within the range of the English reader, as
no other work has done. The tales of ' Tara,' ' Ralph
Darnell,' ' Tippoo Sultaun,' and ' Seeta,' were designed by
their author to mark the principal epochs of Indian history at long intervals of time, and the state of society in
each of them ; and they form a complete work, which
deserves to retain a lasting place in English literature.
And when it is considered that they were for the most
part written by a young officer who spent his life in active
service, remote from all literary society, they are an aston-
ishing proof of natural genius. I mention these things,
not by way of panegyric, but because I hope that many a
young Englishman may enter upon the duties of an Indian
career with this book in his pocket, and may learn from
it what may be done, in the course of a single life, to
develop and improve his own character and attainments,
and to promote the welfare of the people committed to his
charge.

But there is a higher element and a more important
lesson in this record of a life spent in the service of India.
Meadows Taylor gave to the people of India not only his
head, but his heart. He had the liveliest sympathy and
affection for the natives of India. Thoroughly understanding their traditions and their manners, he treated
men and women of all ranks with the consideration and
respect due to an ancient society. The wild Beydurs
whom he encountered upon his first arrival at Shorapoor
—men who were the terror of the country and the myr-
midons of the court—said to him, after their first inter-

view, "We perceive that you respect us, and we will be
faithful to you for ever." And in the more polished
spheres of Indian life he touched the pride of the native
nobility with so light and kindly a hand, that they were
as eager to court his friendship, as the peasantry were to
receive his counsel and his benefits. British rule in India
has, beyond all doubt, conferred the great benefits of peace
and civilisation on the country; but it is sometimes wanting in gentleness and sympathy. There lies probably its
greatest danger in the future. Some examples there are
of men who have touched the hearts of the natives and
enjoyed in return their enthusiastic and devoted regard,
such as the Lawrences, Outram, and Malcolm; but they
are rare. I think the author of these recollections was
one of them. Wherever he went, the natives knew and
believed that they had a protector and a friend. The
sphere of his power and influence was not wide, at least
in comparison with the vast extent and population of the
Indian Empire; but as far as it extended they were complete. Probably there were few men in India who, at the
moment of the Mutiny of 1857, could have crossed the
river into Berar without troops, and held a firm grasp on
the passions of an excited people: and the confidence
inspired by men of this character largely contributed to
save the south of India from the calamities which were
devastating the North-Western Provinces of Bengal. Not
only was the maintenance of peace in the Deccan a matter
of the utmost importance to the suppression of the disturbances in the North-West, but Colonel Taylor was able
most materially to assist the operations of Sir Hugh Rose's
army by moving up cattle and supplies, which were indis-
pensable to the sustenance of the troops.

The chief object we have in view in giving this volume to the world, and the chief object of the author in writing it, is to impress upon those who may be called upon to take any part in the administration of India, and especially on the young men who now annually leave our schools and examination papers for that purpose, that their ability, happiness, and success in the great work before them, will depend very much on the estimate they form of the native character, and on the respect and regard they show to the natives in the several ranks of society. The highest are on a par with the oldest and proudest aristocracy in the world. The lowest are entitled to be treated as members of an old and civilised society.

Meadows Taylor was never, properly speaking, in the civil service of the East India Company or the Crown, nor did he hold any military appointment in the British Indian army. He was through life an officer of the Nizam. He never even visited Calcutta or Bengal. But the administration of the Nizam, both civil and military, is, to a certain extent, that of a protected government, and is largely influenced by the decisions and policy of the Governor-General of India in Council. When it became a question of appointing an officer to administer a province, though that province might be a dependency of the Nizam, it was not unnatural that the selection of an English servant of that prince, without rank in the British service, should be viewed with some hesitation and jealousy, both at the India Board and at Calcutta. It was probably owing to this cause that during the administration of Sir H. Hardinge, and when Captain Meadows Taylor had barely surmounted his first difficulties at Shorapoor, he was disagreeably surprised by a

note from the private secretary of the Governor-General
informing him that the appointment of another agent at
Shorapoor, unconnected with the recent events in that
State, was required, and in contemplation. Upon the
receipt of this intelligence, no motive having been assigned for the intended change, Captain Taylor's friends
in England took steps to ascertain whether there were
grounds to justify it. I find among my own papers the
following letter to myself from the late Mr John Stuart
Mill, better known to the world for his philosophical
writings, than for the eminent public services he rendered
for so many years, in the capacity of Examiner, or Political Secretary, to the East India Company. It may be
inserted here as the highest testimony to the merits of
Captain Taylor as an administrator, from a most competent observer :—

India House, 23d Sept. 1845.

My dear Sir,—You can hardly feel more interested in preventing the removal of Captain Meadows Taylor from Shorapoor than I do myself, because (to say nothing of personal
considerations) I have a very high opinion of the merits of his
administration of Shorapoor. I may say, indeed, that his
being at Shorapoor now is owing to me, for some expressions
of approval and praise in a despatch written by me was what
induced the Indian Government to suspend their intention of
replacing him by a civil servant of the Company, and to refer
the matter home. I have endeavoured to induce the Court of
Directors to negative the proposition. I do not, however, expect to obtain anything so decided, as they do not think it right
to fetter the Indian Government in its choice of instruments.
But as the Court will certainly give no encouragement to the
project, I think it will blow over, and Captain Taylor will remain.—Very truly yours,

J. S. Mill.

And in a second letter, written by Mr Mill a few days later, he added:—

Whatever may be the cause that is working against Captain Taylor, I am convinced that Fraser (the Resident at Hyderabad) has nothing to do with it. Fraser, as far as I know, has always written to Government very much in his favour. Captain Taylor is quite in error if he supposes that the Nuzzerana business has done him any harm. Fraser did not agree with him on that subject, but the home authorities and Sir H. Hardinge did, and do most strenuously.

The cloud did blow over. Captain Taylor's merits were acknowledged at home and at Calcutta, and he remained at Shorapoor many years. Indeed, when the arrangement was made with the Nizam for the liquidation of the claims of the British Government by the cession of certain portions of territory, the district of Western Berar was placed under the management of Captain Taylor; and the services rendered by him were so far eventually recognised by the Government of India, that he retired, after more than thirty-eight years' service, with the pension of his rank in the British service, not unaccompanied with honorary distinctions, which he valued.

The time is past when so adventurous and singular a career is possible in India or elsewhere. The world grows more methodical, and routine takes the place of individual effort. But the same qualities of head and heart are still the only guides to success in the government of a people different from ourselves in race, religion, and manners, but united to Great Britain by a common allegiance and common duties.

HENRY REEVE.

FOXHOLES, 25th Sept. 1877.

CONTENTS.

CHAPTER I.

1808-24.

CHAPTER II.

1824.

CHAPTER III.

1825-29.

CHAPTER IV.

1829-37.

CONTENTS.

CHAPTER V.

1838.

CHAPTER VI.

1839–40.

CHAPTER VII.

1841–42.

CHAPTER VIII.

1843–44.

CHAPTER IX.

1844.

CHAPTER X.

1846.

CONTENTS.

CONTENTS.

CHAPTER XVI.
1858-59.

CHAPTER XVII.
1859-60.

CHAPTER XVIII.
1860-74.

CHAPTER XIX.
1874-76.

STORY OF MY LIFE.

CHAPTER I.

1808–24.

I WAS born in Slater Street, Liverpool, on the 25th day of September 1808. My father, Mr Philip Meadows Taylor, was the only surviving son of the Rev. Philip Taylor, of Old Court, Harold's Cross, in the county of Dublin. My mother was the youngest daughter of Bertram Mitford, Esq., of Mitford Castle, in the county of Northumberland, one of the most ancient Saxon families of England, which still flourishes, from its origin, beyond the Conquest, to the present time, in the enjoyment of its ancient privileges and estates.

My father's ancestors were of a North Lancashire family, and have been traced to Lancaster, where they were known in the fifteenth century. They reckoned many men of sterling worth and reputation among their number; and one, Dr John Taylor, author of the 'Hebrew Concordance,' is well known to this day. The Taylors intermarried with the Martineau family, after the former had removed to Norwich, which became their stronghold; and there the pleasant friendly gatherings and intercourse

A

with Mr and Mrs Barbauld, Sir J. E. Smith, and other celebrities of the time, are not yet forgotten.

Without making any boast of pedigree, I can at least claim descent from two ancient families of England—one Puritan, the other Royalist—and my parents faithfully preserved these hereditary distinctions to the last.

My father was educated partly in Germany, and there learnt to appreciate the advantages of rifles over ordinary muskets. He assisted in raising a volunteer rifle corps in Liverpool, which he commanded as executive captain, the Earl of Derby being the colonel; and thus had, I believe, the merit of being the first to introduce the rifle system into England. This fact was recognised by the War Office at a comparatively late period. In 1807, my father and mother were married at Walton Church, Lancashire. Five sons were the issue of this marriage, three of whom survive, I being the eldest.

Soon after my birth my father removed from Slater Street to Brookfield, a pretty country-house near Liverpool; and later, for convenience in business, then very prosperous, to a house in Rodney Street, the most fashionable locality in the town at that time. I remember but little of Brookfield; and indeed my first memories of Rodney Street are dim and vague. The chief one is of my being attacked with croup, followed by a long severe illness, which changed me from a healthy, sturdy child into an ailing, delicate one, and necessitated my being sent to Ireland, to the care of my grandfather and aunts, for change of air. I grew querulous and weak, and, I fear, was a trouble in the house. I had named myself "King Pippin," and remember lying on the rug in the room I am now sitting in, piping out miserably that "King can't" or "King won't" when required to do anything. I grew stronger, however, and soon became my grandfather's constant companion in his strolls about the garden, holding on by his finger, and gradually losing my

awe of his deep sonorous voice and imposing manner, as
was proved by a speech recorded against me, when, as he
was seized by a violent fit of sneezing, I looked up in
my grandfather's face, and said, gravely, "Grandpapa,
what a chap you are for sneezing!"

In due course I returned to my parents in Rodney
Street, and many memories flit across me while I write.
On one occasion, while on a pond with some skaters at
Street Court, Herefordshire, where my mother's sister
resided, I had a narrow escape of my life. The ice broke
under me, and I was with difficulty rescued—my cry
being, "Help King! help King!"

I believe I could at this time read fairly, and could
repeat a good deal by heart at the age of five. No great
feat, truly; but I was never set up as a prodigy, nor did
I begin Greek at three years old, like Mr Stuart Mill!

My wish was to become a merchant in those days, and,
watching my opportunity, I ran away to find "papa's
counting-house," and was discovered by a friend of my
father's crying in the street, and restored to my dear
mother, whose agony when she found I was missing was
extreme. She feared I had been decoyed away for my
beauty, and that she would never see me more. I was
ordered to bed, without supper, by my father; but I well
remember, as I lay there sobbing, that my mother stole
into the nursery with a bowl of hot bread-and-milk in her
hand, and gave earnest thanks for my restoration to her
beside my little bed.

Soon after this escapade, my brother Robert and myself
were sent to a day-school to keep us out of mischief. Of
what we learnt at the Rev. Mr Fearon's I remember but
little. I suppose the rudiments of English and the
earliest lessons in Latin; but we were very happy,
and it was the beginning of the little education I ever
received.

Among the most distinct memories of these early days

is that splendid illumination of Liverpool, the year of the peace of 1814. We elder boys were taken by our parents through the streets of the town ; and although those were not the days of gas and other brilliant effects, very beautiful devices were arranged with coloured oil-lamps, and our delight was unbounded.

Nor have I forgotten the chairing of Mr Canning and General Gascoigne, on their return as Members for Liverpool, after a severely-contested election. I remember my mother presenting a nosegay of flowers (bouquet would be the word used now) to Mr Canning, and the scarlet streamers with which it was tied, and how we children, standing on the steps, were cheering with all our might, and were shown to him. I remember his laughing face and shiny bald head as he kissed hands to my mother and drove on—the flags too, the shouting crowds, the bands of music, and the windows filled with gaily-dressed ladies ; and I remember how my mother, a true Mitford, insisted that her boys should wear the Tory colours, red and blue, in opposition to my father, whose sympathies were with the pink or Whig colours of the Seftons.

The same year I accompanied my parents to Norwich, where there was a gathering of the Taylor family ; of this I have little recollection ; but of our stay in London— including being taken in a wherry to Greenwich, and seeing Madame Saqui dance on a tight-rope sixty feet high— I have a very distinct impression, and also that I was a hero in the eyes of my brothers on my return.

It must have been about the year 1815-16 that my father's affairs became involved. He rejected all tempting offers to reinstate his business on borrowed moneys, which were freely pressed upon him ; and having honourably discharged every claim, and given up the luxurious home in Rodney Street, to which his previous position had entitled him, he took a pleasant little villa called Olive Vale Cottage, about three miles from Liverpool, to which he removed his family. My mother accepted her change of fortune with all the resignation, devotion, and nobility of her character, and was ever the true helper and comforter of her husband.

At Olive Vale Cottage we boys lived a very happy life. There was a pretty flower-garden which was our mother's great delight, and her carnations, pinks, and auriculas were the finest of their kind; a magnolia and scarlet japonica were trained round the drawing-room windows, and showed her exquisite taste. There was a capital fruit and vegetable garden, which was my father's pride, and where he laboured diligently when he returned each day from his work in Liverpool. There was a poplar-tree too, in the highest branches of which we established a sort of nest to which we mysteriously climbed, to my mother's great dismay, and I remember my father calling to us to " Come down, you monkeys, and don't frighten your mother," while he at the same time betrayed no small pleasure in our accomplishing so manly an exploit. Although they were very poor, my parents were very happy and very proud of their troop of noisy boys, who throve well in the sweet country air.

The next event was my being sent to school. The one selected was kept by Mr Barron at Holt Hall, near Prescot, and I entered as a boarder. There were, I believe, about a hundred boys, and the school had a wide reputation. It was a rough place, although scarcely equal to the Yorkshire school of Mr Squeers ; but I, fresh from the gentle presence and teachings of my mother, felt the change keenly, and was almost inconsolable—so much so, that I was sent home after a while, and when I returned to Mr Barron's, it was as a parlour boarder, a distinction which caused much jealousy, and subjected me to much torment. I was the youngest boy in the school, teased and bullied by all ; but after I had received an enormous cake from home, which was divided among the boys, I grew more into favour, and even became a "pet" among them.

We rose at six in summer, partially dressed ourselves, and, with our jackets over our arms, went down to a stone bench in the yard, where stood a long row of pewter basins filled with water, and often in the winter with ice. Here, in all weathers, we washed our faces and hands, combed and brushed our hair, and went into the schoolroom a while to study; then were let out to play till the bell rang for breakfast, consisting of fresh new milk, and a good lump of bread. At ten we were all in school again, and work went on, only interrupted by the instances of severe punishment which but too often occurred. The rod was not sparingly used, as many a bleeding back could testify, and I have often been obliged to pick the splinters of the rods from my hands.

We were well fed on meat, cabbage, and potatoes, and rice or some plain pudding; on Sundays we had invariably roast beef and Yorkshire pudding. We went into school again at three. At five school broke up, and at seven we had our suppers of bread and milk; afterwards we could study or go out within bounds as we pleased. Good Mrs Barron attended to our personal cleanliness and to our health; and at stated seasons, especially in spring, we were all gathered together in the dining-hall, where the old lady stood at the end of the room at a small table, on which was a large bowl of that most horrible compound, brimstone and treacle. The scene rises vividly before me, as we all stood with our hands behind our backs, opened our mouths and received each our spoonful, swallowed it down as best we could—and had to lick the spoon clean too! Surely this was a refinement of cruelty! I presume I learnt something while at this school, for before me lies a letter from my father, praising me for the good conduct and diligence I had shown, and exhorting me to further exertions, with much sound advice on many points. A like letter was also received from my grandfather, the replies to which I had to write with great care and no blots, and which was afterwards found carefully preserved among his papers.

I could not have remained at Mr Barron's school longer than the close of the year 1817. The ill-usage I received increased, and I ran home at last and showed my mother my bleeding hands, and also my father when he came in. The distance I had run was no great feat for me, who was always selected "hare" in our games at "hare and hounds." Thus the Barron bubble burst. What was to be done with me next? Had I really learned anything, except spelling, which was well knocked into me, and has stood me in good stead all my life? I doubt whether I really had profited much.

My brother attended a small day-school in the village of Wavertree, and when I got home I was also placed there under Mr Newby's care. I believe he was a competent teacher if he chose, but he was incorrigibly sleepy and lazy; and when her husband fell asleep and we boys became uproarious, Mrs Newby walked in, quelled the tumult, and read her lazy helpmeet a sound lecture, which used to afford us intense amusement. She was a tall grim woman, with decided beard and moustache, and a strong Cumberland accent; but she was very kind to us boys. A short time after my attendance at this school began, I received a bite from a dog as we were going along the lane one morning, It proved a very severe one, and I was very ill; my parents were much alarmed, as I was delirious for some time, and it was three months before the wound healed. How vividly I remember my dear mother's anxious face and gentle loving care, and my little brother Selby throwing himself down on the grass and crying that he saw the sky open and the beautiful angels hovering over him and saying to him, " Meadows won't die! " What did the child see? Long years after I questioned him about this, and he said the vision was firmly rooted in his memory!

Time passed on, but I fear my father's affairs did not improve, and there were many anxieties and privations at the Cottage; and at length, after a visit to Dublin, on which I accompanied him, my father accepted the charge of a large brewery in James Street, of which he was to be executive manager.

Does any reader remember the Dublin and Liverpool packets of fifty years ago? Stout cutters, with one narrow cabin for passengers and berths all round it; no wonder no one went across who could avoid it. We were three days and nights at sea; and as provisions were reduced to salt junk and ship's buscuit, we amused ourselves by catching gurnards off the Kish Bank, and these split and broiled were very good.. After a short stay in Ireland we returned to Olive Vale Cottage. My father wound up his affairs in Liverpool, and we embarked with all our belongings for Dublin.

The house we occupied in James Street was large and handsome, and the brewery was a source of constant and varied delight. We helped, or imagined we helped, John Reilly, the cooper, to make and mend casks; and often shared his dinner of salt herring, potatoes, and butter, with old Segrave, the porter at the gate, who had a wooden leg.

My brother and I attended Dr Hutton's school as day-scholars. Dr Hutton taught Latin and Greek himself, and there were masters for French and mathematics. The discipline here, too, was very severe. Was everything I learned always to be beaten into me? I made but little progress in classics, but delighted in mathematics and French, and even gained prizes in these.

There was little variety in our Dublin life. I well recollect the entry of King George IV., the procession, his portly figure, and gracious salutations to the ladies in the windows, and the deafening cheers of the crowd, on that

glorious summer day. The event was a remarkable one
in the history of Ireland, and its people accorded to their
King a right royal welcome.

All this time my dear mother's religious teachings to us
became, it seems to me now, more earnest and constant
than before. From her I learnt the doctrines of the
Church and the sublime sacrifice and atonement of our
Lord ; and how lovingly and carefully she taught us will,
I am sure, never be forgotten by my brother or myself,
and led to the feelings I have all my life experienced of
love and humble devotion to our glorious Church.

In those days it was considered effeminate to teach
boys to draw, or sing, or play on any instrument; accom-
plishments, therefore, were denied us. I had much desire
to learn both music and drawing, but it was not allowed.
I was getting on with Latin and Greek, had entered the
first class, and took a goodly number of prizes in French
and mathematics.

Every boy, I suppose, has one decisive fight to record ;
mine was with a big boy, the bully of the school. We
had one encounter in which I was severely handled. My
father encouraged me, however, not to give in, and gave
me private instruction, until I began to " see my way into
science." Reckoning on another easy victory, my enemy
one day called me a coward, and hit me. I returned the
blow sharply. The odds were scarcely fair, as my adver-
sary had on a jacket with a row of metal buttons down
the front; however, I fought on, hitting out as my father
had taught me, and at last my foe lay down, begging my
forgiveness, which of course was accorded. When I got
home it was very evident what had occurred.

" You have been fighting again, sir," said my father,
severely.

" Yes, sir, with J——," I replied.

" Did you lick him ? "

" I did, father, though he had buttons on his jacket."

"Bravo, my boy! here's half-a-crown for you. Go off and treat your backers, and J—— too, if you like."

And so I did.

I do not know how it came about, but at the close of that half-year I was told that I was to go to Liverpool and enter the office of Messrs Yates Brothers & Co., West India merchants, and be articled to them for seven years. I did not like the prospect at all. I should leave my darling mother and my studies, in which I was beginning to take such pleasure. Why was I sent away? I am at a loss to imagine, and it is useless to speculate now, but so it was; and to the intense grief of my mother, I was taken away, young and utterly inexperienced, and placed as a boarder and lodger with Mr Hassal, a clerk in some office in Liverpool, who had been recommended to my father. I was duly introduced to Messrs Yates's office, in which were several young boys — learners like myself. Mr Ashton Yates, the senior partner, was invariably good to me, and I have a grateful memory of his kindness while I remained in the office. At first I was set to copy circulars, and such easy work; then I was promoted to being post-office clerk—not an easy task in those days, as the postage on letters sent and received was of considerable amount and variety. I afterwards became one of the clerks for attending the discharge of cargoes, sitting in all weathers in a wooden shed with the Custom-house landing-waiter, entering, under their various marks, cotton bales, sugar hogsheads, and goods of all descriptions from the East and West Indies. It was a hard life; and day after day, in snow, frost, or rain, I have sat for hours together, shivering and benumbed with cold, being allowed an hour for my dinner, in which time I had to run two miles to eat it, and run back again. Sometimes a friendly captain would ask me to partake of his meal; and I have frequently shared a landing-waiter's lunch when offered. Our nominal hour for closing office was six o'clock; but

I have often been kept till ten when there was a press of
work. My last office was "assistant dunner," as it was
called—*i.e.*, the collection of moneys due ; and late in the
dark evenings have I, mere boy as I was, been walking
the streets of Liverpool with thousands of pounds in bills,
notes, and gold in my pocket. I was getting on ; but I
had enemies—why, I know not—who played me many a
scurvy trick. My petty cash was often pilfered, my desk
being opened by other keys. I was ordered on private
errands for other clerks, and when I refused to execute
them, I was "paid off" by extra work and malicious
accusations. These were, however, entirely disproved.
I had a steady friend in Mr Yates, and persevered in my
work. The pleasantest part of my duty was arranging
the samples of cotton according to their quality ; and I
have been often called into the "parlour" to assist the
partners in their decisions. I had a fine sense of touch,
and became an adept in the manipulation of samples.

One incident I have never forgotten. I was returning
to the office late one evening, when, passing by the door
of a chapel, and hearing groans and cries, I looked in. A
person stationed at the door invited me to enter and "save
my soul." The place, a large one, was in profound darkness ; a candle here and there only made the gloom more
impenetrable. People of both sexes were sitting in the
pews, and shrill piercing cries arose of "Save me !" "I'm
going to hell !" "I'm damned !" "The devil has me !"
"I'm burning, burning !" "Go away, Satan !" "Jesus has
got me !" and the like, with prayers so profane and shocking that I dare not write them down. Sometimes one got
up, man or woman, and gave his or her experience of
sins and crimes, horrible to hear, but which, nevertheless,
fascinated me. I know not how long I stayed, but a girl
sat down by me at last and whispered, "Come and kiss
me, you beautiful boy—come away." I gained the door,
and fled rapidly in the darkness up the street.

Early in 1824 the wretchedness I endured in the office reached its highest pitch, and malicious tales against me increased frightfully, accompanied by threats. I retorted by saying to those who were badgering me, that if I were not let alone I would tell certain things I knew of them. I. was of course defied; but I felt ill—I had a fearful cough, and the doctor said I was threatened with consumption; so I wrote the whole story to my father, who had left Dublin and was settled at Apsley, near Hemel Hempstead in Hertfordshire, telling him that I must come home for change of air at once.

I went into the "parlour" to consult Mr Yates, who agreed I had better go for a while. I was not strong enough for work, and my enemies in the office were very malicious.

"And," he added, "tell your father, if there is any other opening for you he likes better, or that you wish yourself, I will give up your indentures."

I had enough money of my own to pay my journey; and on a bitterly cold morning I mounted the roof of the London coach at the Saracen's Head, Dale Street, with a thankful heart, and was in my mother's arms on the following afternoon. How happy I need not say.

My indentures were returned by Mr Yates, after some correspondence with my father, and I had ended that phase of my life, richer in experience and general knowledge, but weak and delicate in health. With home care this soon improved.

I was not long in suspense as to my future. My father became acquainted with Mr Baxter, a Bombay merchant, who wanted a young man to assist in the house at Bombay, and proposed to me to go out at once. It had been previously decided that I should go to Madeira for my health, so the proposal fitted admirably. We dined with Mr Baxter, who lived in splendid style, and the terms offered seemed to me and to my father exceptionally good.

I was to receive a large and yearly increasing salary, live in Mr Baxter's family, and to be admitted as an eighth partner when I became of age. My mother's cousin, Mr Newnham, was holding the high office of Chief Secretary to Government at Bombay, and would no doubt look after me; and I was considered a very lucky boy with excellent prospects.

My outfit was at once ordered, my passage taken in the Upton Castle, permission having been obtained for me to reside in India, and I returned for a few short precious days to Apsley. I will not dwell on this period; it is even yet sacred to me: but at length the 15th April came, and I parted from my dear mother in bitter grief, never to see her again. My father took me down to Greenwich in a wherry, with my boxes, and we found the Upton Castle there. We dined at the Falcon, and in the evening went on board. My father gave me much excellent advice and bid me good-bye, both he and I firmly believing that I should return in "no time," rich and prosperous, a partner in Baxter's house.

When I awoke next morning, our ship was anchored off Gravesend waiting for the captain and some of the passengers: when these arrived, we put to sea. So ended my boyhood in England. I had completed my fifteenth year the previous September.

CHAPTER II.

1824.

WE knocked about for a week in the Channel owing to strong adverse winds, and at last anchored off Spithead to wait for a fair breeze, and I wrote to my brother a long cheery letter detailing many a " castle in the air," and hope of great things to come. On the 26th April we finally put to sea. We reached Funchal, Madeira, on the 26th May. I had excellent introductions from my father's relations, Mr and Mrs Leacock, and I was very kindly received on my arrival. I saw a great deal of the island, many new sights and much wonderful scenery, which I find described in a long letter written to my mother. We were about ten days at Madeira taking in wine for India. I was on shore all the time, and I believe some of the passengers were surprised to find " the boy for Baxter's " at dinner-parties and the chief houses of the island. Certainly, several who had not before noticed me now began to do so. The captain and chief officer taught me the use of the sextant and to make observations, and I was soon able to be of use. Some one lent me Gilchrist's Hindostanee Grammar, and taught me to pronounce the words, so I was able to make some progress.

The Upton Castle was frigate-built, and carried eighteen guns, and it was necessary to keep a good look-out against pirate cruisers about the latitude of the Azores. We were all told off to quarters, and I was constituted captain of

the mizzen-top, my favourite resort for reading, and which
now was garrisoned by six stout boys besides myself. One
night I was keeping the first watch with Mr Duggan the
second officer, when just as the lights were being put out
I raised the glass, and saw a large felucca close to us on
the windward quarter. I raised an alarm, and although
we hailed her several times, no answer was given. I think
I hear now Mr Duggan's order to me to "fire," and see the
long dark ship, with all its moving dusky forms, plunging
past us. I fired two muskets in rapid succession ; but the
stranger did not turn, and we sent a parting shot after her.
Our ship was in a state of wild excitement, and groups of
passengers, ladies and gentlemen in every variety of costume, were gathered on deck. We had no further alarms
after this. We were becalmed on the line for nearly three
weeks, dull and insufferably hot. We welcomed Neptune
and Mrs Neptune on board in the approved old fashion,
and I was scraped with a hoop and well ducked, but was
spared the tarring.

We had one terrible gale off the Cape, but got off without much damage. I had a narrow escape of my life, one
day : I was upon the dolphin-striker and had struck two,
and hit a third, and the "quiver" held ; but instead of
disengaging the line from my arm, it became twisted
round my wrist, and had I not been lashed to the dolphin-
striker I must have been inevitably dragged into the sea.
The wounded fish turned in a last struggle, and I got the
line free. My arm was very painful for some time, and I
made no further attempts to strike dolphins.

As we neared Bombay one of the passengers took me
aside, and asked me concerning my past life and future
prospects very kindly. I told him all, and the arrangements which had been made for me in Baxter's house, and
that I believed it to be a great mercantile firm. On this
point I was now undeceived, as my friend said Mr Baxter's was simply a large shop ; that they had been in a fair

way of business, but that Mr Baxter's extravagance in London had been such that it was possible the firm might no longer even exist. However, he added, you have made many friends among us; we are all interested in you, and will help you if we can. I told him of my letters to Mr Newnham and others, and he said it was impossible to have a better or more influential friend. "I think," he said, "you will not be long at Baxter's, and we shall soon see you take your proper place in society." Among the ladies, especially, I had excited an interest by rescuing one of them, a lovely girl, from a watery grave. She had incautiously opened her port-hole during a storm, keeping the cabin-door shut. A great green sea poured in, flooding the whole place. I fortunately heard the rush of water, and forcing open the door of her cabin, found her lying face downwards in the water, which was pouring over the steerage deck. I carried her to the cabin of another lady and put her in, and next day was very sweetly thanked for my services.

All things considered, my voyage had been a very pleasant one. We anchored in Bombay harbour on the night of the 1st of September 1824, having been four months and a half at sea, and the whole of that glorious panorama opened on my sight as I rose early in the morning to have "a look at India."

I find a long letter written to my mother, dated September 3, part of which I am tempted to insert as my first impressions of Bombay:—

" BOMBAY, *September* 3, 1824.

"MY DEAREST MOTHER,—After a long but fine passage of four months and some days, I have arrived at the house of Mr Osborne, with whom I have every expectation of being extremely comfortable; but having been only here a day, I can hardly judge how I shall like the business that I am about to embark in, in the town of Bombay.

"I have arrived at a very good time of the year, as the weather, with the exception of next month, which is a hot one, will get cooler and cooler every day. Even now the evenings and mornings, which is the only time you can stir out, except in a palankeen, are delightfully cool and pleasant.

"But one of the greatest annoyances here are the mosquitoes, which bite terribly; but as yet I have escaped their torments.

"At about half-past ten on the morning of the 1st, land was descried from the mast-head, which proved to be the high land outside Bombay harbour.

"I was employed below, packing up all my goods and chattels, so that I did not come on deck till about three in the afternoon, when by that time we were close to it. It is fine high land, and is covered with green in many places—a welcome sight for us who had been so long at sea. We passed, also, two very pretty small islands, called Hennery and Kennery, all covered with trees to the water's edge; but as it was by this time six o'clock, we could not see the beautiful verdure of the trees; and as we entered the harbour by night, we missed a very fine sight, as the entrance to the harbour is reckoned one of the finest in the world. At half-past twelve we cast anchor in Bombay roads, about three miles from the town, intending to drop down early in the morning. Accordingly, when the pilot came on board about four o'clock, we weighed, and dropped down opposite the town, where we cast anchor for good about a mile from the shore. As soon as we had come to an anchor, we were surrounded by boats filled with black fellows, naked excepting a piece of cotton-stuff tied round their waist, offering fruit, eggs, milk, &c., of which you may be sure we all ate very heartily by way of a treat. About twelve o'clock I hired a boat and went ashore, taking with me all the clean clothes I had, which had dwindled to about half-a-dozen

B

clean shirts, as many stockings, and one pair of trousers
—rather a slender stock! The moment I got ashore, I
hired a palankeen and went to Baxter Bros., where I was
received by Mr Osborne, the manager, who did not know
of my appointment, but was very kind. He offered me
his palankeen to go about in, and recommended me to
deliver my letters ; and I set out for Mr Newnham's, who
was very kind, offered me his advice whenever I stood in
need, and told me if he could do me any service, he would
with the greatest pleasure. I then went to Mr Wodehouse, who asked me if I was entirely engaged to Baxter's ;
and when I told him I believed I was, I thought he looked
disappointed.

" . . . Nothing goes down here but the ' Company,'
and it is indeed an excellent service. There are the
writers, for instance ; as soon as they arrive in India, they
have their three hundred rupees a-month, and nothing to
do but to learn the Hindostanee and Persian languages,
and ride about in palankeens, with a score of black fellows at their heels. In this country there are lots of
servants, and they are the laziest lot of rascals under the
sun. One fellow will not do two things. If you have a
fellow to brush your shoes, he will not go on an errand.
One of our passengers hired eighteen servants the moment
he landed! But their wages are very cheap. You get
these fellows for 2, 3, 4, and 6 rupees a-month, and have
not to clothe them or anything. . . . A shirt here
lasts only a day—sometimes not even that. Fortunately
washing is very cheap, only three rupees a-month, and
you may dirty as many things as you like. I think the
climate will agree with me ; I do not find the heat oppressive. . . . Last night I had a walk on the esplanade, which was crowded with vehicles, carriages, gigs, and
buggies, of all sorts, shapes, and sizes. Bombay is a fort ;
but the fortifications are not in good order. It is a pleasant walk round the top of the ramparts. I have not seen

any of the passengers since I came ashore. I suppose they will all be too proud to speak to me now; but, fortunately, there was not one I cared twopence for, except young Shepheard; that's a comfort. . . . The language is not difficult to get a knowledge of; but to be a good grammatical scholar is difficult, as it is not a written language. But Gilchrist, of London, has invented a way of writing it in English letters. The natives transact their business in Persian, which is a written language. This is a festival day, and the natives walk in a sort of procession, with a kind of drum, making a terrible noise. They dress up in the most ridiculous manner, carry torches in their hands, and go on with all sorts of antics. . . . I have written you a long letter, and told you all I could think of. I shall be in daily expectation of hearing from you, and can assure you there is nothing so disappointing as a ship from England without a letter from yourself.—I am your affectionate son,　　　　　　　　　　　　　　M. T.

"*P.S.*—Pray give my love to all friends at home and in London, where, I daresay, they have not forgotten me. Also to all dear friends in Dublin. When you see the boys, kiss them for me, and tell them the black fellows are such queer 'jummies,' with large bracelets on their arms and thighs made of silver, and rings through their noses, and strings of beads round their necks, and almost naked.

"Kiss dear Johnny for me a hundred times. I daresay he still remembers me; and give my love to Bella.

"We are going to have a new Governor, as Mr Elphinstone is going to Madras, and a Mr Lushington of the Treasury is coming out to succeed him. The present Governor is very much liked, and the inhabitants will be sorry to part with him.

"Mr Osborne lives in a very pleasant part of the town, fronting the esplanade, close to the fort-walls. We can see the sea—in fact, it is close by—so that we have the sea-breeze all day long, without which it would be miserably hot. The houses are all built very large—large rooms, &c.; and the staircases are wide and airy.

"And now, dearest mother, I must close this letter, wishing you health and happiness; and that God may send His blessing upon you and my dear father is the constant prayer of your affectionate son."

I had a comfortable room at Mr Osborne's, and lived with him and his wife. He was in much perplexity about me, as he continued to receive no instructions, and the affairs of the house grew worse and worse. I could be given no salary, and as to the eighth share which I was to receive after five years, Mr Osborne considered it purely imaginary, and his hope seemed to be that Mr Newnham or Mr Wodehouse would provide for me and relieve him of the responsibility. I did not write home any complaints or misgivings, but set to work to give what I could in return for the food, shelter, and indeed clothing, that Mr Osborne kindly supplied me with. I could do but little in the office, or help in accounts I did not understand at first. I could, however, make out bills for goods supplied —wine, beer, and groceries; could draft copies of outstanding accounts, and letters for Mr Osborne to sign. I had to sell in the shop both to ladies and gentlemen. I even one day sold some articles to the young lady I had rescued on board, and she presented me to her father, Colonel ——, with a pretty little speech, telling him the story; and the old gentleman shook me warmly by the hand and thanked me.

I often breakfasted with Mr Newnham, but Mr Wodehouse seemed almost more anxious on my account, and often looked into the shop. So I plodded on, Mr Osborne looking anxiously for letters about me that never came, and vexing himself by vain regrets.

My time of deliverance was not far distant. Mr Newnham one morning sent his palankeen for me, with a note

saying he had something to tell me, and he showed me a
letter from Sir Charles Metcalf, then Resident at Hyderabad, stating that he had procured me a commission in his
Highness the Nizam's army, and the sooner I went up to
Aurungabad the better. I was of course astonished at
this, but without any hesitation I accepted it at once,
feeling very sure I had found a better opening than before. Only, how to get free of Baxter's? Mr Newnham
wrote to Mr Osborne asking that my indentures might be
cancelled. Of course Mr Osborne was surprised, but very
kindly said he would not stand in my way; that I was a
fortunate fellow to have such a friend and get such an appointment, and next day gave me back my indentures.

I find in a letter from Mr Newnham to my mother that
"he is happy to tell her, her son will now quit the shop
and move in his proper sphere. The Nizam's service," he
continues, "holds out the most flattering prospects; and
if he qualifies himself in points of duty and in acquaintance with the native languages, the road to high and
lucrative employment will be open to him. He will
remove to my house, where he will remain till he is ready
to proceed to Aurungabad, where his military service will
commence. I shall be very happy if this change in his
circumstances should prove agreeable to you and Mr
Taylor. He is a fine intelligent lad, and I saw him, with
regret, articled to a house which is not in as flourishing a
state as you were led to believe.—Yours very faithfully,
                            "WILLIAM NEWNHAM."

I removed to a small bungalow within Mr Newnham's
"compound," and a Parsee servant was appointed to
attend me, who spoke good English; but I had not been
idle, and could make myself understood pretty well, my
ear guiding me to a good pronunciation. Arrangements
for my military outfit proceeded. I needed of course
uniform, tents, clothes, &c., and my generous friend, Mr

Newnham, gave me a splendid chestnut Arab, which had belonged to his late wife. How pleased he was that I was out of "that shop"—that I was no longer "Baxter's boy"! indeed I am sure he felt his own dignity insulted as long as I was there. "Now," he said, "you are Lieutenant Meadows Taylor of his Highness the Nizam's service, and we all drink your health, and wish you success."

One other temptation assailed me. Mr Shotton, the head of the great mercantile firm of that name, pressed me to throw aside military service and join his House. The prospects were very tempting, and Mr Newnham was greatly troubled as to what was best for me to do. Finally it was arranged that Mr Newnham and Mr Wodehouse should decide; and their fiat went forth that I was to be a soldier. They were right; the great House perished too, and I should have been again on the world.

So when my kit was ready I left Bombay. Mr Newnham had generously advanced every rupee of my outfit, and I was to repay him as I could; and on the 18th November 1824 I started for Aurungabad.

CHAPTER III.

1825-29.

WHAT was I to see in the new strange world now opening before me? What was I to do and to be? My heart
was full of hope, and my ambitions ran high that morning
as I parted from my kind friend Mr Newnham, whose last
words rang in my ears—"As soon as you have proved
that you *can* be useful, you will be *made* useful," he
said; "be diligent and be steady, and I have no fear for
you. Now go." My things had been sent on in advance,
and what little I had with me was already in the boat at
the Apollo Bunder, in charge of Dorabjee, my Parsee servant. We pushed off as I entered the boat, and dashed
away over the clear water. The harbour was gay with
shipping, and the giant Ghâts in the background were
wreathed with fleecy white clouds about their summits.
I was in wild spirits, and could scarcely restrain myself,
it was so glorious and so beautiful.

I found my horse and pony, tents and baggage, at Pan-
well, where I landed, and in the evening went on to
Chowke. There I had the first sight of a splendid Indian
encampment; the Resident at Nagpore, Sir Richard Jen-
kins, being on his way to Bombay. The scene was very
strange to me. The stately white tents, the camels depositing their burthens, the huge elephants, the native
gentlemen arriving in palankeens, surrounded by their
numberless attendants, the camp bazaar, with its booths

and stalls, the variety of dresses, colours, and equipments —all formed a scene of Eastern splendour such as I could never have imagined.

As I was strolling idly along, I was accosted by an officer, and we fell into friendly chat; and when he knew where I was going, and who I was, he invited me to breakfast, assuring me that any friend of Mr Newnham's would be welcome to Sir Richard.

I was kindly received by the Resident, and again invited to dinner in the evening, and I felt no small gratification at such kind notice being bestowed on me.

Next morning I reached the foot of the Ghâts, and proceeded by the military road. How grand it was! Deep glens and ravines, bounded by tremendous precipices; trees and flowers all new to me; and fresh invigorating air, so cold and bracing, and so like, I thought, to dear old England!

On the 24th November I arrived at Poona, and was hospitably entertained by the officers of H.M. 67th Regiment at their mess. I was shown all the sights during our evening rides, and the temple where the "Peshwah" sat in state to see the English annihilated by his army, which, instead, was defeated at Kirkee, in 1817,—and many other scenes of interest; but I knew little then of Dekhan history.

We reached Ahmednugger on the 29th, and were hospitably entertained by Mr Seton, Assistant Commissioner. I spent a most interesting day there, and finally arrived at Aurungabad on the 5th December.

The last marches had been through dull dreary country, endless stony plains, with scarcely a tree to break the monotony. But as I approached Aurungabad, I saw the beautiful dome and minarets of the tomb of Aurungzeeb's daughter glistening in the sun, and troops at drill in the parade-ground. My tent was pitched near the mess-house; but Dr Young came forward to meet me, and

hospitably insisted that I should be his guest till I had
a house of my own. I reported myself to the officer in
command after breakfast, was put in orders, and directed
to attend drill.

A few days later, it was arranged that I should live with
Lieutenant John Stirling, who had recently joined the 6th
Regiment from the Bombay army, and who had a house
much too large for him. He was a noble fellow, both in
person and disposition, and his untimely death ended, too
soon, a friendship to which I look back as one of my
greatest pleasures.

I was not long in learning my drill, and was put in
charge of the two centre companies, was shown how to
keep the books and pay accounts, which soon became very
easy to me. The adjutant took great pains with me; and
I engaged a Moonshee or native teacher, and began Hindostanee in earnest.

I witnessed a curious spectacle at Aurungabad, in the
shape of a miracle-play, which was annually performed
under the auspices of one Major Freeman, who commanded
the invalid battalion at Aurungabad. During the early
Mussulman period, the kings of Beejapoor had received
and endowed many Portuguese Christian missions, and
one had been located at Aurungabad, where delicious
oranges and purple and white grapes still attest the fact
of its former presence. A miracle-play of the life of our
Lord was performed there by them, beginning with the
scene of His birth, and ending with the Crucifixion. Although, no doubt, it could not bear comparison with that
of Ammergau, yet it was very curious and strange. Portuguese monks chanted the story in their own tongue,
interspersed with bad Hindostanee, but the effect was
very impressive; and the last scene, a real man hanging
to the cross, was the signal for wailing and groaning from
the spectators, who looked on with awe and wonder.

The ceremony may have died out with its patron and

supporter, Major Freeman, but when I saw it the spectacle
was complete.   This Major Freeman was a strange character.   When his wife was very ill, a religious friend
offered to read and pray beside her, but he declined, saying, in his broken English, "My dears friends, I do not
want yous.   I'se got Catholic priests, they prays for my
wife; Brahmins makes *jâps** for my wife; Gosains sits in
de water for my wife; Mussulmans fakeers makes prayers
for my wife; I prays myself for my wife.   Little of alls
is best, dear friend.   Now you goes away, if you please."

I must apologise for the above digression, and continue
my story.

We were often out shooting and coursing, and one day
heard of a noble boar at a village some twelve miles off.
We determined to slay him without delay; and sure
enough I soon saw the great grey brute emerge from
behind a bush, and Stirling and I dashed after him.   My
horse, however, struck his chest against the opposite bank
in attempting to clear a small water-course, and both he
and I were a good deal bruised.   But I followed Stirling
as soon as I could, and met him on foot covered with
blood.   "The beast has upset me and my horse," he said;
"go and kill him."   I rode on some little way, and encountered the hog with Stirling's spear sticking through
him behind the ear.   My own spear had been broken in
my fall, and was useless, and I sent for another.   Meantime the brute took to a sugar-cane field, and could not
be dislodged, charging all who ventured near him; and at
last, when one poor fellow had been badly wounded, I
thought it better to send for my gun, and I fired exactly
between the two fierce red eyes that I saw glaring at me
a few yards off, and the huge beast rolled over dead.
What a reception I had!   I shall never forget it.   Stirling abused me soundly for spoiling the fame of the affair
by shooting the hog, and it was quite in vain that I pro-

* Incantations.

tested that no amount of "buksheesh" would induce the
beaters to go near the sugar-cane. At last he was paci-
fied, and we set off home again. My friend's wound was
a bad one, and we had it properly dressed. The boar
arrived soon afterwards, slung on two poles, and the whole
station, ladies and all, came out to see it. I killed many
a hog afterwards, but never one so large.

These were jolly days—plenty of hunting and coursing,
and association with many bright, noble hearts now gone
to their last long home. Erskine, Harris, Seton, James
Outram, and others whom I proudly called my friends,
were among that goodly-spirited company. Who of them
are left now?

This is no place to detail hunting exploits or tales of
hard riding; but I am sure my association with these bold,
true sportsmen gave a manlier, hardier tone to my mind,
and was of great service to me.

I suppose I acquitted myself well as a soldier, for I was
chosen for detachment duty in the rainy season of 1825,
and ordered to Kanhur, with 200 men, to support a detachment of the Company's 23d Regiment, then acting against
the Bheels, who were in rebellion. I do not remember
that we caught any of the rebels, although we followed
them into their fastnesses; but instead, I caught very
severe jungle fever, which nearly put an end to me. I
partially recovered, but had a relapse on my return to
Aurungabad, and barely escaped with my life. I was
allowed four months' leave, and my kind friend Mr Newnham wished me to come to him. I was put into a palankeen, but was so ill at Ahmednugger that I was given
over. At Poona I was again despaired of; but I reached
Bombay at length, and the pure sea air and Mr Newnham's kind nursing soon restored me, and I regained my
strength rapidly. My financial affairs were by no means
satisfactory. No pay had been given by the Nizam's
Government for the last six months, and there was no

such thing as getting it. I had been obliged to borrow
very considerably; and it was a weary business perpetually borrowing at from 24 to 35 per cent when my pay
would have covered all expenses had I been able to get
it. I explained all this to Mr Newnham, and also the
rumours current that the East India Company were bent
upon doing away with the Nizam's force altogether. He
had heard the same, but bid me not despair. He thought
things would improve, and there was always " Shotton's
House," then flourishing, to fall back upon.

I remained with Mr Newnham for three months, and
then returned well and strong to Aurungabad. I found
letters from home awaiting me. I do not think my father
liked my change of profession much. He thought we had
decided hastily; and there was also a very curious letter
from my grandfather, who had a remarkable dislike to a
military career. " He could only protest," he wrote, " that
it was against the laws of God that men should deliberately slay their fellow-men; and what would my feelings be if I had to kill a man (though he might be a
black one) with my own hand?" and much more to the
same effect. My dear mother, however, encouraged me to
persevere diligently in the career I had adopted, and her
counsels had most weight with me, and her words went
straight to my heart.

Major Sayer had succeeded to the command of the
Aurungabad Division, and proved a very valuable friend
to me. He assisted me in my Persian and Hindostanee
studies, and told me to bring him my translations occasionally to look over. What could be kinder! I was a
stranger to him, and had no introduction; but he interested himself about me, and encouraged me to work on.
With his help I soon made considerable progress. There
were no formal examinations in those days; but as a test
of efficiency, I was directed to superintend regimental
courts-martial, and record the evidence in English, and

the finding of the court. In these I took my turn with
Lieutenant Johnston, the adjutant, and as a reward the
command of the Light Company was bestowed upon me
for " good conduct."

With the exception of one month's leave, which I spent
out tiger-shooting with a friend, I was very busy at home.
I enjoyed my month's sport very much. We slew several
tigers, and an occasional hog-hunt was not wanting. Small
game, too, abounded—partridges and quail, pea-fowl and
hares—and our bags were often heavy. One accomplishment I began to practise at this time. My friend was an
artist, and took beautiful sketches from nature. He encouraged me to try also, and from this period dates one of
the greatest pleasures of my life. He taught me as far as
he could. I have the original sketches of that time—very
minute, and highly finished with a fine pen—the buildings
rather on the incline, and the style stiff and formal ; but
everything has a beginning. When my leave expired I
returned to Aurungabad, and began a course of reading
with Colonel Sayer, which was of great use to me. Better
times came—my pay was more regular, and the debt to
Mr Newnham was almost paid off. I was very comfortable—had a good house and pleasant garden, plenty of
friends, and a hopeful spirit.

About the middle of the year I was appointed interpreter to a general court-martial on a native officer of
artillery—the highest linguistic test that could be applied
to me in those days. I had some misgivings as to the
result, but I ultimately performed my task so much to the
satisfaction of the officer who had conducted the trial,
that he wrote a special letter on the subject, commending
my usefulness to him in " this protracted and difficult investigation." " Now you are fit for any staff duty," said
the colonel, " and I hope you won't be long without it "—
a wish I devoutly echoed.

My Light Company was a fine one—mostly picked men

from Oudh and Behar, handsome and athletic. I worked hard, and my men seconded me well, and the result was to me very satisfactory. We were reviewed, and I received the following flattering compliment from the officer in command : " I beg," he said to our colonel, " you will convey to the officer in charge of your Light Company my very best thanks, and tell him his performance this morning has been of the highest credit to him. I have noticed, with particular satisfaction, his unwearied exertions during the whole of the morning; and the appearance of the men under his command, and their steady conduct, bear testimony to his zeal as an officer." This to me! and before every one too! Need I say how full my heart was?

About this time Mr Martin, now Resident at Hyderabad, who also, *ex officio*, commanded the whole army, issued an order, " that he was about to start on a tour of inspection, and with a view to rewarding merit wherever it should be found, he should advance such officers as were specially brought to his notice, and as a proof thereof, had selected Lieutenant Hampton from the whole army to the honorary post of commander of his escort," &c. Now Hampton was only a local officer like myself, and I, like many others, began to speculate on the possibilities of good things in store.

Meanwhile I was very busy. Colonel Sayer had wished me to acquire some knowledge of military surveying and fortification, and I had made a survey of the cantonment with only a compass, a chain and cross-staff, and a perambulator. I should have done my work better with a sextant; but there was not one to be had. However, as it was, I received thanks for my report when it reached the Residency at Hyderabad, and I was much gratified.

At last the Resident arrived with a brilliant staff; the station was very gay, and I was presented with all the other officers. Hampton had been promoted, and therefore the command of the escort was vacant. The Resident's camp was to move on next morning. After dinner Colonel Sayer took me up to Mr Martin, saying, "Allow me, sir, specially to introduce my young friend here, of whom I have had already occasion to report favourably, officially; I beg you to keep him in mind." "Will you take the command of my escort by way of a beginning?" said the Resident. "I shall be happy to have you on my personal staff if you are sufficiently acquainted with the native language." This the good colonel answered for, and I was told to prepare without further delay. I don't know how I got away: I only remember trying to keep down a big lump that rose in my throat, and the colonel saying to me, "Now you've got a start—you will never disappoint me, I know."

All the ladies and gentlemen of the station were present, and crowded round me with congratulations; one of my friends came back with me to my house; my things were packed; we sent to the city for camels for my tents and baggage, which were despatched as quickly as possible. The night passed—I do not think I slept—and by dawn I was in my saddle, and joined the officers of the Resident's staff as they were starting on their morning stage. It was a sudden change in my life: what might be the next?

The Resident expressed himself much pleased when I presented myself at breakfast when the camp halted at a short stage from Aurungabad. We had killed two foxes by the way, my dogs having been posted beforehand. "So you can ride," said one of my new companions. I was then 9 stone 8 lb., and well mounted, as I had my chestnut, and a splendid bay hunter which Stirling had given to me. Yes; I could ride.

After breakfast Mr Martin sent for me, and asked me about my family and what I could do. He then set me to converse with his Moonshee, which I found very easy.

I had learned to speak Hindostanee like a gentleman;
and here let me impress upon all beginners the great advantage it is to learn to speak in a gentlemanly fashion.
It may be a little more difficult to acquire the idioms;
but it is well worth while. There are modes of address
suitable to all ranks and classes, and often our people unintentionally insult a native gentleman by speaking to
him as they would to their servants, through ignorance of
the proper form of address.

I was also examined in Persian, and Mr Martin complimented me on my diligence. The march was delightful, and the sport plentiful; small game abounded, and
we had an occasional stalk after antelope—sometimes, too,
a tiger was reported. The Resident always gave me some
work to do, and the days flew by very pleasantly. We
halted at Mominabad, a large cavalry station, where there
were brilliant reviews, and *levées* of native officers, and
much feasting. My dear friend Stirling had been promoted to the civil department, and was Superintendent of
a large district to the south; but the day after we reached
Mominabad, the Resident received an express stating that
Stirling had been killed in a fight with some Arabs who
had gained possession of the town of Dundooty; that
Major Sutherland was about to march there with his
whole force, and if the Resident had any instructions to
give, they were to be sent to meet him at Owsa. I was
inexpressibly shocked at this sad occurrence: not only
had Stirling been very dear to me as a friend, but he was
in all respects a *preux chevalier*, whom it had been my
wish to imitate. On consulting the map I found Owsa
was not more than thirty-five miles distant, and that I
could ride on there and join the force. I went to Mr
Martin and entreated permission to go; and I prevailed.
Before leaving him, he said very kindly, " I find you quite
qualified for civil employ, and shall therefore nominate
you to succeed your friend; but the appointment must be

confirmed by the Supreme Government, so you had better come to me at Hyderabad straight from Dundooty."

I was fairly astonished. The department into which I was to be transferred was the height of my ambition; the pay was 1500 rupees a-month! How I thanked Mr Martin, or how I got away, I know not; and between my sorrow for my friend and my own unexpected stroke of fortune, my head was in a whirl. I left the camp that afternoon with two troopers as escort, but the road was unfamiliar, and we were often misled, and it was not till early morning that we reached the cavalry camp as the bugles were sounding to " boot and saddle." We were just in time to join the forces and ride on with them another twenty *coss*, or forty miles. Of course Major Sutherland was surprised to see me, but the letters I had with me explained everything; and after a cup of coffee we rode on. We had a good rest at the end of the stage, and then proceeded to Gulburgah, another twenty miles, whence, after resting, we were to go on to Dundooty, eighteen miles further. It had been arranged that the Arabs in possession of the fort were to be at once summoned to lay down their arms and submit unconditionally; if they refused, the place was to be stormed at daylight next morning. To me was allotted one division of the stormers with their native officers, and all preliminaries were arranged. I think few of the Arabs would have been left had the attack been made, as Stirling was very popular and all were anxious to avenge his death; but as we approached the town we heard the beat of the Arab drum and saw the enemy moving off with their colours flying, by the Hyderabad road. The Commissioner had given permission to the Arabs to depart in peace, and thus they escaped our vengeance.

I had not felt tired, and even came in first in a race proposed by one of the officers. As I slid from my horse, however, I felt very stiff, and sitting on the ground, found

C

I had no power to rise. The surgeon declared my condition to be caused by temporary paralysis of the spine
consequent on my long ride of 113 miles, and I did not
recover at all till the afternoon of the next day, when a
painful tingling sensation set in in my legs and back, and
I soon was able to sit up. It was very clear if we had
had anything to do, I should have been unable to join
in it.

After-investigation proved that my poor friend Stirling
had met his death by his own rashness, in proceeding alone
to force the gate of the town with only twelve men against
more than a hundred Arabs. As soon as the gate was
opened, he fell dead, riddled by four balls which pierced
his chest. In a few days the inquiry ended, and there
being nothing to detain me, I was to proceed to Hyderabad. The evening before, Major Sutherland came to me
as I was sitting on the grass near poor Stirling's grave,
and said, " I know you have been appointed by the Resident to succeed Stirling, and that you are only awaiting
the confirmation of your appointment by the Supreme
Government. Now this is very creditable to you ; but I
have considered the matter very deeply, and I do not
think it likely that your appointment will be confirmed.
Mr Martin's patronage in the civil department will be
curtailed considerably ; and what I propose to you is this
—do not go to Hyderabad. I want an adjutant here for
one of the regiments. I will appoint you, pending your
final transfer to the cavalry. You ride well, our men like
you, and the pay is very good."

It was a tempting proposal. My first wish had been to
join the cavalry ; and yet, when the offer was made, could
I give up the chance of the coveted civil employ and the
splendid opening it afforded me ? Nor could I find out
that my kind friend was sure of his nomination being confirmed either. How, too, could I disappoint the Resident ?
or how encounter the heavy expenses of a rich cavalry

uniform with equipment and chargers? All this flashed through my mind in a moment, and I was not long in making my decision. I could only thank Major Sutherland, and say that "if I did not succeed in obtaining the civil appointment, I would request Mr Martin to put me into the cavalry."

"It will be too late then, Taylor," he said, smiling; "the Military Secretary will fill up the appointment at once, and I wanted you."

"I cannot give up," I replied, "what may be already settled for aught I know."

"Be it so," he answered, "I can say no more." Then he, his brother, and I discussed the matter in all its bearings, and they thought I was right in adhering to my resolve.

So next morning I started; but at a place called Purgy I was taken ill, and but for the kindness of the native Talookdar, Nawab Futteh Jah Khan, who sent his physician to me and nursed me tenderly, it would have gone hard with me. At last he sent his own palankeen, with orders that I was to be brought to his house for change of air. In vain I pleaded weakness and want of time. He would take no denial, and I went. This was my first introduction to the house of a native gentleman. "You are to be one of the family," said my host; "you are only a boy, and the ladies will not mind you. My wife will look after you, and the children shall play with you, and I will send on your letters to Hyderabad."

I stayed with these good people for a week, and was entertained most hospitably, and on leaving, presented my host with my old gun, to which he took a great fancy. He gave me a valuable sword and embroidered sword-belt, while his good lady begged my acceptance of a beautiful patchwork quilt and the bed I had slept in, which had very elaborately painted and gilt feet. I used these as long as they lasted.

When I arrived at Hyderabad Mr Martin sent for me. My appointment had not been confirmed, and he was very sore about it; I told him then what Major Sutherland had offered me. "Ah," said he, "bad luck pursues you: thinking you were surely provided for, I gave the cavalry adjutancy away where, indeed, it was already promised. You must not leave me though; if you will join my household I will have you returned 'on special duty,' till something offers worth giving you." Yes,—it was a great fall of all my castles in the air; I was not to be a civil superintendent, I was not to be an adjutant of cavalry, and I had nothing to do but to wait on, I hope patiently.

Mr Martin was very kind to me. I did what I could to help him in return, and found his splendid library an inexhaustible treasure-field.

The State of Hyderabad in itself is by far the largest and most important Mussulman dominion in India. The city is walled all round, and cannot, therefore, be enlarged, but the adjacent suburbs increase rapidly, and the population cannot now be less than 350,000 souls. I enjoyed my early rides, free from parade and other morning duties, and came upon many a picturesque scene, especially along the river, with the city walls and bastions on the one hand, and the native houses of the Begum Bazaar, with their fine trees, on the other. The river-bed, too, is always a stirring sight, with its countless groups of people bathing, washing clothes, or carrying away water from holes scooped in the sand; elephants being washed or scrubbed with sand by their keepers, and evidently enjoying the operation. These, and many other objects, formed glowing pictures of colour and native costume of endless variety. The scenery, too, is very striking. From one favourite point of view of mine, the city lies stretched before you, the graceful " Char Minar " or gate of the " Four Minarets " in its centre; the gigantic " Mecca mosque " standing out nobly; while the large tank of " Meer Allum " lies at your

feet, and the bold rock of the fort of Golcondah rises in
the distance. From hence, a rising sun gradually lighting
up every object in the clear morning air, and the glowing
glittering landscape terminating in the tender blue of the
distance, is inexpressibly beautiful. There is also a favourite place of resort of an evening for Mussulman gentlemen of the city on a knoll to the right of the Masulipatam
road ; and I was often asked to sit down with them while
their carpets were spread, and their attendants brought
hookahs. Even thus early in my life, I began associating
with native gentlemen, and observing their manners and
customs, modes of speech and conversation. The glorious
view, the air filled with golden light, the gorgeous sunsets,
the mellowness which softened every object, made, I
think, the evening even more beautiful than the morning.
I loved to go there quietly and dream dreams. I was
growing out of boyhood, and that period is always a
momentous one to every man. I was sensitive and shy,
and no doubt romantic. Mr Martin was always kind,
and bade me be hopeful; but I had been sorely disappointed, and felt often sad and dejected as to my prospects. At this time I was often at the house of Mr
William Palmer, where I met the most intelligent members of Hyderabad society, both native and European, and
the pleasant gatherings at his most hospitable house were
a great relief from the state and formality of the 'Residency.

I was not long destined to be idle. One day Mr Martin
sent for me and told me that, under a recent arrangement
in the military department, a small appointment on the
general staff was at his disposal if I liked to accept it. I
was delighted at the idea of having anything to do, and
thanked him cordially for his kindness.

The appointment was Superintendent of Bazaars at
Bolarum, a cantonment of the Nizam's troops twelve
miles north of the Residency, on higher ground, and con-

sequently cooler and more bracing. My duties were simple enough. I had to regulate the markets and the prices of grain in conjunction with the principal merchants and grain-dealers. I was to decide all civil cases, try, and punish all breaches of the peace, and make daily reports to my superior officer at ten o'clock every morning in person. I was to inspect all meat killed, both for the use of the troops and private consumption; in fact, I was a sort of magistrate for the cantonment and its environs; and, as one of the Division Staff, had to attend the "Brigadier" at all parades and on field-days.

I was, on the whole, well pleased with my office. Of course it was monotonous. What Indian staff appointment, with a daily routine of work, is not?

I was enabled to discover and check various irregularities in the prices of grain and *ghee* or boiled butter, which had escaped my predecessor, and this made the sepoys my friends. The stores of grain were kept up at their full complement, and the force could have taken the field at an hour's notice. Every one pronounced the meat and bread better than before; and as I had established a free market for vegetables, they were always plentiful and fresh.

Still, it was a troublesome post. Disputes often arose between masters and servants, debts by individuals, and the like; but I believe I firmly gained the colonel's goodwill by settling a dangerous quarrel between two infantry regiments which had arisen at one of the festivals. During the inquiry that followed, over which I presided, I found an opportunity of reconciliation, of which I availed myself, and the quarrel was made up out of hand.

I did not enter much into general society at this period. High play was the chief amusement which prevailed, and I never was at that time or at any time fond of cards, or did I ever play for money, except for the veriest trifle.

I worked on as well as I could, taking care not to

neglect my Persian studies, and occasionally reading with
a Moonshee or native teacher, and looked forward hope-
fully to the time when, by some possibility, I might gain
an entrance into the Civil Service. The day came at
length. An officer, who was Assistant Superintendent of
Police in the S.W. district of the country, got tired of his
solitary life, and proposed to exchange with me. Mr
Martin at once consented to the step, and wrote to me
very kindly on the subject, expressing his desire to serve
me to the utmost of his power, and recommending me to
accept the exchange.

My arrangements were soon complete. I was to become
proprietor of Captain L.'s bungalow at Sudasheopett, with
one or two tents; he, of my " buggy " and horse, which I
no longer needed. Furniture on both sides was valued;
and when we were respectively in " orders," I betook myself to my new duties, of which the Resident and his
secretary gave me an outline; but nothing very precise
could be laid down respecting them, and I was left very
much to exercise my own judgment.

I left Bolarum with many expressions of kind regret
from the colonel, who thanked me for my services, and
declared himself well satisfied with me on all points,
offering me a testimonial of good conduct and ability in
case of my requiring one at any time.

Now at last I was free !—literally my own master. I
had an immense tract of country to overlook, of which I
knew nothing, except that in going to Dundooty I had
crossed part of it. I took leave of the Resident and of
the Nizam's Minister, Chundoo Lall, who were both very
kind to me; but of all the counsel and direction I received,
I owe most of what was useful to me afterwards to Mr
Palmer, and he offered to assist me by letter if I were in
need of help. His grand-looking old mother, the Begum
Sahib, blessed me, and tied a rupee in a silk handkerchief
round my arm, praying the saints to have me in their

holy keeping ; and I started on my journey, accompanied by my escort of police, and reached Sudasheopett on the fourth day. I had not completed my eighteenth year.

The northern boundary of my district may have been 250 miles in length, extending from Hyderabad to Puraindah, with stations at various intervals, of which Tooljapoor was one of the most important. Its general southern boundary was the Bheema river, to its junction with the Krishna, and its greatest breadth was from 50 to 60 miles, narrowing at either end. In all, it may have included from ten to twelve thousand square miles, and its population must have exceeded one million souls.

My duties in the Revenue Department were not to begin till the Superintendent made his tour through the district after the monsoon. My police duties were very clear. There were stations as nearly as possible every forty miles, where twelve mounted and ten foot police were posted ; and these went periodical patrols from their own station to the next, returning every fortnight.

Foot police were stationed in villages averaging three miles asunder, and patrolled their beat every day. If anything occurred it was reported to the jemadar, and by him to me, if important ; otherwise, it was entered in the diary, which was transmitted to me weekly.

I had altogether 50 mounted and 150 foot police under my command. The road was an important one—the highroad to Bombay—and the patrols had had the effect of keeping off gangs of highway robbers and *dacoits*,* which before the establishment of the force had become very bold and dangerous.

My predecessor had been enjoined to take active measures for the suppression of these pests, but, so far as I could ascertain, had really done nothing.

I assembled all my jemadars and native officers, and endeavoured to find out their views of what was most

* *Dacoity*, robbery with violence.

feasible to be done ; but I found most of them were men from a distance, and possessed little, if any, local knowledge.

A district lay between the tract of land over which I had jurisdiction, and the river Mangera to the north, and it soon became plain to me that unless I had command over this as well, I could do very little to check the depredations of the dacoits, who had, as was evident from the records, become the terror of this part of the country. I therefore applied for, and obtained, the necessary permission, and was soon free to act in all directions needful to my purpose.

My position was a very pleasant one. My little bungalow was situated at the edge of a mango-grove, which lies behind the present travellers' bungalow. It consisted of one centre room, with a division all round, forming a dressing-room, bath-room, and store-room. Without, at a little distance, were the offices and kitchen, and stabling for five horses. I could not immediately start on my tour through the district, as it was the rainy season, but I had ample occupation. I gathered all the information I could with regard to thieves and robbers. I made a large collection of birds and insects for my uncle, Mr Prideaux Selby, of Twizell House, Northumberland, who was engaged upon his great work on Ornithology. Tree birds of all kinds abounded, while the tanks or reservoirs teemed with water-fowl of seemingly endless variety.

I sent to Bombay for a Mahratta grammar, and began the study of that language, without which I plainly saw I could not get on. Teloogoo was the language of the people about Sudasheopett, and it changed to Canarese a little distance further; but neither was a language of business. Mahratta was evidently the most useful of all.

I had plenty to do. Every morning brought in reports from my officers and men, which had to be answered and investigated. Then my early bag of birds had to be skinned and prepared ; English correspondence and my

Mahratta lesson followed; and I had always a box of books from the Secunderabad or Bolarum library to occupy my evenings. I kept Mr Newnham well informed of my doings, and his delight when I obtained this appointment was very sincere.

I rode in to Hyderabad towards the close of the monsoon to see Mr Martin, and I told him what I was doing, and that I was collecting all the information I could about the district. He desired me to march quietly up to a spot near the western frontier, as he might have occasion to employ me actively, but said he could not be more explicit just then. So, at the beginning of October, I joyfully betook myself to my tent-life, with a sense of freedom and of joy which I still can vividly recall.

I journeyed leisurely on. The country was open and beautiful, the various crops were being sown, the air felt dry and fresh, and the march was very enjoyable. I halted near Hominabad, and rode over to see the old city of Beeder, than which, I think, nothing could be more picturesque. Hominabad was a central point, where was concentrated all the trade in salt and spices from the western coast for Berar, receiving in return cotton, oil-seed, ginger, grain, &c. I found I could serve the merchants considerably, and one, Seth Atmaram, became my good friend; but first we had a quarrel. Some of my escort complained of short weight in their flour, and I had the persons who sold it fined: whereupon the other flour and retail grain dealers shut their shops, and went in a body to a grove, where they declared they would remain till I went away. I was certainly not to be intimidated; so I set up a bazaar of my own, which was well supplied by some Brinjaries, the old chief of whom had certificates from the Duke of Wellington for services in the Mahratta war. Provision-sellers came from other villages, and I was independent. An effort was made to induce me to send for the fugitives, but I refused; then a complaint

reached the Minister at Hyderabad, Rajah Chundoo Lall,
that I had desolated the town by my violence, and ex-
torted large sums of money from the chief merchants.
Mr Martin requested an explanation from me, which I,
of course, gave at once. Meantime my friends began to
think they had gone too far, and brought a petition to the
effect that I had been misled, and that they knew the real
culprits, with whom I could deal as I pleased, &c. Mr
Martin was now satisfied, and I received his commendation. The Minister sent down a special officer, who used
a very lofty tone to the merchants, threatened a fine of
10,000 rupees, which I begged off; and he departed
finally, with, no doubt, a very handsome private *douceur*
in his pocket. When I next visited Hyderabad, old
Chundoo Lall, giving me a poke in the ribs, said, grimly,
" Ah, Taylor Sahib ! you should have let me put the screw
on those Hominabad people. You had them down so
completely—and they always defied me—I might have
got a lakh out of them." "And lost your good name,
Maharaj," I replied. " You should bestow half a lakh
on *me* for being so careful of your good name and
honour ! "

There were no more complaints of false weights. The
Dean of Guild and Town Council were made answerable
for them, and the police had authority to inspect them
from time to time.

My next halt was at Tooljapoor, which I found a most
picturesque, delightful spot. I have made it the scene of
my historical romance, ' Tara,' because of its beauty and
of its history, when in 1657 its temple was plundered by
Afzool Khan, whose subsequent murder by Sivajee is still
considered by the people as but a fitting retribution. The
day I arrived, a Brahmin entered my *cutcherry*, or office-
tent, sat down quietly in a corner, and after remaining a
while silent, rose and said—

" I hear you speak Mahratta ; is it so ? "

"I am only a beginner," I replied; "but I daresay I can follow you."

"I am struck with your face," he continued, "and I should like to see your hand and cast your horoscope. Do you know when you were born?"

I gave him the date, and he proceeded to examine first my forehead and then my left hand. "It is a long and happy life on the whole," he said; "but there are some crosses and some deep sorrows. You are not yet married, but you soon will be, and you will have children—not many—some of whom you will lose. You will never be rich, nor ever poor; and yet much, very much, money will pass through your hands. You will not now stay long here; but after many years you will return, and rule over us. Fear nothing; your destiny is under the planet Jupiter, and you will surely prosper."

He added further details when he brought my horoscope some hours later, one which especially struck me being that I should become a Rajah, and rule over a large tract of country to the south.

I thought the affair curious enough, and wrote out a translation of it, which I sent home; but, to my regret, have failed to find more than allusions to it in my father's letters to me.

During that day my tent was beset by hundreds of pilgrims and travellers, crying loudly for justice against the flour-sellers, who not only gave short weight in flour, but adulterated it so distressingly with sand, that the cakes made of it were uneatable, and had to be thrown away. I sent for the civil officer of the town, who declared the flour-sellers to be incorrigible, and that the complaint was perfectly true; so I determined to take my own course.

That evening I told some reliable men of my escort to go quietly into the bazaars, and each buy flour at a separate shop, being careful to note whose shop it was. The flour was brought to me. I tested every sample, and found it full of sand as I passed it under my teeth. I then desired that all the persons named in my list should be sent to me, with their baskets of flour, their weights and scales. Shortly afterwards they arrived, evidently suspecting nothing, and were placed in a row, seated on the grass before my tent.

"Now," said I, gravely, "each of you are to weigh out a seer (two pounds) of your flour," which was done.

"Is it for the pilgrims?" asked one.

"No," said I, quietly, though I had much difficulty to keep my countenance. "You must eat it yourselves."

They saw that I was in earnest, and offered to pay any fine I imposed.

"Not so," I returned; "you have made many eat your flour, why should you object to eat it yourselves?"

They were horribly frightened; and, amid the jeers and screams of laughter of the bystanders, some of them actually began to eat, sputtering out the half-moistened flour, which could be heard crunching between their teeth. At last some of them flung themselves on their faces, abjectly beseeching pardon.

"Swear," I cried, "swear by the holy mother in yonder temple, that you will not fill the mouths of her worshippers with dirt! You have brought this on yourselves, and there is not a man in all the country who will not laugh at the *bunnias* (flour-sellers), who could not eat their own flour because it broke their teeth."

So this episode terminated, and I heard no more complaints of bad flour.

I received notice soon after that I was to proceed to Puraindah and take charge of a squadron of cavalry, which was to meet me there, and that I was to co-operate with the civil authorities of the Bombay Presidency for the suppression of the rebellion of Oomajee Naik—this being the special service that Mr Martin had hinted to me. I

marched at once, and found the squadron already there—
two troops and their native officers. We were not idle.
Oomajee Naik seemed to be ubiquitous, and we had many
a weary, fruitless search for this noted and most mischievous brigand, whose robberies, often attended with violence,
cattle-lifting, and all manner of villany, had become the
terror of the country. Oomajee had a spite against all
authority, hated both priestly and secular Brahmins, and
enjoyed nothing more, if he could catch one, than cutting
off his nose and ears. By his own people he was considered a hero. He was hunted down at last, after many
years, by an English officer, who captured him as he was
bathing in the river Bheema. He led us many a dance
through the country, and often we were misled on false
information. I scoured the hills and plains equally in
vain, and became notorious by wearing a pair of red cloth
trousers, made by a native artist, having worn out my own
riding trousers completely. At last Oomajee found the
place was getting too hot for him, and withdrew, and we
were released from our harassing work.

I paid a pleasant visit to the Collector of Sholapoor,
who, I remember, was much surprised at my youthful
appearance, and we discussed together the best way to
repress the great crime of cattle-lifting, which had been
actively carried on for years. I was amused to meet at
the hospitable Collector's table some of my old shipmates
of the Upton Castle, and to witness their surprise to see
"Baxter's shop-boy" transformed into a grave Political
Agent for the whole of the Nizam's frontier. They all
congratulated me, and showed me every possible attention
during my stay. Mr Newnham wrote me a very gratifying letter, saying he had heard me praised officially, and
that he was quite satisfied with my progress.

I returned to my own quarters, and on consulting with
my native friends, found I had not sufficient power to
carry out my scheme of organising the police as I wished,

at once; but I was advised to take one *pergunna*, or county, work that first, and then gradually extend my system. My district was much cut up by private estates, whose owners or managers defied or evaded the orders of the Nizam's executive government, and would only obey their own masters, some of whom were powerful nobles of Hyderabad, who jealously resented any interference by the executive minister, while their agents were well-known protectors of thieves and robbers, whose booty they shared. Evidently mine was no easy task, and I must make sure my footing before I could establish or carry out any measures of reform.

I had a note from the Collector of Sholapoor requesting me to meet him at a town called Bursee, which I did; killing two splendid hogs on the road, single-handed, and receiving much commendation from my friend, one of the greatest sportsmen of the Bombay side. A complaint was made to us by one of the native officers about the executive department of the Revenue Survey, which was then proceeding: it was averred that bribes were taken and other corrupt practices carried on, and numerous documents were sent in as proof. We looked into the matter, and found not only much ground for complaint, but also that a great deal of the work was good for nothing. I had the pleasure afterwards of learning, through Mr Newnham, that I had been the means of bringing heavy frauds to light, and had done essential service.

In regard to my plan of frontier police, the Collector saw many difficulties, unless, indeed, a regular force were organised; and I had yet much to learn.

I determined, therefore, to begin at my own end of the district first, quietly feeling my way. In some places my orders had met with a hearty response, in others they were totally disregarded.

My camp was pitched at Ekhailee, when one afternoon I saw some persons carrying a native bedstead, which was

put down opposite my tent: there was something lying
upon it concealed by a bloody sheet; when this was withdrawn, I saw a young Brahmin literally covered with
sabre-cuts. He was very faint, but after the barber had
dressed his wounds, he told his story, saying that the
night before, the Rajah, as he was called, of Kurrumkote,
had attacked his house, had murdered his father, uncle,
and grandmother, and had then proceeded to plunder the
dwelling; that the Rajah was still abroad, and purposed
committing another dacoity that night at a village he
named.

There was no time to lose; this at any rate might be
prevented. I had ten mounted men and five available
foot police, and I prepared in all haste.

The perpetrator of the outrage was a noted character,
Narrayan Rao, and I had heard of him as being a very
dangerous man. His village was very strong, and he had
recently repaired the *garhy* or castle, with its gates and
bastions, and it held a strong garrison of desperadoes. I
was determined to have him if I could. My friend, Bulram Sing, knew the country well, and was our guide.
We had thirty miles to march, but eventually the night's
work proved far more.

It was dark as we neared the village of Cooloor, where
the proposed dacoity was to take place, and leaving four
men for its protection I took on the other nine, including
Bulram Sing and another jemadar of police; I had also
two grooms who rode my baggage-ponies; and these constituted my little party.

We rode first to a town called Sooloopett, where Narrayan Rao was reported to have been seen in the bazaar;
but we were at fault, as he had left it and gone, the
people said, to Cooloor; but as there was no other road
than the one by which we had just come, we knew this
could not be the case. Bulram Sing fancied the Rajah
must have heard of the wounded Brahmin having been

brought to me, and therefore had retired to his fort; and
he was right.   We all partook of some refreshment, as we
were tired, and then started for Kurrumkote—the Rajah's
village.

It looked very strong as we approached in the early
morning; the fort stood out in the centre with its large
bastions and loopholed walls, all in excellent repair.   We
halted under a little grove of mango-trees, and when the
gate was opened to allow the cattle to come out, we rode
in boldly, and though the guard seized their matchlocks,
no one attempted to fire.   In reply to their questions I
answered, " I have been travelling all night, and am tired,
and intend to rest here a while."

" We will send word to the Rajah," said several.

" No," I answered, " I will speak to him myself;" and
we rode up the main street.   I thought for a moment that
it was rather a rash proceeding, for on the bastions of the
fort many men appeared, showing themselves on the parapet and calling to us to go back.   The Rajah lived in the
fort, and some men came out and stood on the steps leading up to it, and asked me what I wanted.

" The Sahib Bahadur wishes to see your Rajah Sahib,"
said my jemadar, " and he is tired—he has ridden all night."

" My master is asleep," rejoined the man, " and I dare
not disturb him."

" I must see him, and at once," I said ; " if he does not
come, I shall go in myself," and the spokesman went in,
returning directly with a young fair man, who was tying
a handkerchief round his head.

He saluted me, and inquired haughtily, " why I had
come into his town, into which no Feringhee had ever
before entered without his leave ? "

I stooped down and said in his ear, " You are my
prisoner, and must come quietly with me; if you or your
people resist, I will drive my spear through your body.
Now we will go, if you please."

The street was narrow, and as my horsemen spread themselves behind us, no one could get near us. I do not remember ever feeling so excited as I did when the Rajah and I went down to the gate by which we had entered. He said nothing: but his men were crowding on the walls and house-tops, all armed and calling to each other. Perhaps they noticed that my long hog spear was within six inches of their Rajah's back!

When we reached the gate he merely said to the guard, "Don't follow, I shall return soon;" and we all passed out safely.

"Now," said I to one of my men, "let the Sahib ride, Bhudrinath;" and as he dismounted from his mare, I bade Narrayan Rao get up.

"If you don't, you're a dead man," I said; and Bulram Sing advised him to obey; "for," said he, "if you do not do as my master orders you, he will put his spear through you."

So the Rajah mounted, and as this was seen from the gate towers not a hundred and fifty yards from us, one of my men happening to look round, called out, "They are going to fire;" and we had scarcely time to put our weary horses into a canter, when a regular volley was discharged, knocking up the dust behind us.

Bhudrinath had scrambled up behind the Rajah with a merry laugh, and kept consoling his companion by telling him the shot would hit him first. Narrayan Rao, however, maintained perfect silence, and told me afterwards he expected to have been hung upon the first tree, and supposed this to be my reason for ordering him to mount.

Now I had my prisoner, where was I to put him? My camp was forty miles distant, and I resolved at last to take him to Chinchola, where there was a fortified court-house, which could be easily defended in case of a rescue being attempted; and when we reached it the Rajah was safely located there, having been first put in irons.

The surviving relations of the murdered Brahmins came that evening, and were confronted with the Rajah, who did not attempt to deny the murders. The family were his own near relations, but they had a good deal of silver plate, which had excited his cupidity.

All that night we were kept in constant alarm. Shots were fired at our gates and bastions, and dismal and un- earthly shriekings and howlings were kept up by our enemies. I was glad when morning came, and brought my servants with clean clothes and a guard of five soldiers. It was a busy day; people crowded in with complaints and accusations against the prisoner for ex- actions and dacoity. Strange to say, he admitted them all, and directed us where to find the plunder. I sent for it, and it was brought: massive silver, copper, and brass vessels, and a quantity of valuable cloths and silk. The villagers sent me eight men who had assisted at the dacoity, and their confessions enabled me to apprehend ten more.

I determined to take the wretch himself to Hyderabad. This he heard of, and sent me a private note, which ran thus:—

" You are all powerful and merciful. Send the enclosed to Hominabad, and you can get cash or bills for 24,000 rupees. When you get this, allow me to depart."

" So that is your game, my friend," I thought; " per- haps you may be corrupting my people." So I ordered my bed to be taken down and placed across his door, and talked to him most of the night.

" I was a fool," he said, " not to shut the gate when you were inside. My people would have killed you."

" It wouldn't have helped you much," I replied; " your village would soon have been knocked about your ears, and you would have been hanged. Now you are safe. Chundoo Lall will not hang a Brahmin."

" Not unless your gentlemen make him," he said, " as

you do your own people when murder is done. I hated
them. I only killed my uncle. He was the worst."

"And your grandmother ? "

"Ah !" he said, and was silent. He then asked if I
had sent for the 24,000 rupees in money or bills?

"No," I said, "English gentlemen do not take bribes.
The Minister will get the money at Hyderabad."

"God forbid!" he exclaimed; "take 50,000, take a
lakh. Ah, sir! for your mother's sake let me go. I cannot go to Hyderabad alive!"

It struck me he might have poison concealed about
him, so I had him stripped and searched. I told him
frankly, he must go to Hyderabad, for that I had no
power to deal with him.

But it did not seem an easy matter to get him there.
My scouts brought in word that the Rajah's people were
out in great numbers on the road, and intended to dispute
my passage. My escort was very weak; I had nineteen
prisoners. But a happy solution occurred to my difficulties. My men on the look-out reported that some English troops had arrived, and going up myself, I saw the
flags of an English regiment being set out for an encampment. I dressed quickly and went to the officer in command, who at once ordered a native officer and twenty
men to accompany the prisoners. I started early next
morning, and made a long march, clearing the jungly
tract in which the rescue had been planned, and which
would very possibly have succeeded had my escort remained as it was. I reached Hyderabad on the third day,
and was immediately summoned to the Residency, red
trousers and all; told Mr Martin my story, which amused
him very much, and showed him the order for the 24,000
rupees. He desired me to go on at once to the Minister, and
we did, hot and travel-stained as we were. Chundoo Lall
was very cordial and gracious, and his keen grey eyes
twinkled when I handed him the order for the 24,000

rupees, and he laughed heartily at my account of the whole scene.

"Why did you not get the lakh, Taylor?" he said; "now it will be hidden."

Narrayan Rao sat trembling in the corner, making frantic appeals for justice, and I took my leave as I heard the order given for "close imprisonment."

"The Minister might have given you a present out of the money you brought," said Mr Martin; and indeed I thought so too, especially as three of my best horses died soon after.

I received a very handsome official acknowledgment from Mr Martin for the service I had rendered, praising my "zeal and promptitude in an arduous and trying business," and much more that was very flattering and pleasant. I left Hyderabad within a week; but, alas! my horses had been in an infected stable, and I lost all except my white pony. It was in vain that I asked for some help to replace them, although they had done valuable service, and were a loss of 3000 rupees.

I mentioned my loss when writing to Mr Newnham, and he sent me most kindly and generously a magnificent bay—a timely gift, and one I highly prized.

When I returned to my district, in company with my chief, Mr Colvin, we determined to look into the revenue settlement of the country. We stayed a few delicious days at Beeder, roaming through the grand old city, revelling in its beauty, and recalling its past histories. We could have stayed there dreaming on, but work was before us, and we pushed on to Hominabad.

I am not going to inflict details of revenue settlement on my readers. We found the Bengal system, with which Mr Colvin was familiar, would not suit the country at all, and that the best plan was to continue the former settlements, with here and there some slight alterations; and as I could do this alone, he left me. I worked at this and

my registration of village police in every county and along
the road, getting on as well as I could, and my old hope of
having a district to myself was renewed, as Mr Colvin
was dissatisfied and would not stay, and thought it likely
that I might be appointed in his place.

Some very curious and difficult cases of disputed inher-
itance came before me. One I very well remember, in
which two families claimed the same land under a grant
from King Yoosuf Adil Shah, who began to reign A.D.
1480. The papers were exactly similar. No forgery could
be detected either in the registries or seals ; both seemed
genuine, and we were fairly puzzled, till, after dinner,
holding up the paper to the light, I saw an unmistakable
water-mark — a figure of an angel, with " Goa " underneath. Now Goa had only been taken by the Portuguese
in A.D. 1510 ; therefore, there could have been no Goa
paper in existence in 1488, and Indian paper has never
any water-mark. The falsification, therefore, of the deed
written on Portuguese paper was conclusive.

Mr Colvin was obliged to go back to Hyderabad, as his
health was suffering, and I had an immense increase of
work ; but I determined to make myself acquainted with
every detail, in order to fit myself to succeed him if he
should leave.

Returning after an absence of a month through my district, I was met by some very startling revelations. The
police, and chiefly my faithful Bulram Sing, had reported
some very unusual occurrences. Dead bodies, evidently
strangled, and in no instance recognised, were found by
the roadside, and no clue could be discovered as to the
perpetrators of their death. In two places, jackals or
hyenas had rooted up newly-made graves, in one of which
were found four bodies and in another two, much eaten
and disfigured.

The whole country was in alarm, and the villagers had
constantly patrolled their roads, but as yet in vain. All

we could learn was, that some time before, two bodies of
men had passed through the district, purporting to be
merchants from the north going southwards, but that they
appeared quiet and respectable, above suspicion. During
these inquiries it transpired that numbers of persons of
that part of my district were absent every year from their
homes at stated periods. These were for the most part
Mussulmans, who carried on a trade with Belgaum, Dar-
war, and Mysore, bringing back wearing apparel, copper
and brass vessels, and the like. Who could these be ?
Day after day I tried to sift the mystery, but could not.
I registered their names, and enjoined Bulram Sing to
have the parties watched on their return home. But as
the monsoon opened that year with much violence, I was
obliged, most reluctantly, to go back to my bungalow at
Sudasheopett.

I was very anxious about this time also on another
point.

Lord William Bentinck, then Governor-General, had
adopted as one of his political measures the alteration of
the treaties between several native States with the Honourable East India Company, which provided for the support
of Contingent forces established during Lord Hastings'
government. When it was known that the Nagpore force
had been abolished, and all the officers of the Company's
army remanded to their regiments, and the local officers
discharged with gratuities of a few months' pay each, it
was impossible not to feel the direst anxiety as to the fate
of the Nizam's Contingent, which occupied a perfectly
similar position.

It was expected that we should receive four months'
pay each, and then I should be thrown again upon the
world.

Had the old Nizam lived, or had he been in a condition
to transact business, he might have yielded to the offers
made him ; for the force was a very expensive one, cost-

ing forty lakhs or more, and it was expected the Nizam
would gladly pay twenty or thirty as an escape from
further liability. But his end was now approaching, and
for a time we had a respite.

Mr Newnham wrote to me bidding me "come to him
again and he would do his best to further my interests ; "
and in the event of our force being abolished I should
have done so. Mr Palmer advised my remaining at
Hyderabad and becoming a merchant, and promised me
a rapid fortune. So waiting and speculating I kept on,
often very weary and anxious.

The old Nizam, Sikunder Jah, died at the end of June
1829, and was succeeded by his eldest son, not of the
highest degree of marriage ; but he was favoured by the
Minister, Chundoo Lall, and was confirmed as his father's
successor at Calcutta.

The first use he made of his power was, at the " durbar "
which the Resident attended to congratulate him on his
accession, to demand roughly, " That the Feringhees, who
were interfering in his country, should be recalled." Of
course no immediate reply could be given, as the establishment of the civil control had been at the request of his
father, who was sufficiently wise to see that the best chance
of prosperity for his country was its being placed under
English gentlemen.

It was the general opinion that the withdrawal of the
civil officers would be the prelude to the total abolition
of the Contingent. Reference was made to Calcutta, and
it was decided to accede to the wishes of the Nizam.
After living some months in a state of feverish anxiety as
to my fate, I received orders in October to rejoin my
regiment at Hyderabad, as the civil control was to be dis-
continued. I earnestly entreated to be allowed to remain
even a short time to prosecute my inquiries respecting the
mysterious murders which had been perpetrated in my
district. At first the Resident listened to me incredulously

as I unfolded my tale; but he soon saw I was in earnest, and he wrote to the Minister to request permission for me to stay; but Chundoo Lall replied that the Nizam had become so impatient and imperious that he dare not sanction my continuance; and with a very heavy heart I rejoined my regiment, the 6th, stationed at Bolarum. Had I been allowed to remain, I should have been the first to disclose the horrible crime of Thuggee to the world; but it fell to the good fortune of Major Sleeman to do so afterwards. My inquiries were very active, and I found that parties of apparently most respectable Mussulmans occasionally passed through the district, having charms, amulets, and medicines to sell. "Our trade," said one to me, "is to take with us from Allund, old and new *sarees* and waistbands and trade with them, getting in exchange brass and copper pots, and gold or silver ornaments; these we exchange again when the rains begin. We don't take our wives; they and the children remain at home as hostages for the rent we owe." What could seem more plausible; and who could conceive the horrible crimes that were concealed under so fair a semblance?

The subject haunted me; why should so many men follow the same calling? Where did they go? Were they speaking truth? My people were at fault, and Bulram Sing shared my suspicions. He and Bhudrinath volunteered to follow and watch these men, and they were both absent disguised as fakeers when I was recalled to my regiment, and thus the mystery remained unsolved!

All chance of civil employ was now over, but still the service was safe, as the Nizam had promptly refused to do away with the Contingent and substitute a payment of twenty lakhs, as had been suggested. He took pride in the force, and the English Government now declared that it should not be disturbed, but that its cost should be lessened by sundry reforms. The pay was made to assimilate with that of the Company's army, without any consideration of the pensions, passage - money, and other advantages of the Company's service: we "locals" were to have our bare pay only—in my case as a lieutenant it was 290 rupees a-month instead of 400. New regulations were drawn up providing promotion to the rank of captain after twelve years' service: but no pension was allowed; and the whole was summed up by a sentence which carried despair to many a heart—

"The Nizam's Government can grant no furlough to Europe."

No more sight of home! no future meeting with my mother! never again to visit England, unless I left the service and returned to be a burden to my people. I can never forget the numbness which crept over me as I thought of it, now that all pleasant anticipations were gone, and my congenial employment exchanged for the dull routine of regimental duty. My old company received me with affectionate greeting, and I made up my mind, for the present at least, to remain. I was now twenty-one.

CHAPTER IV.

1829-37.

I HAVE, perhaps, no right to intrude upon my readers the doubts and fears, crude hopes and impossible aspirations that filled my mind, as was only natural in one so young. I had met with some disappointments, bitter ones, already; but I had courage and good health remaining, and I always look upon this period as a turning-point in my life. I was exposed to much temptation. In those days in India men drank hard and deep, and high play was the rule, not the exception. However, I cared for none of these things, and kept much aloof; I was esteemed exclusive and unsociable, but I did not mind. I had my own recreations after my own taste; among these my boat on the large Hoosein Saugor Tank was my chief one, and scarcely an evening passed that I did not drive over from Bolarum to have a sail. I had rigged her myself with three sprit-sails, after the fashion of the Liverpool ferry-boats, and I fully enjoyed sailing her in company with the other tiny yachts which were always out. I studied Persian and Mahratta, and if I had been drawing all day long I could not have complied with the requests that were made to me to fill the albums of my fair friends.

Mr Martin was removed from the Residency at Hyderabad and transferred to an appointment at Delhi. He had never been popular, and his manner was cold and formal except to those he really liked. To me he had been invariably kind, and the tears stood in his eyes when I took leave of him. "I would have done more for you if I could," he said; "I feel as if you were among the few really true to me." He soon afterwards took furlough to England, and did not resume his public life.

In November 1830, Colonel Stewart, formerly Resident at Gwalior, was promoted to Hyderabad. From him and his charming family I experienced kindness and hospitality unbounded. He was generous and open-hearted, and belonged to the school of "non-interference" politicians. The Nizam expressed himself anxious to effect reform in many departments, but ended by doing very little.

At the end of the Mahratta war of 1818, the finances of the Nizam's State were in the utmost disorder, and the Government of the Nizam had no credit whatever in the money market. Had it not been for the continuous loans made to it by Messrs Wm. Palmer & Co., it must have become bankrupt in all its State obligations. The Nizam had large private hoards, but these he refused to allow his Minister to touch for any public purpose. The loan of £600,000, authorised by the Indian Government, from the house of Wm. Palmer & Co., did for a while satisfy some pressing needs; but no attempt was made to introduce economical reform, or to raise depressed revenue to the ordinary standard. Therefore, financial distress continued. Villages were deserted; large tracts left uncultivated; rebellions ensued which the Government was too weak to check; and it was when things were in this condition that Sir Charles Metcalf proposed the introduction of the superintendence of English officers into the civil departments—a measure sanctioned by the Court of Directors, and approved by the old Nizam.

The measures enforced by these officers were the settlement for five years of every village which duly received its lease. Waste lands were let at small increasing rents, till a fair average should be attained in five or seven years; cultivation increased rapidly; emigrants returned; much good was done, and much exaction prevented. The officers of the Nizam's Government made the collections, and generally managed their own districts, but no demand for extra cesses or oppression of any kind was left unnoticed. These native officers considered the check and superintendence of the English a great grievance, and appeals were entered against them; but on the whole the system worked harmoniously and beneficially to the people.

Now, however, that the civil control of the English was abolished, the country was thrown open to the Minister and his creatures, and the old scenes were enacted anew. The fine rich cotton-growing country of Berar suffered terribly, and many more likewise. Districts were farmed out to speculators, or money-lenders—whoever chose to make the highest advance; and it was a grim joke at Hyderabad that every man who took a district rode the first stage with his face to his horse's tail, to see who was following him.

To Chundoo Lall's policy Colonel Stewart appeared indifferent. The Nizam had been offered power to dismiss his Minister, and had refused to do so, professing himself perfectly satisfied; so things grew worse and worse.

I have not yet mentioned the prosecution of Obeed Hoosein, the late Resident's Moonshee, on the part of the trustees of the house of Wm. Palmer & Co. This person had been an immense favourite of Mr Martin, I think. But for his influence the Resident would have given Mr Palmer every assistance in the recovery and liquidation of the large sums lent by the House to the Nizam's Government: but from the moment of his arrival there was a perceptible difference; and not only was no help given in recovering sums which had already been decided in favour of the House by the Mussulman Civil Court of Hyderabad,

but every difficulty that ingenuity could suggest was
thrown in the way, and Chundoo Lall and others amused
themselves by telling Mr Palmer how much money they
were giving to the Moonshee to get the claims altogether
quashed. Sir Charles Metcalf's opinions were adverse to
the House, and debates ran high. There were Palmerites
and Metcalfites; and I, young as I was, took part in the
discussions, maintaining only that " if the whole of the
claims were dishonest, why did Government pay any of
them? Why had the English Government applied to the
Court of King's Bench for a mandamus to adopt a despatch in Messrs Wm. Palmer & Co.'s favour? And why
had the Hyderabad Courts given awards in their favour
amounting to £100,000, the payment of which was hin-
dered by the intrigues of Mr Martin's Moonshee?" No
doubt I spoke as a lad, and with all the zeal of youth;
but now, forty - four years after, I find my opinion un-
changed.

Mr Palmer's house continued my chief resort. There
was a fascination about him quite irresistible to me, his
knowledge was so varied—classical, historical, and political. His father, who had been secretary to Warren
Hastings, had taken part in all the most eventful scenes
of early Anglo-Indian history, and had married, as was
very usual then among English gentlemen, a lady of high
rank, one of the Princesses of the royal house of Delhi;
and his fund of knowledge and great store of anecdote
made him a delightful and improving companion.

In 1830 (I forget the exact date), my prospects brightened. The adjutant of my regiment, having completed
twelve years' service, was promoted to the rank of captain.
I was the next in seniority, and my claims were recognised by the Resident, Colonel Stewart. I passed my
examination in Hindostanee "with credit," and my name
appearing in orders, I assumed my new duties. My pay
was increased considerably; and I was much amused,

when I asked a young lady to dance at a ball one night,
to overhear her ask her mother's permission, "as I was
now an adjutant."

"Are you quite sure, dear?" said mamma; "if you are,
you may do so. He is quite eligible *now*."

I could not repress a smile as I led the young lady out
to our dance. Are mammas still so watchful?

During the rainy season of 1830, I met with a very
severe accident in riding after a panther, which led us a
long chase. He got away through some high grass at last,
and mounting my horse, with my gun in my hand, I
made after him. My horse put his fore legs into a deep
hole, as we were going at speed, and I was shot out of my
saddle, and thrown on my shoulder with great violence.
I got up directly, ran on to the garden where the panther
had taken refuge, and pushing through the hedge I saw a
fine young sepoy keeping him down with his bayonet, and
another poor fellow sitting at a little distance holding his
arm, which was nearly severed above the elbow. I tied
his arm up with my handkerchief, and soon after the
doctor arrived. He asked me if I were likewise hurt,
remarking I looked very pale, and I owned to much pain
in my right shoulder. On examination it turned out that
I had not only broken my collar-bone, but also the scapula
and the socket of my right arm. I did not recover the
use of it for many months.

At the close of the year, H.H. the Nizam expressed a
desire to review the whole of the troops at Secunderabad
and Bolarum. I had then charge of my regiment; and
the unusual size of our men, and their steadiness, excited
the envy of officers of the Madras corps. As the Prince
passed slowly on his elephant we dropped our colours,
which no other regiment had done; and he then learned,
perhaps for the first time, that such troops belonged to
him. After parade we were all to breakfast with his
Highness. I was late, and could not easily find a seat,

which the Resident observing, offered me one close to himself. The Nizam, a fine-looking man over six feet in height, with a fair skin, ruddy complexion, and blue Tartar eyes, at once recognised me and inquired my name. "He has already done me a delicate but important service," he said, to Colonel Stewart, "and I am glad to have this opportunity of thanking him. He will tell you what it was."

So I related how, one evening, my camp being pitched at the town of Kullianee, I was told that a lady of rank, attended by her secretary and a few followers, was without, in a palankeen, asking to see me. I went out at once, and my fair visitor told me that she was the youngest sister of the Nizam, married to the Lord of Kullianee, who had ill-used and even struck her; that she had left his fort, daring his people to molest her; and had come to my camp, where she was sure the English flag would protect her. Now she wanted an escort of police-horse to conduct her to Hyderabad. This I gave her, and provided escorts from stage to stage until she reached Hyderabad.

"Did you report this?" asked the Resident.

"No," I replied; "the Begum especially desired the matter should be kept private. I have recorded it in my Mahratta diary, but it is not a circumstance I could report officially."

"You are right," he said; "and you see your service has not been forgotten."

The Nizam was quite at his ease, conversing with Colonel Stewart, and occasionally asking me various questions about the country and what I had done.

Shortly after this, the Nizam's brother, Moobariz-oo-Dowlah, collected a number of Arabs and Afghans, strengthened his house in the city, and proceeded to press claims against his brother which could not be for one moment entertained. The case becoming serious, and disturbances being imminent, Colonel Stewart was called upon to repress the disorder by sending in a force from

Bolarum. I was still in charge of my regiment, and, preceded by two guns, we marched into the city. Had there been any fighting we should have fared badly in those narrow streets, lined with terraced houses, all covered with armed men; but happily not a shot was fired, though the guns at the palace gates were unlimbered. The officer commanding the brigade had preceded us and induced the rebel to proceed according to orders to Golcondah, and to trust to his brother's generosity to settle all disputed claims; and so, for a time, there was a hollow peace patched up.

Moobariz-oo-Dowlah, however, could not rest content, and the Minister had overlooked the fact that in his personal retainers he possessed the means of doing much mischief. The treasury at the Fort of Golcondah is one of the most ancient in the State, and at this time contained 100 lakhs, or a million sterling; and the Nizam, wishing to remove some of the money, sent his treasurer, with a small guard, for the purpose. Moobariz-oo-Dowlah refused admittance, and the others, being too weak to fight, placed a guard at the entrance. There was great consternation at Hyderabad. Five thousand Arabs, Rohillas, Sikhs, and other foreign levies, including some of the old French "Ligne," were marched out to Golcondah, and took up a position in the outer *enceinte;* but they made no impression on the Prince, and indeed were supposed to be well affected towards him. After days of useless negotiation, the Minister, on the part of the Nizam, requested the assistance of the Bolarum Contingent; so we all marched out on the 6th January 1831, and encamped opposite the north or Delhi gate, on the plain on which stand the noble mausoleums of the Kootub Shahy Kings. It was an absurd state of affairs. The interior was held by the rebel Prince, the outer *enceinte* by the Nizam's levies, who also treated us as enemies, not only refusing to allow us to enter, but threatening to fire on us, and training the

E

fort guns on the wall so as to command our camp. I rode
to the edge of the counterscarp one morning, but was
warned off. However, I managed to have a look at the
ditch, and saw that it was wide and deep; and by dint of
exchanging good-humoured " chaff" with the men, escaped
unharmed.

We remained inactive until the 15th February, when
we were suddenly ordered into the fort, and the Nizam's
troops at the same time ordered to leave it. We took up
a position not far from the Prince's palace, between it and
the treasury, and pickets were immediately posted. I
held the advanced pickets with two guns and four companies. I had my guns loaded with a double charge of
grape each, and as the Prince's men were watching us
very closely, they must have seen that we were in earnest.

The Nizam's people began removing the treasure, but it
was slow work, and for four days and nights I had not
even time to change my clothes; the weather, too, was
very hot. I believe mine was the post of honour, as it
would have been of danger had any fighting occurred.
But it was annoying to be kept there perpetually on the
stretch, with constant alarms that the Arabs were coming
to attack us, and with the sound of their peculiar drum
and their war-songs constantly in our ears.

I was not sorry when, on the fifth morning, one of the
staff rode up and told me I might withdraw my men, for
the Prince had agreed to send away his levies and keep
only his immediate retainers.

A scene followed which affected me very deeply. I
had drawn up my four companies, and released the guns
from their position, when the men burst into loud shouts
of—

"Bolo, Mahadeo Baba Ke Jey!" ("Victory to the son
of Mahadeo!")

I hardly understood it at first; but my friend S., who
came to look after his guns, clapped me on the back and

said, "I do congratulate you, Taylor, with all my heart; no truer proof could have been given you of the men's affection; you will never lose your title—it will follow you all your life." "Bolo, Mahadeo Baba Ke Jey!" he shouted to the men, and heartily did they respond; while, as I proceeded to dismiss them from parade, the cry was taken up by hundreds of both the regiments present.

Even our chief came out to say a few kind words. Captain S. was right, my *sobriquet* never left me, not even in the Mutiny, and it may still linger among the descendants of those who conferred it.

The force was to return to cantonments, but the request of the Nizam was complied with that six companies should remain in charge of the fort, and I was appointed to take command. I was to see that no levies joined the Prince, and I was to be the medium of communication between the Prince and the Resident. "You can read Persian," the Resident said to me, as he gave me my orders, "and you are to open and read all letters the Prince sends you, whether to the Nizam, the Minister, or me: what he has hitherto written are so insolent in tone, that if the others are like them, you need not forward them. If you can make up this quarrel between the brothers, do so, and I shall be obliged to you; but on no account make it worse."

So I remained at my post, and for a few days no notice was taken. I sent for my boat, and used to sail about on the fine tank which washed the walls of the fort, and see the Prince spying at me through a telescope. At length his Moonshee came out, and I offered him a sail one evening. In return, dishes arrived for breakfast and dinner, delightfully cooked, and I reported this friendly intercourse to the Resident. At last letters were sent—one to the Resident, another to the Nizam, very violent in tone, which I returned; others followed daily for more than a fortnight, gradually improving in tone, but not right yet. "You've hooked your fish, Taylor," said the Resident, laughing, " but he is too strong to land yet; I'll not help you or interfere at all;" and I was very glad he did not.

By-and-by my friend grew sulky, but this did not last long; and one evening the Moonshee arrived with some extra good dishes for me, and food for the whole detachment. " Would I be pleased to draft a letter that would satisfy all parties—his honour was in my hands," this was the message delivered by the Moonshee. I did draft a letter, and the Prince flew into a violent rage over it, and abused me for having so small an idea of his dignity. We wrangled over it for a week, and he ended by placing his case unreservedly in my hands, and writing what I dictated. I made the draft in English so as to be sure of my meaning, and it was afterwards translated by me into Oordoo with my own hand, to assure the Prince that it was really mine. The letters were brought to me the next afternoon; and as the Moonshee and I sailed about, the Prince waved a white flag by way of salute, which we answered from the ' Zora' with twelve shots from her little pieces.

I took the letters next morning to the Residency. That to the Nizam was forwarded at once, and was pronounced very satisfactory. He would send his mother directly to Golcondah with his assurances, and would make proper arrangements for his brother's return. When I returned to Golcondah, I found the old Begum Sahiba had already arrived, and two female servants were sent to my tent to report that she and her son had fallen on each other's necks and wept much; and in a day or two Moobariz-oo-Dowlah was escorted to the city with all possible respect.

I received the thanks of the Nizam for having "for the second time rendered a service to his family."

Moobariz-oo-Dowlah sent his secretary to me afterwards, when my intended marriage was announced, with a " Fard " or memorandum in Persian, which was presented on a silver salver covered with a napkin of cloth-of-gold.

He hoped I would accept for my future wife the articles
mentioned in the list, as a mark of the gratitude he felt
for the services I had rendered him.   The presents he
wished to give were very valuable, including shawls, necklaces, ornaments for the head, bracelets of diamonds and
other gems, a zone of gold set with precious stones, and a
necklace of seven rows of pearls with diamond pendant,
the aggregate value about 20,000 rupees ; but alas ! I
could only thank him for his kindness, and tell him I was
not permitted to accept his gifts.   He afterwards got into
trouble by his connection with the Wahabee conspiracy of
1839, and eventually died a State prisoner at Golcondah.
During my stay I was only once permitted to ascend the
hill whereon the fort stands, and I wrote my name in the
mosque, now disused ; but I never could even enter the
gates afterwards, nor, since the temporary occupation of
the place in 1831, has any Englishman ever been allowed
to enter its precincts.

On the 25th August the following year, I was married
to Mary Palmer, daughter of Wm. Palmer, Esq., Hyderabad, by the Rev. W. J. Aislabie, chaplain of the station,
at Secunderabad Church ; and in December of that year
my regiment was ordered to Hingolee, where we took up
our abode.

Hingolee was a dreary place enough—scarcely a tree
near it, no gardens, and altogether desolate.   There was
no amusement to be had at the station, and we passed our
evenings in reading French and Italian, and my wife tried
to teach me to play the harp; but suddenly one day the
sounding-board and back split up under the heat, and my
progress was rudely interrupted.

On the 4th of June 1833 we were ordered to march to
a place called Goleegaum, the chief of which, Jalloojee
Naik, had rebelled against the Government, garrisoned his
fort, and was plundering the country.   The town was reported to be forty miles distant, and we started under a

blazing sun. We were obliged to halt several times, but by dint of resting during the heat of the day and going on at night, we at last sighted the place, lying in a hollow beneath us, and keeping up a sharp fire from its walls. We had, in reality, come upwards of a hundred miles, and the thermometer had been 114° under the shade of a thick banian-tree at our last halting-place. How our men, laden with forty rounds of ammunition and two days' provisions each, did it, I don't know. I helped them as much as I could by dispensing with pantaloons, which were tied up in bundles and placed on the spare carriage-bullocks. Many a Hindoo song was sung in chorus as we marched, relieved by the old cry, " Bolo, Mahadeo Baba Ke Jey !" and on calling the roll, when we reached the camping-ground, I found that, with the exception of five men who had been left to burn a man that had died of cholera on the road, every one was present, and apparently fresh.

Jalloojee Naik, the rebel, was still in the fort, and maintained a continuous fire, some of the balls cutting the branches of the tree we were under ; and it was arranged that we should attack the fort the following day. It was a very strong place—a square mass, with a large bastion at each corner, loopholed for musketry and wall-pieces. The height of the wall was fifty-two feet from the parapet to the ground ; the whole was in excellent repair.

We held a council of war, and arranged matters as follows :—

First, the fort was to be shelled by the howitzer. I was to occupy the crest of a rising ground opposite the village, and advance through the village in case the shells did not take effect, and attack the outworks. Captain T—— was to set fire to the village, so that the sparks and burning thatch might be carried over the fort by the wind, which was very strong.

I reconnoitred my post that evening, and had a narrow

escape, a ball passing through my cap; but I saw enough
to show me the place was "ugly," and might prove tough
work for us. I think we all felt it so, though little was
said as we parted for the night.   We were to take up our
position at earliest dawn. The stars were very bright,
and the ceaseless firing kept up from the parapets of the
fort had, I remember, a very beautiful effect. The place
seemed full of men.

   Suddenly a sentry challenged, and we all sprang to our
feet. I called out not to fire, and ran forward with some
of my men. A moment later a short figure advanced and
threw himself at my feet, and I found it was Jalloojee
Naik himself, with five or six attendants, who all gave up
their arms. I sent him in at once to Captain T——'s
tent, and received orders from him to take two companies
and occupy the fort at daylight.   I felt very thankful for
this termination to the affair, especially when I saw the
place we were to have attacked. As soon as it was light
we marched to the entrance-gate, and desired the garrison
to come out singly, first depositing their arms inside.
There were eighty-five men only, as the remainder of the
three hundred were absent at the Mohurrum festival, not
expecting our visit. What a place it was! The courts
and their entrance-gates grew narrower and narrower, till
the last one would not admit two men abreast. There
were store-houses filled with grain, rice, and *ghee*, stables
and cattle - sheds, stores of forage and provisions. It
seemed deserted now, except for a few women; and my
men began to remove as much as possible of the grain and
other property, which was sold at the drum-head, and the
proceeds divided among them.   I secured the rebel's
household gods for my share, and a matchlock inlaid with
gold.

   Some camp - followers had set fire to a house in the
village, and the wind blowing strong towards the fort,
brought with it pieces of burning thatch and volumes of

smoke. The stacks of forage took fire, and the wood-work of the buildings followed. I was about to depart when I fancied I heard the wail of an infant, and searching hurriedly about, I found a young woman lying insensible upon a bed, with a very young baby beside her. I took both in my arms, and staggered out through the fire and smoke, and meeting two of my men, who were anxious about me, they relieved me of my burden, and we left the place to the flames. The rebel Rajah was told of the rescue of his wife and child, but he only replied, " They had better have died," and relapsed into sullen silence. His atrocities had been fearful. Persons had been suspended by the heels over the battlements of the fort; others had had their ears stuffed with gunpowder, which was ignited; but I may spare the reader these. He was made over to the Civil Superintendent of the district, and I do not know what his fate was eventually. His surrender alone prevented his being hanged on a bastion of the fort.

We returned to Hingolee on the 21st June by twelve easy stages, instead of the three we had marched the distance in before. Some rain had fallen, and it was cooler.

Now I became very busy. Those famous discoveries in regard to the practice of Thuggee had recently been made at Jubbulpore and Saugor by (then) Captain Sleeman, which made a sensation in India never to be forgotten. By the confessions of one gang who were apprehended, many Thugs in Central India were brought to justice; and at last the Thugs of the Deccan were denounced by these approvers, and as many lived near Hingolee, they were at once arrested. I volunteered my services in the labour of collecting evidence, and they were accepted. Day after day I recorded tales of murder, which, though horribly monotonous, possessed an intense interest ; and as fast as new approvers came in, new mysteries were unravelled and new crimes confessed. Names of Thugs all over the Deccan were registered, and I found one list containing the names of nearly all those whom I had suspected in my old district. The reader will remember my intense anxiety on this subject in 1829, and my conviction that deadly crime existed and was only awaiting discovery ; now it was all cleared, but I felt sore that it had not fallen to my lot to win the fame of the affair.

Some men of the artillery and some camp-followers deserted at this time. They were also Thugs ; and it was a horrible thought that these miscreants had been in our midst, and it made many in the station, and especially the ladies, very nervous. We had searched for bodies of murdered people wherever we were told to look by the approvers, and invariably found them, sometimes singly, sometimes whole parties, and the details were so sickening we resolved to open no more graves. I wrote and sent home to my father an article on Thuggee, which was shown to Sir Edward Bulwer, who sent me word that had he possessed any local knowledge of India or its people, he would write a romance on the subject ; why did I not do so ? I pondered over this advice, and hence my novel, ' Confessions of a Thug.'

The year did not end pleasantly. A horrible plot, said to be of Wahabee contrivance, to murder all Europeans at Bangalore, and sell their women as slaves, was discovered. There were disturbances in Oudh and other northern provinces, and famine was rapidly spreading from Kathiawar and Goozerat over the Deccan. We did what we could at Hingolee, first individually, then by general subscription. A Brahmin cook was engaged, whose bread and boiled pulse all would eat, and a good meal was given to each person once a-day. The system worked well, and our relief-books showed that three thousand persons received food daily and were all in good health. But in the rural districts thousands of people and cattle must have perished ; the gaunt attenuated forms of some who arrived to ask for aid were pitiful to behold, and the roads were strewn with the bodies of those who died on their way from weakness and starvation.

During the next three years I had much domestic trouble. The birth and subsequent death of two dear children, the severe and continued illness of my wife, and my own very narrow escape with my life from terrible jungle fever, contracted at Goodaloor, at the foot of the Neilgherry Hills, whither we had been ordered by the doctors for change of air for my wife,—all these events saddened our lives and caused us much distress.

Of the beauty of the scenery on the Hills I need not speak here. It has often been described and enlarged upon since, but at that time it was less familiar to those at home; and I find my letters teeming with descriptions of our journey—of wooded hills and towering mountains, of trees and waterfalls, of precipitous crags and deep wooded glens, of ferns and blackberries and violets to remind us of dear old England, of sunsets and sunrises, rolling mists and cool fresh breezes—and, above all, of gratitude for my wife's returning health. My enemy, the fever, however, came back when I was at Ootacamund with renewed violence, and the medical men looked grave, and spoke of a voyage to England as my only hope of life. How could this be accomplished? Furlough was prohibited, and the only chance was a voyage to the Cape— dreary enough, but still it must be tried; and meantime we stayed on, mostly at Coonoor, where I amused myself trying to sketch some of the most striking views, and was always enchanted with its beauty, so varied and so picturesque on every side. It was at this time, when I was in sore trouble at the loss of my second child, that I had the good fortune to be introduced to the then Gover- nor-General, Lord William Bentinck. He was staying at the Hills and had often noticed my boy, not knowing whose child he was. When he died, he wrote me a kind

letter of sympathy, asking me to come and see him. I
did so as soon as I was able, and so faint and weak was I
that I could not stand when I entered his room. He took
me in his arms, laid me down on a sofa, and sent for some
wine. I told him, when I was stronger, that I had two
letters for him which I had been unable to deliver before
—one from Mr Newnham, and the other from my uncle,
Captain Robert Mitford.

"You don't mean it," he said, as his face beamed with
pleasure; "he is one of my dearest friends; why did you
not come to me at once?"

"I have only just received this letter," I replied, "and
I did not like to intrude before having received an introduction."

"Now what can I do for you?" he asked.

I mentioned that the Paymastership at Hingolee would
soon be vacant—could he appoint me? and he promised
to assist me if he could. "Only," I added, "I fear I shall
be obliged to go to the Cape on leave, this fever has so
shattered my health."

"Why not to England?" he asked.

Then I poured forth the tale of the furlough grievance,
and he could scarcely credit that such an order had been
passed. He sent his secretary for a copy of the orders,
and saw it was all true.

"I shall put in a minute at the next Council," he said;
"we can get over this, and I shall record that my friend
Mr Taylor is to be allowed leave to England when necessary. That will be enough for you."

"But, my lord," I said, "though I am more grateful
than I can express for your kind consideration towards
me, my case alone will not help my brother officers. May
I plead for them as well?"

"Certainly," said Lord William, "you are quite right;
and though my minute as regards yourself will stand in
case of urgent necessity, yet all of you shall be released

soon from this restriction. Write to-day to the senior
officer of your 'locals,' bid him send in a memorial without delay, and I will have it passed."

The friend I wrote to despatched the memorial as soon
as he could obtain the signatures, and the question passed
through Council without difficulty.

After this interview I dined frequently with the Governor-General, meeting there many charming and interesting
characters, amongst others the then Mr Macaulay, whose
conversation I found intensely fascinating ; his seemingly
boundless knowledge of life, his acquaintance with history
and philosophy, his fiery zeal in argument, and his calm
eloquence in oratory, opened to me new subjects of thought
for future study. Oh, if I had been among such men
always, I thought, I should have been very different!

I grew stronger in health, and my regiment being
ordered to Ellichpoor at the end of December, we left
the Hills about October 10. We did not return by the
way we had come, for we had only too much cause to
dread it, but went by Coonoor and Coimbatoor, where
there was a most extraordinary collection of large figures
of horses in terra cotta. I have never heard of these in
any other part of India, and could obtain no tradition of
their construction or their origin. They were reverenced
by the people as offerings to a divinity they locally worship, but possess no particular value.

At Bangalore I was pressed to stay and act as interpreter to a court-martial about to sit, as, strange to say, no
competent linguist was available ; but I could not do it
without much loss of time, so we pushed on, and finally
reached Ellichpoor on the 3d February. We found two
infantry regiments, one cavalry, and some artillery, at the
station, so that there was no lack of society. I practised
my drawing, and began to paint in oils, victimising many
friends to sit for their portraits, and finding endless occupation and delight. Thus with military duties, and

shooting, and excursions to various places of interest
within reach, our time passed pleasantly.

It is not fitting for me here to undertake political discussions, or to comment on the career of the illustrious man
who at this time quitted India; but I feel I must add my
tribute to his integrity of purpose, liberality of action, and
the commencement of that system of progress which is
now bearing ample fruit. No more eloquent tribute to a
statesman was ever written than that by Mr Macaulay, engraved on the pedestal of Lord William Bentinck's statue
at Calcutta. It contains no flattery, but a simple record
of the real motives of the man "whose constant study it
was to elevate the moral and intellectual character of the
Government intrusted to his care." To me individually,
and to our service, he had rendered inestimable benefit. I
was told a testimonial was to be presented to me for what
I had done, but I checked the scheme as soon as I heard
of it. There was only one man to whom gratitude could
be expressed, and that was the Governor-General. He
was succeeded by Sir Charles Metcalf.

Mr Palmer's affairs seemed mending. An award was
made by Mr M'Leod for a portion of the debt, and twenty-
four lakhs were paid in, the Nizam advancing most of the
money, and the creditors were paid in full. But the
other awards of the civil courts against other debtors, for
whom the Nizam's Government was security, were not
adjusted ; and these, together with the first balance of
twenty lakhs upon the great loan, remained to be settled.

The balance was not disputed, and they were left for
payment, and still remained unadjusted and due, in spite
of many memorials to successive governments, which have
been hitherto without effect.

In December I was promoted to the rank of captain,
having completed twelve years' service ; but I was allowed
for a time to fulfil the duties of adjutant.

The following year I began my tale 'Confessions of a

Thug.' I had never attempted any work of the kind before, and I found it intensely fascinating—the work seemed to grow so rapidly in my thoughts and under my hands, and I enjoyed the sensation ardently. I remember giving the first few chapters to one of my brother officers to read, and his constant demands for "more," and his perpetual scoldings for my "laziness" in writing so slowly, were accepted by me as a high compliment.

Mr Palmer, too, encouraged me to proceed. He criticised and commended, and his marginal notes were of great use to me, and often very amusing.

In 1837 we made a charming excursion to Boorhaunpoor. My old friend Major Sutherland had been appointed Resident at Gwalior, and invited a party to meet him and shoot tigers. It was a very beautiful journey, and I could fill pages with descriptions of all the places of interest through which we passed. I took several sketches at Boorhaunpoor, every street and turning abounding in subjects for the pencil, so that the difficulty was in knowing where to begin.

Boorhaunpoor has been always famous for its brocade-weaving. We visited some of the looms, and watched how the gold and silver threads were deftly woven in. But the most interesting part of the work was the making of the gold thread itself, which we followed through all its stages.

A piece of silver about the length and thickness of the middle finger is first gilt several times, according to the value of the thread to be produced. It is then hammered out into a long bar, as it were, and drawn through plates of fine steel, perforated with holes, which are changed each time to one smaller, till the wire becomes as fine as a hair. This is then drawn, two wires at a time, through a still finer plate, over a bright steel anvil by a man who hits each a sharp blow with a steel hammer. Thus the whole becomes a flattened wire of exquisite fineness and ductility, which is then wound on a reel. A long and very thin silk thread, with a spindle at the end, is now passed over a hook in the ceiling, and a man, giving the spindle a dexterous twirl, applies the gold wire to it, which he runs up as far as practicable. The gold thread thus made is wound upon a reel, and the next length begun. The manual dexterity shown, and rapidity with which the process is accomplished, is very curious. I have never read any description of it, and hence am tempted to make this digression.

We had capital sport and a series of tiger-hunts while enjoying the splendid hospitality of the Resident. One incident occurred which amused us all. I had given up my seat on Major Sutherland's elephant, and my guns also, to another gentleman, as I was disinclined to go out that day, when one of the sirdars came up and asked me why I was not going.

" Oh," said he, " take my elephant and see the fun, even if you do not shoot. He is very small, but very easy, and will not jolt you."

I accepted his offer, and mounted the little beast, on which I sat comfortably astride on a well-stuffed pad. As I passed my tent I called for my sun-hat, and my old tent-pitcher ran out, crying—

" You are not surely going without a gun, sahib ? Take mine ; I have just cleaned it, and I will load it for you with ball to shoot the tiger."

This ancient weapon was a French musket of the last century, only known to explode on rare occasions. I had myself seen its owner sitting behind a bush snapping it at a hare which was calmly sitting at a short distance quite unmoved, but he was unable to get it to go off, and when it did, the hare had taken its departure after all. This venerable piece, which had taken part in the wars of Bussy, was brought to me.

" It will kick a bit," said the old man, as he placed it

in my hands; "but you won't mind that when you kill the tiger." He then made a salaam to it, patted it, and said to it: "Do well, my son; you will be with the master;" and we started, I flourishing my weapon, and being not a little "chaffed" on my accoutrements.

"Never mind," said I, "I'll kill the tiger;" but at the same time I had not the smallest intention of discharging the gun at all.

The place was reached—the tiger found. Every one fired—no one hit him. I retired to a piece of waste ground some distance off to be out of the way, when, with a great roar, the tiger dashed forward, ready to spring, within a few yards of my little elephant, which stood like a rock. I fired instinctively, I think, though the recoil nearly knocked me backwards, but the tiger did not move. I told my driver to get off, as he was going to spring, when the man exclaimed—

"He's dead, sahib—quite dead!" and as he spoke, the fierce grim head fell to one side. The old "Frenchman" had for once done its duty, and the triumph was adjudged to me.

I had had a very narrow escape, for my little elephant was not higher than the door of a room, and the result must have been terrible had the tiger made his spring.

The hot-weather season was especially trying, and brought back my fever, with severe neuralgia, and I was racked by pain.

"This won't do," said the doctor. "You must go away; we can do no more here."

My wife answered quietly, "Yes, doctor, we will go;" and so it was settled: and on the 1st November I received my certificate and three years' leave of absence.

Had the old furlough rule still existed, I must, humanly speaking, have died.

We travelled on by easy stages, visiting Adjunta and its marvellous caves, now so well known by photographs,

and Major Gill's splendid fresco-paintings, which met so
untimely a fate in the great fire at the Crystal Palace.

We also visited the Ellora caves, and the cool air in-
vigorated me, and brought back a feeling of health to
which I had been long a stranger. At length we reached
Bombay, pitching our tents on the esplanade.

I had been ordered not to proceed direct to England,
but to linger in Egypt or Arabia on account of their dry
climate, and I set to work to see how this could be
effected.

The only steamer about to start was already full, cabin
accommodation being very limited. Various schemes
were thought of and failed. At last my agents told me
one day that an Armenian gentleman had taken his passage on board a large Arab *buggalow* bound for Mocha,
which had capital accommodation, and we could manage
well if we took our servants.

We went to see the ship, a large one of her class, about
400 tons burthen. She had come from Batavia, and was
going to Mocha, with a light cargo. She had a poop
and stern cabin, which occupied the whole breadth of the
ship, with a bath-room attached. In front, the cuddy and
two cabins—one for the captain, the other for our Armenian fellow-passenger, who, fortunately, spoke Arabic like
a native.

We found our servants very willing to go with us, and
we laid in our stock of provisions, live-stock and liquors,
not forgetting abundance of bottled water, several goats,
two small tents, carpets and rugs.

Some of our friends thought us very rash, but I argued
if a vessel could come safely from Java, she could go to
Mocha with a dead fair wind, and we felt no alarm. So
early in January we sailed out of the harbour, all things
promising us a fair voyage.

F

CHAPTER V.

1838.

I AWOKE the next morning and went early on deck. How delicious it was, the cool pleasant breeze and the ship rolling lazily along under her enormous sail! The captain, mate, and some others were on the poop, and I was greeted with a general "salaam aliekoom," which I returned, Arab fashion, and we all sat down. Presently the captain's breakfast was brought, rice and fried fish. "Bismilla, sit down with us," cried he; "here we are all one, Arabs and Christians. Thank God! we have got away from those Kafirs of Bombay, who were no better than Hindoos! Come, sir, and eat with us." I did eat heartily, and found the viands very good indeed.

At noon the mate, to my surprise, brought out a sextant, took the sun's altitude, and worked it out in English figures. He had three chronometers for longitude, and said he would take a lunar for correction in a day or two. All seemed so perfectly regular—for I had checked the calculations—that I was quite satisfied we could come to no harm through bad navigation. We had plenty of air and room, our own servants, and in our Armenian fellow-passenger an intelligent, agreeable companion. He had brought with him large stores of Armenian beef, which was delicious, and is prepared in this wise.

"Take pieces of lean, but good juicy beef, two or three cubic inches in size, boil them partially, then rub in salt,

pepper, and a *soupçon* of onion. Fry in melted butter,
or lard, or oil. Put loosely into jars, and pour boiling
water over all till the jar is full. The beef will keep for
years if closely covered."

Altogether it was like travelling in one's own yacht,
and was most enjoyable. I had told the captain that I
belonged to H.H. the Nizam's service, and knew all the
Arab sirdars of his court—Abdoolla ben Ali, Oomr ben
Ooz, and others—and he said I should find their names
very useful to me on my journey.

We sailed past Cape Partak, with its grand bold precipices descending into the sea, and its perpetually varying
colours and tints. Then headland after headland, all of
the same bold type, succeeded, until we cast anchor not
far from shore opposite the town of Shahar.

Presently the sheikh left the fort, and his procession
looked very gay as it wound down to the beach, where
several boats were waiting; they then put off with slow,
measured stroke, the rowers singing in chorus as they
approached our vessel. The sheikh, a fine old man, courteously invited us on shore and made us welcome. My
wife was carried off to the women's apartments, and I con-
versed with our host, gravely smoking *nargailés* (water
pipes) and sipping coffee the while. In the evening he
took us to his garden without the town, and after that
more pipes and more coffee, till the sun went down, when
one of the men cried the invocation to prayer: carpets
were spread, and all present performed their devotions.
We then took our leave and returned to the ship, the star-
light being more brilliant than I ever remember seeing
it before. We continued our voyage next day, having
landed our cargo and halted at Macullah. This proved
a very picturesque and curious place, lying at the foot of
huge mountains dipping into the sea. We went ashore,
but the sheikh here was surly and indifferent, and after
pipes and coffee we took our leave. The captain told us

the sheikh was in a bad humour about the "Aden affair," and we should soon find out all about it at Aden, which we reached in due time, casting anchor in the back harbour as the sun was setting.

"I do not see any English ships," said the captain; "I wonder there are not some here."

Next morning he and I landed, and took donkeys to ride into the town. When we came to the barrier fortifications, the guard at the gates refused to let us pass, but eventually allowed us to sit in the guard-room till permission should be obtained from the sheikh for our entrance.

The sheikh himself soon appeared, followed by a numerous company, and sitting down ordered pipes and coffee. I did not like his look or that of his people, who swaggered about stroking their moustaches in a very Hyderabad fashion. I was not noticed; and in a conversation which ensued between the sheikh and our captain, I saw the face of the latter become very grave, and my Arab servant, as he handed me some coffee, stooped down and whispered, "You must get back quickly or they will seize you." This was not a pleasant prospect, as the gate was closed and resistance would have been hopeless. I could not understand a word of what was going on. At last I heard "Nizam" and "Abdoola ben Ali" occurring in the wrangle; and after a while the captain told me I might go, and with a smile the sheikh offered me his hand and bade me "depart in peace."

"Go at once," said the captain. "I will tell you all afterwards."

You may be sure I was only too thankful to make my way back to the ship, and I learned afterwards that my being in the Nizam's service and knowing two of his Arab chieftains intimately, had alone saved me from a very unpleasant detention. The English, said the sheikh, had been intriguing with a member of his family to get possession of the place, and he disapproved of the whole transaction. The English had fired from their ships and killed many people, and he had determined to keep me in irons till an indemnity had been paid.

What an escape I had had! The people were much excited, and but for my Hyderabad friends, I had a poor chance of getting away. I was indeed very very thankful for the great mercy shown to me, and we were heartily glad when the captain weighed anchor and we left the dreary rock behind us.

We continued our voyage to Mocha, where we parted company with our good captain, who transferred us to another Arab vessel commanded by a friend of his, " Salim ben Ahmed," son of a rich merchant at Jeddah. At Mocha I found an English agency house, and some officers of the Indian Navy, who scarcely believed that I had visited Aden and had got out of it again. I had been in the greatest danger, for as soon as a force could be sent, Aden was to be attacked, and my life would surely have been forfeited.

Our new captain was anxious to proceed. We were to sail inside the reefs in smooth water, by day only. It was strange work threading our way in and out of the reefs. The weather was delicious, and every evening we made for some rocky island and were moored to it for the night. We often, in the evenings, took the boat and went out among the islands, occasionally landing to collect the lovely shells which abounded, or we took out our lines to fish, and were generally very successful. Such strange creatures we fished up ! Such varied forms and brilliant colours ! I began to make a collection of drawings of them, which I afterwards exhibited at the meeting of the " British Association at Newcastle-on-Tyne," and eventually presented to the Linnæan Society, for which I received the distinction of being elected an honorary member.

The beauty of the beds of coral on these still evenings was indescribable : they were like huge beds of flowers—

pink, red, emerald, yellow, and purple, mingled with grey
and brown; and the extraordinary clearness of the water
gave us a feeling of hanging in the air which was very
strange. We were really sorry when we neared Jeddah,
and cast anchor in the harbour. Salim and I had con-
cocted a scheme that I was to leave my wife at his house
at Jeddah under the care of his mother, while he and I
went to Mecca to see the *haj* (pilgrimage). "No one will
recognise you," he said; "you are browner than I am,
and I will lend you clothes: we shall do the journey in
the night." So we landed, and next day we were to start.
We had, we thought, kept the secret safe; but it had
leaked out somehow, and our consul at Jeddah came to
me and told me the Pacha had sent for him, and asked
him whether I was going to Mecca.

"He will be in danger without a firman from the
Sultan, tell him," said the Pacha, "and I cannot give
one."

"You had better come and tell the Pacha you will give
it up," said the consul, "for the gates will now be carefully watched, and you are not safe."

I saw there was no use resisting, and very reluctantly
I went to the Pacha. He laughed heartily when I assured
him I would not go, and answered in French—

"I do not care, but others do, and your life would be
in peril."

An English ship lay at anchor in the harbour, and
proved to belong to Messrs Palmer of Calcutta, my wife's
relations. The captain insisted on our coming at once on
board, and we lived there most luxuriously for nearly a
month. I had little hope of getting on to Suez during the
haj, and our good friend, Captain Hill, offered to send us
on to Tor, at the entrance of the Gulf of Akaba, in the
beautiful long-boat, in which a cabin could easily be
rigged up by awnings, and which would be under the
command of the boatswain; but this plan was frustrated

by Captain Hill receiving orders to return sooner than he expected, and the long-boat would not have time to rejoin the ship.

I heard of a good *buggalow* about to sail for Suez. We took our passages in her, and left our kind friends with regret. We intended to land at Tor, go to Mount Sinai, and thence to Jerusalem for Easter.

The morning we sailed I awoke hearing an unusual shuffling of feet and a buzz of many voices. On going on deck, to my horror I found it and the poop both crowded with pilgrims from Mecca, who, the captain said, had been sent on board by order of the Pacha.

In vain I remonstrated, representing that I had taken the whole poop. The captain would or could do nothing, and I told him I should appeal to the authorities at Yembo for redress. On arriving there, I sent my servant to the Pacha, requesting him to come and see the plight we were in. Men and women constantly intruding into our cabin, a frightful crowd, the effluvia and vermin from which were sickening, and quite impossible to describe ; added to this, we suffered terrible abuse for being "infidels," and my wife was afraid to leave her cabin.

The pilgrims lived mostly on dry biscuit, and very pungent bitter cheese. Few only had the privilege of cooking any food; and I very much feared that some frightful epidemic would break out among them soon.

At length a Kavas, one of the Pacha's messengers, arrived, with the servant that I had sent before ; he brought a kind message from his master, entreating us to come ashore at once. This was impossible, as we durst not leave our baggage ; but the Kavas carried off our captain, who was in a terrible fright, and then returned with a handsome boat belonging to the Pacha, and orders to take us and all our belongings to a Government vessel, where, he said, the Pacha would meet us in the morning. We were not long in complying with this civility ; we

once more breathed the fresh air, and the last I saw of the
vessel was a scramble among the crowd to get near our
cabin and flock into it.

Next morning the Pacha visited us, accompanied by
his secretary and staff. He was dressed beautifully, in a
costume made of fine brown cloth, with a profusion of
braiding of a darker shade of the same colour, and had
several decorations on his breast. He spoke French with
fluency, and a little English, and nothing could exceed his
courtesy and kindness. "I am afraid to treat this rascal
as he deserves," he said. "If I had the power, I would
have bastinadoed him severely; but he belongs to the
English agent at Suez, and I dare not; but I can at least
release you from your present uncomfortable position. I
will put a crew and Reis on whom you may depend on
board this vessel, and you can dismiss them whenever
you please. All you have to do is to give them their
wages and food, which amount to very little. Take the
ship to Tor, and if the wind is against you, you can take
her on to Kosseir." I accepted his kindness most gratefully. That afternoon our new Reis arrived, and early
next morning we left Yembo with a handsome present of
dates, Turkish sweetmeats, and new live-stock, fodder for
our goats, and all we needed, from our kind friend.

I was now my own commander, with a crew of twenty-
four men and a pilot. I could go where I pleased, and
the Reis proved a good navigator. Yembo, from the sea,
was the handsomest Arab town I had yet seen. It is
built on the margin of the shore, up a rising ground, and
the lines of whitewashed houses had a pretty effect. This
town is the port of Medina, and the residence of the provincial governor, and there seemed to be a good number
of Turkish troops stationed there. We gave passages, at
their earnest solicitation, to a Turk and his wife, who had
been with us on our former ship. He was old, and in bad
health, and their state was really pitiable. His wife pro-

mised to be useful, and proved eminently so during our voyage.

We had a delicious sail up to Tor, between the reefs and the mainland, and at night we made fast to one of the islands, or cast anchor in shallow water, and then went off in the boat seeking endless treasures in shells, fish, and coral. The colours of the shallows seemed to grow more intense and vivid—of all shades, from the deepest violet and purple blue, to the most brilliant turquoise, emerald green, and red; and as we threaded the often narrow channels the effects were charming. The coast up to Yembo had been comparatively flat and uninteresting, but from thence it grew much bolder in character. Fine headlands were seen in front of us dipping into the sea, and the voyage increased each day in interest, till at length the rocky peaks and precipices of the Jebel Antar range stood out before us, and behind them lay the Gulf of Akaba. In this portion of our little voyage the scenery was very striking, and the atmospheric effects wonderful, as the sun ran its course, and the shadows of the peaks and ravines changed till all was merged in a soft violet tint as evening closed in. We were alone; we saw no fishing-boats or other craft, no sign of dwelling or life upon the shore, which looked utterly desolate and barren in its grandeur. Very grand, too, is the mouth of the Gulf of Akaba, with the range of Jebel Antar to the south, and the far more lofty and imposing mountains of the Peninsula of Sinai to the north. The gulf itself was like a large lake shimmering in the mid-day sun as we entered it, the ranges of mountains on either side being veiled in lovely violet mist.

Very soon the little town of Tor lay before us, and as we anchored, and hoisted our English flag, a boat put off with one likewise flying at her stern; and we found our visitor was the secretary to the English agent, who brought his chief's compliments, and asked what he could do for us.

We ordered pipes and coffee, and sat down to talk.

"If this wind holds," said our friend, "you can go on to Suez; but if a *shimal* or north wind blows, you may be kept here for a fortnight; the sea is dangerous then for your small vessel."

"And Akaba?" I asked.

"Impossible," he answered; "even the Sultan's firman is at present useless. The Arabs are fighting, and the passes quite closed. You must give up that idea."

"Well, then, can we get to Mount Sinai, and to Jerusalem?"

"I fear not," he replied; "but I will go on shore and ask the sheikh. Perhaps you will come with me?" and I went.

The old English agent was very civil, ordered pipes and coffee, and we proceeded to discuss the business, the Arab chiefs having come in.

"You could only do it by yourself," they said; "we could not carry you there with the lady: you would not fear a few shots if you were alone. Have you a firman from the Sultan?"

"No," I said; "only a passport from the Bombay Government."

"Ah!" said they all, "that is of no use; we could not be responsible for any Englishman without one from Constantinople."

So Sinai was given up, and a *shimal* coming on, the Reis said we could not stay where we were; there was no use in staying—the wind would soon moderate, and we could cross over to Kosseir very quickly and safely. So next morning we started with a fresh cool breeze, and we had, at least, the whole of Egypt before us, and the sights that we had to see would be ample compensation for our disappointment.

Our voyage was most propitious; we reached Kosseir very quickly, without touching a rope. On our arrival

we found no difficulty in procuring camels; and my servant "Abdoollah," who had been there before, and knew
several of the principal people, was a great help to me.
We remained on board our ship till all our preparations
were complete, and our tents pitched under some date-
trees, near the town. Then we landed, and walked
through the place, once the ancient Berenice, with no
trace left now of its former greatness, except the ruins
which lay on either hand.

No accommodation for my wife's journey could be devised, except large *kajawas* or panniers, slung upon a huge
camel, with an awning above to keep off the sun; and
with soft bedding these were made endurable enough.
For myself, I had a camel, and two donkeys in reserve.
The Turk rode a donkey, and his wife a camel, on which
were all their worldly goods.

So we set out on our first march into the desert which
lies between Kosseir and Keneh, the old beaten track of
Egyptian, Greek, and Roman traders, each in their turn
through ages of the past. My previous idea of a desert
was that it would be flat and sandy, but instead our road
lay through a hollow, with considerable hills on either
side, affording striking and pretty views at every turn.
Here and there the valleys were very narrow, and high
precipices towered on either hand. Again they widened
into lateral ravines, which seemed interminable. In many
places the rocks had Egyptian, Greek, or Roman characters carved upon them. Does any one know of these, and
of their purport?

It was not very hot, for the north wind blew cool and
fresh, and we could travel all day. I had never left my
camel, and towards evening became very tired. I lay
down on some warm sand near our tents, and gradually
stiffened, to the great alarm of my wife; but my servant
and the camel-men said they would soon cure me. I was
turned on my face, and my back rubbed with castor-oil

well heated. By this time some large cakes of *dhoura*
meal had been prepared and partly baked, and these
smeared with oil were bound on my back, the whole
length of the spine, and partially covering my ribs. They
were almost too hot to bear, but I obeyed orders, and
allowed myself to be swathed up like a mummy. Next
morning, to my great delight, I had neither pain nor ache;
the remedy, rough though it was, had been effectual.

On the fourth morning we met some men driving
camels, and carrying water-melons on their heads—how
refreshing they were! I think I see now our old Turk,
whose lips were much chapped by the dry wind, sitting
on a stone, intensely appreciative of the large slice I
handed to him. A few miles further from the crest of
the pass, we had our first look at Egypt.

It was very beautiful; the cultivation reached nearly
to the foot of the descent, of a vivid green, and most luxuriant; wheat, barley, pulse, cotton, and sugar-cane, with
fields of yellow and blue lupins in flower, patches of crimson clover, with date-trees, and sycamore, and our Indian
babul, or mimosa, everywhere.

My Hindoo servant cried out, excitedly, "India! again
India! are we come back to it?" No, it was not India
certainly, but it was inexpressibly lovely; and our hearts
were full of gratitude to God for His goodness in bringing
us so far in health and safety. No more rough travelling,
no more privation; but instead, a sojourn among glorious scenes of antiquity and beauty which we had longed
to see.

A few miles more and we had reached Keneh, which
seemed exactly like an Indian (Deccan) town, with its
clay-roofed terraced houses; and we were taken at once
to the house of the English agent, who placed very comfortable rooms at our disposal, and took all the trouble of
dismissing my camel-men off my hands.

The house was scrupulously clean, and our friend's wife

was a first-rate cook. I remember two dishes in particular
—one of quails, fried somehow in vine-leaves, and another
of long cucumbers, stuffed with delicately-flavoured mince-
meat—that would have satisfied much daintier palates
than ours. We often wished to be able to converse with
our host, who was a Copt, apparently a merchant, in good
circumstances; but the only mode of communication was
Italian, of which he knew a very little, so we did not
make much progress.

I had some pleasant shooting—quail were plentiful, and
I found snipe, too, in the little swamps, so that my bag
was generally a good one. One day we sent out our tents
a little distance from the town, and had a picnic, spending
a quiet, dreamy day under the shade, enjoying the delicious cool wind, the great river flowing past us, and the
peaceful scenery beyond. "You must see Dendera to-
morrow," said our host; and we went, crossing by a ferry-
boat, and finding donkeys waiting for us on the other side.
We breakfasted at the vestibule of the temple, and then
set to work to examine it, and the old Roman town beyond
it. My servant declared we must be in India, because there
was a real Hindoo temple; but the temple of Dendera was
more imposing than any I had ever seen, and its grand
proportions, at first not easily understood, grew upon one
hour by hour. The roof is covered with names, modern
and ancient; Greek, Roman, Egyptian, and Arab, as well
as every European nation, has its record of the "John
Smith" of the inscriber, and I added mine to the number.

The Roman town interested me very much; for not
only were the narrow streets clearly defined, but some
of the houses and walls, which were nearly perfect, and
the round arches, though built only of sun-dried bricks
cemented with mud, remained as they had been first
erected, perhaps two thousand years before. We left the
place with regret, grim and desolate though it was. The
temple looked very grand in the evening light. No rain

falls here, which accounts for the preservation of mud walls and arches. No rain for 2000 years — can one realise it ?

We had seen all the sights, our clothes had been washed, our boat was ready—a small *dahabieh*, very clean and comfortable—our luggage was stowed away on board ; but what were we to do with our Turk and his wife ? He was very feeble, and she was of great use to us, so they were allowed a corner on board ; and we bade farewell to our kind friends, who gently declined any recompense, until at length I bethought myself of my small tents, which I offered them, and which were gratefully accepted. On our arrival at the river, we came upon an Arab woman frying pancakes and omelets for the boatmen. The woman had good fresh butter, and the smell was very appetising; so we sat down and had our meal of the pancakes and omelet, with salad and hard-boiled eggs, and ate till we could eat no more. How good it was !

Our intention was to go up to Assouan and Philæ, then return and stay a while at Thebes, and so go down to Cairo. If the *shimal* lasted, we should run up to Thebes very fast. If we lost it, we might have varying winds ; but not a *khamseen* for a good while. It seemed a very pleasant programme; we should see all the wonders of Egypt, we should sit in the gate of Ethiopia ; and as our boat was very light, there was no fear of the Cataract.

The Nile is far better known now than it was in those days—drawings, engravings, paintings, and photographs have been made of the scenes along its banks, and are familiar in England to all, so that any description of mine from memory now, would, I fear, be incomplete and tiresome. Yet there are some scenes which can never fade or change as long as memory lasts. Who that has seen them could forget the granite quarries above Thebes, with the blocks of granite split from the native rock ready for transmission down the river ? or cease to wonder at the

means of transport and erection? Who can forget the
grandeur of the giant figures of "Abu Simbel," or the perfect temple at Edfu? Above all, who can forget the wild
scenery of the Cataract and Assouan—the shouts during
the ascent amid the seething waters; or the welcome
change to the placid pool above, with exquisite Philæ
beyond, sitting a queen indeed upon the waters, glowing
in the bright sunlight?

We stayed at Philæ for five days, living in the temple
during the day, and sleeping on board our boat at night;
and our enjoyment was intense. English visitors were
rare then, and many boat-loads of natives came alongside
to have a look at us, and bring us presents. I think,
among all the many scenes which rise in my memory as
I write, that those evenings spent at Philæ were the most
beautiful, when the still, long pool reflected the brilliant
tints of the sky, among the dark basalt rocks, till all faded
into dim grey; and the moon, near the full, cast over all
a flood of silver light, and the temple, the ruins, and the
feathery palms were bathed in it, till they seemed hardly
of this world, and we sat on and watched the stars appearing, one by one, and drinking in the strange "eerie"
beauty around us. If there is a place on earth where
one's heart swells, and one's throat seems to tighten, it
is Philæ.

Back again to Thebes, very pleasantly. Our crew were
hard-working, good-humoured fellows, full of fun of one
kind or another, singing merrily to their oars when the
sails could not be used, and their voices sounded mellow
and sweet in the choruses. No doubt there is monotony in
Nile boat-life, and yet it is very pleasant, and very restful.
If I pleased I could go ashore and have a day's shooting.
My crew delighted in acting as beaters, and game was
plentiful enough. Frequently we received presents from
the chief man of the village—sour milk, the same as in
India, live pigeons, vegetables, melons, or anything he

thought might be of use to us; and he would beg in return a little English powder for firing, or a pencil, or a little tea. Sometimes I accepted an invitation for the evening, and smoked my pipe and drank coffee with the village elders, longing always to be able to talk to them without an interpreter.

They were much interested in India, and I had to answer many questions about its people and religion. I enjoyed these homely, but to me very interesting, meetings exceedingly; and I read in after-days, with deep interest, the story of her life in Egypt, so touchingly described by my cousin, Lady Duff Gordon, in her delightful letters, and was able to feel how real and true are her descriptions.

We remained at Thebes, I think, a fortnight, visiting all the places of interest, and especially the ruins of Karnak, where I made many elaborate sketches, now, alas! lost. We crossed the river to the Memnonian Palace, part of which we had swept out for our abode. We were close to the great sitting statues, and could watch them at all times of the day, and in all the changing lights. In the morning and evening nothing can exceed their grim, uncouth grandeur. How they were brought from the quarries, how erected, who can say? One can but look and wonder!

Of course, too, we visited the tombs of the kings. I need not enlarge upon them, or on the interesting fresco-paintings which illustrate not only the costume and customs of ancient Egypt completely, but also its wars and processions, the employment of the Jews during their captivity in making bricks, helping to drag large building-stones, and the like—the Jewish features being always discernible. The passages were hot and stifling, full of bats, and the smell of the castor-oil lamps almost unendurable; but we persevered, and saw all there was to see, enjoying our return into the cool fresh air afterwards.

" Should we like to have one of the tombs on the hill-
side above us opened ? " asked Abdoollah ; " the Arabs
were willing, if we wished, to open one for a certain
amount of *buksheesh.*"

I agreed at once, and next evening they returned with
many curious objects : a chair, perfect except for its rush
bottom, which had decayed ; a necklace of beads the colour of turquoise ; several scarabei, and small blue enamel
figures ; and best of all, two most elegant terra-cotta boats,
one of which had good, well-modelled figures at stem and
stern, and an altar in the centre of the boat, at which a
priest was offering.   There were also some mummies of
ibis, one of a small crocodile, and another which seemed
to be a cat.   They had likewise picked up a woman's
mummied hand and part of an arm ; the hand was plump
and beautiful in shape.   The boats, and two of the scarabei, when examined at the British Museum, were found
valuable, as they proved the establishment of different
kings, filling up gaps in one of the dynasties ; and I received, I think, £47 for them.   All the minor articles I
gave to Dr Abbott, the famous collector at Cairo, for his
museum.

The north wind had moderated very much, and we were
anxious now to get on.   We stayed a day or two at Keneh
with our old host and hostess, who would take no denial.
A fantasia of dancing-girls was to come off in my honour :
I had never seen one, and was curious to see what the
Ali-meh of Egypt were like.   Certainly their dancing, or
rather posturing, was very strange, some of it both elegant
and spirited, as they twisted scarfs about each other, and
waved their arms and bodies in time to the music.   It had
an almost mesmeric effect upon me.   Again, nothing could
be wilder than some of their rapid movements, appearing
to lose all consciousness of self in their ever-varying ges-
tures.   Their singing was wild and plaintive by turns, but
it did not interest me, as Egyptian music is very mono-

tonous, the chief aim apparently being to produce long, high, quavering notes, which received due applause from the bystanders. Their costume was rich and good ; far more elegant, as were also their performances, than those of Indian nautch girls. They wore necklaces and brace-lets in profusion of what appeared to be gold. I saw nothing indelicate or indecent in what they did during the whole performance.

Laden with gifts from our kind friends, of flour, eggs, semolina, vegetables, sour milk, and fresh bread, we re-entered our boat, and started again down the river. There was not much variety in the scenery, but it was very pleasant, and the tall sails of the Nile boats, both traders and *dahabiehs*, and the towns and villages which we passed, always formed pretty objects in the landscape.

We were still seven days from Cairo when I was attacked with ophthalmia in its worst form. The pain was horrible, and we were very thankful when we reached Cairo, where I was at once taken to the hotel, and put under the care of Dr Abbott, through whose skill, under God's blessing, my eyes were saved ; but he said another day's delay would have been fatal. I was quite blind for some time, and I can never forget the joy and thankfulness I felt when I saw again, though very dimly, my wife's dear face. With very great care I eventually recovered, but for a long time I appeared to be looking through milk-and-water with opal tints upon it. At Cairo, I was told by the English vice-consul that a long complaint had been laid against me by the owner of the *buggalow* from which I had been delivered at Yembo. I was accused of breach of faith, violence to the Reis of the vessel, and other mis-demeanours ; and the official was stiff in manner, and far from agreeable. I showed the decision of the Pacha at Yembo, which he forthwith entirely ignored. My copy of the agreement made at Jeddah, and signed by Mr Ogilvie, was, however, very different to the one filed on the plaint and unauthenticated, and my friend began to doubt. "Had I any witnesses?" he asked. I had only my servant and the old Turk, who were desired to proceed next day to the vice - consulate. Their account of the affair simplified the matter very much, and the vice-consul told me they gave evidence in no measured terms, and descriptions of our state which I dare not record ; so the question was referred to the consul-general at Alexandria, and I promised to appear when called for. I was not allowed to go out, except with my eyes closely bandaged ; but after some time we were given leave to prepare for our journey. A boat was engaged, and we left Cairo, the scene of so much suffering and so much mercy. As we rode on in the early evening after leaving Boulak, Cairo, with its groves, minarets, and domes, and its lofty citadel, with the rugged hills beyond it, was before us on one side. On the other, date-groves, villages, green fields, and the mysterious Pyramids in the distance, behind which the sun was setting, and a glory of crimson light-tinted clouds hung above them, and spread over the southern and eastern sky, reflected in the broad still river ; and as the sun sank lower, the distance changed to the deepest violet, and at length a still misty grey veiled it from our eyes. What a picture it would have made !

On my arrival at Alexandria I was summoned to the consulate at once, and most courteously received. My affairs were under investigation, and the result was that all my passage-money was returned, and the owner of the *buggalow* fined into the bargain, and threatened as well with the loss of his agency if he ever attempted imposition again.

My cousin, Mr Philip Taylor of Marseilles, was then inspector-in-chief of the " Messageries Royales " steamers, and knowing I was on my way home, had desired the captain of the steamer then at Alexandria to inquire for me. Finding we had arrived, he very kindly sent off for our baggage, and when we went on board we found the best cabins reserved for us. We had to take leave of our faithful Turk and his wife; the latter clung to my wife, crying, "Take me to England with you!" and refusing all payment. "Why should you ask me to take money?" she said; "I have plenty—my husband has plenty; why should you think of it?"

All I could persuade her to take was one of the Deccan goats. The other I gave to the mistress of the hotel at Alexandria; and when I returned on my way back to India it knew me again, and rubbed its head against me!

Off again,—to Smyrna first, in such luxury as we had long been strangers to—such delicious beds and sofas! such a cook! such excellent wine! and a captain who could never do enough to make us comfortable, and help to pass the time agreeably. We had English and French books on board, chess, piquet, and other games; but my great delight was to lie lazily watching the sea, to feel the delicious climate, and, as they express it in Indian idiom, to *eat* the air.

We ran across from Smyrna to Crete, coasting along its eastern shore to Syra, where we were to stop; threading our way among the islands before a balmy wind, through the Ægean Sea, now passing barren uninhabited rocks, again fertile islands, all combining to form sea-pictures of surpassing beauty. Leaving Syra, where I did not land, being satisfied with our captain's account of its dirty streets, and strange pyramid of terraced houses, which looked sufficiently picturesque from the sea, we bounded on past more islands, more headlands, those of the south of Italy being very grand; and so to Malta, where we were boarded by the officer of health, and carried away to the gloomy-looking quarantine lazaretto.

Here we had airy rooms, and a *guardiano* appointed to us as our sole attendant. As we had a clean bill of health we thought it very hard, but we had to submit to twenty - one days' detention nevertheless.   Our *guardi-ano*, " Michele," was a merry fellow, and did his best to cheer us.

"Did he know Mrs Austin ? " I asked ; " and was she still at Malta ? "

" Who does not know that kind lady, who is as a mother to us all ? " was the reply.   " Was I her brother ? "

" No, her cousin," I said ; " and she will come and see us when she hears we have arrived ; " and so she did, coming to the Parlatorio, which had a double iron grating, too distant one from the other for us even to shake hands. I told her how we had travelled, and what we had done, and she seemed wonderstruck that we had performed such a journey so well.   I also confided to her about my book, ' The Confessions of a Thug.'   She was about to start for England, and asked me to give her my MS. to look over on her journey.   I did so ; but the three volumes were first scored through with knives, then smoked with sul-phur till the ink turned pale, and finally delivered to her, by means of a pair of long tongs, through a narrow slit in the grating !

A few books had fortunately been left in our quarters by charitable predecessors ; and with these and bathing, swimming about within the prescribed limits, our time passed somehow.

At length we were released, and took up our quarters in the town ; but the glare was trying to my eyes, and the heat very great, as it was June, so we were not sorry to leave Malta, and embarked again, passing Etna, then Messina, where we stayed a few hours ; and Stromboli, casting up its red-hot stones into the dark heavens answering Etna, whose illumined pillar of smoke towered grandly to the sky miles astern.   On to Naples, where we were refused permission to land, owing to a dispute about port-dues between the French and Neapolitan Governments.   So to Leghorn, and the lovely gulf of Spezia, and all the glori-

ous beauty of the Riviera, till, finally, we arrived at Marseilles on the 3d July, and were met by a hearty welcome
from our relations.

One amusing incident occurred. I had two large jars
of Indian preserved tobacco, and our captain assured me
these would inevitably be confiscated. I had no wish to
lose my tobacco, and was determined to pass it if I could.
My panther and tiger skins were ruthlessly seized, to my
great dismay, and I trembled for the precious jars. I
wish I could give the conversation in the original French
as it occurred.

"What is this?" asked one of the *douaniers*, politely.

"Oh, taste it," said another. "I daresay it is a preserve."
That gave me my cue.

"Yes, gentlemen," I said, "it is an Indian preserve
that I have brought with me. Will you do me the favour
to taste it?"

"Is it sweet?" asked one; "it has a strange smell,"
and he sniffed at the open jar.

"Ah, yes," said I—"peculiar, no doubt; there are many
strange things in India."

"No doubt, sir—no doubt; but is it sweet?"

"Surely," said I; "it is prepared with sugar and spices;
do try it."

"Well," he returned, "here goes," as he put in his fore-
finger, and swept out a good lump, which he put into his
mouth.

Now if there can be anything more inconceivably nasty
to the taste than another, it must be prepared Indian
tobacco; and the man, after sucking well at the lump,
spat it out upon the floor with a volley of oaths, while
the others stood round in fits of laughter.

"You do not seem to like it, sir," I said, as gravely as I
could; "but it was surely sweet?"

"Sweet! yes," he cried, "the devil's sweetness. Horrible! horrible! *sacre!* . . . horrible!"

"Perhaps," said I, looking round, "some other gentleman would like to try it."

"Is it hot?" said one; "Indian things always burn one's mouth."

"There is no pepper whatever in it," I replied.

"And how do they eat it?" asked another; "is it with bread-and-butter?"

"Well," I returned, "there are many ways of using it—every one to his taste, you know."

"Certainly, sir, certainly; every country has its peculiar tastes; may we try it?"

"By all means," I said.

Then there was a rush at the jar, and all put in their fingers and hooked up bits to taste. It was impossible not to laugh, and my cousins fairly roared at the scene that ensued, the *douaniers* spitting, spluttering, swearing, declaring the preserve only fit for the devil to eat, and getting rid of their quids as fast as they could; but one turned his head on one side, and said—

"Do you know, my friends, I rather like it? one would soon grow fond of it. May I take some home to my children?"

"Shut up the jars!" cried the chief, gruffly; "let us have no more of such nonsense! Let them go to the devil! I beg you pardon, monsieur, but the taste will not leave my mouth—like rotten cabbage with sugar on it! Bah! we cannot charge duty on poison like that. Take it away!"

So I carried off my two jars in triumph.

We pushed on after a few days' stay at Marseilles, where for the first time in my life I saw and examined machinery of the highest interest. Mr Philip Taylor had lately embarked in marine engineering work, as well as in the manufacture of powerful machines for oil-mills and the silk trade, and his comparatively small establishment grew rapidly into a large concern.

We found the journey by diligence to Paris very fatiguing, and probably we suffered more than others from having led such a free open-air life, and the close cramped-up vehicle seemed stifling. However, Paris was reached at length, and after a few days' delay, spent mostly at the glorious Louvre, and also in refreshing our, by this time, very dilapidated wardrobes, we set off again, reaching London at last, after a weary night journey from Dover in the coach.

CHAPTER VI.

1839–40.

I received an affectionate welcome from all the members of my family who were in London. I had left them a boy, and had entered on a life which was quite new and strange to them; and I think some were surprised to find I " had the manners of a gentleman," as one remarked to me, " and did not show traces of contact with the savage tribes of India!" nor could he be persuaded that the people among whom I had been living were highly civilised, and in many ways resembled ourselves. I determined not to speak of India unless I were asked direct questions, or to tell Indian stories, which might not be believed.

Mrs Austin, to whom I had confided my precious M.S. at Malta, had been much interested in its perusal, and kindly introduced me to Mr Bentley, in whose hands I left it; and to my infinite delight he eventually accepted it, and the agreement was duly executed. Thus one great wish of my life was to be fulfilled. I had hopes, too, of obtaining further literary employment, and as my long journey had been terribly expensive, and my means were slender enough, I looked forward to both pleasure and profit in my work.

I attended the meeting of the British Association held that year at Newcastle-on-Tyne. I exhibited my drawings of Red Sea fish, but as I had no knowledge of ichthyology, I could only explain the localities and circumstances in

which I found them. As I have said, I gave them to the
Linnæan Society, and was not a little proud when I was
elected an honorary member. I paid a visit, too, to my
uncle, Mr Prideaux Selby, at Twizell, and was pleased to
find the collection of birds and insects I had sent him from
India in excellent preservation, and much appreciated by
him.

We spent a happy time visiting among my dear mother's
relations at Mitford, Twizell, and North Sunderland; and
my book was going slowly through the press. My MS.
proved too voluminous : much had to be curtailed and
condensed; a great deal was pronounced really too horrible
to publish ; and at last I found it advisable to return to
London to see about it. Mr Bentley wrote to me that I
must come and hurry it, as " Her Most Gracious Majesty
the Queen " (to whom Mr Bentley was Publisher in Ordinary) " had directed sheets, as they were revised, to be sent
to her—and having become interested in the work, wished
for further supplies as soon as possible."

I worked hard at my proof-sheets, and was very busy.
I was asked to write an article for the ' British and Foreign
Quarterly,' on " The Disposition of the Native Princes of
India towards England " in the event of a protracted
struggle in regard to the Affghan war, and I freely confess
I was afraid to undertake it. However, I set to work, and
did my best, and it was approved of, and, I was told, excited much interest in England, and particular attention
on the Continent, and that it was translated into several
languages. I founded my article on Major Sutherland's
little book upon Native States, which he had written while
Secretary to Sir Charles Metcalfe, and which I unearthed
in the department of the President of the Board of Control,
uncut.   I referred to my article lately, and among the
native states there recorded, some, as Oudh, Nagpore,
Satara, and Jhansi, have been annexed to the British
dominions, and are now integral portions of its empire of

India; but the remainder exist as they were, the treaties being strengthened by her Majesty's proclamation on the assumption of the government of India by the Crown ; and though some modifications of older treaties have occurred, they in nowise alter those which are recorded in Major Sutherland's work. I received ninety-five guineas as my honorarium for this article, the first money I earned by writing, and I do not think I ever felt prouder or more pleased. In this, and all my undertakings, I have ever had the soundest advice and most steady help from my dear cousin, Henry Reeve, whose faithful love and friendship have never failed me all my life.

I went to see Lord William Bentinck, who was then in London. He received me very kindly ; and I felt more and more, as the intellectual aspect of London society was opening upon me, that, but for his generous interest in me when I was in sore strait, I should never have returned to my native country. He was much interested in the introduction of vernacular education into India, and also of translations of English works ; and he charged me, as I agreed with him, to do my utmost to support the cause in England, and to assist it in India. I never saw him again. His health was terribly broken, but his interest in these subjects never flagged.

I got back to the north for Christmas. Such cold, as I had long been a stranger to, set in ; and as I could not get further than Manchester by railway, I had to mount the coach, there being no inside seat. Well do I remember that drive, the biting north-east wind, and the keen frost— I sitting by the coachman ; and at last, when he could hold out no longer, I took the reins ; and I believe the excitement of driving the " wild teams," as the coachman called them, kept me up, for I had never felt such cold before. At every stage we found hot tea ready ; and if possible every team was wilder than the one before ; but we drove in turn : and when, on reaching Leeds, I tendered my half-

crown, the man would not take it. " No, no, sir ; not a
penny from a genl'man as helped a fellow like me to get
through such a night ! If it hadn't a bin for you w'd ha'
been on top of Blackstone Edge a-lyin' in the snow, for I
couldn't a-drivin ye ! " And I assure you I felt proud of
the good fellow's hearty commendation.

The year that was expiring had been very memorable to
me. When I reflected on the great distance we had safely
traversed, the variety and interest of the scenes we had
witnessed, the merciful protection we had enjoyed, my recovery from long and severe illness, and the restoration of
my sight—my heart was lifted up in thankfulness to the
Almighty Giver of all these mercies. Besides, there was
the reunion with my family : all had received me with
open arms. A few dear faces were missing, certainly—one
I never ceased to mourn, who would have shared my
pleasures and my troubles, and whose loving sympathy
was always ready for her boy; but my life was a very
happy one, and the dawning hope of literary employment,
however humble, was very precious to me.

Returning to London in spring, I found my book, ' The
Confessions,' had been received with much greater interest
and success than I had ever ventured to hope for ; and
not only did the London papers and periodicals take it
up, but the provincial press teemed with flattering reviews
and long extracts from it. It was curious to hear people
wondering over the book and discussing it ; and evidently
the subject was a new sensation to the public. It passed
rapidly through the first edition, and a second was in pre-
paration. I was asked also to write another book, which
should take the place of an historical novel, and become
the forerunner of a series of such Indian works, and Tippoo
Sultan was chosen as the subject. I remonstrated, as I
considered the theme too recent ; and what could I make
out of it ? To be sure, I had travelled through Mysore,
and could describe local scenery and objects, but I fairly

despaired of making a readable story out of Tippoo. But my publishers were not to be convinced, and I promised to do my best.

I required some information in regard to points in the Duke of Wellington's transactions with the family of Tippoo Sultan, and I wrote to him asking him to be so good as to help me. To this request I received a short and very characteristic reply, written on a scrap of foolscap paper, dated from the House of Lords.

"The Duke of Wellington is too busy at present to answer Captain Taylor's note ; but if he will attend at Apsley House to-morrow at eleven, the Duke will endeavour to remember what Captain Taylor requires."

The note was the merest scrawl, but was precious to me in remembrance of the very courteous interview that followed. His memory was perfectly clear, and he had forgotten nothing in regard to his own part in the first Mahratta war. He told me 'The Confessions' had fairly taken him back to India.

I spent the summer in Ireland, principally at the dear old house at Harold's Cross, in which I now reside. We travelled, too, to Killarney and Limerick, and visited my father, who was then living in the Co. Clare.

On our way, I had the strangest speech made to me by an old beggar-woman that I think I ever heard, even in Ireland. As we drew up at Naas, the usual clamour for charity began. I was on the box-seat, wrapped up in a coat bordered with fur, and doubtless looked very cosy.

One of the old women called out—

" Ah, thin, comfortable gintleman, throw us a copper!"

I was dubbed "comfortable gintleman" by the crowd till I could no longer resist, so I threw down a shilling to be divided. On this my old friend dropped on her knees in the mud, and raising her clasped hands, cried—

" Ah, thin, that yer honour might be in heaven this night, sittin' wid the blessed Vargin Mary upon a binch ! "

At Killarney we fairly bothered the beggars by speaking to them in Hindostanee, and thereby escaped importunity.

"Hasn't he moustaches?" said one. "He is a furriner. What's the good o' axing the likes of him? Bad cess to him."

In spring I went to London again, having devoted the winter to the writing of my new book, and to enjoying Dublin hospitalities.

I had the *entrée* into much delightful society in London, and became acquainted with many distinguished characters.

Lady Morgan was insatiable about Indian stories, and I had to invent or improvise when my memory failed me. At her house we had rich treats in music, Moscheles, Liszt, and others frequenting her rooms constantly, besides many gifted amateurs.

I was free of Gore House too, and look upon the evenings spent there as among the pleasantest reminiscences of that period.

It was most interesting and fascinating to me to meet so many men of note under such charming auspices as those of Lady Blessington. Most of these now, perhaps, are gone to their rest, and there is no need to mention names. Does any one remember the strange, almost "eerie" speech that Prince Louis Napoleon made one evening there, when, leaning his elbow on the mantelpiece, he began an oration declaring the policy he should adopt when he became Emperor of the French? And I remember, too, when this really happened, how his actions actually accorded with that strange speech. When Lady Blessington rallied him good-naturedly on what he had said, he put his hand on his heart, bowed gravely, and told her that he was never more in earnest in his life, and that she would understand it all by-and-by. Maclise and I walked home together, and could speak of nothing else.

As I came to know Prince Louis Napoleon better, he proposed to me to join him in a tour through India which he contemplated, taking with him Count D'Orsay. He was to apply for my services as long as he required them, and the plan appeared delightful.

I heard from him direct, after I had returned to India, asking for information on various points of equipment, &c.; but the Boulogne affair and what followed put an end to the whole scheme, to my infinite regret.

I remember, too, another very interesting evening at Gore House, when I was presented to the son of the great Russian Minister, Count Nesselrode. He had been specially sent over to glean intelligence of the English designs in Asia, and he set himself steadily to pick my brains on all sorts of Indian subjects. He was, or affected to be, surprised at my account of the number, discipline, and equipment of the native army in India, of the condition of the cavalry and artillery, and especially when I told him that I should not hesitate to put my own regiment of native infantry in brigade with H.M. Guards, and that they would work with them as well and as effectively as any regiment of the line.

I was complimented afterwards by several present on having spoken out some very home truths fearlessly, and I hope they were of use. That night Lablache and Tamburini sang by turns, and imitated the singing of Grisi and Persiani, in the most surprising way, in falsetto, quarrelling over it very amusingly. But I may not linger over these memories, which few who shared them could have forgotten. It was to be my last season of such society for many a long year, and I prized it accordingly.

I pass over the intervening time which we spent in farewell visits among our friends and relatives, and we left London in November, on our return to India.

I had attended the last *levée* of the season, " on departure for India," and as I knelt to kiss her Majesty's hand, she said to me very graciously, " I wish you a safe voyage, and trust I may see you again." And so she did, exactly twenty years later.

Back again, through Paris and Marseilles, from Malta to Alexandria and Cairo, and so to Suez, down the Red Sea, always hot and uncomfortable, and we were glad at last to reach Bombay early in January, after our long absence.

We sent on our luggage on carts to Poona, and ourselves started, just as I had done seventeen years before, on my first journey to Aurungabad to begin life.

How was I to go on? Was I to rejoin my regiment, and continue its dull routine of duties, or was a fresh career before me? My mind was filled with speculations on these and many other points.

I need not go over again my old route to Poona, where we did not stay long, but went on to Sholapoor. All along the route I found luxuriant and continuous cultivation, instead of the waste land and deserted villages of 1824. The original survey operations had been improved, the assessments had been reduced and arranged on a proper valuation of the land, and the change in the aspect of the country was as remarkable as it was beneficial. The early millet and pulse of the first crop of the season had been reaped on the uplands, but in the lower ground the later millet and wheat were fast ripening, and the sheets of golden grain were truly beautiful. All over the upland stubbles were large flocks of ortolans, of which I shot numbers, affording us delicious eating ; and every afternoon I rambled out with my gun, and seldom failed to bring in a bag of hares, quails, and partridges.

It was a most enjoyable journey throughout. We had a very pleasant party of fellow-travellers : a lady and her family, who came with us from Bombay on her way to join her husband ; and the children were charming companions, boys and girls both accompanying me in my rides, mounted on stout ponies, and scrambling all over the country. The only uncomfortable member of the party, I believe, was their tutor, a Frenchman, who found the people barbarians, the country barbarous, and the language worse. Above all, there were no hotels, no wayside inn, even, where one could procure a cup of coffee. His chief delight was to come out with me, and see partridges and quails shot *flying*.

We reached Sholapoor in due course, and found tents sent for us by Mr Palmer. We halted there for two or three days, and then pursued our march by the Nuldroog and Hominabad road, through my old district of 1827-29. From Sholapoor to Hyderabad in those days there was, strictly speaking, no road, only a track; but I knew every mile thoroughly, and that I could obtain assistance everywhere if it were required.

The tents were very comfortable; the children, and even Monsieur, were enchanted: they were lined with pretty chintz, and carpeted, and had double walls and roofs to keep off the sun, and were a luxury we had not expected.

I received a perfect ovation through my old district, and it was very gratifying to find I had not been forgotten. At Nuldroog, where we halted a day or two, the townspeople visited me in great numbers; and both from the Nawab's agent in the fort, and from the zemindars, came presents of provisions, trays of sweetmeats, barley-sugar, and almonds, not only for ourselves, but for all my servants and followers. At every village, as we entered it, the authorities came out to meet us with jars of milk, baskets of eggs, and humble offerings of flowers, while the piper played us past the village.

At one resting-place, parties of women came to visit my wife, and tell her stories of me, and how " at first they used to be afraid of the gentleman with the ' red trousers ; but he had done them no harm, and the country was not so quiet now as when he had been with them," and more that was pleasant to me to hear.

H

At Hominabad, in particular, the welcome given to me was on a great scale; all the merchants and others assembled about half a mile from the town headed by my old friend Atmaram, the dean of guild; and there were baskets of flowers, sweetmeats, and fruits, which I had to accept. The town pipers and drummers played us to our tents; provisions were provided for all the party; and in the afternoon crowds came to visit me, and have a talk over old times in their simple, homely fashion.

They were very curious about England, and I had to recount all my doings since I had left them. My wife, also, had her assembly of women; and told me afterwards, with tears in her eyes, how precious it was to her to hear how these people really loved me, and wanted me to come back to them.

Next day we proceeded to Ekali, where it may be remembered I had marched after the insurgent rebel before-mentioned. He was still confined at Hyderabad, and had been fined heavily; but was said to have become a reformed character, and to have grown very humble and religious.

At Sudasheopett, my old residence, I had another similar ovation; but my little bungalow had been removed, and a larger one built for the accommodation of travellers, and I was rather sorry not to see it again.

On the 26th February we arrived at Hyderabad, having been just a month on the road; and Mr Palmer was overjoyed to see us again. I put a copy of my new book, 'Tippoo Sultan,' into his hands, and in some respects he liked it better almost than 'The Confessions.' He told me that nearly every one doubted my really being the author of 'The Confessions;' and said it was fortunate that I had sent him the work in manuscript as I did, so that he could assure all sceptics that he had read it in my handwriting before I had left India, thus ending all discussion.

General J. S. Fraser had succeeded Colonel Stewart as

Resident at Hyderabad, and received me most cordially, recommending me very earnestly to pursue my literary work, and prophesying that I should find ample occupation for my pen.

My regiment, the 6th, was at Bolarum, and the men and officers came to see me in numbers, and to welcome me back again; but General Fraser was making other arrangements for me. I was to go to Hingolee to take command of the 8th, whose commandant had gone on furlough to Europe. It was a long march in the hot weather; but orders had to be obeyed, and we started on the 13th March, making as long stages as we could.

During our stay at Hyderabad the festival of the Mohurrum had occurred; and I was gratified to find that my description in the 'Thug,' although written from memory, was correct in every particular, yet hardly giving an idea of the grandeur of the scene.

One sore disappointment awaited me. I had hoped that my little savings, upon which I had not drawn during my absence in England, would have increased materially; instead of this, all had been swept away, with a very small hope of recovery, and I had to begin afresh. Had I died then, my dear wife and child would have been left penniless; but God was merciful to me in all things. Before I left Hyderabad, General Fraser warned me to make no arrangements to reside at Hingolee, as I might be sent on to Ellichpoor to act as staff-officer and paymaster. And so it proved. We again marched on the 19th April, and reached our destination safely. Since our departure from Bombay we had travelled very nearly seven hundred miles, and we were truly thankful to be at rest, and with a delicious climate to live in. The brigadier had the privilege of residing at Chiculdah, upwards of 4000 feet above the sea, where there was no heat, and the nights and mornings were almost cold. My eyes, which had suffered much from our march in the heat and glare, now improved rapidly, and I would fain have remained at Chiculdah during the monsoon; but as soon as the rains set in, the brigadier and the doctor moved into cantonments, and we were forced to follow.

I then began a new book, but my eyes proved too weak for writing, and I was obliged to give it up. I could paint better, and amused myself by taking portraits of my friends.

I managed, however, to send an article to England on " Educational Measures for the People of India," which was called forth by a controversy then raging between the Arabic, Persian, and Sanscrit party, and the English and vernacular, whose cause I espoused, not only in the Indian press, but in my letters for the ' Times,' which were then regularly sent by every mail.   My advocacy of their measures did not slacken until they were finally adjusted; for the practical benefit to the people by their adoption far exceeded what might be looked for from the ancient system and languages so ardently insisted upon by Wilson and others.

I need not now enter into the particulars—they are matters of history, and out of date; but I have never re-gretted the part I took in this discussion when I see the noble results which have been already attained, and are rapidly advancing year by year all over India, in all its regions, and in all its vernacular languages.

At the latter end of October my tenure of staff employ-ment came to an end, and I was ordered to rejoin the 8th Regiment at Hingolee.   A pretender to the person and claims of Appa Sahib, the ex-Rajah of Nagpore, who had escaped from custody after the Mahratta war of 1818, had arisen in rebellion in the Nagpore district, and, joined by bodies of Rohillas and others, was plundering where he could.   The 8th Regiment was already in the field, and I was directed to join it without delay.   So I started through a wild and almost depopulated, but very beautiful, tract of

country, and in a few days came up with the regiment.
The campaign, however, was concluded by Captain Johnston's capture of Appa Sahib, after a truly surprising
march of 78 miles in 32 hours. Another brilliant attack
was made on a party of Rohillas by Brigadier Twemlow,
at the head of a detachment of cavalry: 150 of the enemy
were left dead upon the field, and the rest captured; the
cavalry lost eight killed and wounded only. This was a
truly gallant affair, for the Rohillas (Affghans) are well
known for their bravery, and for good use of their weapons.

My contributions to the 'Times' were apparently liked,
for I heard at this time that I had been appointed
"Special Correspondent," on a yearly stipend; and this
honour I continued to enjoy for many years.

Events in India were deeply interesting at this period;
the miserable retreat from Cabul, the failure of Lord
Auckland's Affghanistan policy, and the safety and relief
of Sale's brigade, were universal subjects of interest and
speculation. Before I left Ireland I had become
acquainted with Lord Fitzgerald and Vesci, and was
honoured by his friendship, while I supplied him with all
the information he needed, as far as my experience carried
me. I had now become his regular correspondent, and
so continued as long as he held office as President of the
Board of Control, and by him I was strongly recommended
to Lord Ellenborough, the successor of Lord Auckland.
Although Lord Auckland had not been able to give me
permanent employment, or transfer me to the cavalry in
the absence of vacancies, yet he had, since my introduction to him by Lady Blessington, shown a very kind
solicitude respecting me and my advancement, which, had
he remained in office, would probably have been attended
with good results. Now I had to look to Lord Ellenborough, to whom I sent Lord Fitzgerald's letter of
introduction, and I was much gratified by receiving an
autograph letter from him in reply, which showed more

knowledge of my doings hitherto than I anticipated, and
contained kind expressions of goodwill.

Shortly after I joined the 8th Regiment I had occasion
to return to Hyderabad, and there was appointed to do
duty with the 4th Regiment stationed at Bolarum, where
I took a house, and for some months we led quiet and
happy lives. The weather was delicious, and we had
some pleasant parties to Golcondah, where we entertained
our friends. Although the country is bare of trees, the
locality of the Kings' Tombs presents many picturesque
features. The noble mausoleums themselves, the grim old
fort and its massive walls, the city of Hyderabad in the
distance, and several large lakes or tanks sparkling in the
sun, contribute to form one of the most striking views in
the Deccan. After Golcondah we all assembled near the
tomb of Boorhani Sahib, on the east of the city, the
Nizam's deer-preserve, where, as I had permission, several
fine bucks were shot.

Here, on the 23d November, just as I had ridden in
from Secunderabad, I received a note from General Fraser
desiring me to come to him at once, as he had something
important to communicate ; so I rode in to breakfast,
after which we entered on the business for which he had
sent for me.

CHAPTER VII.

1841–42.

I HAD been aware that an officer of cavalry, a very accomplished and able man, had been employed as Political Agent at Shorapoor for more than a year in adjusting affairs at issue between that State and the Government of H.H. the Nizam, in pursuance of Act 17 of the Treaty of 1800 between the British Government and the Nizam, which stipulated for interference between the Nizam and Shorapoor in case of the latter withholding payment of tribute and just claims due to the former.

The original tribute had been comparatively low; but the Nizam's Government had increased it on various pretences, and on the succession of the late Rajah, who had very recently died, a Nuzzerana, or succession fee, of fifteen lakhs (£150,000) had been exacted by the Nizam's Minister, which was to be liquidated by instalments.

These demands led to many complications, in which the British Government had always been obliged, under pressure of the treaty, to take a part. Money had been borrowed from local bankers under the signature of British officers to pay instalments of tribute and succession fees, which the impoverished State could not meet; and there were disputes between the Shorapoor State and the bankers, the bankers and the Nizam's Government,

which altogether presented a very complicated and eminently disagreeable state of affairs.

The officer in charge had just concluded a proposed
settlement of all these matters, and had submitted an
exhaustive report on the country and its revenues and
resources, when the Rajah, Krishnappa Naik, died suddenly, and his elder Ranee, Ishwarama, assumed the
administration as regent to her son, a boy of seven years
old or thereabouts.

The Ranee was a woman of much energy and clever-
ness, but she was dissolute to a degree—in fact a very
Messalina, and hardly second to the famous Maha Ranee
of the Punjaub. Her infidelities were known to her
husband and his family, but could not be checked. On
the death of her husband she defied all parties, resisted
the settlements made by Captain Gresley, and called out
the military forces of the country, about ten thousand
men, whom she rallied round her, inducing the leaders
to promise to support her on oath.

The late Rajah's family, who headed a strong party in
the State, had declared themselves opposed to the Ranee
because of her infamous character; and acting according
to their declaration, the late Rajah's brother, by name Pid
Naik, had been proposed as regent during his nephew's
minority, an arrangement which was ratified by the
Governor-General in Council. This measure, however,
had been violently resisted by the Ranee, and she defied
her brother-in-law and the British Government alike.

Affairs having reached this point, and Captain Gresley
having no disposition to temporise, he applied for a force
to disperse the adherents of the Ranee, to establish Pid
Naik in office, and to assist him generally to carry out
the measures he had proposed, and which had received
sanction.

General Fraser, however, did not consider an exhibition
of force necessary, nor had he, he thought, a sufficient

number of troops at his disposal to render it sufficiently imposing. Our army was then evacuating Affghanistan, and there was no security in the Punjaub after the death or Maharajah Runjeet Singh. Troops from the southward had been marched northwards, a measure which had caused outbreaks of mutiny in some corps of the Madras army ; and while the movement across the Punjaub was in progress, it was felt that any outbreak of war elsewhere might be only as a spark to a magazine of general treason, which might explode with fearful consequences.

When the assistance of a force was denied him, the political officer reported that he could do no more than he had done ; that the position of the Ranee was growing stronger ; and that if she were supported by Arabs, Rohillas, and other mercenaries whom she had funds to maintain, the result would be a costly and bloody little war, always to be deprecated.

He had already been able, by seizing the ferry-boats on the Bheema and Krishna rivers, to prevent the crossing of those mercenaries ; but the rivers would now soon be fordable, and no security would then exist. He therefore begged to tender his resignation, and to be relieved without delay.

"Will you take up this matter, Taylor?" asked General Fraser of me. "If you succeed, it will be a good thing for you, and you are at any rate independent. I cannot spare any other officer just now on whom I could rely."

I saw it was a very, very difficult matter—one in which a very able man had failed ; but it was a chance of political employment, for which I longed ; and I was confident in myself, and knew that if I should be so fortunate as to succeed, Government would be obliged to me. So I accepted the offer at once, and said I would do my best to bring the refractory lady to terms. No doubt I was rash ; but I could but do my best, and did not anticipate a long absence.

I went at once to Secunderabad, packed up what things I required, took my tents, and marched the following morning to Hyderabad.   I employed the next day in reading up the very voluminous papers connected with the case, and afterwards again visited the Resident to have a final consultation.   He explained his intended line of policy, which was to abstain from using force as long as negotiation could be carried on, and the interest of the Government secured; that, in fact, he had no available troops till the regiments now on their march should reach Hyderabad ; and then, if necessary, he would support me with four regiments.

I started alone the following morning, and on the fourth day reached Muktul, a distance of 120 miles.

On my way to Shorapoor I went to Captain Gresley's camp, and heard from him an entire exposition of his transactions with Shorapoor from first to last.   He told me that the Ranee's paramour, a man named Chun Busappa, was now paramount ; that Pid Naik was in dread of his life ; that the Ranee was insolent and confident to the last degree ; that she knew of the British reverses in Affghanistan ; and that her astrologers were filling her mind with the most absurd stories of the evacuation of India by the English.

"I have twice failed in my negotiations with this woman," said my old friend, "and I could not humiliate either myself or the British Government by trying a third fall with her.   You are a new hand, and may be more successful ; but I advise you to be very cautious, for no one is to be trusted in Shorapoor, where the people, though outwardly civil enough, are at heart treacherous savages, and you would not be safe among them."

This was not encouraging.   I remained two days with my friend ; but the more I heard and the more I considered, the more the business seemed hopelessly involved. His views were convincing enough.   He maintained that

had he been at first supported by a regiment, with other
forces at hand in case of need, all would have been
arranged quietly without firing a shot; but he was quite
hopeless of my success now, as more mercenaries had
already joined the Ranee, and the Beydur militia were at
her entire command.

He showed me, too, a letter from Colonel Tomkyns, part
of which ran thus—

" If Taylor settles this matter without troops, he will be
a cleverer fellow than I take him for!"

Not flattering, certainly, but quite enough to put me on
my mettle; and I had formed a little plan of my own
which I longed to test.

Next day I was at Shorapoor.

It was a grim place to look at, certainly: a mass of
granite mountains rising abruptly out of the plain, and
though apparently several miles long, had no connection
with any other range.

To the north, a second line of lower rocky hills ran
parallel to Shorapoor, and a flat valley about a mile or
mile and a half wide lay between. The Shorapoor hills
were masses of granite, whose denuded tops appeared in
strange *tors*, and piles of rocks exceeding in magnitude
any I had before seen. There was no appearance of a
city.

My tents were pitched in a pleasant tamarind-grove
close to a suburb, and I was told that the town was over
the brow of the hill before us, and lay in a hollow between
the highest part of the range to the east, and a somewhat
lower portion to the west. I found two companies of my
old regiment, the 6th, and a few cavalry, as my escort.

About mid-day I was visited by Rajah Pid Naik, who
brought his nephew, the little prince, with him, several
members of his own and the Ranee's family, and a banker
named Luchmangeer, a Gosain; and I read out the letter
from General Fraser, which announced my mission, and in

which he hoped that the measures of Government would
be adopted without further delay, and recommended all
parties to sink their differences in the common good of the
State. I then warned them of the fate of many other
States which had from time to time rejected and opposed
the Government, and had perished under their own eyes,
and entreated them not to be over confident, but to be
very careful.

The Ranee's brother formed one of the audience, and
seemed very attentive. I told him that as Pid Naik had
been selected by Government, no other could be admitted
as regent; and after the warnings Captain Gresley and I
had both given, any opposition to these orders would be
considered rebellion, and without doubt would be dealt
with as such.

I could see, however, that Pid Naik had no party, and
that to set him up and pull the others down was almost
a desperate matter; and I nearly inclined to Captain
Gresley's opinion that force would be necessary. I requested that all the officers of the State troops, and the
heads of the Beydur clans, might be sent to me next day,
that I might explain to them the views of Government;
and to my surprise they came to a man—about a hundred
of as wild-looking fellows as I ever saw—and were introduced to me one by one, by one of the State officers. Pid
Naik stayed away, and I was glad he did not come.

I spoke to them for some time. A few grew violent,
and swore they would acknowledge no authority but the
Ranee's, and would fight for her and Chun Busappa to the
death. Others were quiet, and, I thought, determined;
and some appeared irresolute. I had done enough for that
day, and dismissed the whole assembly with the cere-
monious gifts of *atr*, and betel-leaf, and a garland of
flowers.

" You treat us with respect," said one of the jemadars or
officers, " and we thank you for it."

"I always treat my friends with the respect I hope to receive myself," I replied; and I believe this simple act of courtesy at least softened many.

Next day I went to return the visit of the little Rajah, and to submit my demands to his mother.

If I had listened to all the warnings I received, I should never have ventured at all. Many, I was told, had vowed to make an end of me: the town was full of the Beydur militia, who had sworn to turn me out of Shorapoor, and the like.

I had to ascend by a roughly-paved road, about 400 feet, into the city, which appeared well built and well populated, lying between portions of the rocky range which varied from 400 to 500 feet in height. Being completely screened from without, it seemed, as it had been described to me, a very stronghold of freebooters.

I was politely received in the outer court of the palace by the little Rajah, where a great crowd of armed men were assembled, and then led into another court, and through a passage into a third, well built of red brick, and of two storeys. It contained two open halls, neatly covered with white cotton cloths, with large pillars at intervals. The little Rajah, who was a delicate-looking though cheerful boy, was by no means disconcerted, and asked me many questions pleasantly, and at last invited me to come and see his mother.

She was in the next room, and sat at the door behind a bamboo screen—through which, however, she could see me, though I could not see her. She spoke neither Hindostanee nor Mahratta; but I had a good interpreter in one of the members of the family, who had been at Hyderabad, and was quite a gentleman. For a time she spoke very pleasantly, and the little Rajah had, of his own accord, come to me, and was sitting in my lap. "See," said the Ranee, "my son has gone to you, as he never did to his father, and now you must be father to us all."

This speech led the way to business; and when I told
her it would be far from wise to pull her own house about
her ears as she seemed to be doing, she replied, in the
most innocent manner possible, "That she was quite
unaware of having offended any one, and could only look
to the British Government to protect her and her son, as
it had already done for several generations."

We talked for four hours without ceasing, and at last I
handed her a paper, in which I had embodied my demands.

1st, To give an account of the revenue for the last three
years.

2d, To give over the Rajah's seal of office.

3d, To make over all the armed men to Pid Naik.

This sadly bothered her, and she was as slippery as an
eel; but it would not do. I said I would not leave her
till I had her determination from her own mouth; for I
had no faith in letters or messages, and I doggedly kept
my seat.

This did good: for, though arguing bravely, the Ranee
was driven from her positions, one by one, and at last
agreed to all my demands. Would she keep to her word?
That remained to be seen. The only objection which I
thought was a reasonable one was about the seal, which,
being the Rajah's, could not be used by his Minister; but,
as she suggested, a seal of regency might be engraved and
used. After this interview was over, I walked to Pid
Naik's house through the crowd outside, and saw his three
fine boys and two girls, while his wife sent me a kind
message. He appeared more hopeful, and thought we
were getting on.

Next day the leaders of all the armed men came to me
again by appointment, and I requested they would at once
give me agreements to serve Pid Naik and not the Ranee.
How I had to argue and coax by turns, I can hardly
describe; but at last one came over to me, then another and
another; but some remained unconvinced and went away.

I then wrote to the Ranee ; and, after a day's interme-
diate delay, she sent me about 400 men—those on whom
she could least rely—and I made them over at once to Pid
Naik.   The Ranee now began to see that she must either
come down quietly or be pulled down, and in two days
more I had secured 600 men.   But still I was not satisfied.

The Beydurs had not come to me, and I was very anxious
about them, as they were the representatives of the 12,000
militia, and the Rajah's body-guard, on whom the Ranee
had lavished much money.   I also had much anxiety respecting the garrison of Wondroog—a very strong fort,
about ten miles off, in which there were 300 picked men.
On the seventh day after my arrival I had secured 1400
men in all.   The last 700 were Beydurs, as fine and bold a
set of fellows as ever were seen, well armed with sword,
shield, and matchlock.

"Tell us," cried their leader, "are you going to make
Pid Naik Rajah ? "

"By no means," I replied.   "He will only be Minister.   Your little Rajah is my son, and I will put him
on his throne with my own hands before I go."

" And you give us your word about this ? " they asked.

" Certainly I do," I cried, " and the word of the British
Government."

"Enough !" was the general shout.   "And now put
your hands on our heads, and we will be your obedient
children henceforth."

Then they crowded round me, and I placed my hands
on a number of heads, many prostrating themselves before
me, some weeping, and all much excited.

I had sent for baskets full of wreaths of flowers and
betel-leaves, and I gave each of the leaders a garland,
hanging it about their necks myself, while my attendants
distributed the same to the others.   As they filed down
before me, each division gave me a hearty cheer : " Jey

Mahadeo Baba!"—the old cry of Golcondah! How had they learned it? I confess it moved me deeply.

No fear now, thought I; and I was right, though there were some trials yet to undergo. All these men were sadly in arrears, and I took up money sufficient to give to each two months' pay. I did this solely on my own responsibility; but I saw the necessity, and felt sure I would be supported by General Fraser.

That evening they went of their own accord and made salaam to Pid Naik, who could hardly believe his senses when he saw them. The day after, all the horsemen of the State came to me. They had Chun Busappa in their charge to protect him from me, but promised obedience like the rest. I saw it was the time to demand him at their hands. To this most of them demurred, as they were on oath to the Ranee; but they said, "Though as a point of honour they could not give him up, yet they would have nothing more to do with him."

Next day the Ranee's agent came to try to get a promise of probation for Chun Busappa; but he found me utterly obdurate, and I suppose he went and told him it was no use resisting, for in the afternoon Chun Busappa himself came to me alone, and threw himself at my feet, making no conditions. "He had now no protector from his enemies," he said, "and submitted himself to me to be dealt with as I pleased."

I quote here the following passage taken from one of my letters to my father:—

"I hear the Lady is very sore, and I hope she is. There is a long account to settle with both—that is, with the Ranee and Chun Busappa. They owe the Nizam's Government two lakhs, arrears of tribute which I must get; and they have paid none of the bankers whose instalments are in arrear. It will be no easy matter to get this money; but patience will do a great deal, and as yet no force has been used. Collectors have been sent into the districts to collect the revenue now due, and to establish Pid Naik's government; and I have only to hope all may go on quietly. Besides the papers to Pid Naik, I have taken others from all the mercenaries and the Beydurs, in the name of the British and Nizam's Governments, pledging themselves to obedience and allegiance, on pain of punishment if they go in opposition to the future management of the State.

"I have already found out that four days after the Ranee had reported to the Resident that she had made over the Government to Pid Naik, she bound down all the Beydurs by oath, and many others, not to obey him, but to stand by her; and if she could have been joined by the Arabs and Rohillas, which Captain Gresley's vigilance alone prevented, she would have caused the Government of India much anxiety."

I had now been at work ten days, and hard, anxious work it was.

So far, I had carried all my measures. My proceedings were entirely approved of, and I received the following official letter from the Resident on the 22d December, after my report had reached him :—

"These despatches demand from me nothing further than the expression of my entire approbation of the temper, judgment, and firmness which you are now exhibiting in the discharge of the duty intrusted to you; and it will be very gratifying to me to state to the Supreme Government, that under your judicious management the affairs of the Shorapoor State may be arranged in a satisfactory manner and without the necessity of having recourse to arms. . . . Nothing remains to me but to transmit to you my entire and unqualified approbation of all your proceedings."

(Signed)   "J. S. FRASER, *Rest.*"

Captain Gresley also wrote from Muktul—
" You have managed admirably, and deserve very great

I

credit. I could never have done the thing so well. General Fraser ought to be much obliged to you."

These letters were very gratifying and encouraging; but the following, which the General was so good as to write to my wife, was even more so :—

" MY DEAR MRS TAYLOR,—I cannot resist the pleasure of telling you, because I am sure it will give you pleasure, that I have received three despatches from my *chargé d'affaires*, your good husband, at Shorapoor, and that he is succeeding admirably in the duty intrusted to him—even getting the better of a lady!—the Ranee Ishwarama—which of all diplomatic transactions is probably the most difficult.

" He has exhibited the most perfect temper, tact, and judgment, and I have been delighted to express my entire and unqualified approbation of the whole of his proceedings.

" The requisite communication has also, of course, been made to the Governor-General, and it gratifies me to think the despatches must equally meet the approval of this higher authority.—Very faithfully yours,

" J. S. FRASER."

And the following extract from a letter from the Secretary of Government followed very shortly afterwards :—

" The Governor-General directs me to express the great satisfaction with which he has perused these reports, and his entire concurrence in the just approbation you have bestowed upon the temper, judgment, and firmness evinced by Captain Taylor in the several transactions he has detailed.   (Signed)   T. EDWARDS, *Assist. Secy.*"

In addition to the above, I had almost daily private letters from the General, which were very encouraging; but I have kept no copies of them, nor, indeed, are they needed here.

I had not, however, by any means, done with the Ranee yet. After my first flush of success, her party again assumed formidable dimensions, and I feared might incite her to fresh opposition. I had only myself to rely upon, for Pid Naik was utterly useless and helpless. I did not relax in any of the demands which I had made, for which the Ranee alone was responsible, having collected the revenue for many years; and finding I would not give in, she sent to me to say she was preparing bills for a lakh of rupees.

These were, however, so long in making their appearance, and there were so many evasions and excuses for which I could not account, that I grew more suspicious, and discovered at length that Chun Busappa, who was in my camp under surveillance, was sending the Ranee private messages to delay; that I " should soon be turned out, as Captain Gresley had been, and that I had no force at hand to use in case of resistance."

At last the Lady sent the banker to me with an impudent message, to the effect that if Chun Busappa were released unconditionally by me, and if she were allowed to have her own way in the direction of affairs, she would then pay the lakh of rupees.

This was displaying the cloven foot with a vengeance, and it was evident that so long as Chun Busappa remained, these secret intrigues would go on. I heard, too, that she was endeavouring to incite some of the 12,000 Beydur militia to attack my camp and rescue her paramour, and my men had noticed a great number of them prowling about, and posted on the hillsides at night. I therefore determined to send Chun Busappa at once to Linsoogoor, the cantonment of the south, where he would be quite safe and kept out of mischief. One of my *chuprassies* or messengers knew the road perfectly, and the Krishna river was fordable.

Twenty-five of my cavalry were therefore ordered to

prepare for a night march; and about nine o'clock, when all was quiet, I went to Chun Busappa, and told him he had forfeited his word, and was leading his mistress into fresh trouble. He did not deny the charge, but confessed the Ranee had sent him word that she would rescue him. I told him I had likewise heard the same, and that he must gird up his loins at once and mount the horse that awaited him.

In five minutes more he was on his road, guarded by the cavalry escort, and reached Linsoogoor the following morning in safety.

Long afterwards this man thanked me, with tears in his eyes, for having saved him, and the Ranee too, from much evil—perhaps even from death; and told me, also, how narrowly I had escaped myself. If I had not been very vigilant, I would have been attacked by clans of the 12,000 whom I had not seen. I wrote to my father thus:—

"Great was the indignation and consternation of the Lady in the morning. She beat her head, and, as it was reported to me, knocked it against the wall, roared and cried, and then, in a violent passion, rushed into the outer court of her palace, and called upon all good men and true to help her to get Chun Busappa back again. This was the crisis that I expected, and upon it would turn everything, hostile or peaceable. But nobody stirred. Only six negro slaves loaded their guns, and threatened everybody; but, being threatened by others, quietly fired them off, and were placed under surveillance.

"Well, my Lady then was down on her marrow-bones for a few days, and my humble servant. She had her palankeen prepared to come and see me, which I declared, without my wife's presence, would be indecent. Then began a series of sorrowful letters, with presents of partridges and quail, fruit and vegetables; but it would not do: I must have my lakh of rupees; and it came in two days in bills, which I very gladly despatched to Hyderabad."

I now determined to discharge certain of the mercenaries ; and in consequence of the Ranee's obstinacy
about the money transactions, the Resident thought it
would be too hazardous to attempt the measure without
some backing up. The 26th Regiment, Madras Infantry,
which was on its march to Secunderabad, was therefore
ordered to make a diversion to Shorapoor, and to await my
orders. In reality I did not want the regiment ; but the
Resident was more cautious than I, and thought preven-
tion better than cure. I had no trouble with the mercenaries. Those who were needed for ordinary duty were
retained ; superfluous men discharged, their arrears for
four years being paid to them according to their amounts.
I thought the garrison of Wondroog were inclined to be
restive, but the men all came into camp,—a very fine set
of fellows ; and when I had inspected them, looked at
their arms, and complimented them on their steadiness, I
called for volunteers for a hog-hunt, and I think more
than half the men responded at once : so we started, the
officers of the 26th Regiment joining heartily, and showed
them good sport before we returned.

Another very anxious crisis thus passed over ; but the
Ranee said she had no more money, though her own
accounts showed she had more in hand than the 75,000
rupees I had asked for, and I told her that I had no
alternative but to attach her private estates if she remained
obstinate ; and at last I did so by sending small parties of
cavalry into her villages, and this so completely humbled
her, that, in consideration of her having complied with the
former demands made, I begged that the balance still
remaining might be remitted. She was literally at my
feet for one day : though I told her not to come, she
arrived in her palankeen at my tent, to lay all her sorrows
before me. I could not turn her away ; and as she entered
she fell prostrate on the ground, and placed her son in my
arms. Both were weeping bitterly. She begged hard for

her estates; but as the attachment had been made at the
instance of the Nizam's Government, I could not take
upon myself to withdraw it, and could but assure her that
I did not wish to punish her more, and that I trusted
Government would be lenient in the end. The Ranee had
arrived just after breakfast, and sat with me till sunset,
surrounded by her women and secretaries, unveiled, nor
did she ever seclude herself afterwards.

I had sent for my wife, who, with her brother, soon
afterwards arrived from Hyderabad, and I selected an open
spot within the walls, about 500 feet above the plain, to
which we removed. The Ranee now asked permission to
come and visit us, and I was glad that she should do
so. She offered many valuable presents—shawls and
ornaments—and tried to put a large string of pearls round
my wife's neck; so that I was obliged to tell her firmly
that if she attempted again to force presents on my wife,
or to talk to her about her affairs, I should be forced to
forbid all communication between them.

The next day we returned the visit, and were introduced
to all the family.

The late Rajah had had three wives, and in all there
were fifteen children. Among these, one lively child, of
about ten years old, became our prime favourite, and she
engaged me in a game of romps, pelting me with roses,
and laughing merrily. There was not the slightest attempt
on the part of any of them to hide their faces, nor was
there any of the stiffness usual among native families.

The more I became acquainted with the State affairs,
the more anxious I grew to have the remainder of the
Ranee's debt to the Nizam's Government remitted. Under
cloak of British authority, it had, on the late Rajah's accession, not only imposed a fine of fifteen lakhs (£150,000),
but an additional yearly tribute of 56,000 rupees. It was
no wonder, therefore, that under an improvident and
neglectful Government, the State affairs had fallen lower

and lower, and it required very careful treatment to enable them to recover.

Eventually, at my suggestion, a new arrangement was entered into between the Nizam's Government and the State of Shorapoor. Another division of the *pergunnas* or counties was authorised, ceding that of Deodroog to the Nizam, and retaining that of Andola on the frontier line, whose people were most unwilling to be transferred.

The Nizam's Government was to give up all claim for arrears of tribute and succession fine, and the annual tribute was now fixed at 60,000 rupees a-year. These were the best terms I could get; and it was only by showing how entirely the successive Residents at Hyderabad had been misled by reports from temporarily deputed officers to Shorapoor, and how the original sum demanded under the treaty of 1800 had been increased, that I gained my point. If, as in justice ought to have been the case, past exactions had been repudiated, the Nizam's Government would have been obliged to refund ; but all these exactions had been recognised by us, English officers had been deputed to levy them, and their transactions were immutable. The retention of Andola and remission of all arrears of tribute—the interest on which, at the ordinary market rate of 12 per cent, would be 60,000 rupees—were certainly some service done to the State, and were the most favourable terms I could procure. But the Nizam's Government grumbled terribly at being obliged to give up its dominant position, and revert to its original status. It could no longer make extra demands through us, and get us by treaty to enforce them. It could not impose a succession fine on the young Rajah. It could only get what I had proposed, and which was ratified by the Supreme Government.

Of course, owing to these arrangements, my friend the Ranee got back her estates and the revenues collected, which had been kept in deposit ; but her appanage was reduced from 30,000 to 18,000 rupees a-year, the Rajah's expenses been borne by the State. I think at the time she was very grateful, and the reduction of the Nizam's Government demands seemed to strike every one —most of all Pid Naik. Indeed, with careful management the State would be easily able to pay them.

I soon perceived that it would be necessary to lose no time in placing the young Rajah on his *guddee*, or throne, that he might be publicly acknowledged. My reason was this. For some years after her marriage, the Ranee had had no male child, nor had any of the other wives. In fact, the late Rajah had formed two other marriages, in hopes of having an heir.

If there were no male heir born to him, his brother Pid Naik naturally succeeded; but Pid Naik declined succession for himself, and put forward his eldest son for adoption, who had been generally acknowledged, although no ceremony of actual adoption took place.

However, when hope was nearly at an end, the Ranee had a son, and Pid Naik's son was thrown out. It came to my ears that Pid Naik, encouraged by his boon companions at his drinking-bouts, had said that "now he could do as he pleased, and had at the ball at his feet, and he would show them all so after I had been withdrawn." In any case, whether this were true or not, he was very cool about the ceremony of placing the young Rajah on his *guddee*. He made many excuses. It would cost a great deal of money; the Beydur clans must be brought together, and he was by no means sure of them; an auspicious day must be selected, and was far distant, and the like; and if anything went wrong, he would get the blame. However, I simply told him I had received orders from the Supreme Government to proceed with the ceremony on the earliest possible date, and according to the rules and customs of the family on such occasions, and that it must be done forthwith.

And so it was. Arrangements were made of all kinds.
There proved to be enough money in the treasury to pay
the expenses of the ceremony. Invitations were sent to
the neighbouring families and people of rank, and the
State observed its usual profuse hospitality to all, and its
charitable doles to beggars, dancers, jugglers, acrobats,
&c.; and for three days previous to the ceremony, the
feasting was perpetual. Finally, when all the Hindoo
rites had been concluded, I took the little Rajah, who had
been sitting close to me, as his mother had implored me
not to allow him out of my sight, and leading him to his
guddee, or cushion of embroidered velvet, placed him upon
it in the name of the Government of India and the
Nizam.

"Whoever," I said to the crowds about us, "is the
friend of your Rajah Enketappa Naik" (and I added his
titles), "is the friend of both Governments; and whoever
is his enemy is our enemy, and will be dealt with as he
deserves. The British Government will protect your
Rajah and his interests till he reaches his majority, after
which his possessions will be made over to him. It is,
you see, a long journey to travel: some will faint and fall
by the way—some will fail; but in the end, if ye are all
of my mind, ye will joyfully repeat this ceremony."

Then followed great clapping of hands, and again the
old cry, "Jey Mahadeo Baba!" and afterwards the dis-
tribution of *pan* and *atr*, with handsome shawls and
dresses of honour, according to degree. The ceremony
being ended, the little prince rose, and thanked all present
in, for his age, a very dignified manner; and I took him
back to his mother, who embraced him passionately.
Whatever the Ranee may have been, there was no question
that her love for him then was devoted, and that she was
very grateful to me.

"This would never have taken place but for you," she
said to me, as she embraced my wife, who had been with

her all the afternoon. "What can I give you ?—how can I thank you both? My child is in truth yours, and you must guard him henceforth as a son."

We submitted, as a matter of form, to be enveloped in rich shawls, and soon afterwards took our leave. Pid Naik had accompanied us to the entrance of the inner court, but it was not etiquette for him to proceed further, and he waited for us and went with us to our tents, amidst firing of guns and noisy music.

So far, I hoped I had done my duty, but I felt uncertain as to the future, for no definite position had been assigned to me as yet.

CHAPTER VIII.

1843–44.

My position, however, had meanwhile been considered by the Governor-General, and shortly afterwards I received the following despatch from General Fraser, dated 18th May 1843 :—

" I transmit for your information and guidance the accompanying letter from the Secretary of the Government of India.

" The sentiments of the Governor-General regarding the administration of the Shorapoor State during the minority of the Rajah Enketappa Naik are so fully and clearly expressed in this despatch, that it is only left for me to request that you will be strictly guided by them.

" I shall be glad, however, to be informed that the caution enjoined in the fourth para. has been observed, and that the system upon which it has now been determined that the administration of Shorapoor shall be for some time conducted, is in conformity with the wishes, not only of Rajah Pid Naik, but also of the most influential persons in the State.

" You will be so good as furnish me with such occasional reports of your proceedings as may be necessary for my information, and for eventual submission to the Government of India ; and I shall be glad to be informed of the measures you may deem it advisable to adopt, with a view to give a good practical education to the Rajah ; and I beg that you will from time to time make me acquainted with the character and disposition he manifests, and the extent or degree in which he profits by the instructions you may have the opportunity of giving, or causing to be given to him.

"It will be highly gratifying to you to have received the Governor-General's entire approbation of your conduct; and I am happy to be able to add, as the expression of my own personal sentiments towards you, that I place the utmost reliance on the judgment and discretion which you have hitherto manifested, and which are so essentially necessary in the official connection of every British officer with the natives of India."

(Signed)   "J. S. FRASER."

Copy of despatch from the Secretary to the Government of India with the Governor-General, to Major-General Fraser, Resident at Hyderabad :

"POLITICAL DEPARTMENT, AGRA,
3d May 1843.

"SIR,—

"1. The Governor-General has read with regret Captain Taylor's letter, and its enclosures, transmitted to me in your letter of the 20th ultimo.

"2. The Governor-General was in hopes that the administration of the Shorapoor State might have been carried on during the minority of the Rajah, ostensibly by Rajah Pid Naik, with the general advice and support of Captain Taylor, but without his assuming a prominent part in the government.

"3. The facts stated by Captain Taylor, and the decided opinion expressed by him, in which you coincide, with the admission of Rajah Pid Naik of his inability to carry on the government, and his request that you will appoint a gentleman who, in conjunction with himself, will arrange the affairs of the Shorapoor State—all these circumstances compel the Governor-General to adopt, most reluctantly, the conclusion that a British officer will be necessary, in order to secure to the inhabitants of the Shorapoor State, during the minority of the Rajah, a just and beneficial government, and to enable the State to perform its pecuniary obligations towards the Nizam and its creditors.

" 4. The Governor-General considers it desirable that, notwithstanding the transference of the administrative authority in Shorapoor to a British officer, Rajah Pid Naik should, as far as possible, be put forward as the head of the State during the minority of the Rajah ; and it will be obviously expedient that the British officer should act in concert with Rajah Pid Naik, and place the young Rajah upon the Hindoo throne (*guddee*) with the usual ceremonies.

" 5. The Governor-General therefore authorises your directing the adoption of such measures as will be necessary for the adoption of these objects ; it being understood that the proceedings be in conformity with the wishes, not of Rajah Pid Naik alone, but of the most influential persons of Shorapoor.

" 6. The Governor-General intimated, on the death of the late Rajah, the interest he took in the welfare of the minor Rajah succeeding under such painful circumstances ; and his Lordship particularly directs that every consideration be upon all occasions shown to the young Rajah ; and that every measure be adopted which the judgment of yourself and the British officer at Shorapoor suggests, for the purpose of imparting to him a good practical education, such as may render him capable of administering the government of his State with benefit to his subjects.

" 7. It is not sufficient to place in the hands of the Rajah, on his attaining his majority, a prosperous and well-ordered State.   It is due to his people—it is necessary to our character—that the State should be confined to hands by which prosperity and good order may be preserved.

"8. The Governor-General has much satisfaction in seeing the difficult task of restoring the State of Shorapoor to the condition it seems to have once enjoyed, confided to Captain Taylor, whose good disposition, ability, and discretion have been manifested in all the transactions in which he has been engaged.

"9. The Governor-General requests that you will communicate to Captain Taylor his entire approbation of his conduct."

(Signed)   " J. THOMASON,
Secy. to the Govt. of India."

It was in consequence of these instructions that the young Rajah had been placed upon his throne, and I was very grateful for this proof of Lord Ellenborough's entire approval of my conduct. I had received neither from General Fraser nor the Governor-General any specific instructions as to the details of the future government of the State, and I felt, as these appeared to be left entirely in my hands, that no greater proof of confidence could have been manifested. I had given Pid Naik a fair chance from the time I had put him in charge as regent. I had assisted him to the very utmost of my power; but he was utterly helpless and incompetent. I had suggested many systematic improvements for his treasury; for collection of the revenue; for provision for the tribute he would have to pay, and the like,—not one of which plans was there the slightest intention, apparently, to carry out. On the contrary, he seemed to be surrounded by a new set of harpies and obstructors of order. He gave himself up occasionally to fits of intoxication, from which no one could arouse him.

His excellent wife made piteous complaints to me and to my wife on the subject, and so did his sons, giving me

sad accounts of his bad habits, and how sometimes for
days together no one saw him, when he and his special
favourites continued their drunken orgies night and day.
If I remonstrated privately he cried like a child, promised
most humbly to amend, and was as bad as ever directly
afterwards. His brother, his uncle, and all the Government officers reasoned with him, but in vain; he was
indeed hopeless.

I had explained the purport of the Government despatches, and had quoted to Pid Naik and all concerned,
including the chief bankers and merchants, the points
to be observed, and they expressed themselves perfectly
satisfied. The population, too, of the villages and districts
seconded the others with every expression of confidence ;
but still, I thought more was necessary ; and as I was
summoned to Hyderabad as a witness on a court-martial
then about to sit, I wished to take the opportunity of
laying the whole subject before General Fraser, with a
view to obtaining his specific instructions with regard to
Rajah Pid Naik.

There were many important matters to arrange. The
local bankers had claims, they alleged, upon the State for
nearly twenty lakhs (£200,000). There had been no
revenue settlement of the land for more than half a century ; but I need not describe the condition of an effete
State which had been going rapidly to ruin under heavy
pressure from without and absolute neglect within. No
hand had been stretched out to save it; and I think, more
pity and consideration ought to have been shown to the
oldest princely family in the Deccan, which, through all
wars and revolutions, had preserved its possessions without
committing itself with any one since the earliest period of
the Adil Shahy dynasty of Beejapoor.

Fortunately, I was not obliged to leave Shorapoor till
August, when the first violence of the monsoon was over,
and the weather was delightfully cool and pleasant. Al-

though we had lived all through the hot season in tents on the open ground, none of the party had suffered in the least, and our time had passed very pleasantly. My wife was a great favourite with the ladies of the palace, and with the children, who came sometimes to spend the day, playing very much like other little ones, and bringing their dolls with them, for whom feasts were made. Sometimes the Ranee herself, or one of the other matrons, accompanied them, and the young Rajah came too ; sometimes Pid Naik's sons and their mother, who was very delicate : in short, there was no constraint among them, and they went and came as they pleased.

I had heard these Beydurs called "savages ;" but in truth they are no more savages than other nations of India. They are perhaps somewhat more blunt and less obsequious, far more natural in manner, and we liked them all the better for that. My own tent was open to all comers from breakfast-time to sunset—no one was refused ; and although I did not personally inquire into cases of complaints, I referred all such petitions to Rajah Pid Naik by endorsement. If I could have spoken Canarese, I should have felt more at my ease; but many who came spoke Mahratta and Hindostanee, so that I managed to get on very comfortably on the whole. I had selected a site for a house during one of our evening rambles—a small level plain on the top of the plateau to the west of the city, and directly overlooking it, the mountain beyond it, and the plain beyond that again. The view was certainly very fine ; and as the site was 400 feet above the town, it would not only be cooler, but more healthy than below.

The ground was being cleared, and the places marked out for house, stables, and servants' offices. I hoped, on our return from Hyderabad, to find the building had commenced ; and there were plenty of first-rate masons and other work-people in the city. It was impossible to say how long we might be detained at Hyderabad, so I could only leave all the directions in my power to Pid Naik; and having done this, we started, and marching as rapidly as we could, we reached Hyderabad on the tenth day.

Before leaving Shorapoor, however, I had the great pleasure of receiving the following extract from a private letter from Lord Ellenborough to General Fraser, who wrote—

" It gives me great pleasure to send you the subjoined extract from a *private* letter from Lord Ellenborough, on the subject of your management of recent affairs at Shorapoor."

(*Extract.*)

" The account Captain Taylor gives of the proceedings of the Beydurs, and of the arrangement with them, is very satisfactory.   He has managed the affairs in which he has been engaged extremely well."

And I considered that a private letter from the Governor-General was much more complimentary and comforting than a public and formal despatch.

After all, I was not long detained at Hyderabad, and arrived once more at Shorapoor on the 1st September. My presence was very necessary, but as everything was going on well and quietly, there was no need for any anxiety about me.   During my short stay at Hyderabad, General Fraser and I had fully discussed the Governor-General's despatch, which I had already communicated to Pid Naik, and all the principal persons of Shorapoor, including the Ranee ; but it was necessary, I was of opinion, for the Resident to write himself to Pid Naik on the subject.   The commencement of an English direction of local affairs was a momentous event for Shorapoor; and no room for doubt ought to remain, or any question of the purpose of the British Government.   My own position, and that of Pid Naik, should be clearly defined.   General

K

Fraser desired me to prepare the draft of a letter in English and in Persian, to be sent to Pid Naik, embodying the wishes and directions of the Governor-General. This I did; but the Resident did not approve of it, and said he would make one himself. When the two were compared and checked by the best Persian scholars, who were called in, mine at last was adopted.

I had availed myself of Mr Palmer's directions in correcting my own draft. He was a first-rate Persian scholar, and could at once suggest the most expressive, as well as the most courteous, and plain, and decided phrases that a paper of the kind required, as applicable to persons of Pid Naik's position and understanding. Mr Palmer's assistance to me had proved very valuable. I wish I possessed a copy of this document, but I do not find it amongst my father's collection of my letters and papers.

My position at Shorapoor was declared to be supreme, and that of Pid Naik executive; and sound advice was given him to practise rigid and systematic economy, until the financial difficulties of the State were overcome.

Pid Naik was styled " Rajah Pid Naik Dewan," * and was to be allowed a seal as such. He had claimed the same title as the Rajah, " Bulwunt Bhyree Bahadur ;" but this was a ridiculous assumption, and would have been resented by the Rajah, the Ranee, and others of the family. Doubtless he would feel chagrined by the title proposed, and by the whole matter ; but I had no resource but to do my duty, and let him down as easily as I could.

As soon as I arrived at Shorapoor, Pid Naik paid me a visit. Everything had gone on smoothly during my absence, and I complimented him upon all he had done. I then delivered to him the Resident's letter, and he sent away his crowd of attendants and followers in order that we might discuss the subject unrestrainedly between us. It had been left optional to him to accept the orders of the

* Regent.

Governor-General or not, as he chose ; and I was ready to transmit his wishes, whatever they might be, whether of entire and *bonâ fide* acquiescence in the orders issued, or his objections to them, as he pleased. If he acquiesced, it would be my duty and care to make the execution of these orders as light and pleasant to him as possible ; but if he objected, I could only transmit any letter or paper that he might give me.

He said his honour and reputation were in my hands, and he would think over the letter from the Resident, and give me an answer as soon as possible. This he did ; and the reply, when it came, was quite satisfactory, and expressed his desire to work faithfully with me for the good of the State. Between us we made out a budget of the State revenues for the year, and I found that we might have 240,000 rupees, out of which the local charges would be 100,000, leaving 140,000 for payment of tribute and interest, with a balance to go on with.

A few days after this interview there happened a disagreeable affair in Shorapoor. One of my *chuprassies,* or messengers, was buying some grass in the market-place from a Beydur woman, and was badly wounded by an armed Beydur standing near. Whether my *chuprassie* had insulted the woman or the man, or whether they quarrelled over the price, I never knew ; but he was never accused of having done so. I had just set out from my house to ride up to my new works on the hill, and had turned into the market-place, when I saw the Beydur run off, brandishing his bloody sword ; and after procuring what assistance I could for my wounded *chuprassie,* I went after the Beydur who had cut him down. I met him in the main street, and ordered him to give me up his sword, which strangely enough he did at once (I had only a slight riding-whip in my hand), and telling my prisoner to go before me, I took him to the palace guard, and gave him in custody to the men on duty there, to be kept safely until Pid Naik, who

was out shooting, should return. I then rode on towards
my new buildings, and returned shortly before sunset.

It was still quite light as I rode back into the town, and
I found a crowd of armed men before the palace gate,
shouting and much excited. The first idea that occurred
to me was that there might have been some collision
between my escort of twenty infantry and the Beydurs ;
but I had sent my people word to remain quiet, and they
had done so.

As soon as I appeared I was surrounded in an instant
on every side, so that it was impossible for my horse to
move one step, and the shouting and peculiar shrieking of
the Beydurs were indescribable. Many matchlocks were
pointed at once close to my body; and I saw one fellow's
match pressed into the priming-pan by the trigger twice,
and grains of powder igniting on the end of it each time it
was withdrawn. For a moment I gave myself up ; but, by
the mercy of God, the piece did not go off. Drawn swords
were also brandished close to my face, but no blow was
made at me ; and the whole passed in less time than it
takes me to write.

At that moment several men ran out of the palace gate,
one of whom I knew to be the Rajah's own body-servant.
He pushed through the crowd, struck up the matchlock
then touching me, and calling out to the crowd, pushed
them aside right and left, telling me not to be afraid. He
then accompanied me to my house, where I found my
escort under arms and much excited.

The Ranee sent me word that both she and the Rajah
would come to me at once, if I would allow them, and
stay with me ; or would I come to them ? But there was
no need now, though I felt in my heart I had nearly tasted
death. The men of my escort were very savage ; and it
was as much as I could do to prevent their marching to
the palace court and taking the offending Beydur into
their own custody. Pid Naik shortly after arrived in a

terrible fright, and offered to stay with me all night ; but I
felt no further alarm.   The Beydurs, however, went to the
palace guard at night and carried off the prisoner to the
hills.   He was a champion among them, a wrestler and
athlete, and had the appellation of " Bich Kuttee," or
" Thrower away of the Scabbard."

In the morning all the clans of the " Twelve Thousand "
were found to have gone out upon the hills, where they
were shrieking, blowing horns, and beating their drums all
day, vowing they would not surrender the man unless
they had a guarantee from me that his life would be
spared.

A row with the Beydurs would have been very serious,
and I was determined not to have one if I could help it ; at
the same time I was equally determined not to give way
an inch.   Pid Naik was in a desperate fright ; but I would
not allow him to give in, and he obeyed my orders, insist-
ing that the prisoner should be sent back to him.

By evening the Beydurs grew tired, and made over the
prisoner to Pid Naik, who forthwith put him in irons, at
my suggestion, though he was more than half afraid of his
own people.   I daresay they did not like it ; but it was no
time to show the white feather.   Having waited for a day
to see that all was quiet, I urged Pid Naik to make the
Beydurs bind themselves down by strong bonds to behave
quietly for the future.   At this they took fresh alarm ; but
they did not go back to the hills, and I knew my game
was safe ; and so it proved in the end.   I made known to
them that I would take no further steps in the affair until
the issue of the wounded *chuprassie's* case was known ;
and I was very glad for all parties concerned that he
seemed going on well.   I sent them all away, with a
present for the wife and family of the imprisoned Beydur,
as it appeared they subsisted entirely on the fruit of his
labour, and all seemed satisfied and happy.

I daresay my *chuprassie* was a good deal in fault—for

he was a bit of a coxcomb, and no doubt had given himself airs—and I only put the Beydur in irons in order to make an example.

A few weeks after, on the occasion of the "Dussera"—a great anniversary festival of the Hindoos—the head men of all the clans of the "Twelve Thousand" came to me with a very humble petition on behalf of the Beydur still in confinement, and said they would esteem it a direct favour if the man were released to them. They were ready to make any agreement or bond with me, and to obey me implicitly in all things. My *chuprassie* had nearly recovered from his severe wound; at all events, his life was no longer in danger from it: and as he too joined in the request that his assailant should be forgiven, and the young Rajah, Pid Naik, and his brothers, and other influential persons, backed up the petition, I saw no reason to refuse. By consenting, I had a fair hope that this hitherto utterly lawless and uncontrollable body of men might be brought under some kind of subjection for the future. I therefore complied with their request, and the Beydur prisoner was released before them. He came blubbering to me, falling at my feet and begging pardon. He then prostrated himself before my *chuprassie*, who also forgave him. But I had impressed upon Pid Naik the necessity of requiring from all the heads of the clans much more stringent and more formal engagements than they had given before, which, it now leaked out, they repudiated as irregular and not binding. At the first hint of what was intended, the Beydurs took fright, but they did not go back into the hills; and after a consulation among themselves, under their great tree of assembly in the centre of the town, they gave in, and professed themselves ready to do as I wished. The agreements, which contained several clauses, were drawn up by me. They secured to the clans all hereditary lands and privileges, but made me, as the chief authority in the State, supreme judge in criminal cases, and in any other trials which could not be settled by their own *punchayet* (court). My drafts were copied by their own chief registrar, and signed by him, and by all the chiefs, and many others. When the agreements were ratified in all respects, I held a court, and the papers were presented to me formally, and I crossed hands over them with the chiefs of every clan. It was a very anxious period, and the complete success of the affair was a very great relief to me. General Fraser, too, had been very anxious; for any disturbance among the "clans of the Twelve Thousand" would have been most embarrassing after what had at first occurred. However, in the end he was satisfied that I was in reality now stronger than ever.

Several years afterwards, I heard the truth of the whole affair, and I was thankful I had not known it at the time. The plot had been originated by Kishnaya, Pid Naik's especial favourite and boon companion, whether with his master's knowledge and connivance or not I cannot say; but Pid Naik was, whether accidentally or on purpose, absent that day on a hog-hunting expedition.

The plan was this: One of my men—any one—was to be quarrelled with and cut down by the Beydur champion, on which it was presumed that I would immediately attack the Beydurs to recover possession of him, and thus a general *mêlée* would ensue, in which I would be made away with. The scheme, I daresay, seemed perfectly feasible, for no blame would have attached to any one, except, perhaps, myself. But, through God's great mercy, I escaped.

As soon as I could leave Shorapoor after the Dussera festival, I determined on making a short tour to see the country and become acquainted with the rural population, and also to give directions concerning the first settlement of revenue. I had, too, some cases of border raids and robberies of cattle by Beydurs on the northern frontier to inquire into and adjust. I found that for generations past no notice had ever been taken of such depredations by the Rajahs, and the issues had been left to the strongest. This, however, would not do now. I found that, wherever the land was under cultivation, the crops were, for the most part, very fine, but that there was comparatively little under tillage, when the large areas of village lands were considered. For these the people were clamorous for leases. I was obliged to tell them at present I could do nothing, but that I hoped to return as soon as I could. Meanwhile I was picking up all the information in my power, in my rides over village lands. There was plenty of game everywhere, and my bag was generally well filled; the people were exceedingly well-disposed and civil, and my time was passed very pleasantly. In November I received official notification of my promotion :—

"Captain Meadows Taylor, 6th Nizam's Infantry, is promoted to the rank of 'Captain Commandant,' with effect from 7th July last, *vice* Doveton resigned the service. Captain Commandant Meadows Taylor is posted to the 7th Regiment, but will continue in charge of the affairs of Shorapoor."

I was therefore secure of a regimental command in case of any alteration in the arrangements at Shorapoor. I returned there about the middle of November, and was distressed and vexed to find that Pid Naik had been at his old work, drinking very hard.

"I find," I wrote to my father on the 22d November, "Pid Naik is seemingly on his last legs, morally and physically. He looks very shaky, and has been seriously ill, after some days of beastly drunkenness; and I am sure more will follow when I leave again.

"I had to counteract endless petty schemes and dirty tricks. 'Who is the man who prevents these?' said his Brahmins; and he replied—

"'Ah, it's all very well for you; your knuckles are not rapped: it is only mine.'

" I would not be put off with excuses that so-and-so had peculated or intrigued, but would only exclaim—

" ' You are the executive, and you have full power to check all irregularities. If I did the work myself, you would grumble, and I look to you. Why cannot you go on comfortably, and in a broad, straight road with me? You know you always suffer in the end. Why are you so foolish? If you want money, say so—come and ask for it. The treasury (for I had established one with some difficulty) is not yours or mine; it belongs to the State. You can have what you require for State purposes; but do not steal from it, or allow cheating.'

" Personally we are very good friends, and now and then he really does some trifling business; but where the State moneys are concerned, he has no idea of honour or principle. He has not been seen for the last two months in public, except when he has come to visit me; and the people whom he employs have largely increased their power. Here is an instance of what goes on :—

" A learned man and very holy Brahmin who returned from the annual pilgrimage to Trippetti, and had charge of the State funds and expenses there, was asked to send in his accounts; and when examined, a debt of 2500 rupees (£250) was proved against him, which I directed he was to pay — and he promised to do so in fifteen days. This caused a very great sensation.

" ' So great a Brahmin! so holy a Shastree! That he should be made to pay!'

" ' Why not?' said I. ' Has he not cheated the State, and Trippetti also? and, moreover, acknowledged to having done so?'

" ' Oh yes,' was the reply, ' but he is a Shastree, and has spent it at the shrine of Sri Ballajee.'

" ' So much the better,' say I. ' But Sri Ballajee is just. He did not like the stolen money, and he sent the Shastree back to pay his debts!'

" ' Ah, truly, that may be the case,' said a knowing old
clerk ; and after a very long discussion, the assembly
finally gave it as their opinion that I had hit the right
nail on the head.

" Pid Naik had, I knew, been offered 500 rupees as
his share of the spoil, if, indeed, he had not already
bagged the money; and he not only proposed that *no*
demand should be made against the Shastree, but that
he should be given another 500 rupees, as a mark of
approbation ! "

My house was getting on very well. Building was very
cheap, and I hoped to finish it for 2000 rupees. It was
all of granite, which the stone-cutters sold in large blocks
1½ foot long and 4 to 6 inches thick, 6 to 10 inches
broad, for 3 rupees a thousand. I got the wood for the
roof for nothing, for there was a lot lying at an old
fort in the Nizam's country, which the land revenue
officer seemed delighted to get rid of, as no one had
claimed it for years.

There were about forty-six beams of various sizes,
which answered my purposes capitally, and were well
seasoned, saving me a very great expense, both in procuring wood and conveying it perhaps a hundred miles.
Lime, too, was very cheap; but the building was principally done with mud and stone, and only pointed on the
outside so as to keep out damp.

I employed about forty people. They did not work so
fast as English workmen, but on the whole I was very
well satisfied. A mason's wages at this time were about
6d. a-day, and the women, who assisted largely, had from
1½d. to 4d. On this they lived well, and many possessed
gold and silver ornaments purchased out of their own
earnings ! I was obliged to write to Bellary, seventy
miles off, for an estimate of carpenter's work, as the
making of doors properly was an art quite unknown in
Shorapoor. The fitting stones to the corners of the doors

and windows involved employing a different class of masons, those who worked with chisel and hammer, and were quite distinct from the wall-builders. Their wages were higher, and they had to find their own tools, which were all of the best steel.

The arch between the two centre rooms was turned in one day by two men in good stone and mortar work : it was 12 feet span, and 2 feet thick. I suggested to them to make a rough wooden frame to build over, but they shook their heads, and so I let them alone ; and they proceeded to build up the form of the arch between the piers with rough stones and mud, then struck the circle at the top, and smoothed it over with mud ; this soon dried in the sun, and the next day the arch was built over it, and was as firm as a rock. I often wondered what English work-men would have said to it all.

I laid out a flower-garden too, and the soil turned out very good. I had to clear away some rocks, and make the ground tolerably smooth. The Ranee kindly gave me a piece of ground in one of her gardens, at the foot of my hill, in which was a good well, so I did not despair of having plenty of plants, and wished to try and induce a taste among the people for English flowers and vegetables. I sowed beans, peas, cabbages, broccoli, and cauliflowers, which eventually throve and flourished. I was often amused on a holiday to watch the crowds of people who came up from neighbouring villages, and from the town, to see what was going on. Sometimes one, wiser than the rest, endeavoured to explain to the others " all about it ;" but they only put their forefingers to their teeth, shook their heads, and marvelled silently.

My friends the Beydurs were now very peaceable, and conducted themselves very quietly, cultivating their fields, and sometimes coming down from their hills with presents to me of partridges or other game. They generally had their dogs in leashes, and carried falcons on their wrists.

As soon as I could leave we went out again into the districts, and I began my work in earnest through the country.

I found the people very distrustful at first, and I was not surprised at it, as their own Government had never kept faith with them at any time; and it was but natural that they should be suspicious of me.

" How do we know," they said, " that your agreements with us are binding? " and I replied—

" I shall inquire into your condition before I sign your leases, and I shall visit your villages and look into your accounts; and, moreover, I give you my word, the word of an English gentleman, which cannot be broken."

" But you may go away? "

" If I do, another will succeed me."

" Well, we shall see. If you keep faith with us for one year, we will take heart, and cultivate all the waste lands in the country."

These scenes and conversations were of constant recurrence, and soon the people began to talk to me, and to consult me on their business affairs, and I felt pretty sure that when the revenue settlement was begun, the people would trust me, and get over their shyness and suspicion. I had determined to admit no strangers as clerks; clumsy as they were, the hereditary officers of the State had the first claim for employment, and must be educated into regular system if they were to be of use afterwards. I therefore made my selection, leaving the others with Pid Naik. An extract from a letter, written in December 1843, will give some idea of the condition in which I found the head village of the *pergunna* or county which I first visited :—

" These districts are in the worst conceivable condition. No accounts whatever have been kept; no record of the revenues, or of the land in and out of cultivation, for sixty-seven years, and you may well imagine the work of cleaning out and reorganising the Augean stable of abuse and corruption. Whole villages in this county are deserted, and are little more than heaps of ruined houses. This village, Hoonsigee, had formerly a weekly market and many dealers in grain, a hundred families of weavers, and a host of other tradesmen. Now, there are left only one grain-dealer and two weavers. Half the cultivators' houses are in ruins, and the land is more than two-thirds waste. The revenue used to be 4900 rupees a-year, or £490. Now, it has declined to 875 rupees, or £87, 10s., and is collected with difficulty; what could be done? I will tell you what I have done. I invited back the weavers on a low tax of three rupees a-year—they ought to pay twelve; but then they have to rebuild their houses. With them come other tradespeople, cultivators, grain and flour sellers. While we have been here, fifteen families have returned from the British territory, and more are coming in. I can get no better terms than three rupees per *cooroo*, and I have accepted that for three years, with an addition of three for the next three years, when the land is to be reassessed; the present assessment being thirty rupees per *cooroo* per year—that is, 40 acres for £3 per year. Matters may differ a little in each county, but I can get land taken on no other terms. People cannot trust the Shorapoor authorities, and mistrust me too for the present. They are very shy—however, that ; is wearing off very fast, and during the last three days they have come forward pretty freely. It is hard work, however, but I don't despair, and hope to lay a foundation for future revenue arrangements. Oh that I were rid of Pid and his crew, who grow more and more obnoxious, idle, and altogether mischievous!"

The year 1844 opened very brightly upon us. I had arranged three small counties; the rent had been only 2000 rupees a-year—it would now be upwards of 3000 rupees, and hereafter would produce 8000 on the new leases. I was beginning to see my way ; and as we approached the Bombay frontier, farmers came in numbers, asking to be allowed to settle and take up new land, as much as I would give them. Of course I made no objection, and they became registered landholders.

We were in excellent health, and found our tent-life very agreeable.

The people came in crowds wherever we encamped. I have had a couple of hundreds about my tent, and they seemed much interested and amused by our ways, which of course were quite new to them. It pleased us to see the confidence they had in us ; and they constantly brought some little gift as token of their friendly feeling. I felt very thankful for all this.

I never worked harder or felt stronger in my life— sleeping soundly, and eating heartily, and the climate was delicious.

My wife and I used to take our morning rides together over the fields. I had to inspect the lands, and sometimes very amusing scenes took place when gross peculation and roguery were discovered. One was in reference to the *patell*, or head of the village at which we were encamped, " Kembavee." This personage had a fine estate and farm of 2410 *beegahs* under excellent cultivation. Some of it was a free grant for services performed by his forefathers ; but by the original deed of grant he was to pay 1600 rupees, or £160 a-year for the whole. The land was all under rich crops of *jowaree* or large millet, wheat, cotton, linseed, and pulse. The *patell* had being paying only 600 rupees a-year for the last sixty-eight years! and had the assurance to ask me for a remission of 200 rupees out of the 600, as some of his crops had failed ! This led me to examine into the case carefully, and to go over the whole property, and we rode over literally miles of fields, which were far more like 10,000 *beegahs* than 2410. Of course I gave no remission, and the *patell* voluntarily agreed to pay his full rent of 1600 rupees next year if I would not charge him for arrears !

Here is also another instance.

The *patell* of a village near asked me to come and look at his land, as the crops had dried up. I told the people to meet me on their boundary at sunrise, and I went. The crops were certainly poor ; but I said, " In the Company's territories no man has more land than he pays rent for, therefore remissions are allowed. You seem to have a great deal more than you write down, suppose we try one field ;" there were in it about 15 *beegahs* of wheat, the same of linseed, the same of pulse and cotton—all very fine ; and a patch of *jowaree*, poor and dried up. Altogether, by pacing it, it appeared to me 90 *beegahs*, of the best quality, and all well tilled.

" How much do you pay for this piece ? " I asked ; but there was no answer.

One fellow nudged another, but no one spoke. I asked a second, and a third, with the same result. At last a fine old soldier of the village, a Mussulman, spoke out.

" Please your lordship," said he, " the *patell* pays two rupees (four shillings) for it per year."

" Two rupees ! " cry I. " O *patell* of bad destiny, two rupees for all this land ! Say, how much am I to remit out of that ? Are you not ashamed of yourself to enjoy all this land for two rupees ? Now let me see more of your fields."

" They are all the same," cried the sturdy soldier. " Please your highness, that *patell* takes all the fine land and puts off the poor land upon us poor people, paying what he chooses to the Government ; and they are all the same."

" Well spoken, O Khan ! " cried a chorus of people; " it is the truth ! "

Looking at the honest soldier, I asked him, " Now,

where are your fields ? if they are bad, you shall have a
remission."

He drew himself up, proudly enough, and replied—

" My fields were sown in the rains, and God has been
good to me. I have reaped and stored the crop, and my
children are eating it. I have paid my rent too, and want
nothing but your favour."

So I patted him on the head, and bade all the rest go
and do as he had done, and I heard no more of remissions.

So it was in every village; the powerful paid no rent in
comparison with the poor, and thus the revenue had been
diminishing year by year. No accounts of land had been
taken for fifty years or upwards ; no one had paid the least
attention to the subject, and it would necessarily take some
years to get to the bottom of all the defalcations, and to
establish a new and honest system.

Nor had even the rent which had been collected been
forwarded to the treasury; in some places half the sum,
or even less, was expended on the village itself, and the
balance handed over to the collector. What wonder that
the revenue declined ?

It was very hard work, beginning at seven every morning, and lasting till after midnight, except one hour for
each meal ; yet I was very well, and the work had to be
done somehow. At Shorapoor everything was quiet and
prosperous ; but Pid Naik's good wife was very ill, and he
wrote despairingly about her. I was very sorry for this,
for I knew well if she died he would be enticed by his
other wife, who was as great a drunkard as himself, and
both would go rapidly to the dogs ; but remonstrances, and
even entreaties, were of no use. He made promises which
he never fulfilled.

As, after much inquiry, there was no specific charge
proved against Chun Busappa, except that of wasteful
extravagance, and even this seemed to be more the Ranee's
fault than his, I had him released from Linsoogoor,

and he came direct to my camp. Whether he had been
the Ranee's paramour or not was no business of mine.
His account of the whole matter was of course a different
affair altogether. He said he had been trying to do what
I was doing, but the corrupt practices prevailing were too
strong for him. He said that Luchmangeer, the Gosain
banker, had desired the management of affairs; but that
the Ranee had preferred him, and therefore he had become
a mark for slander and misrepresentation to Captain
Gresley. He would not permit almost unlimited peculation by the *duftardars* and other ministerial officers, and
they resented his interference with them, and as he
was a "Lingayet," all the Brahmins hated him; and
no doubt there was a good deal of truth in these justifi-
cations.

As to Rajah Pid Naik, I knew now very well what he
was, and it was scarcely likely that the Ranee, a shrewd,
clever woman, who had known him since she was a child,
would give in to him, or allow him and the Gosain banker
to domineer over her; and she had never forgotten the
proposed adoption of Pid Naik's son by her husband.
That feeling rankled at her heart, and until her own son
had been formally recognised by the Government of India
she had never been free from anxiety. With me, and to
me, I must say that Chun Busappa behaved extremely
well. His office was an hereditary one as keeper of the
treasury and wardrobe; but he did not wish to resume the
actual performance of these duties, and he never interfered
with the current business in any respect, while, if I required information on any point, he gave it readily and
clearly if he could.

In one respect, indeed, he was highly commendable; he
had taken under his charge certain detached villages, and
all the Ranee's private estates had been managed by him.
In these the people were content and prosperous, the lands
were well tilled, and the accounts had been well kept for

several years; while he was evidently much liked and respected by the people.

Early in February Rajah Pid Naik's good wife died. She had been the mother of seven children, and was much respected for her charity and piety. I went into Shorapoor to pay him a visit of condolence, but I found him very low and despairing about himself.

His chief anxiety, however, appeared to be that the State should allow him 3000 rupees for his wife's funeral expenses, gifts to Brahmins, &c., and that a market should be founded in her name. I could do nothing without instructions, at which he did not seem pleased; and I felt no doubt that, had I not come in from the districts, he would have taken advantage of the occasion to have appropriated at least 10,000 rupees—so dishonest was he. I told him I could not lay out the Rajah's money on his private expenses, but if I received permission from the Resident, the expenditure should be authorised. I saw more clearly every day that had it not been for my presence, the whole of the money would have been made away with, as Pid Naik's people put it into his head that he was in truth Rajah of Shorapoor, and none else; and the poor little Rajah would have scarcely been able to hold his ground unaided.

I also visited the Ranee and the Rajah, who were overjoyed to see me. I had appointed Mr Murray, the medical attendant attached to me, as instructor in English to the Rajah, and I found he had made very fair progress, being able to read easy stories, and write very fair copies. I was much pleased, and told him when I came to reside in my own house I would look after him myself. He was very intelligent, and never tired of asking me questions about my country, its customs, and its people. He was also learning Persian, Mahratta, and Teloogoo, the language of business, and got on very well with all. I found three rooms of my new house were roofed in, and the walls plastered inside ; the rest was in active progress, and I hoped all would be ready for us by the time we wished to return.

Meanwhile my work continued, and the condition of some of the towns and villages was truly distressing to witness. One, the town of Narribole, used to pay, according to the accounts given me, 26,000 rupees a-year, comparatively a very few years ago. Now 5000 rupees were collected with difficulty per annum, while no regular accounts had been given in or taken for eighty years !

By this time, however, it was well understood that I should require accounts and returns properly made out by next season ; and there was less trouble when they saw I was in earnest.

Personally, Lord Ellenborough had been very kind to me ; but as special correspondent of the most influential paper in the world, it was impossible to pass over his policy in regard to events in Affghanistan or elsewhere. His proclamation in regard to Scinde, and other transactions, are now matters of past history, but live fresh in the memories of those who were contemporaries of that time, and still survive. He had been appointed Governor-General, and had arrived in India at a very critical period. Not only had Lord Auckland's policy, as regarded Affghanistan, broken down utterly, but the force at Cabul had perished miserably in their retreat ; an attempt under Pollock to force the Khyber Pass and relieve the brave garrison of Jellalabad had failed. The Sikhs were to the last degree unquiet, and had been so since the death of Runjeet Singh in 1839. The Mahratta State of Gwalior was in a very shaky condition ; there were strong indications of disturbance in Scinde ; and instances of mutiny in the Madras army had occurred, under the impression that the native portion of it would be required to proceed to Affghanistan. It might have been supposed that Lord Ellenborough, considering his undoubted high character and reputation, would have struck out some definite policy, so as to meet the crisis in a spirit suitable to the emergency.

It is true that, thanks to the indomitable spirit of Pollock and Nott, Cabul was again occupied, and all the captives were rescued, and that the forces under these generals were successfully marched out of Affghanistan. But there were no indications of support from the Governor-General; on the contrary, for a time timid vacillation, and in the end pretensions of having achieved the success which was due to others. This was very painful to witness then; and when the force actually returned, safely guided through the tumultuous upheavings of the Punjaub, the famous proclamation issued by the Governor-General, which was to be read at every native court, was treated as it deserved by the press of India and of England.

I, in my humble capacity, never had so humiliating a task put upon me as the reading of that proclamation to Rajah Pid Naik and all the authorities of Shorapoor. Not only did they not comprehend it, but they considered it, as it really was, a piece of bombast, only intended to conceal the disaster of Affghanistan, of which every one knew perfectly, and many no doubt rejoiced over in private, and of which the most exaggerated details were given. If the policy in regard to Gwalior shows finer and more generous features in the non-annexation of the State after the victories over its mutinous armies—long the nucleus of every discontented and ambitious chief of Central India—what shall be said in regard to the policy in Scinde, which, placed in the hands of an unscrupulous man, ended in the destruction of that ancient State, with whom the British Government had made treaties of eternal friendship?

These are now, however, subjects of history, and I need not revert to them; but I cannot accord with the opinion, in regard to the actors and the acquiescers in this tragedy, —"De mortuis nil nisi bonum;" and posterity will deal with them as they deserve.

CHAPTER IX.

1844.

I RECEIVED during this time an official despatch from the Military Secretary's pay department fixing all my future allowances, which relieved me from further anxiety on that score. The Resident had behaved very handsomely to me, and I had every reason to be grateful.

We spent three days on the banks of the Krishna—a glorious river, with grand rocks and streams, and dark pools below. I tried fishing; but although fish were plentiful, I could not succeed at first owing to the want of proper tackle. The beauty of the scenery was very great —wild and striking—and the river was much broken by islands: the water reached above a man's waist, and in one place the river divided into five large streams, each more than two hundred yards in width. Higher up I heard there was a fine waterfall, which I should have liked to visit, but I did not care to delay just then, so we deferred it to another time. We remained out in the district until the end of March, when the heat became suddenly very oppressive and unbearable, and we began to long to inhabit our new house, which, from its lofty position on the hill, would insure our having plenty of air, and cool refreshing wind at any rate at night. I found the house entirely roofed in, and several rooms, quite enough for our accommodation, ready ; and we were very soon greatly the better for the change.

But I was not happy about Pid Naik's goings on. He was engaged in an intrigue at Hyderabad, through Luch-mangeer, the Gosain banker, the object of which was, absurd as it may appear, to get himself recognised by Rajah Chundoo Lall, the Minister of the Nizam, as Rajah of Shorapoor. This scheme was to be backed up by the Nizam himself, in order that, as in the case of the district officers in 1829, the interference of the English might be withdrawn. I personally did not care about this ; but I saw it would unsettle the little mind Pid Naik possessed, and that he was conducting himself now far more like the Rajah than the " Dewan." He spent and threw about money just as he pleased, in defiance of his own promises and my directions, and this could not be permitted. I therefore desired him—

1st, To give no orders upon the treasury without my counter-signature.

2dly, To allow no persons except the regular Govern-ment officers to interfere with State affairs ; and

3dly, To appoint any day in the week most convenient to himself for a General Durbar or Court, at which I, with the Rajah, would attend to receive reports, hear petitions, and transact general business.

I never received any reply to these proposals in writing; and though Pid Naik came over and over again to see me, and promised most faithfully that he would do all that was required of him, I was told by some of his own people that he had not the slightest intention of fulfilling his promises.

In May the reports of the Shorapoor intrigues became so notorious at Hyderabad, that my friend Captain Malcolm, assistant to the Resident, wrote several times to warn me of them, and desired me to keep well on my guard against them, &c. As affairs stood at present, according to Captain Malcolm's account, Luchmangeer had got the support of the Minister and of the Nizam himself. The Minister had been promised 30,000 rupees, with 20,000 to some subordinates; the Nizam himself was to have 100,000 rupees, or £10,000. And all had been led to believe that the Shorapoor treasury was full, and that the amount could be paid over to them at once.

"If you will refer to my previous letters," I wrote to my father, "you will find, I daresay, that a balance of five lakhs of rupees was said to be due to the Nizam's Government when Captain Gresley made his settlement. When I became perfectly acquainted with these affairs I thought otherwise, and was convinced the balance was due to the other side, and to a large amount. I therefore wrote a letter on the subject, and a very earnest one, to get the Shorapoor estate excused the balance on account of its poverty. To this the Resident would not listen; but as I had no reply from the Governor-General, I thought my letter would have struck him, and that he might have referred the subject to England. Whether he did so or not I know not; but orders have since come out from the Court of Directors that the balance is *not* to be taken, and whatever may have been paid by the Shorapoor State since the late settlement (£16,500) is to be refunded.

"Now the Nizam's Government does not like this at all, and has not answered the Resident's note on the subject. Malcolm thinks the Nizam will make a reference to the Governor-General, which will not be successful; for this balance of five lakhs is sheer robbery. What the end of all will be I know not; but if the Governor-General abandons the policy he deliberately undertook, it will be most strange and unaccountable. I do not think he will; and I believe when he hears of their intrigues he will take the bull by the horns, and place the country entirely under my direction, or that of some other English officer, which would be the only means of retrieving the State from ruin and destruction. As to the intrigue, I am not uneasy since I heard it was known at Hyderabad; and if the Governor-

General comes down on the Nizam to refund the £16,000,
I shall be all right."

Shortly afterwards General Fraser wrote again to Pid
Naik, enclosing copies of extracts from his former letter,
to which no reply had been vouchsafed. The General's
letter now required replies, even in the ordinary course of
politeness and etiquette. Pid Naik evaded an answer for
several days, offering to send his agents ; but I would take
no verbal answers, and he said he was too ill to write ; and
so we continued to skirmish, and still Pid Naik would
give no reply either to the Resident's letter or to mine.
His chief counsellors now were a boon companion of his
who was once a religious mendicant, and went out accompanied by a boy begging for rice—another, the holy man
who was dismissed for cheating in his district last year.
The third was the chief spiritual adviser of Luchmangeer,
the Gosain banker (whom I had sent to Hyderabad), a
man who had again and again complained to me of Pid
Naik's indifference to him, at the same time extolling his
own holiness. This holy man came to me when he saw
that his friend Pid Naik must soon go to the wall, and
abused him and the rest, betraying all their confidence.
What a pack of scoundrels they all were, to be sure !
Contemptible and most villanous ! Pid Naik was gullible
to a degree, and believed all these rascals told him. He
asked for money on the most foolish pretexts. He wanted
musical boxes, and an English carriage, although there was
not a road within miles of Shorapoor where one could
possibly be driven,—indeed, I had long been endeavouring
to persuade him to mend the roads into the city ; but he
objected, urging that his so doing would impair the im-
pregnability of the place !

Every day he promised to do exactly as I asked him,
and every day he did the contrary, or evaded, or shuffled
in some way, till I was obliged to be very imperious in
my demands. Then he came cringing and begging me not

to tell of him, and agreed to some trifle, by way of a *sop*, and the whole scene was re-enacted. However, I did not keep silence, and I regularly sent copies of our correspondence and details of our communications up to Government, accompanied by some very severe remarks, and I could only hope that Lord Ellenborough would give them his attention in time ; and as Pid Naik was perfectly deaf to all remonstrance from me, I could but look to Government to support me.

At last, after much weary waiting, a note came which ran as follows :—

" I have understood the letter of the Resident to *you*, also the Persian extracts which accompany it, in every respect. I consider you to be in the place of the Resident. According to his orders to you, do you act truly."

Pid Naik was evidently determined not to reply to the Resident himself, and I sent a copy of the foregoing to Hyderabad, to which the Resident answered privately :—

" I need not say how much I regret the difficulties you have experienced from the incapacity and unaccountable obstinacy of Rajah Pid Naik. It is now a question before the Government of India whether he can at all be retained in the office of Dewan, or altogether removed, and yourself installed as the sole and exclusive manager of the district. Recent despatches from the Court of Directors have, however, intervened regarding Shorapoor, upon which I have been obliged to write largely, and these circumstances may perhaps occasion some delay in the coming to a specific decision in the case of Rajah Pid Naik."

After much vexatious delay, I received an account of receipt and expenditure, of which no details were given whatever.

Revenue, ...	235,000 rupees.
Expenditure by Rajah Pid Naik, ...	110,000 ,,
Government debts, including tribute, . . .	110,000 ,,
Reserve fund, ...	10,000 ,,
Losses and extras, ...	5,000 ,,

Now the Nizam's Government had only received 50,000 rupees on account, and thus 60,000 were due from Pid Naik on that head! Every one ought to have been paid out of the sum set down, but there were 40,000 rupees of arrears due; and thus a deficiency of one lakh, or 100,000 rupees, had occurred in the financial year. There were about 4000 rupees in the treasury, and about 10,000 rupees of outstanding balances difficult of realisation. Now there was a new debt of quite a lakh, and how much more had been concealed from me I could not say. If affairs had been honestly conducted, we should have had a surplus to carry on to the next few years. How Pid Naik had got rid of the lakh of rupees which he had thrown away I could never discover; but I imagine much of it had gone to support the intrigue at Hyderabad. Now the accounts would have to be forwarded to Hyderabad, and would tell their own disgraceful story, needing no comment from me. Nothing had come of the intrigue at Hyderabad; and nothing was likely to come of it. The Nizam and his Government had taken warning by the movement of the Supreme Government of India and the Court of Directors, and had thrown off Luchmangeer and his false promises with contempt.

.   .   .   .   .   .

In August I took my wife to Linsoogoor for medical advice—she was ill and suffering. I had arranged to send her home to England for a time to recruit her strength, which had suddenly and unaccountably declined. I trusted that the means used would enable her to undertake the journey, and that the complete change would set her up. God saw fit to take her from me very suddenly at the last.

Of that time I cannot write. It is many years ago, and all the scene with its sad details rises fresh before me. I tried humbly to bow to the will of God; but I had lost in her not only my loving and beloved wife, but my steady, true friend, my comfort and my happiness; so tender in her love, so gentle; so firm to do right, and so keen to detect wrong. Henceforth I must be alone at Shorapoor, and work on as best I could without her loving presence and her wise, calm counsels, without human aid or sympathy of any kind. Well—it was a bitter grief, and it had to be borne; so, after a very severe illness which detained me for some time, I returned to take up my work again at Shorapoor alone.

I found my house quite finished now, and looking really beautiful inside and out. What a mockery it seemed to me! The dear presence that would have made it home to me; the deft, skilful hands that would have delighted in making it habitable and homelike — these were at rest now, free, at all events, from future pain and suffering; and in this thought was my only comfort. . . . Fresh anxieties were in store for me at Shorapoor.

. . . .

I had been hearing for some weeks past very disagreeable reports in relation to a conspiracy at Shorapoor to destroy the young Rajah at the " Dussera " festival, when great crowds usually assembled. Pid Naik's favourite, Krishnaya, was at the head of this most villanous scheme.

The young Rajah of Gudwall, a neighbouring principality, had been shot in his Durbar with his father and brother, and their bodies had been cast out of the town.

My watchful friend, Captain Malcolm, wrote to me to be on my guard, and look well to the river ferries, because reports were rife that Arabs and Rohillas had moved in my direction, so as to arrive at Shorapoor at or during the " Dussera " festival.

The Ranee was in the wildest state of alarm about her son, and about me; but I had brought another company of the 6th Regiment with me from Linsoogoor, and I had now 170 men—quite enough, I considered, to prevent any disturbance. I had also requested Pid Naik to send

Krishnaya to me, as I suspected he was implicated in the plot; but instead he had despatched him to the fort of Wondroog, nine miles off. To my surprise, however, General Fraser ordered a regiment of infantry and 200 cavalry to march on Shorapoor, and they all arrived the day before the festival. Evidently the Resident was anxious and determined to use every precaution in his power. Very soon after the arrival of the troops, Pid Naik came off to see me in the direst alarm. "What was the meaning of these troops?" he asked. I verily believe that he imagined they had come for him! And as I did not care to erase this impression altogether, I only told him that there were reports of a dangerous and bad character afloat at Hyderabad, relative to some intrigues going on at Shorapoor, and that the troops had been sent by the Resident's orders to be ready in case of emergency and to prevent trouble; but that no one would interfere with him, or molest him in any way, if things went well and quietly.

Two days afterwards, two of Pid Naik's confidential servants came to me privately, saying they had something to disclose; I therefore took down their depositions. A sad revelation, indeed, of contemplated treachery! They professed to have warned their master, but in vain, and therefore came to tell me, in the hope that mischief might be prevented. Evidently I had arrived just in time—the scheme was already to be carried out. My informants were fearless men, and gave their information clearly and unhesitatingly. In all respects it accorded precisely with Captain Malcolm's private information received at Hyderabad.

The heads of the depositions were these:—

That for a long time past Pid Naik had tacitly allowed Krishnaya to intrigue; and that he, finding all his efforts at Hyderabad unsuccessful and thwarted by me, had at last grown desperate, and had laid this diabolical scheme to make away with the poor little Rajah and with me also during the procession, by means of some villains whom Pid Naik had sheltered (although he had denied having done so to me), and who were rebels from the Nizam's country and notorious desperadoes.

The man who gave the best evidence was manager in Pid Naik's late wife's household. He deplored what had occurred, and how Pid Naik had gradually been brought to listen to Krishnaya's vile plot. He said he did not think his master had any bad intentions of himself, but had been talked over by the others whose names he gave me, and they agreed with those against whom I had received warning from Hyderabad. He said he thought Pid Naik had despatched Krishnaya to Wondroog because he felt certain that I had discovered the plot, and he would wish to appear well disposed towards me by punishing the chief offender. For as the man said, "If there had been no plot, he would have written to you evasively; as it was, why should he put his favourite directly into prison as soon as you asked for him ?"

The *karkoon* or clerk who sat at Pid Naik's gate also gave similar evidence. I requested Captain Stoddart, who was in command of the troops, to move his force nearer, so as to command the entrance to the gate below my hill; but owing to a deep ravine coming in the way, he could not post them nearer than a mile from the gate ; however, the road was a good one up to it, and the force could easily move along it in case of necessity.

This movement created some fear, but I sent word to the townspeople not to be afraid—that no harm was intended, and that the procession was to go on as usual.

I was also much surprised by a visit from Krishnaya's most confidential Brahmin, who came to me openly—a man I had never before seen ; but he said he could keep quiet no longer, and was most willing to give evidence before Krishnaya himself on oath anywhere. I was indeed delighted, and encouraged him to make a clean breast of it, and a very pretty revelation it proved. He told me he it was who had sent me anonymous warnings and hints on several occasions, and appealed to me whether they had not turned out to be true. And in the present case he said it was he who "had told it to a friend, who had told it to my agents, who had told it to me"! Now all he desired was to be openly confronted with Krishnaya. I took down this deposition also and forwarded it to the Resident; it accorded with the previous ones in every respect.

I then sent for Pid Naik, and without informing him how far he was implicated, told him of the horrible plot that had been discovered, and informed him, before Captain Stoddart as a witness, that I should hold him responsible in life and person for any riot or disturbance, and also for the safe custody of Krishnaya. He did not like this at all, and pretended to be greatly shocked at the contemplated villany; but when I told him further particulars, and what conclusions had been arrived at from his recent acts, he seemed to comprehend the danger to himself if he did not at once exert himself to prevent mischief. He agreed to give the necessary orders, and to see that peace was preserved during the procession, and in fact I think the shock quite sobered him, for I never saw him so collected or so earnest and clear-headed.

The procession takes place at night, and the Rajah had to proceed from his palace to an open space about a mile off. All the Beydur clans were present, all the State soldiers, and crowds of people. I had a party of a hundred picked men, giving them orders to keep close to the Rajah. We went down to the palace about five o'clock, a rather formidable-looking party. I was on my elephant, with Captain P——, who had come in from Linsoogoor; and then my little force of picked men followed. When we arrived at the palace we dismounted,

and each taking the little Rajah by the hand, we led him
between us to his elephant, which was waiting, placed
him upon it, and then remounted our own. We proceeded very, very slowly, any one might have taken a
shot at us that pleased; but God protected all — the
fatherless boy and those with him—and we were unhurt.
Not a word was spoken, every one was most respectful to
us, and we passed on to the place where the ceremonies
were performed, under the hill whereon my house was
situated. The crowd baffles description. After the ceremonies were ended the fireworks began, and were very
fine; one bouquet of two hundred rockets was superb.
About eleven o'clock we returned to the palace with the
Rajah, whom I restored to the arms of his anxious
mother. She had been in a state of the wildest alarm
and anxiety; and of her grateful feelings when her child
was brought back safely to her I need not speak here.

Thus was I again, through God's great and infinite
mercy, preserved through imminent danger.

The next day I demanded Krishnaya from Pid Naik.
I hoped that when he was delivered up, the Government
would be convinced of the rascality prevailing at Shorapoor, and would be disposed to assume a firmer aspect,
and make a final settlement of affairs.

Pid Naik, finding he could make no impression on
the Nizam's Government, now began writing letters to
Hyderabad complaining of me—and very much calculated
to set the Nizam and the British Government by the ears
—and sent an agent with them to Hyderabad to deliver
them to the Resident and to Colonel Tomkyns. I warned
the Resident of what was coming, and then sent for Pid
Naik, told him I had heard of his proceedings, and asked
him what he had been doing, and what he had written.
Then he swore solemnly "on his children's heads" that all
was false. However, in due time Pid Naik's agent arrived
at Hyderabad, and delivered the letters to Colonel Tomkyns

and to the Resident. Colonel Tomkyns took the letter, but turned out the man who brought it, and the Resident did exactly the same. Both of them forwarded the letters to me without having opened them, and I sent for Pid Naik as soon as I received them, and showed them to him with the seals unbroken. He could say nothing, he could make no excuse or frame no lie, he was so utterly dumfoundered ; but he went home, and was dead drunk for the next three days !

Meanwhile Pid Naik's agent at Hyderabad had again, through Luchmangeer, the Gosain banker, got the ear of the Nizam's confidant, and he reported to his master that the Nizam was going to interfere on his behalf; and Captain Malcolm wrote to me privately confirming this report. The Resident, however, had already written a spirited note to the Nizam's Minister requesting that these disreputable intrigues might be put an end to once for all, and the reply was all I could wish for. Orders were issued to seize Pid Naik's agent; but he had been evidently informed of his danger, and had made his escape. I showed all these letters and documents to Pid Naik, who begged me to transmit a letter of apology to the Resident, denying that he had ever sent an agent, and requesting that if any person came hereafter, purporting to have been sent by him, or by his orders, he should be at once forwarded either to me or to himself.

That evening the young Rajah and Rajah Pid Naik came up to my house to hear the band of the 2d Regiment play on my terrace. It was a glorious moonlight night, and I had never seen Pid Naik so pleasant. In the morning, of his own accord, he sent all the treasury orders to be countersigned by me, and the accountants with all the accounts, imploring me to try and *save his credit*. It would have been poor spite in me to notice the past any longer. I did my best to set him upon his legs again, and I told him I intended to hold him up as long as he deserved it.

I believe the reason of this very sudden change for the better was that I took the fate of the rascal Krishnaya into my own hands, and placed him in confinement, heavily ironed, reporting proceedings *afterwards* to the Resident. I felt it was a case where decision was needed, and I exercised it at the risk of being found fault with. I considered it due to the welfare of the State, and the safety of the Rajah and myself, to keep this mischievous character safe, as he was always inciting Pid Naik to some villany or other. Another evil influence was also at an end by the sudden death of Krishnaya's friend, Bheem Rao. He, it was said, took poison on hearing of Krishnaya's arrest, fearing awkward disclosures.

With the removal of these two, all opposition to me ceased, and, as I have said above, all my demands were complied with without further hesitation. Would it last? I often wondered; but I hoped Pid Naik had had a severe lesson, and that he had found both the Government and me too wary to look for success in any future plot.

The effect of all this was very successful; the first proof of the confidence it had inspired was given me in a very gratifying visit from the heads of the Beydur clans, who came to me with offerings of flowers, begging me to forget the past, and from henceforth to consider them as my children. I took the opportunity of making them a little speech, and with good effect. I told them it had pleased God to afflict me in the loss of my dear wife, and that I had no tie now to bind me to Shorapoor, except my wish to serve their young Rajah, and to do my duty to those who had sent me there, and that it was very hard to have to bear all this anxiety and my own sorrow too. " Relieve me of that," I cried, " and you take a heavy load from me."

This touched them deeply; they crowded around me, placing their hands on my feet and neck, and earnestly exclaiming, " They would never *vex her spirit* by causing me pain or anxiety."

M

I saw my opportunity, and spoke at length. I warned them against crime—cattle-lifting and dacoity, both of which had before been considered honourable achievements—and I offered them advances for trade or for land cultivation to the utmost of my power. They listened very attentively, and I believe I won them entirely ; having done so, I determined to keep them. When I had ended I offered them *pan* and flowers, and sent them away.

Another proof of confidence in me was the increase of revenue in the contracts, the contractors having previously held back to see how matters would go. They would not give Pid Naik last year's amount ; but they agreed with me for 13,000 rupees above it, which was no unwelcome addition to our finances. The crops promised well, both grain and cotton, and the price of grain rose from 12 to 20 rupees a *candy*, owing to the increased demand.

I endeavoured to show Pid Naik the folly of his previous course, which would have been to levy additional heavy taxes, that he proposed as soon as the people were at all more prosperous. For this year I was content to have a moderate increase of revenue, to bring peculation to light, and to see the people more contented and more happy.

Pid Naik and I worked away at the accounts, and he could do his work very well when he was not drunk!

The treasury arrangements were concluded, and the pay of the establishment settled, which amounted to 90,000 rupees a-year. The contingencies, which last year amounted to 73,000 rupees, would be only 25,000, and there were 100,000 set aside for Government demands and arrears. I had the control of the whole, and not one anna could be disbursed without my counter-signature.

I also, at *Pid Naik's request*, began several roads, which were much needed. I had to study road engineering as well as I could, and lay them out, and superintend the

whole ; those leading from the several gates of the town
were specially essential.

Shorapoor was a regular mountain fortress, a robber
stronghold. To make it stronger than it was by nature,
it had been fortified, and all the gates were rendered nearly
impassable to any one except footmen by large loose stones
being thrown down upon the passages to the plain. These
had gradually become a horribly rough kind of pavement,
so slippery and so loose that any horse unaccustomed to it
tripped and stumbled at every step. No cart could have
attempted to enter the town ! Pid Naik's people had been
laying out a road to the river Krishna, and part of it led
over a gap in the hills, rough and bad. They told him
they could not clear it, and advised him to apply to me,—
hence his making this request, which had surprised me not
a little. I instantly set thirty men to work, looking after
them myself morning and evening. The road was now
complete, twenty feet wide, and made of rotten granite,
which became almost as hard as stone in a very short time.

When I had completed about 1200 yards, all were
delighted, and crowds came to see the wonder.

" Why not carry it through the gateways ?" said some
one.

" Why not ?" I rejoined ; " and then no more necks will
be broken on those polished stones."

Pid Naik assented, and I instantly put on additional
workmen, thirty-five to each gate. From the gates the
roads were carried through the town, and up to the Rajah's
palace, and I could scarcely get them done quickly enough
to satisfy the people. This was indeed a great step in the
right direction. I had high hopes now, and even dreams
of a good school, public dispensary, and suchlike institutions ; but I was obliged to be very cautious.

One day we very nearly had a row. One of my English
household shot a dog which was carrying off a fine fat
duck in its mouth. The dog, it appeared, belonged to

a Beydur. A body of these went off to Pid Naik to com-
plain, and I told him to settle the matter as he pleased; but
he would do nothing, and one of the scoundrels thought it a
good opportunity to make a disturbance. So next morning,
as Mr A——— was going into the town to see the Ranee's
brother, he found about a hundred armed men on the road,
who refused to let him pass, and threatened him. He
came to me to make his complaint, and during that time
about fifty men went to his tent and bullied his wife,
terrifying her by yelling, screaming, and pointing their
guns at her.

I wrote to Pid Naik at once that if these people were
not punished immediately I would leave Shorapoor ; but
I did not expect he would have the courage to do as I
asked. However, to my surprise, the ringleaders were
seized, and the row was put an end to. The whole had
been a got-up affair to try and pick a quarrel with me, and
had been instigated by one of Pid Naik's bosom friends
and boon companions.

I wished to reach Linsoogoor in time for Christmas-day,
and as I had a good deal to do before the year closed, I
went out for a while into the districts, and worked very
hard. From eight in the morning till eight in the evening
people crowded in, and I only allowed myself half an hour
for breakfast and dinner. It was weary work, neither
gratifying nor amusing,—a constant unveiling of acts of
tyranny and oppression, lying and cheating ; but it had
to be done, and the more I worked the more intricate it
seemed to grow.

"Why," said a fellow to me one day, quaintly enough,
" do you take all this trouble in combing people's hair?
You only break your combs, and don't get out the tangle-
ments ; the best way would be to shave it off and let it
grow again, and then you could make it as smooth and
straight as you please." But this was rather too severe a
measure, and I preferred plying the comb with patience.

I had my reward in seeing the people more prosperous,
and the trade of my little State increasing, and apparently
in a fair way to become the high road of commerce from
the Company's districts into those of the Nizam and others.
I lowered the duties, and the carriers were now protected
at every halting-place by the very Beydurs who used to
plunder them, steal their cattle, and annoy them in every
way !

During this year there was not one single complaint of
border outrage or cattle-lifting, and the country at large
seemed to know that such doings must cease under the
new *régime*. The people came forward boldly with their
complaints, instead of going about in armed parties against
those who had wronged them, burning their stacks of corn,
and perhaps wounding or vexing inoffensive people in
revenge for their injuries.

Pid Naik now was quiet and obedient, and having
placed the expenditure on a proper footing, I trusted all
would go on regularly in that department. I had as yet
made no proper report on the state of affairs generally, but
intended to do so after Christmas, on my return from Linsoogoor. I did make one special report on the state of the
accounts, showing the waste that had occurred, and the
Resident agreed with me that it had been very deplorable ;
but ended by saying, that as long as everything showed so
fairly for the present, and as Pid Naik had no means of
making up the deficiencies, and had listened to reason, he
should be excused from any demand on account of it, and
this was what I had myself proposed. I am sure this decision was a very great relief to Pid Naik himself, while to
me the General wrote :—

" Your despatches contain ample proof of a most unwearied and unremitting attention to business, and a zeal
in the discharge of the duties of your office that can
scarcely fail to be attended with the happiest results. It
may be expected that time and patience should be neces-

sary for the purpose among a people so entirely unaccustomed to any kind of regular and just government."

I left Shorapoor on the morning of the 24th December, at 1 A.M. Such glorious moonlight, as I well remember, and very cold. I was glad to stretch my legs with a walk of five miles, and arrived at Linsoogoor a little after sunrise.

And so the year 1844 ended—one very eventful to me—one full of sad, sad memories, and bitter, grievous trial. Yet through all I had been strengthened and upheld by my heavenly Father to bear the burden He put upon me; and He too, in answer to my earnest prayer, gave me courage and hope to cheer me on. I had, in some measure, succeeded beyond my hopes—I had won the hearty approbation of the highest in the land. I had gained, and was hourly gaining further, the confidence of the people; they were more peaceful and content, improvements were progressing, trade and crops were promising. I had good health and constitution, and though often weary and sadly sick at heart, the thought that my efforts had so far succeeded gave me strength to fight on; and somehow I had a liking for my work, and a certain pride in it, which carried me through many a difficult task. If I had not felt at times so unutterably lonely, I should have been quite happy; but the thought of what I had lost in her who would have cheered and supported me, was at times almost too much to bear.

India, too, had made a great stride that year. Mercantile and other projects were advanced. A new Steam Navigation Company was started, the shares in which were bought up directly; so with the banks, of which there were three, if not more, in North-western India, and others in Bengal, Bombay, and Madras, all doing well, and paying interest at 10 or 12 per cent on their original capital. Also there was the plan for the Bombay Railway, of which all the shares were snapped up by English and

Indian capitalists. Yes, India was stirring in these respects, and was likely to advance in all peaceful undertakings under our veteran General, who apparently thought of anything but fighting, and busied himself with roads, bridges, education, and trade—one and all of which his predecessor seemed to think out of his line altogether, and perhaps beneath his notice.

The new year opened brightly enough. On my return to Shorapoor I found the Rajah well and happy ; and as I had persuaded some of my friends to accompany me from Linsoogoor to see my house and my little State, I had quite a gay time of it. My party consisted of three ladies and four gentlemen, and their advent created quite a commotion in the town. We pitched our tents at Bohnal, a small village seven miles west from Shorapoor, where there was a very pretty tank or artificial lake, of considerable size.

I had drawn out a plan for a sailing-boat of tolerably large dimensions, and had had her built at Linsoogoor ; and finding her quite finished, I put her on a heavy artillery-waggon, and conveyed her to Bohnal with many a misgiving, as she had been built altogether by the drawings I had given. She was now quite ready to make a start, and was put into the water on her trial trip, and I was very glad to have so large a gathering on the occasion. We awaited the great event with much anxiety, and it was looked for by all the natives with intense curiosity and eagerness. First, out came the Ranee and all the *élite* of Shorapoor, to have a look at the boat, and their admiration was unbounded, and most amusing. As to the little Rajah, he was wild with delight, and hugged me with all his might for having made the boat for him. The Ranee was for being out half the day ; and once, when there was " a bit of a sea," and the little vessel was dashing through the water, throwing up the spray about her bows, she was in absolute glee. She, the English ladies, and the children went out thus with me two days running, and great was the fun and merriment among us all.

It was certainly an unprecedented thing for the Ranee and me to be together in the "same boat;" and it was wonderful to see how the native ladies, wild and secluded as had been their life hitherto, opened out under the influence and companionship of their English sisters. Indeed, my friends told me they had imagined the Ranee a perfect tigress, and that they were most agreeably surprised to find her so pleasant and so polite. My boat had turned out a pretty thing—20 feet keel, and 24 feet over all, a good beam, and three masts—old Liverpool ferry-boat fashion— a bowsprit and jib, topmast and sails. She was very stiff in the water, and very safe; in fact, she worked well, and was beautifully finished in every respect, built of teak, copper-fastened throughout; yet she had been entirely the work of two common carpenters of the country. I felt rather proud of my first experiment in ship-building; and my boat was a constant source of amusement and recreation, as, although the lake was not very large, it was sufficiently so for an hour or two's sail in the evenings when work was done. It was about a mile across, and one and a-half long. Its depth, when full, was 20 feet; but as the "Rajah" only drew $2\frac{1}{2}$ or 3 feet, there was always plenty of water for her. The exclamations of the natives were very amusing sometimes. "Dear me," said one, after we had been sailing along briskly for some time, "see how that grass is running! was ever such a thing seen before!"

"But," said another, "that hill is moving away, and there goes a tree! Well, to be sure, it is miraculous!"

And so they would go on till I convinced them of the truth.

My party soon broke up. They expressed themselves charmed with the novelty and beauty of all they had seen, and it certainly must have been a change from the dull routine and gossip of station life.

I determined to build a cottage at Bohnal for a refuge
from toil at Shorapoor, and before I left I marked out the
foundation. It was to consist only of two rooms and a
small bath-room, with a veranda round them. The view
was very pretty, looking over to the old fort of Wagingera,
and across a wide plain with the Deodroog Hills in the
distance. Stone was to be had for the picking up, lime
was plentiful, as also was long grass for thatching, so that
the cost was very moderate.

I made a contract for a road between Bohnal and Shorapoor, which promised to be very pretty, as there was a
good deal of wood and firm red soil, and I hoped that all
these plans and projects of mine would in time produce
a civilising effect upon the natives, and induce them to
follow my example.

I now returned to my district work, and the conflicts
over false returns were as troublesome as before. Still I
observed a good deal of progress, and the demand for
taking up waste lands was very great. Numbers of old
Shorapoor families had returned to their villages, and there
seemed to be abundance and prosperity everywhere. An
insurrection had broken out in the month of February in
the southern Mahratta country, and the British authorities
were most anxious about the Beydurs of Shorapoor, as the
movement was within sixty miles of them, and had they
joined in it, things might have taken a very serious turn.
I lost no time in sending an urgent appeal to them all,
not to be enticed into the rebellion ; and they responded
most warmly and joyfully, and proved their loyalty to me
in the most practical manner, as not one Beydur of my
district joined the rebellion. At last I felt I had them
well in hand, and I know that the Bombay Government
were very thankful to me for my control over so formidable a body.

In March another great ceremony took place—the first
removal of the young Rajah's hair ! It is usual in some

Mussulman, and most Hindoo, families, not to cut the hair of a male child until he has attained a certain age. In the Rajah's case, his father and mother had fixed the period at nine, eleven, or fourteen years of age. It had not been done in the ninth year, and the present was the eleventh, which could not be passed over; and I was glad of it, for the boy suffered greatly from the weight and heat of the tangled and matted hair falling about his shoulders.

As this was a State ceremony, I requested the Resident to allow me to bestow what was needful in the way of funds, and I was permitted to give the Ranee five thousand rupees from the State treasury, to which sum she added as much of her own, and the following is the description of the affair which I sent home :—

"There was a great gathering of all classes of people to partake of the Ranee's hospitality. I don't know how many Brahmins and others were invited; all were fed and received gifts of clothes and alms. The crowds were enormous. All the members of the family were feasted for two days, and received turbans, scarves, and other presents, and every one seemed pleased and happy. The ceremony itself took place in a tamarind-grove near a suburb in the plain on the south side of Shorapoor; the Ranee had had comfortable tents arranged for me, and I arrived from camp in time for the beginning of it. I did not see what was taking place, as no one entered the enclosure but the Brahmins; but the beating of kettle-drums, blowing of horns, and firing of guns, announced the ceremony completed. I was sitting with the Ranee the whole time, and she was very thankful to me for my presence there, and the assistance I had been allowed to give.

" As the camp could not move into the city that night, I remained, and there was a grand *nautch* under the trees, and fireworks, which had a very pretty effect, the whole grove being lighted by torches, with occasional Bengal and blue lights. Next evening all went up to the city in grand procession — the Rajah on his superb elephant, with his little wife beside him, who had arrived from the Mysore country just in time. She is rather dark, but a pretty child about eight, with glorious eyes. I rode and *drove* another elephant, and we were surrounded by all the horsemen and foot-soldiers, and the Beydur clans. Such a scramble! When we got into the city we were joined by others, and there were literally thousands, and all the house-tops were covered with well-dressed women and children. By this time it was dark, but there were hundreds of torches and blue lights ; and the effect of the crowds in the streets, the horsemen, and the women on the flat roofs, was very fine. It was the best procession I have seen. We proceeded to the great temple, where the Rajah and his people went to return thanks and make offerings. I remained as I was. I joined them afterwards, when we all went on to the palace ; and after sitting a short time in Durbar, the little Rajah told me he was very tired, as well he might be—so I broke up the assembly, and took him to his mother, thanked her for her hospitality, and came away. I stayed the next day at Shorapoor, because Pid Naik was beginning his old tricks of spending money without authorisation. He complained that his people did it—they would not listen to his advice or orders ; and the latter was the truth. What could I do but preach and caution ? I found the little Rajah getting on very fairly, and I send you a note of his in English as a specimen. He reads easy stories nicely ; but is best in Teloogoo and Mahratta, which, after all, he needs most. Would that I could send him to England ! but that is impossible."

Inquiry had been in progress at Hyderabad regarding the alleged debt to the Gosain bankers ; and a suspicion arose in the minds of the Resident and Captain Malcolm that the interpolation of *one line* in the Mahratta docu-ment was a forgery. This provided a bonus of 15,000

rupees on one transaction, and interest at two per cent
per month on the whole; and the bonds were sent down
to me. There could be no possible doubt of the forgery.
The writing and the colour of the ink were quite different
from those of the remainder of the document. I took
the deposition of the clerk who had written the paper,
and he declared at once that the line in question had been
interpolated, and that the writing was not his. The
original draft of the bond was then produced. I took
depositions from a number of experts, and also from all
the secretaries and clerks who were present when the
bonds were written and sealed—all unanimously declared
the line to be an addition, and false. If the forgery could
be proved, the State would be relieved of debt with
interest to the amount of two lakhs, or £20,000.

These inquiries led me into an investigation of the
sums paid by the Shorapoor State for fifty-two years to
the Nizam's Government, and I found it to have been no
less than one crore and seventy-nine lakhs (£1,790,000),
on various pretences; whereas all it was entitled to
was 50,000 × 52 = 26,000,000 — twenty-six lakhs only
(£260,000); so that the excess paid to the Nizam's
Government was £1,530,000, and yet more was required!
My father very naturally asked me what law there was in
Shorapoor, and I find I wrote as follows:—

"As to administration of justice, it lies entirely in my
hands. Pid Naik will do nothing. He does not see the
necessity of any law or justice; therefore I have to
decide all minor cases myself. No court of justice has
ever existed in Shorapoor; but the people are used to
punchayets or arbitrations, which seem very fair. They
are properly courts of five members—two plaintiffs, two
defendants, and one person named by them; but here
as many as will, sit—and their judgments are really
excellent."

In June I was rendered very anxious by a report from

Hyderabad, apparently to be relied on, that a Bengal civilian was to be sent to Shorapoor, which was to be entirely severed from Hyderabad. This, it was said, had been resolved on by the Court of Directors, on the examination of correspondence for many years past, and the discovery that the security Government had entered into for the Shorapoor State amounted now to £90,000.

It was strange that no answer had been given either to the Resident's despatches or my own, on the subject of Shorapoor management, for upwards of a year now; neither he nor I knew whether we were doing right or doing wrong—we had only acted to the best of our judgment and capacity; but for some time past I had begun to find the Resident very reticent, and apparently unwilling to take further responsibility on himself.

For my own part, I was satisfied I had done my duty to the utmost of my power. I had reported all irregularities and their consequences; I had requested special and detailed instructions as to the wishes of Government, and I had received none beyond what I have already given here. Lord Hardinge was now Governor-General. I wrote to his private secretary, and pleaded what I had already done; showed what further measures I had in view, and their results for the good of the State, if they were carried out; and left my case in the hands of the Governor-General, awaiting an answer with considerable anxiety.

It came at length, and was unfavourable. It ran as follows:—

" DEAR SIR,—In reply to your letter of the 12th instant, I am directed to state that the arrangements contemplated by the Governor-General for the arrangement of the Shorapoor affairs will require the appointment of another agent unconnected with the recent events which have passed in that State, and I very much regret that I

cannot hold out any expectations that the retention of
your services will come within the scope of the measures
now under consideration."

(Signed)   "C. S. HARDINGE,

Private Secy.

" CALCUTTA, 28*th May* 1845."

However, I was determined not to let the matter rest
here.   What I had at first written was in general terms ;
what I wrote the second time were more particulars
referring to the many despatches I had forwarded, in
which I had made urgent application for the instructions
of Government as to the arrangements of the Shorapoor
State.   This letter, like the first one, was transmitted
through the Resident, General Fraser, and he wrote a
long despatch on the subject, which, Captain Malcolm
informed me, was the clearest and most complete State
paper he had ever seen from the Resident's pen.

As many small matters constantly arose which required
references to the Nizam's Government, and also in regard
to other local business, I had maintained an agent at
Hyderabad, by permission of the Resident, and the
Nizam's Minister, Suraj-ool-Moolk ; and my agent now
reported that he had been directed by the Minister to
acquaint me with what had occurred at the Nizam's court
in reference to Shorapoor ; and this was the substance of
his communication.

The Governor-General had applied to the Nizam to
have the State of Shorapoor made over to the British
Government during the minority of the Rajah, and to have
all its affairs managed quite independently of the Nizam's
Government and of the Resident.

To this the Minister, Suraj-ool-Moolk, had replied, by
direction of the Nizam, that Shorapoor was a State tributary to him, and not to the Hon. E.I. Company, and had
been so recognised in the treaties.

That when the late Rajah died, his Government had made no opposition to the appointment of a " Dewan ; " and if the Company were dissatisfied with him, he should receive no support from Hyderabad, and might be removed from office at the pleasure of the Company.

That no opposition had been offered by the Nizam's Government to my appointment; and as I had hitherto acted in the interests of both Governments, being a servant of both, so I ought to be allowed to continue to act, the Nizam's Government, on its part, having perfect confidence in me.

That the Nizam's Government could not see on what principles the British Government could take its tributary out of its hands, especially as there was now profound peace at Shorapoor.

" If " (I quote from one of my letters to England) " the Nizam's Government has really written this, as I am informed, I cannot but think it will have its effect upon the Government of India ; and it tallies with what Captain Malcolm wrote to me some time ago, that the Nizam had sent a crusty note about Shorapoor, and my agent was told the purport of it as above, with orders from the Minister to tell it or write it to me on the first opportunity.

" Meanwhile a new subject of anxiety to Government has sprung up. I wrote last month that Pid Naik was very ill of combined drunkenness and disease, and that I did not expect him to live. He has lived, however, but at the expense of his intellect. He is now quite foolish, sometimes insane. His people have sent for two Mussulmans, who are famed for making charms and amulets, and the belief is that he is bewitched. With one charm he rubs his eyes, another is burnt by his bed, a third is washed off the paper, and he drinks it. My apothecary reported some time ago that he had an attack of *delirium tremens*, which, as no one here knew how to treat it, has resulted in insanity. When I went to see him, a few days ago, he

knew me ; but I could not make him understand, except
that, when I asked him about his seal of office, he said,
'Do you use it while I am ill.' I have reported all to
Government; but until the larger questions are settled,
the lesser ones lie by. It is useless to enter upon speculations : God only knows what turn things will take ; and to
Him I have committed all, most sure that, whatever His
will is, it is good.

"Since I last wrote, my new road has been completed,
and it is the best and prettiest I have ever made, the
ground being so nicely wooded. My greatest achievement
has been the driving of my new phæton to the end of the
road every morning to exercise the horses and look after
the workmen, and it ran beautifully, and indeed is, I flatter
myself, a very stylish thing. The horses did not like the
hills at first, but now are quite accustomed to them, and
I shall soon take the little Rajah out with me for a drive.

"This new road has opened out Shorapoor completely :
all the artillery and troops in the kingdom could march
straight through it without difficulty. I have been finishing a picture of Shorapoor for you in oils, and I hope it
will give you some idea of the town. In the foreground is
the Rajah on horseback, attended by his usual retinue,
nearly a hundred figures. I have attended closely to
detail and costume in those nearest the eye. It is perhaps
too ambitious a subject for me ; but I have done my best,
and it has afforded me much amusement and pleasure. I
have also been attempting my own portrait for the Rajah,
who wished very much to have it."

The cholera broke out with great severity during the
months of June and July. When I returned from a short
holiday I had taken to Linsoogoor, it was still very prevalent, attacking children very fatally, and in fact sparing
neither age nor sex. Fully five hundred souls were swept
off in Shorapoor alone. On one day I remember fifty-one
persons died, and for several days the average was twenty

to thirty per day.   Thank God! the disorder did not come up my hill, but was confined to the town below.   A good fall of rain checked it, and it ceased as suddenly as it came.

The people were greatly rejoiced at its departure, and there was much sacrificing of sheep and buffaloes, and, rather to my dismay, the clans of the Twelve Thousand asked my permission to hold a grand sacrifice to their ancient divinities in Shorapoor, which do not belong to Hindooism, but are remnants of original beliefs.   The authorities came to me in a great fright, and said this *pooja** had not taken place for eighteen years, and that on the last occasion the Beydurs had fought among themselves, and that some of the State soldiers had likewise been killed and wounded; and that if the ceremony were allowed, guards must be posted around the place of sacrifice.

"But," I said, "why do you not trust the Beydurs?"

"They are not to be trusted," was the reply.

I, however, sent for the head Beydurs, and told them if they would promise *by my feet* not to make a disturbance, I would let them have their *pooja*, and feed them well; and as their little Rajah was a child, and the Dewan, Rajah Pid Naik, ill and imbecile, they had only me to look to, and I hoped that as I was about to place great confidence in them, they would not disappoint me.   They declared they would not.

"Send one of your *chuprassies* to us," they said, "and he will be as much as an army."

So I sent the one *chuprassie*, and one or two steady old Brahmins who knew the people.   About 6000 Beydurs assembled.   There was plenty to eat and drink.   About 400 sheep and 50 buffaloes were killed during the ceremonies; and there was not one drunken man in the streets, nor a quarrelsome word spoken, yet all were armed to the

* *Pooja*—worship, a religious function.

N

teeth! I wondered whether at a gathering of Irish, or
English even, such order would have prevailed.

I had never before been so perfectly satisfied with the
Beydurs, and was very glad to be able to forward good
accounts of their steady behaviour to Hyderabad. I had
felt great anxiety, owing to the evident reluctance of the
authorities of the place to have this *pooja ;* but I knew if
I flinched at all, or had put them off with promises, there
might have arisen ill-feeling against me. Now all was
right—and fortunately a good deal of rain fell, which was
attributed to the goddess being pleased.

The great suspense I had now for some time been
enduring, was happily relieved on the 19th July by a
private letter from General Fraser, which ran as follows :—

" MY DEAR TAYLOR,—I have several times informed
you that the whole circumstances of your removal from
Shorapoor were to me a perfect and most unintelligible
mystery, and I am happy to tell you that I have just
received the extract of a despatch from the Court of
Directors to the Supreme Government, of 19th March
1845, in which the whole of your conduct is spoken of in
the highest terms. This, with some other matters, will
form the subject of an official communication from me to
you in the course of to-morrow or next day.

" It gives me great and sincere pleasure to add, that
the Government have intimated to me that, pending the
receipt of the honourable Court's reply to a letter from
Government, dated 12th April last, the Governor-General
in Council has determined to suspend the resolution which
related to your removal from Shorapoor and the appointment of another officer. On this latter part of the subject,
however, it is not probable that I shall have occasion to
address you officially, as I do not think I have ever informed you officially of the resolution of Government to

remove you.—Believe me, my dear Taylor, ever sincerely
yours,

"J. S. FRASER, *Resident.*"

"*P.S.*—I have just received your letter of the 12th. I
think you ought to report to me officially the good conduct of the Beydurs on occasion of the late grand *pooja.*
This is very creditable to yourself personally, and I shall
be glad to report it for the information of the Supreme
Government."

The official despatch which came from the Court of
Directors is too long for insertion *in extenso,* but I subjoin a few extracts.

*Extract from a despatch from the Honourable the Court of
Directors, No. 9, dated March 19, 1845.*

Para. 64. "Captain Taylor's reports, dated 30th December 1843 and 18th January 1844, afford very favourable indications of his capacity for the task intrusted
to him, that of reforming the administration of a State
always one of the most backward of the petty States of
India, and now much debilitated in condition by over-
exaction and other mismanagement.

"In this difficult enterprise Captain Taylor seems to
be in no respect aided, and in some degree thwarted, by
the Dewan, Pid Naik, who, from indolence and weakness,
rather than from evil intention, is, though profuse in
promises, sparing in performance. If Captain Taylor s
ability and perseverance should fail in sufficiently over-
coming this obstacle, Pid Naik must be reminded that
he occupies his position solely by your appointment, and
that not he but your Government is the guardian of the
young Rajah and real regent of the State. At the same
time, Captain Taylor should by no means lose sight of the

importance of maintaining a good understanding with
Pid Naik. Great allowance must be made for the natural
mortification of that personage at his supersession in the
supreme authority which, on being nominated Dewan, he
expected to exercise. His rank in the State must render
the tone of feeling displayed by him greatly influential
in the country, and the measures of Captain Taylor cannot
fail to be more acceptable to the population, if taken with
his concurrence and approval. Captain Taylor therefore
should endeavour to conciliate his co-operation by every
token of conciliation and respect."

Then follows approval of my plans and arrangements
for the collection of revenue, leasing lands on five years'
leases, and inducing the ryots and weavers to return, and
proceeds :—

"We are of opinion that it is both right, and the duty
of our Government as the Rajah's guardian, to do what,
according to the ideas and practice of the country, he will
have a full right to do when he assumes the Government
—namely, to resume all alienations of revenue which
were either excessive in amount or improperly bestowed.
The time and mode of effecting such resumptions, and
the extent to which they should be carried, are subjects
for the consideration of the local authorities, under your
general guidance.

67. "Captain Taylor's attention is vigilantly directed
to the reduction of expenses, and he has proposed a
schedule of expenditure amounting only to one lakh
instead of 179,303 rupees as formerly,—independent, however, of all payments to the Nizam's Government and
creditors.

68. "We are glad to observe that Rajah Pid Naik's
opposition will not be allowed to defeat the needful arrangements for the young Rajah's education and gradual initia-
tion into public business.

70. "Captain Taylor has hitherto abstained very pro-

perly from introducing any judicial changes, the revenue
system and the regulation of the public expenditure being
matters of more immediate urgency.   When these subjects,
however, shall no longer engross his attention, we shall
hope that he has been able to introduce some tolerably
constituted court of criminal justice.   Heretofore, he says,
there does not appear to have been any administration
of justice whatever.   There is no kind of court, civil or
criminal.   The place, however, of civil courts, is in some
degree supplied by the ordinary native expedient of
punchayet.

   " True extract.   F. CURRIE,
                              Secretary to Government of India."

   Rajah Pid Naik's earthly career was fast closing now.
He was not only very dangerously and incurably ill, but
the following correspondence will show that the Government of India had at last come to the determination of
dispensing with his services :—

*From F. Currie, Esq., Secretary to the Government of India,
   to Major-General Fraser, Resident at Hyderabad.*

                    " FORT-WILLIAM, 18th *July* 1845.

   " SIR,—I have received, and laid before the Governor-
General in Council, your two letters of 10th and 27th ult.,
Nos. 64 and 69, with enclosures from Captain Taylor, and
in reply I am directed to state that the Governor-General
in Council authorises your instructing that officer to set
aside Rajah Pid Naik entirely should he be living when
you receive these orders.   And his Excellency directs
that Captain Taylor assume the entire charge of the administration of the Sumusthan pending further orders,
which, as instructed to you in my letter of the 4th inst.,
No. 1913, will be communicated to you on receipt of the

sentiments of the Honble. the Court of Directors on the affairs of Shorapoor.—I have, &c.

"F. CURRIE, *Secy. to Govt.*"

General Fraser wrote as follows on July 30th :—

"I have the honour to transmit for your information and guidance the accompanying letter from the Secretary to the Government of India to my address, No. 2024, under date the 18th inst.

2. "It may be almost superfluous that I should suggest to you the propriety of carrying into effect the measures therein directed, with every consistent regard for the feelings of Pid Naik, and in such a delicate and cautious manner as shall avoid giving any offence or jealous suspicion to the Beydur population or other inhabitants of the Shorapoor Sumusthan.—I have, &c.

"J. S. FRASER, *Resident.*"

I found it, however, quite a hopeless task to communicate the contents of this letter to Rajah Pid Naik, who lingered on, suffering from the effects of his paralytic seizure, and was now both speechless and insensible. He lived till the 8th of August, and then died without apparently further suffering. I went to visit him a few days before he breathed his last, and as he revived a little, his sons believed him to be sensible. I think, perhaps, he was conscious for a few moments, for he took my hand in one of his, while he passed the other all over my face and person, trying the while to speak, but no articulate sound came from his lips. I promised his sons, who were in bitter grief, that I would return if he revived at all ; but he did not, and passed away quite quietly.

I made every arrangement for his obsequies, and for the expenses necessary for their performance ; and the morning after his death attended the funeral in full dress as a mark of respect. When I went to the house, I found the late Rajah dressed in rich garments, with all his jewels on, set out on a terrace in the courtyard, the body placed leaning against a wall, and seated on his velvet cushion of state, and his sword and shield lying beside him. The face was disfigured by paralysis, bloated, and under the pale hue of death was most distressing to see; but all his retainers, many of the chiefs of clans, and friends were bidding him a last farewell, and were saluting him. When the ceremony was concluded, the body was taken up, and placed sitting in an open chair, and then, taking his two eldest sons by the hand, I led them after him, amidst the firing of guns and the wailing of the crowds all around us, to the place of cremation, where, divested of its jewels, the body was placed on the pyre, to which the eldest son applied the first torch; and as the wood had been thoroughly saturated with oil and *ghee*, or boiled butter, together with camphor and incense, it burst into a fierce blaze, and the cremation was soon complete. I remained with the boys till all the ceremonies were ended, and then conducted them home,—paid a visit of condolence to the sorrowing widow, and then took my leave.

It would have been indelicate, it appeared to me, to open the subject of my succession at once; but when the first few days of mourning had expired, I held a court, in order to explain publicly what I had previously made known privately to all.

There was at first some little difficulty with the heads of departments. I laid down my plan of proceeding very decidedly, and adhered to it. At first they greatly wished that the Ranee should have a voice in all that went on, and that nothing should be done without her concurrence. A few trifling orders even had been given in her name; but I cut all this very short, and distinctly stated that I would stand no sort of interference whatever; and to put an end to all controversy on the subject, I went to visit the Ranee after my Durbar was over, and she protested vehemently, not only that she would never attempt to hinder me in any way, but, on the contrary, that she would assist me to the utmost of her power.

I arranged that the State seal with my signature was to be the only authorised authority for documents in the State. The seal was a mere matter of form, as all orders, receipts, and the like, were examined during the week, and on Monday mornings were produced, and explained to the little Rajah, and sealed up in his presence, so as to show the people that he was in reality considered their Rajah, and the head of the State. The people were glad to see him put forward, and all discontent soon subsided. Even the keys of the treasury were brought up every night and put under my pillow ; and those of the stores and groceries were kept by the Ranee, as she wished to have them.

Another great blessing was vouchsafed to us ; a plenteous rain fell at last, which had been sorely needed. Grain had risen in price, and I was growing anxious, for a famine seemed inevitable. The young leaves of the early grain were withering ; but still all knew if rain fell it would sprout again. The wells were dry ; but they filled rapidly, and in a few days the grain looked green again, and everything seemed cheerful. My lake at Bohnal was now really a noble sheet of water—good two miles from corner to corner, and six feet more in depth than the previous year. As if, too, all I had endeavoured to effect had taken place at once, I heard privately from Captain Malcolm that the Nizam was about to remit the payment of four lakhs and a half, which was still due on the old accounts. He had seen the Minister's draft of an official note on the subject, and assured me I should soon have it officially. I need not say how great a relief it would be to me when it came.

I continued to pay frequent visits to the Ranee, and

took her and the Rajah drives in my new carriage. Her
ecstasies were very great, and her remarks most amusing
when she was driven to places where she had never been
before. I visited Rajah Pid Naik's family also very often.
He had left no will, nor any directions as to the disposal
of his property or estates ; and as, several times when he
was sensible, he had put the hands of his wife and children
into mine before all his people, so now they all requested
that I would take sole charge of their estates and affairs,
and manage them for the benefit of all—and I consented.
The head steward and accountant, with all their papers,
were then made over to me, and so long as I had charge
of their affairs, I never had trouble with any of the family.

Poor Pid Naik! with many faults he had many kindly
qualities ; but he was utterly unstable, quite unable to
resist temptation, and too obstinate and puffed up by the
people about him to attend to orders issued by Government. He fancied himself Rajah of Shorapoor, and at
heart desired to gain the succession for his eldest son.
Brahmins, mostly of bad character, had obtained complete
ascendancy over him, and he was too weak, and too credulous and superstitious, to resist their suggestions. I do
not think he ever went into extreme wrong but once, when,
if he did not actually embrace crime, he certainly shook
hands with it. The temptation was great, for if the Rajah
had been killed, his son would have become Rajah in his
stead. Pid Naik left eight children,—six by his excellent
wife Mádama, one by the other wife, and another illegitimate.

CHAPTER X.

1846.

I was obliged to be absent for a short time on private
business, and there had been many attempts made to
induce the Ranee to defy my authority, but as yet she
appeared firm. She had, however, set up a new paramour,
one of the menials, and under such circumstances was not
to be depended upon, and I was obliged to watch very
narrowly. Not long after my return to Shorapoor a letter
was intercepted by one of my Beydurs, who had obtained
it for a few rupees from the messenger that was to have
taken it to Hyderabad. The writing and the seal were
those of an old Brahmin of rank, who I knew aspired to
be head manager under the Ranee, and the letter was
addressed to one of the Nizam's confidential servants,
urging him to send 1200 Arabs and Rohillas without
delay.

Before the copy of the letter and my report could reach
General Fraser by express, Captain Malcolm wrote to me
privately that 400 Arabs had actually left Hyderabad, and
begged me to stop them.

I showed this letter to the Ranee in confidence, and
warned her; but she protested entire innocence, and the
old Brahmin suddenly and mysteriously disappeared. I
found out that my absence had been interpreted as a recall,
and that the Ranee had been making profuse promises to
her adherents; but I took no notice of these stupid in-

trigues, which could only be stopped when they came to a crisis.   The authorities at Hyderabad were very busy sifting this plot, and its intrigues seemed interminable.

The year 1845 closed pleasantly for me.   In the first place General Fraser sent me a copy of a despatch which he had received from the Secretary to Government on the subject of Shorapoor affairs, which was very gratifying, as the first from Sir Henry Hardinge.

" Foreign Department.

"Dated CAMP ZEIT, 7th November 1845.

" SIR,—I have received and laid before the Governor-General your despatch, dated 17th October last, No. 129, submitting copies of correspondence with Captain Taylor, in regard to the Shorapoor Sumusthan.

" In reply, I am desired to state that his Excellency does not consider, after perusal of the papers submitted, that they call for any orders from him beyond the expression of his opinion that Captain Taylor would appear to have shown zeal, ability, and judgment in the conduct of the affairs of the Sumusthan during the past season.—I have, &c.   F. CURRIE, Secy."

Lastly, it had pleased God to grant to the people one of the finest harvests ever remembered, though in the beginning of the season the anxiety, owing to the want of rain, had been so great; and what could be a happier opening for 1846 than a cheery letter from my father, bringing good news of all my dear ones at home?   I had recovered from a sharp fit of fever and ague, which left me as weak as a child for a time; and the people were orderly and quiet through the country—no cattle-lifting, no robberies or outrages—and some of the most notorious thieves and robbers had taken to farming quietly and contentedly, and I endeavoured to encourage more to follow their good example.

The Ranee and her intrigues were the only cause of anxiety, and she certainly was in a queer humour, exalting her new favourite with all her might and main in the most shameless manner; but the townspeople seemed quite weary of her profligacy, and were very gentle and perfectly easy to manage; but I never saw in any place, or among any natives, morality at so low an ebb among the higher classes, or such entire absence of the commonest truth and honesty. I often felt there was no chance for the poor young Rajah among them all. I went out into the districts as usual, and got through all my routine of work just the same as the year before, and a few extracts will suffice.

"*February* 1846.—I got to my camp all right, and yesterday moved on to Andola, six miles. Such fields of *jowaree!* such glorious crops I never saw before, and the people say have not existed for ten years. One ear of *jowaree* I pulled, which contained a countless number of grains, all nearly ripe, and like so many pearls. The cotton, too, is very fair, but not quite so fine as the *jowaree*, perhaps; and there is a good local demand for manufacture on the spot, so my farmers will make a handsome profit.

"All hands are very grateful to God. Their worship is not ours, but their gratitude is the same, and we may well hope will find acceptance in His sight. . . .

"I don't know how *jowaree* would mix with wheaten flour. I don't think it would rise, as the flour wants the gluten of wheat; but it is highly nutritious, as the robust frames of our peasantry testify—no fat, all sinews and muscle—enduring vagabonds as ever helped at a border fray or drove their neighbours' cattle. Now, all are as quiet as mice. . . .

"I am informed that the Ranee is now in great admiration of me, and swears she will have nothing to do with any nonsense such as was going on. I wonder what she means, and what is in the wind now !

" The Governor-General's hands just now are too full of the Sikh war to attend to anything else, and the post has brought the news of the victory over them, about which I was not a little anxious.　.　.　.

" *February* 24*th*.—Bitter cold wind till noon; worked hard all day. In the evening I went into the village, carpets were spread on the terrace, and we had a *nautch.* I sat in state for an hour, and then went and saw the children who had been married; one about eleven, very pretty and fair for a native ; she came and sat in my lap very confidingly, but would not open her eyes till I put my watch to her ear, showed her the works, and the 'tic tic' within. Such eyes they were ! well worthy to be painted. The other was a sly puss, but came at last to me. Then fireworks, and I took my leave.　.　.　.

" The General has authorised a new line of post, which has saved me at least three days, and is a great comfort. Are not these wonderful victories over the Sikhs ? The Peninsula can hardly boast a more brilliant series. We have fought no such battles in India before.　.　.　.

" I have quite secured the additional revenue I hoped for; altogether my accounts will show 30,000 rupees extra over last year, and I hope the big folks will be satisfied."
.　.　.

On the 24th April, as the heat was very great, with scarcely any shade, and the thermometer averaging from 125° to 127°, I returned to Shorapoor. There was also another very severe visitation of cholera, and the poor little Rajah was very ill, with terrible inflammation and sup-puration of the glands of his neck. Native remedies had proved useless, so I insisted upon being allowed to see what I could do, and I sent to Linsoogoor for some leeches, which I applied, and afterwards lanced the place, putting on soothing poultices. He slept all that night, and he recovered his health and strength, which had been greatly reduced; and I believe my renown as a physician was widespread.

There were great rejoicings on the recovery of the Rajah, and among other entertainments a Hindoo play, which I had never seen before, taken from the Bhagwat, or recitation of the poem relating to Krishna.

The chief performer was a handsome young girl, who was a capital actress and singer, very richly dressed. She personated one of Krishna's wives, lamenting his absence from her. The text was all given in recitation, with here and there an air and chorus, the language Canarese, which I could not follow. One plaintive air with a chorus was excellently given, and I wish I had been able to take it down. Her acting was admirable: grief, sadness, hope, jealousy, despair, all depicted in turn, and her joy at the last when she found she had been tormenting herself for nothing after all'! Yet the whole was performed by stone-cutters, who could neither read nor write; and the plays had been learned by rote, and were traditional in their families.

Some of the Hindoo dramas acted in this way must be very beautiful. Sir William Jones has translated "Sa-kontala," "The Toy Cart," and others admirably. Rude as it may appear, one can trace the ancient system of chorus—the actor appealing to the chorus—and the chorus answering the actor or actress, advising, pitying, &c. That which I saw was not strictly a play, but one of the sacred books dramatised. There were comic interludes, to enable the female performers to rest, and these, too, were very clever. Altogether, the children, for whose enter-tainment it was given, were highly delighted, and so was I; and we all sat on the ground together.

It seems absurd to mention more intrigues, but I was forced to check one which was growing troublesome. The

head of the *duftar*, or account department, one of the
chief peculators in Pid Naik's time, set himself up as the
Ranee's champion, and she gave him valuable presents,
and abetted him very shamelessly.   At last he took it on
himself to declare to her that he had been appointed by
the Nizam her Minister, and gave her a sum of money
out of the treasury.

This could not be allowed.   I therefore suspended him,
put the *duftar* papers into the hands of the real hereditary
head of the office, a clever young fellow, and sent the
defaulter to his house, under a guard of twenty of my
Beydurs, who kept him safely.   No one grieved at his
degradation, for he had been insolent to all classes.

In a few days the Ranee came to me, and was very
penitent, wept very much, and promised to be so good in
future ; but I cannot say I trusted the lady !

From the first I had determined to allow no outsiders
in hereditary offices.   I had to teach those who held these
posts what their duty was, and how to keep systematic
accounts.   I had a day-book and a ledger in the treasury,
and they were kept very neatly and correctly.   On examination at the end of the financial year, I found that,
after paying the Nizam's tribute and other debts and
arrears, I had still 70,000 rupees of surplus balance, notwithstanding all the extra expenses of the family in ceremonials which could neither be delayed nor avoided.   The
account stood thus in the final reckoning of the year :—

Total revenue,	.	.	.	.	Rs. 321,716	10	6
Total expenditure,	.	.	.	.	246,818	4	3
Balance in favour of the State,	.	.	Rs. 74,898	6	3

Of this General Fraser sent me ample approval, which I
need not copy in detail ; the concluding paragraph shows
the spirit in which he wrote.

" The mode of accounts which you have adopted is clear

and explicit, and appears well calculated to afford that information to the Supreme Government which it will no doubt desire to possess. With regard to your management of Shorapoor, I highly approve of the zeal, ability, and un-remitting exertion with which you discharge the duties of your present important office, and your gradual establish-ment of order and well-regulated administration in a dis-trict hitherto proverbial for maladministration, corruption, and every species of disorder.

(Sd.)   " J. S. F."

I find that but little of interest took place during the remainder of that year. All was flourishing and peaceful. Now and then petty intrigues occurred on the part of one or another. Luchmangeer and the lady herself were generally at the bottom of the mischief, or her paramour Kasima. He indeed disseminated ill-will between two sections of the Beydurs, with a view to set them all by the ears, and thereby to bring disrepute on me. There was a small riot in the town, and some grain-dealers' shops were injured; but the offenders came to me and "begged pardon" like naughty boys. Happily, in November Luch-mangeer was summoned to Hyderabad, and I obliged him to go, and we had some peace.

Among themselves the Beydurs were rather at strife, one accusing another of having more land than he ought to possess, and suchlike disputes. However, with these I never interfered. I was too weak, and they knew it, to break up a clannish faction of 12,000 men and more, who held the finest lands in all the villages, and so long as they were orderly, it was all I required. Had any serious quarrel arisen I must have interfered, and I often told them it was to their interest in the end to keep together and remain peaceable.

Rather a curious incident occurred during this year. A Brahmin, who had been absent from Shorapoor for two

years, came to me, and said that he had cast up the table
of my nativity, and had brought me the result. As I
had never seen or heard of him before, and as he himself
wished to know whether it tallied with my own experience
hitherto, I was anxious to see the paper, which ran after
this manner. I had not, nor could I have, given him any
sort of information as to the date of my birth or other particulars, as I did not know of his existence.

From birth under the *Sun's* influence. Neither favourable nor unfavourable. I was weak and delicate, sometimes ill. Six years.

Next under the *Moon's* influence. Generally good; few
crosses, and those which occurred resulting in good. Ten
years.

Next under *Venus.* Neither good nor bad. The ordinary run of life. Seven years.

Next under *Saturn.* Bad. Losses; grief. No worldly
advancement; no wealth. Never long in the same
place; unsettled; frequent disappointments. Eighteen
years.

Deduct on account of astrological months, five years two
months.

End of troubled period, thirty-five years ten months.

Since when I have been under the influence of " Brihas-
put" or *Jupiter,* of whose sway one year is already nearly
past, and it will continue, from its commencement, sixteen
years. Add to the previous calculation the one year of
Jupiter, and the result is—thirty-six years ; which was my
exact age. The Brahmin inquired whether that was about
right, as he had been rather bothered in the calculations
regarding the moon's influence, which could not be rendered with as great certainty as the others. No one here
knew my age, that I was aware of; but the result seemed
to me very curious. I wished to know how the calculations had been made ; but my friend could only explain
them in Sanscrit, and this I did not understand. I sent

the paper home to my father, and it afforded a good deal
of interest and amusement to friends at home.

The details of my daily life were too monotonous to
be of general interest—one day passed like another, only
varied by my daily rides and drives to look after my roads
and other public works; and I propose to introduce here a
short sketch of the history of the Shorapoor State, which
may not be uninteresting, and may serve to relieve the
sameness of my story.

The Beydurs are a race of aboriginal descent, numerous
in Mysore and in the southern Mahratta country. They
profess to be Hindoos, some following Sivite Brahmins,
some Vishnavite, and many, perhaps most, the tenets of
the Lingayets; but at heart they are believers in the
original demons, sprites, and local spiritual beings in
whom their ancestors had faith in the earliest period of
their race, and their worship is still actively maintained,
all the opposition of the Brahmins and Lingayets notwithstanding. These spiritual creatures have various names
and various attitudes, merciful, protective, and destructive,
and one or other is worshipped according to necessity—
for children, for good crops, for any vow made in any need
or emergency, for destruction of enemies, for staying of
disease among men or cattle. Sacrifices are made to rude
stones in their honour; but they are not represented by
images, nor do they dwell in temples. Large peepul, neem,
or banian trees, and most frequently deserted spots on
village boundaries, ·are the places which the deities are
supposed to like best. Although the Beydurs arrogate to
themselves pure descent from the Kshettriyas or warriors
of ancient times, they have no pretension to caste, as understood in a Hindoo sense—no Hindoo, even of the lowest
caste, would take water from their hands, or eat food
dressed by them. In short, they are *mlechas* or outcasts,
and form part of that great mass of aboriginal population which—as the Gonds, Bheels, Mangs, Santhals,

and many other tribes — underlie Hindooism all over India.

In character they are violent, fickle, and often treacherous—adepts in lawless pursuits, and often engaging in serious organised crimes, as dacoity, cattle-lifting, &c., in which they take a pride. They are brave, and Tippoo's famous infantry was mostly composed of them; but they are impatient of control and difficult to manage. In the service of the Beejanugger State, in the fifteenth and sixteenth centuries, they were very numerous, and were at times more than a match for the Mussulmans of Gulburgah and Beeder. Among themselves they are merry and quarrelsome by turns, fond and jealous of their women, industrious in some respects, and idle in others; devoted to field-sports of all kinds—hawking, coursing, hog-hunting, and deer-shooting. None of them are mechanics or artisans in any form or degree; and but for their association with civilising Hindoo, Mussulman, and British influence, they would most likely relapse into their original savagery.

The family of Shorapoor came originally from Rutnagherry, in the Mysore territory, where they were lords of a hill-fort and a considerable district. They were one among many such "lairds" who were feudal vassals of the Hindoo State of Beejanugger, and who served their masters with all the clans of their own tribe after the first Mussulman invasion and subsequent settlement of the invaders at Gulburgah, and declaration of independence of Delhi by Alla-ood-deen Hussun Gungoo Bahmany, in 1347. The Hindoo State of Beejanugger was obliged to defend its own frontier against Mussulman inroads; and some of the Beydur clans were settled in the tract between the Krishna and the Tungabhudra rivers, among whom were the Beydurs of Rutnagherry.

In the wars between the Bahmany kings and the Hindoos, these Beydur clans always took a distinguished part, and afterwards in those with the Mussulman dynasty of Beejapoor; but as the Hindoo power declined, the Shorapoor family joined the Mussulman, and became his feudal vassals. The river Krishna had been hitherto the boundary between the Hindoos and Mussulmans; but the latter now occupied the Dooab, a tract lying between that river and the Tungabhudra. Gradually, partly by military service and partly by encroachment, the Shorapoor clans took possession of countries north of the Krishna. They built a fort at Wagingera, on the west side of the Shorapoor hills, where they became more settled and powerful, and their chiefs were raised to noble rank at the Beejapoor Court, with extensive privileges for the collection of dues from the country round, and which was, in reality, "black-mail;" and so matters continued till the Emperor Aurungzeeb captured Beejapoor and annexed its dominions, in 1686. The Beydur chief of Wagingera, however, resisted the Emperor for some time, and refused to come to his Court, though very earnestly and cordially entreated to do so. At length he consented; but being jeered and insulted by the courtiers, he returned to his fastness, more determined than ever to rebel. It was quite in vain that the Emperor wrote him letters of pardon and assurance, impressed with his own right hand dipped in ground sandal-wood—in vain that he wrote, "Would that you were a Mussulman! you would be to me as a brother." No impression could he make upon the rebel chief, who was assisted and encouraged by Sivajee, and his famous commander, Dunnajee Jadow. At last the Emperor attacked Wagingera, was a second time repulsed, and it was not until after a siege lasting seven months that the fort and town of Wagingera were eventually stormed, with the aid of the army from the south, under General Zoolficar Khan. Driven from his fastness, the rebel chief, Pam Naik, selected the secluded spot where Shorapoor now stands. Its proper name is " Soor-poor," the " City

of Valour." Here he was allowed to live in peace, and
eventually became good friends with the Emperor, who
bestowed high titles upon him, created him a " Commander
of Five Thousand," conferred on him a large addition to
his territory, confirming all previous grants by the Beejapoor monarchy, and also extended his collections from
villages over a great portion of the Deccan and Carnatic.

As the Mussulman power declined, the Beydur chiefs
maintained their position, and though nominally tributary
to the Peshwahs, never performed actual service. If their
district collections were interfered with, they plundered
the Peshwah's country till the interference was withdrawn.
They were in a somewhat similar position with Nizam-ool-
Molk, who was Viceroy in the Deccan; and when the Nizam
and the Peshwah concluded their treaty at Yatgeer, on the
frontier of Shorapoor, in 1785, the two Powers consulted
as to whether the Beydur chief should not be at once
attacked, and his dynasty suppressed as a public nuisance.
The reigning Beydur chief, however, partly by showing a
very bold front, and partly by the high reputation of his
clan for valour, and also by agreeing to pay 50,000 rupees
a-year to the Nizam, escaped the threatened danger.

The Shorapoor State was then very flourishing, the
revenue being between twenty and thirty lakhs a-year.
There were two battalions of disciplined sepoys under
European commanders, and a park of artillery, and these,
with the Beydur militia, 12,000 in number, and a considerable body of cavalry, made the reigning Rajah, Enkappa
Naik, truly formidable. Hyder and Tippoo, each in turn,
tried to induce him to join them, but he was content to
remain as he was; and Tippoo, though he overran part
of the neighbouring District, made no attempt to attack
Shorapoor.

Enkappa Naik was a great patron of Hindoo learning,
and established a Sanscrit College, which I found still
existing in a reduced form. He was a good soldier, and

skilful administrator, according to the customs of his tribe, and the manner in which he brought his principality out of the troubles and difficulties of those times was truly admirable; but the fortune of the State passed away with him.

The Mahrattas grew stronger, and sweeping away the Shorapoor dues from their district, imposed instead heavy demands on Shorapoor. The Nizam repudiated Aurungzeeb's grants, and annexed all the territory north of the Bheema river. In the State was not only bad administration, but waste and extravagance. On the death of the late Rajah's father, the Nizam's Government demanded a succession fee, or *nuzzerana*, of fifteen lakhs, which the then Resident at the Court of Hyderabad, Mr Martin, declared to be an "equitable addition to the Nizam's Government." The amount was partly paid in cash, and, except the final balance of four and a half lakhs, by loans taken upon British security from the Gosain bankers of Shorapoor, year by year, until Rajah Krishnappa Naik died, the State being then virtually insolvent.

It was soon afterwards committed to my care, in the hope that, in some degree, the past might be redeemed, and the family placed in more comfortable circumstances for the future.

This short sketch will, at any rate, show the reader that the Shorapoor family was one of the oldest and the most distinguished of the Deccan; that they had attained high rank under the Bahmany and Adil Shahy as well as the Moghul dynasties; had been respected by the Peshwahs and Tippoo; and if, through misfortune and bad government, they had fallen into a lower grade of power and wealth, they deserved better treatment than they had received at the hands of the British Government in its intervention.

After my first tour through my districts the agricultural classes became anxious for a settled revenue, and spontaneously offered me a gradual increase for a term of five years. I could not at once grant it, nor during the uncertainty of political affairs could I even propose any such settlement to the people as an advantage.

Now, however, all hindrances had been removed, and I considered that such an arrangement would conduce to the welfare of the people. I had no actual data, by survey or measurement, for assessing the land; but the old accounts in the possession of village registrars were freely brought forward, and the assessment made by a former Rajah, fifty years ago, " Enkappa Naik the Great," was accepted by all as just, and was a good foundation on which to begin.

Between this assessment and the present one existing, a mean was struck, and the difference in prices of grain, &c., and the amount alienated in grants, were all allowed for. The maximum of settlement was then decided, and fairly distributed over lands under cultivation and waste, for which the rates at first settled by me were the standard.

The people seemed quite content, and in some instances offered an increase on the rates of their own accord; but of course the settlement was very roughly done, and not with the accuracy with which one founded on an actual survey could have been executed. At all events, it opened up the road to the employment of local capital, and, above all, it satisfied the people.

My own work was, of necessity, very heavy, but proceeded very successfully, as one by one the different districts were arranged on five years' leases, and the result in the immediate application of capital to the reclamation of waste lands was most satisfactory. The rents were regularly paid, and the crops and harvest exceptionally good, and I anticipated a very favourable balance-sheet.

One instance I record, among many, which I gave in letters to my father.

" The *patell* or head man of a large village where I was encamped, had been very poor, and was thoroughly disheartened by repeated exactions.   His wife, a homely, excellent woman, had complained to my dear wife that her husband was idle, and begged I would speak to him.   'If he wants money,' she said, 'I will pledge every ornament I have to buy bullocks.'   I, however, assisted him from the State with sufficient money to set him up.   This year the man and his wife came to me together, and she was the speaker.

   "'God has prospered us,' she cried ; 'we have now 32 bullocks, besides cows and buffaloes ; we used to pay 32 rupees, but all our land is cultivated now, and we pay 322 rupees ;' and there were hundreds and hundreds like him, prosperous, secure, and thankful."

   I was then on the right bank of the Bheema, and one day received a deputation from a large village called Sinoor, on the left bank, the estate of an officer of the Nizam's household who had charge of the royal tent establishment, and I went to them next day.   The village women and children, all neatly dressed, met me, poured libations of water before my horse, and offered me flowers and garlands.   A carpet was spread in the *patell's* house, and I sat with the assembly for a long time, hearing accounts of how the Beydurs used to come in bodies, cut down their crops, drive off their cattle, and keep them in perpetual fear.   Now all was secure, not a head of corn was touched, and all their distant lands were under culti-vation, as well as those near to their dwellings.   The same Beydurs who used to plunder them came unarmed to their weekly market, and all was peace.

   Many men showed me scars of sword and bullet wounds received in those affrays, and indeed the whole frontier must have been in a sad state.   I need hardly tell you how very gratifying this visit was to me, and it was followed by many others to my frontier neighbours with the same result.

   If I have as yet left the affairs of Scinde unnoticed, in

regard to the great political transactions of Lord Ellenborough's government of India, it is because they have
long since become subjects of general history, commented
upon by all writers, and therefore beyond the province of
this record of my life. During the process of annexation,
however, I watched the progress of Sir Charles Napier
with the keenest interest. Outram was one of my earliest
and closest Indian friends, and we corresponded as frequently as his and my own heavy duties allowed of. I do
not believe that Lord Ellenborough ever desired the conquest or the annexation of Scinde ; but he was in the hands
of a man who, led on by personal unscrupulous ambition
and daring, which no one can question, formed, as it
appears to me, from the beginning, the resolution of dis-
placing the Ameers, and, regarding its strategical importance, of converting Scinde into a British province. History
and Sir William Napier's ' Conquest of Scinde' tell how
this was achieved : how, by one traitor among their
brotherhood, Ali Moorad, Sir Charles was misled and
deceived ; how the Ameers were literally goaded on to
war, and defeated in the bloody battles of Meeanee and
Dubba, and lost their State and their treasure.

In my letters to the ' Times,' I was able, with my
friend's assistance, to detail the progress of political events
as they occurred ; and I believe I told the truth, without
sparing any. No one could question the high military
capacity and valour by which the victories were won by a
handful, comparatively, of British soldiers against perhaps
the bravest Indian troops that ever took the field, and
whose numbers far exceeded those of the British forces.

By the splendour of these victories, the people of England were perhaps dazzled, and the political events of the
time were thrown into the shade; but they are inefface-
able, and will remain for ever a blot upon the record of
Indian history ; not as the effect of any national or Govern-
mental policy, but as the consequence of the acts of one

man, who, uncontrolled, had entered Scinde under a fore-gone conclusion, and brought about the result. Lord Ellenborough could be just and merciful in the case of Gwalior, the troops of which were more treacherous and more dangerous to the peace of India than the Beloochees of Scinde; and it is difficult to estimate why he confirmed Napier's aggressive policy in the one instance, while he contradicted it in the affair of Gwalior, which he conducted in person. In both these instances the troops of the State were the aggressors, not the principals themselves, and except for one man's ambition the results would have been the same.

In a short time, comparatively, Sir William Napier's glorification of his brother appeared in the 'Conquest of Scinde.'

It was impossible for Outram to remain silent under the attacks made upon him and his reputed share in these political transactions, and I, and many other friends, urged him to write and publish a vindication of his acts, and a revelation of facts, which in Sir William's book were either omitted or glozed over to justify Sir Charles's execution of his mission. Sir Charles had taken £70,000 as his share of the Ameer's wealth. Outram, a poor man, had declined to receive a penny of the proceeds, though his share was a large one, and therefore he was entirely independent. He roused himself to the task, and wrote, sending the manu-script to me for approval and correction, and I cheered him on. At first his expressions were laboured; but his style soon became clear and vigorous. It was the fashion, when his commentary appeared, to say that Outram never wrote a word of it, and that he was unable to do so; but if such an opinion still lingers in any mind, I can at least declare that I saw and read the whole from beginning to end in his own handwriting, bold and large. I advised him to have the document roughly set up and printed in Bombay, and then sent home for final reprinting, after

being duly corrected for the press, and I myself revised all
the proofs, suggesting here and there rearrangement of the
matter, so as to form a more continuous narrative and
commentary; and, so revised, the whole was forwarded to
Edinburgh, where it was finally published. I altered none
of the writing, and the book is as I saw it when in manuscript, with the excision only of any repetitions, and here
and there a slight variation in the arrangement of detail.
I kept the original letters and much of the manuscript by
me for many years.

Whether Scinde was a profitable annexation or not was
a question deeply considered by Lord Hardinge's Government, and by the Court of Directors, who at one time
appeared very much disposed to repudiate the conquest
altogether; and in my opinion it would have been well to
have done so on the discovery of Ali Moorad's treachery.

Sir Charles was very sensitive on this point, and issued
one of his famous proclamations "To his Soldiers," to
prove that Scinde was profitable, and that he had actually
remitted revenue from it. This assertion was taken up by
the press of India very earnestly; but as no details were
given on the other side, Sir Charles had pretty much his
own way. I, however, was supplied from my own sources
of information in Scinde and Bombay with authentic copies
of unpublished public accounts, and was permitted to use
them. I saw I could prove by the details that if Sir
Charles remitted ten lakhs (£100,000) of surplus revenue
from the province, after paying all its civil charges, that
in reality on the military side the cost was a million and
a half sterling, for which there was no provision at all!
And with the consent of the editor of one of the leading
papers, I opened a series of letters on the subject of this
costly annexation and its political character. Occasionally
these were answered by an article in Sir Charles's defence,
very ably and speciously worded; but they could not bear
down the weight of actual results, and after a while the

editor gave judgment in my favour so warmly and heartily
for the public service I had rendered that I was amply
rewarded for my trouble.

Whether the conquest of Scinde now pays its expenses I know not—in any case it is well governed and
prosperous. No question could be raised as to its importance in a strategical point of view; but the mode of its
acquisition is a dark blot on the record of Indian history.

CHAPTER XI.

1847–50.

In January 1847 I lost my faithful friend and manager of one of the largest of my districts, Bulram Singh, who had been an officer of my police in 1827-29. He was one of the best natives I ever knew, most faithful and intelligent. The district under his charge was the worst in the country; but he had managed it well—had encouraged the people to increase cultivation—and had laid a good foundation of eventual prosperity. With his last breath he committed his wife and children to my care.

On my return to camp I had to wait till daylight at a village about half-way, which I reached in the evening. The good old mother of the *patell* being sure, as she said, that I was very tired, had prepared a delicious warm bath for me, and a most abundant and well - cooked supper, consisting of various capital dishes of vegetables and light *jowaree* cakes. The family were strict Hindoos, and did not eat meat. They had also got ready a comfortable bed, with fresh clean sheets and pillows. This spontaneous hospitality touched me very much; and it was just the same wherever I travelled.

As the Resident had applied to me to report what kind of a revenue survey would be necessary for the country, I selected a village of average size, and began a regular survey of it, field by field, partly by cross-staff and chain, and partly by prismatic compass, for I had no theodolite, and finished all, including the map, myself; and then forwarded the whole of the papers, field-books, and registries of pro-prietors to the Resident, with a report.

I was, however, in no hurry to begin a survey. I con-sidered it would be time enough when the present settle-ment was at an end, as many of the occupants had measured out their own lands, and were becoming more and more correct. This season was the coolest I had ever felt in the Deccan. I find on the 25th February the thermometer varied from 68° to 76° in my tents, and at Poona there had been a frost. It did not, however, last long, and was suc-ceeded by extreme heat.

In March the Rajah's youngest sister, a very pretty little girl of six years old, was married to the Rajah of Soondee, near Madras, aged twenty. He was a courteous, well-bred young man, and the little child was a great pet among us all, so pretty, and very fair, even rosy in cold weather, and quick and clever too. She was being educated in Teloogoo, and her favourite book was extracts from the 'Pilgrim's Progress,' which, indeed, was liked by all classes at Shora-poor, and there were occasional readings of portions of it by the Brahmins.

As head of the State, and *in loco parentis*, I had to per-form all ceremonies, except going to the temples, and others of a purely religious character. I wanted the parties to wait till the child was thirteen or fourteen, but her affianced could not delay, as he wrote to me to say he could not be installed as Rajah of Soondee while he was single ; and as royal families of Beydurs were very scarce, he was forced to take this child. There was no use preach-ing in such matters, so I remained neutral, and allowed them to do as they thought proper themselves. The Ranee came to me for 20,000 rupees for the expenses of the ceremony ; I could but refer the request to the Resident, who would sanction only 3000 rupees expenditure by the State, and the Ranee was very much disgusted.

In May the Rajah had another terrible fever, and narrowly escaped death. He was brought up to my house for change of air, when a turn for the better came, and he recovered. If I could have kept him with me longer I would have done so, as the clear cool air on my hill would have renewed his strength, and he much preferred being with me, as his mother's horrible profligacy and want of chastity shocked him terribly: but this he could only tell me secretly, and weep bitterly, poor boy, at the shame it cast upon him.

If Government had removed the Ranee Ishwarama from Shorapoor, as it had done the Ranee of Kolapore, and also at Lahore, all trouble would have been avoided; but it was not to be so.

However, I reported, as it was my duty to do, her now openly shameless conduct; and in June I received a despatch in relation to her, from which the following are extracts:—

"2. It appears to us a preferable mode of disposing of the case would be that of requiring the Ranee to retire entirely from Shorapoor, and to take up her abode in her father's house at Rutnagherry. . . .

"5. I do not apprehend that the mere banishment of Kasima (chief favourite), and other paramours, would be productive of much benefit with a woman of her immoral character. These personages would probably follow each other in succession, notwithstanding any engagements you may receive from her to the contrary, and you would have the same inconveniences, and the same evil influences to surmount which you have at present."

But neither the Resident nor I had power or authority to remove the Ranee, or suggest to her "change of air." It was a question which the Governor-General alone could decide.

My report for the revenue year past, 1256 *Faslee*, was considered by the Resident to be "eminently satisfactory;"

but it is too long for insertion here, and too full of local questions to be interesting to the general reader. The Resident was gratified at the low rate of assessment, which was on the general average eleven annas or 1s. 4½d. per *beegah*,* that for the Nizam's country being upwards of four rupees, or eight shillings; and he was satisfied that the increase did not proceed from extra rates of taxation. The result of the accounts was as follows :—

	Rupees.		
Revenue under all heads, . . .	351,556	2	9
General expenditure—loans, advances, village expenses, ...	245,276	11	6
Cash balance, . . .	106,279	7	3
Balances of loans and advances recoverable,	15,124	7	0
Total in favour of the State, .	121,403	14	3

At last I had a lakh in the treasury! safe after all payments, including tribute to the Nizam. The Gosain bankers' claim, after being checked in England on their own accounts, transmitted by me, dwindled to 121,000 rupees, on the decision of the Court of Directors, after scrutiny by actuaries. I discovered that the bankers had not credited a payment of 52,000 rupees, received by them from assignment on villages, which was proved by their own receipts to the villages; and if I had not had the control of the whole State accounts after the death of Pid Naik, and of those of the villages also, I should never have discovered it. The original claim was admitted to be 380,000 rupees. Now 52,000 with interest thereon amounted to 72,000, which had been deducted, and the balance due was therefore considerably reduced, but Luchmangeer and his brethren were in no case to receive it.

* The standard of the *beegah* varies in various provinces, but it is generally about one-third of an English acre.

They were all quarrelling among themselves, and the Resident declared that, until he knew to whom the balance
was to be paid, he would give no order on the Shorapoor
treasury. He thought it very possible that I might discover other fraudulent transactions, and I was not without
hope that I should.

On my report of the previous year, I had the pleasure to
receive a copy of an extract from the Court of Directors'
political despatch to the Governor-General, which was as
follows :—

"Para. 29. From Captain Taylor's report of 12th September 1845, it appears that the *Faslee* year 1254 had produced an increase in cultivation over the preceding year of
17,656 rupees, and of net revenue 18,852 rupees, and that
the whole revenue had been collected, except some trifling
balances in course of collection.

" 30. We agree with the Governor-General that Captain
Taylor appears to have shown zeal and judgment in the
conduct of the duties of the Sumusth'an during the present
season.   His report contains much valuable information
respecting the landed tenures and revenue system of Shorapoor, and he seems to have adopted means well suited for
gradually improving the revenues of the country, without
introducing such changes of system as might hereafter be
embarrassing to a native Government."

In reference to my official report on the current year,
the Governor-General was pleased to write as follows.

The letter is dated Simla, 23d August 1847, to General
Fraser, from the Secretary to Government with the Governor-General.

" SIR,—I have the honour to acknowledge the receipt of
your letter, dated May 22d last, No. 62, submitting Captain
Taylor's report on Shorapoor for 1846, and in reply, to state
that the Right Hon. the Governor-General considers the
report satisfactory, and very creditable to the zeal and

P

ability of that officer, to whom you are requested to convey the favourable sentiments of his Lordship.

"2. If the removal of the Ranee Ishwarama, the mother of the young Rajah, will tend to benefit the State, the Governor-General will not object to the adoption of the measure. It must, however, his Lordship observes, be done with all the forms of courtesy, care being taken that the allowance she is to have in her own country be not too much contracted; but she must be given to understand that its continuance must be contingent on her discreet behaviour.

"The Governor-General approves of Captain Taylor's proposal to register the military class, and other Jahgeerdars of Shorapoor; and also sanctions that officer's proposition to make a survey of the whole country, with a view to its final settlement.—I have, &c.

(Sd.)   "H. M. ELLIOTT, *Secy.*"

Need I say that I was more than satisfied with this cordial letter from Lord Hardinge? and I felt certain that the issue of the current year's work would assure him that improvement was progressing, slowly perhaps, but I hoped surely.

About this time I had a very strange interview with the Ranee. She had been ailing for some days, and reports were rife as to the cause of her illness, which were disgraceful enough. However, she sent for me early one morning, having, as her servant said, passed a sleepless night, and being very much excited and troubled in her mind. As soon as I had taken my breakfast I went to her. I found her lying on her bed in her private room, seemingly very restless and in pain, moaning incessantly, but apparently dozing. I sat down in the outer room, as I did not wish to disturb her, and the little Rajah came to me crying bitterly.

"She is going to die, she says," he whispered. "She has abused me shamefully. She says I am not my father's child, and bade me go away. Where am I to go to? What am I to do? Indeed I am so frightened, and you are the only one I can look to. I have hidden all her shame and my own, and this is too much! I fear for my life!"

I comforted him as well as I was able, and told him I would bring his mother to reason if I could, and that if he really continued frightened, he should come to my house or go to the cottage at Bohnal. As we were speaking, I heard the Ranee call loudly.

" Is he come? Is Taylor Sahib here?"

I went in at once. She was still excited, and her breathing seemed oppressed. I really thought she was dying, and she complained of being " all on fire inside." I had brought a small bottle of sal-volatile with me, and asking for one of her silver drinking-cups, dropped into it what was requisite ; and when one of her attendants had added water, she drank it up, and fell back upon her pillows. After a time she roused herself, and desired one of her servants to go for the *purohit* or family priest.

" I am dying," she said, " and must tell you all. You are the head of the family and the State, and should know everything."

When the priest arrived—a man I knew very well, as he was always in attendance, and one of the professors, as it were, in the Brahmin Sanscrit College—the Ranee told him to bring a certain box which contained the secret papers of the house ; and when he had brought it she unloosed the key from a necklace she had on, and bade him open it. The man demurred.

" These papers have never been seen by any one but my lord the Rajah, who is gone to heaven, yourself, and me. No one else knows of them," he cried ; " why should you show them to Taylor Sahib?"

The Ranee sat up straight in her bed, and glared at him. I had never seen such a look on any human face before.

" Do as you are told," she cried, savagely; " what is it to you what I do ? "

The *Shastree* trembled all over, and without speaking he unlocked the padlock and opened the lid. The first thing I saw was a roll tied with red silk.

" Tell him first about that," said the Ranee, and fell back again.

" It is not fit you should hear it," said the *Shastree*, who spoke both Mahratta and Hindostanee fluently.

" It is the Rajah's horoscope which I wrote. The moment he was born I noted the time, and the conjunction of planets, and the result was bad."

" Yes, it is bad ! " cried the Ranee, seizing my arm, as I was sitting on the ground by her bedside—" it is bad ! All that concerns that base-born boy is bad ! Why did his father die ? Why did I not strangle him with my own hands rather than let a wretch like that live to be the ruin of the State ? Yes ! he is fated to die *in his twenty-fourth year*, and I shall not see it ! I am dying myself, and you English have made him secure to glory in my death ! Ah, yes ! he will die before he is twenty-four complete ; we, my husband and I, sent that paper to Nassik, to Benares, and everywhere that there are wise Brahmins ; but they all returned the same answer. He must die in the twenty-fourth year after birth. Is it not so, *Shastree ?* Did we not spend a lakh of rupees over this, and it availed nothing ? " and she stopped for want of breath, her eyes flashing with excitement. " Is it not so ? Tell the truth ! "

" You speak truth, lady," said the *Shastree*, who was sobbing. " It is only the truth, Taylor Sahib ; I have tested all the calculations and find them exactly conforming to the truth according to the planets. The Rajah is safe till then ; but when that time comes, how, I know not, but he will surely die. He will never complete his twenty-fourth year ! never ! never ! "

" No ! " cried the Ranee, interrupting him—" he will not

live ; he is the last of his race.   He will lose his country,
and all the lands, and all the honour that the Sumusthan
has gained for five hundred years.   Would that he were
dead now, the base-born dog and slave !" and then she
uttered language that I dare not write.

I was obliged to rebuke her sternly, and threatened to
go away if she spoke so again ; but she cried the more.

"Slave ! slave ! I wish he were dead, and the State
safe !   It might go to you—to the English.   I would give
it freely, now—now—but not to that boy ! Listen ! never
go from him until he is dead—then take the whole yourself.   Behold, I give it to you, and the *Shastree* is witness
I give it to you and your children—they shall have it.
O Taylor Sahib ! you have been as a father and mother to
me, and I have often used you very ill.   I am a wicked
woman, and deserve punishment ; but listen to me—forgive
me !   Never leave that boy, Enketappa Naik, till he is
dead, and burned like Pid Naik—will you promise me
this ? I am dying—dying !" she paused for breath, and
went on.

" Now I have told you all the secret I had in my heart,
do not tell it to any one till he is dead ; do you put your
hands upon my neck and swear this."

" I promise you I will not," I said, " on the faith of an
English gentleman," as I put my hand, with the *Shastree's*,
on her neck.

"Enough !" she cried, " I am content.   Do not suppose
I am mad or excited, I am quite myself, only for the pain
I suffer.   I do not think you will care about the other
papers ; they are some of the emperor's grants to our
ancestry, and there are some foolish letters from chiefs in
the Mahratta country, asking my husband to rise with
them against the English ; but he was too wise to do that."

" I will seal up the box in your presence and that of the
Shastree with the State seal," I said ; " and I will add my
own seal when I reach home ; " and to this she agreed.

I sent for the seal, and the priest and I sealed up the box. There was no one else present. I had desired the Rajah to go to his lessons when I went to his mother, so he was in his private apartments. The women in attendance had been dismissed by the Ranee, so that no one could have heard what passed. I showed the Ranee the box sealed up.

"That will do," she said; "keep it now yourself; it is safer with you, whatever happens, than with me. Now I am very weary, and would sleep. Do not think ill of me; but I have only told you the truth before God! I have given you much trouble in coming here to-day—now leave me."

I went. The Rajah sent word I was to come to him; he was learning his Persian lesson with the *moonshee;* as I entered he bade the man depart and leave us alone.

"What did she say to you, *appa ?*" (father), he said, anxiously; "what is in that box ?"

"Only papers," I answered; "the papers of your house, those from Beejapoor, and the emperor, and others. Your mother is ill, and thought herself dying. I will take care of them in future, and I have sealed them up."

"And what did she say? I heard her so angry."

"It was not with me this time," I said, "though you know we do fight sometimes. She only told me what to do in case of her death."

"And will she die, *appa ?* "

"Not this time," I replied; "but she is in pain, and how it may end, who can tell? Do not go near her at present, she has gone to sleep, and may feel better to-morrow." I could not tell the poor boy what she had said of him.

"I will send you word by-and-by how my mother is," he said, presently; "and now leave me."

In the afternoon they sent to me to say she was better, though still weak and in pain, and that she and the Rajah were playing *chowsr,* a kind of draughts, together.

As I had much to discuss and consult on with the
Resident, and a meeting would save endless correspondence, I proposed that I should go up to Hyderabad, and
he told me to start without delay.

My journey was somewhat deferred by a heavy case
which I had to dispose of relative to a large gang of robbers,
whom I was lucky enough to catch, and who during the
year past had perpetrated several most daring gang-
robberies, attended with murder, in the Company's
districts to the southward. I obtained, as I expected,
great commendation for this capture, as the Bombay
Government had been very hot on the matter, and very
angry with their magistrates in Dharwar about their
apparent neglect. It was not their fault in the least, as
the robberies were planned by men about 60 miles north-
ward of me, and the men who committed them had
travelled at least 140 miles to the scene of their pillage.
They were *brinjarries*, or carriers of grain, and were
quietly encamped at a village about 24 miles off, trading
most unsuspiciously in grain and salt. Captain Hervey—
an able assistant in the department for " Supression of
Thuggee and Gang-robbery "—was lucky enough to get
hold of fourteen of the gang at another encampment
about 40 miles south-west of me ; and having obtained
both information and confessions from them, sent me the
particulars so as to enable me to follow up the trail. It
was not easy at first to discover their whereabouts ; when
I did, I sent out a strong party, and to my joy they
returned with one leader and sixteen men. The other
chief was absent with thirteen more men on some
expedition. I secured, however, their wives and families,
also their cattle (295 bullocks, 438 goats) and other property, amongst which were many stolen articles recognised
by the approvers. Hervey and I broke the power of this
gang very materially. I was anxious about the thirteen
men that had escaped us, and I issued notices to all on

the frontier to be on the alert in the hope of catching them on their return.

I left Shorapoor at last on the 3d October, reaching Hyderabad on the 9th. The Resident and I discussed all our business very amicably, and the Resident agreed with me on several material points. First, that it would be wise to delay the commencement of the survey for a time ; next, to delay also the proposed inquiry into the Beydur lands, of which they were very jealous, and it would be like thrusting one's hand into a hornet's nest ; and again, that it would be well to make a second reference about the removal of the Ranee Ishwarama.

I did not, of course, tell the Resident of the strange scene which had taken place so recently. Since then she had been amicable and quiet ; but who could trust her ?

I remained a short time at Hyderabad, and greatly enjoyed a little intercourse once more with my own countrymen and women. What a treat it was to hear some music, and to exchange ideas with men of one's own kind after the life of solitude I had led so long ! There was a grand fancy ball, too, to which I went as a " nobleman " of the Nizam's Court—a quaint simple dress of white muslin, a small green turban, a shawl and dagger, &c. I wore no beard then, and an artist from the city came and fastened a splendid one on to my chin, so as to join with my whiskers. As I spoke Hindostanee fluently, and could assume all the native manners, nobody found me out ; Captain Malcolm and I went together, he as a Muhammadan Doctor of Laws—a capital dress; and as we went with Suraj-ool-Moolk's nephew, and entered the room with him, we passed off well. It was very amusing to be spoken to by the native gentlemen as one of themselves, and to parry their questions as to where I had come from, &c.

Captain Malcolm soon after left Hyderabad, and was

a very great loss to me individually, and to the people.
They assembled in crowds to see him off, and accompanied him for twelve miles out, and presented him with
an address.   Such a tribute had never before been given
to any Resident or Assistant.

My return to Shorapoor was most unpleasantly delayed
by an accident which turned out very serious.   The
horse I was riding fell under me, and I was injured
internally, and confined to my bed for several weeks.
The Resident was most kind—coming constantly to sit
with me, and I was tenderly nursed at Mr Palmer's house.
My only anxiety was about Shorapoor; but the Resident
comforted me, saying, " If there is any row, Taylor, I shall
go down myself and act for you, so don't be anxious about
your affairs."

Nor was I, at first; but the lady, finding my absence prolonged, began to be again very mischievous.   Her paramour,
Kasima, told her that my being reported ill was only a
blind, and that the State affairs were now to be made
over to her; that I had been removed from Shorapoor,
and was under the heavy displeasure of the authorities,
and the like.   One act of hers annoyed me excessively.
I had desired the Rajah occasionally to write to me as an
exercise in English.   Some time elapsed, and I received
no letter.   I wrote to inquire the cause, and an answer came,
a good specimen of handwriting to show the Resident.
The Ranee had been absent when the note was written
and despatched.   On her return she sent for her son, and
beat him very severely with her own hands for daring to
write to me and to ask when I was coming back.   The
poor lad was terribly frightened, and sent me word
privately to come *quickly*, for that much evil was going
on ; and he afterwards managed to write to me in Teloogoo, urging me to make haste, " for his life was not safe."
The Ranee was gathering all the heads of the Beydur
clans together about her, under Kasima, feasting them,

and giving them silver ornaments and other presents. One day the runner who carried the post-bag was going as usual along the road when four Beydurs jumped out upon him from behind a hedge, and demanded the bag. The man would not give it up, and fought well with a stick ; but this was of no avail against the swords of the Beydurs, and the poor fellow's left hand was struck clean off, and he fell senseless under repeated blows. The bags were then seized, and were afterwards found in a lonely place, but they were empty. A large reward was offered, but no clue could be obtained as to the perpetrators of the outrage. I strongly suspected female curiosity was at the bottom of it, and that the Ranee wanted to find out what was said of her by me. She gained nothing, how-ever, as I took care not to write anything about her or her doings by the post. The town was reported to be full of parties of Beydurs, going about with drawn swords ; and at an assembly a resolution was passed that no orders of mine were in future to be obeyed. This resolve eman-ated solely from the Ranee's party ; the remainder, who were likewise the majority, were yet, or appeared to be, stanch.

I had recovered pretty well from my severe illness, and was growing very anxious to return to Shorapoor. My detention had happened at a very awkward time ; but still, under God's blessing, I believe my life was saved, as had I been at Shorapoor, with no skilful surgeon near, my life must have been in all probability forfeited. So as soon as I could get leave I started, having first had a long consultation with the Resident, who was of very decided opinion that the Ranee must go—and that at once ; and that Lord Hardinge's order should be carried out. A letter from the Resident to the Ranee was soon drafted, and troops were desired to be in readiness to march on the shortest notice upon my requisition.

I reached Shorapoor on the 3d February, having been absent three months. The Rajah came out several miles to meet me, and embraced me, imploring me "not to let him go back to his mother any more." We went up together to my house. The city seemed full of armed men, but I took no notice of them ; my main object was to prevent collision between the two parties of the Beydur clans and the Rajah's personal adherents, which, if it occurred, must have led to disastrous consequences.

The next morning I had a translation of the General's letter ready for the Ranee ; and during the night, she, anticipating being taken to task for her proceedings, had assembled all her men in Shorapoor, and sent out orders for all those in the districts to come in ; and these were fast arriving across the hills in detached parties.   When my letter reached the palace, there were about five hundred of her adherents outside, who rushed about the streets with drawn swords ; but happily there was no collision.   I sent warnings to them in vain, and so did the Rajah ; but his messengers were insulted, and all declared they would obey no orders but the Ranee's.   I had posted all the trusty Beydurs inside the palace, and had sent for the garrison of Wondroog, which was stanch to the Rajah, and thus had nearly four hundred men about him.   My great object was to prevent collision between the parties; and the palace guards behaved admirably. When the rebellious party thundered at the gates, demanding the Ranee and Kasima, who were inside, no one stirred, and the Rajah controlled his people with admirable temper.   As darkness fell the insurgents retired to a high conical hill, the headquarters of some of the clan, and consulted how to make a night attack on my house; but I, as well as my position, were too strong for them ; and finding that but few of the country Beydurs joined them during the night, they sent to me for terms.   I would take none but unconditional surrender of the leaders and their arms ; and in an hour or two sixteen of the leaders were brought to me, and the insurrection was at an end.

General Fraser, the Resident, had written to me to say that he wished to come down to Shorapoor himself; and I thought he expected some disturbance on the Ranee's removal. I therefore awaited his arrival, according to the instructions I received from him, before finally sending off the Ranee. During the night painful scenes had passed between her and Kasima, each reviling the other in no measured terms. He had threatened to murder the Ranee, and had drawn his sword on her. The Rajah had interposed; but Kasima said he would not give up his sword to any one but me. Accordingly the Rajah sent him to me, when he and five of his brothers placed their arms before me on the ground, and all were put into confinement. Several other leaders gave themselves up during the day; but three of the very worst remained at large, trying to rouse the district Beydurs. However, nothing came of their efforts. In the afternoon the Ranee sent for me, and I went. She was quiet enough then, but was crying bitterly. She told me she had been behaving very ill, and that she knew I must carry out the orders of Government. She also confessed to having concealed valuable State jewels, &c.; and when they were brought I sent them to the treasury. Her only hope was that she would be treated with courtesy; and this, I assured her, would be the case. Her son's delight that this interview passed over so quietly was indescribable : he and his little sister and brother clung to me, and I could hardly get away.

On the 11th the General arrived, and I went out to meet him and bring him in. As he entered the town and ascended the hill, a salute of seventeen guns was fired from the ramparts, and a second from the guns near my house. All the officers were assembled at my house to receive him, and a guard of honour of the 1st Regiment presented arms as he alighted from his palankeen. A few minutes after the young Rajah came up, with a great con-

course of people, and was duly presented to the General
by me. He was remarkably well dressed, and behaved
very properly, answering all the General's questions with
the ease and precision of a well-bred gentleman. All the
male members of his family accompanied him, and also
the most respectable inhabitants of the city, who were
introduced by me, one by one; and after sitting for a
while they took their leave, and the General was left to
refresh himself after his journey.

The Resident was very complimentary to me on my
arrangements, and was especially struck with the success
of my plan at the palace for cutting off the Ranee and
Kasima inside from their adherents outside. I told him
the Ranee was ready, and had agreed to go; and he thought
with me, the sooner she was off the better. I therefore
went down to the palace, having previously sent on her
tents and some of her baggage and attendants. I was
busy for four hours, making all final arrangements and
settlements, and at last she was ready. Up to this time
she had been quiet; but of course at the last there was a
scene. Her women set up a howl which was heard at my
house, and she cried a great deal. She refused to see the
Rajah, which I was glad of; and he did not desire to see
her. She asked me for a note to the Collector of Bellary,
which I gave her. She then rose, requested me to take
care of her children; and I led her to the door of the
outer court, where her palankeen was waiting. As she
entered it she said, " I know this is all my own fault. Forgive me. You could not help it." And kissing my hand,
she closed the doors, the bearers took up their burden, and
in ten minutes she was beyond the gates, the escort closing
round her.

I then went to the little Rajah, who threw his arms
round me, saying, " He had only me now, and he hoped I
would take care of him, there were so few he could trust."
I told him not to be afraid. I had had a very painful

task to perform; but now it was over, and I hoped we
should have no more disturbance or anxiety.   I then took
my leave, and returned to my house and to the Resident,
who had been very anxious, and shook me warmly by the
hand, congratulating me that this much-dreaded event had
been so quietly got over.   Indeed, I had again deep cause
of thankfulness for the happy issue of what might have
been a fearful scene of tumult and strife.

The Resident paid a return visit next day to the Rajah,
and was taken to the Ranee's late apartments, where
several members of the family were awaiting us.   After
some conversation the men retired, and I went for old
Kesámá, great-aunt to the Rajah, and all the children, who
came nicely dressed; and the General took two on his
knees, and was much amused by their chat.   He promised
the old lady to be kind to the children and the State; and
then she took the Rajah, and begged the Resident to put
him into my arms, which was done, to her infinite satisfaction.   This over, wreaths of flowers were hung about
our necks, *atr* was given us, and we departed.   We went
round the city on elephants, and I showed the Resident
all through it.   We passed the Beydurs' large "tree of
assembly," where about 1500 of them had congregated, all
armed, and lining the road.   I stopped the elephants, and
the Resident addressed them, assuring them that their
Rajah would be cared for and their State also.   It was now
dusk, and a host of torches were lighted, and blue-lights
stuck on poles preceded us.   The effect was wonderful,
revealing wild rocks and wilder faces, most picturesque
and startling in the fitful glare.

Next day I showed the Resident the lake at Bohnal,
explaining to him my project for enlarging it, which he
approved.   He left next morning, having expressed himself most heartily pleased with all he had seen, and saying
he would write to me from Hyderabad officially, and in
due time the despatch arrived.   I subjoin a few extracts:—

From General Fraser to Captain Taylor, on special duty at Shorapoor.   No. 179 of 1848.

" SIR,—I have the honour to acknowledge the receipt of your several letters noted in the margin.   .   .   .

" 2. Having had an opportunity of fully communicating with you in person at Shorapoor regarding the affairs of that district, I have now the gratifying duty to perform of placing on record my entire and unqualified approval of the whole of your recent proceedings.   .   .   .

" 4. Your very judicious measures, taken previously to their arrival (the troops), had already restored tranquillity, and reduced the insurgent Beydurs to obedience, besides obtaining the assent of the Ranee Ishwarama to remove from Shorapoor to Rutnagherry.   .   .   .

" 6. You will be pleased to order an immediate investigation to be made into the conduct of the Beydur prisoners transmitted to Linsoogoor under charge of the 1st Regiment (Nizam's Infantry).   I think it desirable that this inquiry should be made by a Commission, presided over by yourself, with Captain Commandant Johnston, and any other officers whose services may be conveniently available, as members.   .   .   .

" 9. The proceedings of this Commission will be forwarded by me to the Government of India; and pending the decision of that authority as to the ultimate disposition of the prisoners, you will be pleased to request Captain Commandant Johnston to detain them under custody sufficiently strict to prevent any risk of their escape, but without unnecessary severity.

" 10. I shall submit the whole of your correspondence, now acknowledged, for the information of the Government of India, and I shall be happy to bring to the special notice of the Right Honourable the Governor in Council the ability, judgment, and firmness by which you succeeded in averting the serious danger which threatened the district

of Shorapoor, and perhaps the necessity of having recourse
to actual military operations, which might have proved a
source of much present inconvenience, besides involving a
consequence still more to be deprecated, that of injuriously
affecting the relations subsisting between the Beydurs and
yourself, and substituting fear and distrust in lieu of that
confidence and attachment which I feel assured the majority of the people now bear towards you.—I have the
honour to be, &c.   J. S. FRASER, *Resident.*

  "HYDERABAD, 17*th February* 1848."

To this I, of course, returned a suitable reply; but I
was obliged to go out at once into the districts, as my
long detention at Hyderabad had materially interfered
with my work, and I could delay no longer. The Commission of Inquiry was therefore postponed for a time.
As the settlements now only required supervision, my
labour was comparatively easy; but the crops were bad,
the cotton and wheat were blighted, and other products
injured by excess of unseasonable rain. And I had to
make some material remissions, which in the end satisfied
everybody. Lord Dalhousie had now succeeded to the
office of Governor-General, and took his seat in January,
and the whole of the Shorapoor correspondence would be
laid before him. I was anxious for the result, and it
arrived at length. It was most satisfactory. His Excellency in Council expressed his entire satisfaction with the
manner in which the affair of the Ranee had been conducted, and "directed" that his "approbation of the
ability, firmness, and judgment" I had displayed should
be conveyed to me. It was all very gratifying; but I
could not but miss more than ever the dear face that
would have lighted up with loving joy and pride at my
success, and I never liked to return to my beautiful house.
Old wounds would reopen, and I longed for a kind word
or a loving smile to greet me there. I determined then,

however, to live out my life alone, and that I would never
seek marriage with another ; and I have kept faith to her
who is gone and to myself, and shall do so till I die.
This determination was the result of a very curious and
strange incident that befell me during one of my marches
to Hyderabad. I have never forgotten it, and it returns
to this day to my memory with a strangely vivid effect,
that I can neither repel nor explain. I purposely with-
hold the date and the year. In my very early life I had
been deeply and devotedly attached to one in England,
and only relinquished the hope of some day winning her
when the terrible order came out that no furlough to
Europe would be granted. One evening I was at the
village of Dewar Kudea, after a long afternoon and evening march from Muktul, and I lay down very weary ; but
the barking of village dogs, the baying of jackals, and
over-fatigue and heat prevented sleep, and I was wide
awake and restless. Suddenly, for my tent-door was wide
open, I saw the face and figure so familiar to me, but looking
older, and with a sad and troubled expression. The dress
was white, and seemed covered with a profusion of lace, and
glistened in the bright moonlight. The arms were stretched
out, and a low plaintive cry of "Do not let me go ! do
not let me go !" reached me. I sprang forward, but the
figure receded, growing fainter and fainter, till I could see
it no longer, but the low sad tones still sounded. I had
run barefooted across the open space where my tents were
pitched, very much to the astonishment of the sentry on
guard ; but I returned to my tent without speaking to him.

I wrote to my father. I wished to know whether there
was any hope for me. He wrote back to me these
words :—

"Too late, my dear son. On the very day of the vision
you describe to me, ——— was married." . . .

Shortly after my return to Shorapoor, I succeeded in
catching two of the Beydurs who had escaped. One of

them tried to stab himself when apprehended; but, being prevented in time, only scratched his stomach. They both made a confession which cleared up everything in regard to the late insurrection. It was they who, with two others, attacked the post-runner and took his bag from him by order of the Ranee and Kasima, in order to find out what I had written. In all, they had hoped to raise 10,000 men, and relied on the treasury for payment, which was to be seized by them. I was to be prevented from entering Shorapoor unless I promised to accede to all the Ranee wished; but the Rajah coming out to meet me, which they had never contemplated, put an end to that part of the scheme. So far all was clear enough, but subsequent declarations and confessions by other parties proved contradictory, and others were accused by them as well as the Ranee. So I took the witnesses to Linsoogoor to be examined before the Court then sitting, and left it to the Resident to unravel what he could. I never had had experience of anything at all like the lies and counter-lies recorded on that memorable occasion; they beat all that had come to my knowledge.

I had a letter from my friend the Ranee, who preferred remaining at Bellary, and I was glad she did so, as she was more under surveillance at a large station; she expressed herself content and satisfied, and I answered her note telling her of her children and their welfare.

The accounts of the State would possess no interest for the reader; but the table given below will show how I was progressing.

Balance in favour of the State for 1253, '54, '55, '56, and '57 *Faslee* :—

1844 (1253 *Faslee*), balance,	.	.	. Rs. 45,456	7	6
1845 (1254 ,,	,,	.	. 41,805	11	9
1846 (1255 ,,	,,	.	. 74,898	6	3
1847 (1256 ,,	,,	.	. 181,391	0	6
1848 (1257 ,,	,,	.	. 308,547	0	0

while the whole cash account of the treasury, which included receipts from other sources, shows the balance in hand to be Rs. 348,977 : 14 : 9.

How quiet was everything at Shorapoor for the next two years! No intrigue! no suspicion! no combinations! The Rajah, as he grew up, advanced in intelligence, and daily attended to all the current business, working with me cheerfully and well, and I had no apprehensions on his account. The Nizam's Government had withdrawn their demands for balance claimed, and the Court of Directors had repudiated any claim for interest on the bankers' bonds on the discovery of their forged interpolation. It became now a question whether they were not debtors to the State; and so 1849 opened pleasantly. 1848 had been a turbulent year in many parts of India, but though the second Sikh war was not concluded, there was no doubt now as to its issue, and in March 1849 the Punjaub was annexed to the British Empire.

I was summoned to Hyderabad to report on the proceedings of the Court on the Beydurs, and I was obliged to state that not only had I never been summoned as a witness, or as a prosecutor, but that the Court had wandered into extraneous matter, and had been at the mercy of false witnesses both for and against the prisoners. That the chief points of the insurrection had never been inquired into at all—that is, the assembly in arms, &c. My paper was sent into the Court, and at length I was summoned; after which the final finding of the Court was that the prisoners had been guilty of overt acts of rebellion; but in consequence of their long imprisonment, they were recommended to mercy—and the Ranee, who had never been on her trial at all, was acquitted! The whole proceedings were forwarded to Lord Dalhousie, who eventually confirmed the finding of the Court; and some of the prisoners were released. He blamed me too, for having been misled—why, I could not understand. The

measure of removing the Ranee was one of Lord Hardinge's which I had to see carried out, and it was done
without bloodshed. Perhaps the Court was bewildered
by the great mass of contradictory evidence before it ; and
possibly even his Lordship's astute mind was too, for he
made ample amends to me hereafter.

The Ranee was to be allowed to return, but when or how
was not specified.

In July we had another visitation of cholera, and the
Rajah's half-brother died of it, to the great grief of the
family. He was a very interesting and promising child ;
but no care availed to save him. I sat up myself with
him for four successive nights, and he died, poor little
fellow, in my arms.

I was greatly interested in the extension of the lake at
Bohnal ; it was my first essay at irrigation works, and
proved a complete success. I had taken careful levels of
the whole of the ancient embankment, which was much
higher than was necessary. I added 12 feet to the escape-
weir, and took advantage of some natural hillocks beyond
the weir to extend the embankment in accordance with
the old portion. The lake filled in September, and was a
truly noble sheet of water, $2\frac{1}{2}$ square miles (rather more
than 1600 acres) in area, with an average depth of 12 feet.
I had built a small schooner for the Rajah, and we sailed
matches against each other, to his infinite delight ; he
never cared how hard it blew.

The despatch of the Court of Directors upon my reports
for 1847 and 1848 was very cheering and acceptable to
me. Its length alone prevents my giving it here ; but it
was evident that all I had already done and proposed to do
had been well and carefully considered and approved.

The Rajah had removed from the palace in which he
had lived with his mother to the older and original residence of the family. It was badly built, and during the
heavy rains of the present year, one night a corner of the

building fell, and so shook the whole that repair was impossible. I therefore asked and obtained permission to build a new palace; and I set to work to make designs for it. The building was handsome and commodious when finished, but I could have wished a larger space for it to stand in.

Several other tanks were in progress, and I determined to try, in these ways, to lay out the surplus in the treasury to the best future advantage of the State. Bohnal works cost 6000 rupees, and this was entirely paid back during the very first year by the increased return of rice and sugar-cane produce.

On the 20th May 1850 my friend the Ranee returned! having been away from us for more than two years. She had got terribly into debt, and had nearly been sent away from Bangalore to Vellore in consequence of her intrigues. She had been ill too; but in spite of all, here she was again!

She stayed some days at Linsoogoor, where a house had been taken for her, and I had a very amusing account of her most absurd demands and unreasonable requests.

She wanted three good houses belonging to private individuals, who were to be deprived of them; and if she did not get them, she vowed she would come up to my house and live there! This was indeed an alarming prospect for me! However, I, with the Rajah and all the principal people, went to meet her at the Krishna, the frontier, where the Rajah's new suite of tents had been pitched for the first time for her especial accommodation; and as she crossed the river, we went forward to welcome her, and conduct her to her tent. She refused to enter the large one, but chose a dirty little one belonging to her servants; and a very stormy and disgraceful scene occurred, which, as my last illustration of the lady's temper and disposition, I copy from a letter written to my father.

" We were all there, and after a short interval, glaring at us one by one, she burst out—

" ' Well ! and what have you sent for me for ? '

" ' We did not send for you,' said I, and several others.

" ' Yes, you did. Do you think I would have come of my own accord ? You had better kill me, and throw me into the river, or put me in the guard-house. How very proper and pleasant it will be to be in the guard-house ! Why shouldn't I live in the guard ? Have you got those houses I ordered ? '

" ' No, Ranee Sahib ! ' I answered. ' The houses you ordered are private property, and you cannot have them.'

" ' Can't have them ? ' she cried ; ' who are they to deny me ? Am I not Ranee of Shorapoor ? Can I not do as I choose ? '

" ' No, not quite,' I returned ; ' not with what belongs to other people.'

" ' No ? I can't ? we shall see,' she cried. ' Did not General Cubbon and Mr Pelly, and —— and —— and ——' (hurling at me a host of names), ' and a lot of other people, tell me I could do whatever I liked ? and yet it seems I am not to have my very first wish gratified. Am I less than those people ? Are they not my slaves ? Well' (after a torrent of abuse), ' and where am I to go ? '

" ' To the palace, Ranee Sahib,' I replied.

" ' The palace ! I won't go there ! no, not to my old place ! I won't be taken there except by force. Why don't you tie me hand and foot ? You are powerful, and I am only an old woman.' (Here the Ranee began to whimper.) ' Put me into the river at once. I'll *not* go to Hyderabad, or to Bangalore, or to Bellary. I'll go on pilgrimages. I will not stay here. I won't ! I won't ! No, I won't ! '

" ' But,' I said, ' Ranee Sahib, you seem to forget that your son, the Rajah, is sitting near you ; you should go with him and me, and we will both try and make you as happy and comfortable as we can.'

" ' My son!' she screamed. ' My son! He is no son of mine, the base-born! He my son!' and a volley of invectives followed. ' I wish he were dead! Why did he live, and not my sister's child? Yes! you killed him among you, just to vex me!' (and more abuse succeeded, which I could not translate.) ' He my son indeed!'

" Poor little Rajah; how he bore it I know not: but every now and then he pulled at my coat, or squeezed my hand, and whispered—

" How can you bear it? Come away."

" I told him we would bear it as long as we could, for I was in hopes the storm would spend itself, and that she would be more amenable afterwards; but there was yet a very ticklish subject to introduce—viz., her former estates, or *jagheers;* she being now only dowager, and the young Ranee having the estates; an allowance having been substituted for her lands.

" How she raged and foamed when I told her! What a fierce war of rage and passion waged when I explained matters to her! Her allowance had been fixed at 1000 rupees a-month. She became quite beside herself when she heard this, and made use of language that made one's blood creep. The idea of pay was worse than anything.

" ' Am I a servant?' she yelled, ' that I should take pay? Have not other Ranees their estates? Why do you take mine?' Then a fit of crying, then more abuse; till at length my patience and temper could stand it no longer, and I fairly told her that if she did not come to Shorapoor, as she was directed and permitted to do, I should dismiss her escort, and leave her where she was. That the decision of Government could not change; sooner would the current of the river turn and flow upward. I strongly advised her to return to Bangalore until she was in a more reasonable frame of mind; and I ended by telling her, that if she continued so violent I should report everything that she said to Government, and that she would probably get deeper into trouble. At length, at sunset, after having endured her society for nearly four hours, we left her.

"At eleven at night she sent for me again. What a life this woman led me! I took a relative of hers with me, a respectable man. She was restless and uneasy, said she was sorry for what she had uttered, that she had lost her temper, that she could not sleep because I had left her in anger, and had sent for me to tell me so, &c.; and that she had determined to go to Shorapoor next day, and would do exactly as I bid her. Also she proclaimed that she intended to live privately, and to have no men about her; that they had all cheated her, and brought her into trouble. As I found her cool and reasonable, I gave her a lecture, appealing to what feelings she had, and showing her how her own evil doings had led her into disgrace and banishment, and would inevitably do so again if not controlled. She seemed to feel my words, and kept repeating, ' I have no true friend except you. Forgive me! forgive me!'

"After a long talk I left her and came home to bed, tired and worried enough. Next day we all started, the Rajah riding a fine horse; and about 3 P.M. the Ranee came to his tent, and seemed more pleased to see him. In the evening we started for Shorapoor, about seven miles, she and I in palankeens, the rest all on foot or on horseback—a motley crowd, but very numerous. The Ranee appeared in very good humour, and thanked me for having received her with so much honour. When she arrived at the palace, all the children, with dear old Kesámá, met her; but she took no notice of any one except Kesámá, at whose feet she fell, praying her to forgive her, and to place her hands upon her head—which the good old lady did at once."

Thus the Ranee subsided into her old palace and old associations. She had brought a poor half-caste with her, and amused herself by writing English letters to officials she had known during her absence; but as these were invariably returned to her, she addressed the Resident with the like result. Her allowance was higher than she expected—12,000 rupees a-year—and she professed herself content.

She sent for her old friend Kasima, who came to me in much alarm.

"What am I to do?" he said. "I have had quite enough of her and of her schemes—she is a devil."

"She was kind to you," I replied; "she had you married in state, and made her son, your prince, walk before your palankeen; you should not abuse her. All you have to do is to keep quiet;" and he took my advice.

When I came in from the country in August the lady was very quiet, and returned my visit, bringing some of the children with her, and staying nearly all day amusing herself in my garden; but I found her chief object was to present me with a schedule of her debts! These amounted to 62,000 rupees, and there were more behind. I had no authority to pay any such sum, which had been borrowed by her chiefly in Mysore; and whether permission would be granted for the payment of these debts or not I could not tell. Eventually 500 rupees a-month was deducted from the Ranee's allowance to give to her creditors, a decision which set her frantic; and she announced her intention of appealing to Parliament, though utterly ignorant of what that tribunal was, or where!

CHAPTER XII.

1851-53.

A COPY of a despatch from the Court of Directors reached me in December. It was most satisfactory, and reviewed the transactions of 1847-48. It was full of honourable commendation, which I need not here repeat; but the State had made great advance since then in material prosperity, and I was glad to have an opportunity of showing it to Major Johnston, then military secretary at Hyderabad, and he promised to write to Sir Henry Elliott, at that time secretary with the Governor-General, and to tell him all he had seen, and about the improvements in progress. I found the Ranee very ill and miserable—she had had a stroke of paralysis that had affected all her left side, and more particularly her face, which was now hideous; and there was little doubt that dropsy had set in, in addition. The apothecary who had charge of the public dispensary and hospital did what he could for her, but had a very bad opinion of her case.

In March my public report for the year past went in, and was reviewed by the Resident, General Fraser. He was perfectly satisfied; and on the report of Major Buckle, engineer-in-chief at Hyderabad, sanctioned my estimate for the new tank at Kuchaknoor, near Bohnal. Major Buckle had great experience in irrigation works in the Madras Presidency, and was kind enough, during one of my visits to Hyderabad, to instruct me in the principles of the construction of dams, sluices, and the like. I had put

these instructions into practice, and sent up all the estimates, with survey, plans, and sections, for this new work.
I was very anxious to complete it, if possible, during my
stay at Shorapoor. It would be of considerable magnitude
—the dam 1872 yards in length; the greatest depth of
water-storage 50 ft.; the average of the whole basin about
20 ft.; and the area of water $6\frac{1}{4}$ square miles. It would
be a noble sheet of water, and very profitable, as it would
irrigate upwards of 10,000 *beegahs* of rice. As soon as my
estimates were sanctioned I began the work, and the Rajah
opened it with all due ceremony, turning the first sod, and
carrying the first basket of earth.

The concluding paragraph of General Fraser's despatch
was as follows:—

" I consider it, however, due to you to place upon record
the renewed expression of my entire approval of your
public conduct, and my highest commendation of the un-
remitting and devoted attention which you give to the
discharge of your important duties."

Could I desire more? Still my life was lonely and
dreary: I had no society whatever; and only at rare
intervals a short visit from some friend or passing traveller.
If it had not been for my daily work, which lasted from
seven in the morning till eight at night, and sometimes
longer, I could not, I think, have endured the entire isolation of my life, all official praises notwithstanding.

During my wanderings over the Shorapoor district in
this and former years, I had discovered, in many places,
cairns and dolmens, some of them of very large size, corresponding in all respects to similar monuments in England,
Brittany, and other places. I mistrusted my judgment in
regard to them for a long time: but at length I drew up
a paper on the subject, accompanied by sketches; and
followed it up by another in regard to the contents of
cairns which I had opened. In one spot, near Sholapoor,
I found most curious remains—a large barrow, with a

parallelogram of rocks, 440 ft. by 280 ft. The rocks were
in regular line, some of them 12 ft. long and 9 ft. thick,
and from 5 to 6 ft. high. They had been rolled from the
granitic range, a distance of 1½ mile. Another place contained an immense number of large rocks, placed in regular
rows, direct and diagonally, leaving squares of from 5 to 6
yards between. In this area were some cairns. I sent my
article on the subject to the Royal Asiatic Society in
Bombay, who did me the honour to elect me a member.
These stone monuments of Shorapoor tallied exactly with
European examples; but it seemed to me so strange a discovery that I almost doubted whether European archæologists would admit it. They did so most fully afterwards,
and my discoveries at Shorapoor were followed by others
even more interesting in other portions of lower India.

For a long period the affairs of the Nizam's Government
had been in a critical state. It owed nearly one million
sterling to the British Government, which it could not pay.
The Contingent was constantly in heavy arrear, and Lord
Dalhousie, urged by the Court of Directors, pressed for
a settlement. The subject had been under reference to
England for several years, but it appeared now nearer a
conclusion.

The Nizam had tried several Ministers in succession,
who had failed. He then attempted to govern himself,
and failed more signally than his Ministers. The State
had no public credit, and the administration in the provinces was oppressive to the people, and utterly corrupt.
Now affairs seemed to have reached a climax. Provinces,
detailed in a minute I wrote by desire of the Resident in
January 1851, were to be made over to the British Government, and I was to be put in charge of one of them.

"The experience and past services of Captain Meadows
Taylor," wrote Lord Dalhousie to General Fraser, "at once
point him out as the proper person for undertaking the
direction of those districts which lie near Shorapoor, if his

present occupation will admit of his entering on this additional charge."

It would have admitted of it, for no new measures were required at Shorapoor, and the Rajah was gaining enough experience to manage fairly for himself, with a little assistance now and then. He transacted most of the current business, and did it very well. His new palace was finished outside, and nearly inside also, and the upper apartments were very airy, cool, and spacious.

My only dread was on account of his mother, who, I feared, was endeavouring to drag him into her toils by the worst possible means. However, the new arrangement with the Nizam was not to come into force at once. I was summoned to Hyderabad, to be given charge of a province, but returned as I went—the appointment being delayed. When there, I ascertained many more particulars of the condition of the Nizam's Government than I previously had knowledge of, and in some respects it was worse than I thought.

The first instalment of the Nizam's debt, 40 lakhs, £400,000, had been remitted to Calcutta, and the second was due ; but there were no funds to meet it. The Nizam sent to his Minister, Suraj-ool-Moolk, jewels, which his Highness valued at 30 lakhs, to be pledged for that amount ; but the bankers only valued them at 10 lakhs, and they even declined to give four for them. The principal bankers were so shaken, in fact, by their previous loans, that not only were they unable to make money, but some were even threatened with insolvency. At the instance of capitalists at Madras, an advance had been made on the Nizam's jewels of five lakhs ; but this was a mere drop in the ocean.

The first 40 lakhs had been raised by officers newly appointed to several large districts, assisted by the bankers. It was now proposed to raise a similar sum by putting in new men and turning out the others. Nobody

dared to mention "cession of territory" to the Nizam, and
thus the vessel of the State drifted on without sail or helm
to the rocks, on which it might go to pieces at any time.   I
was sorry for the Resident, who, if he trusted to Suraj-ool-
Moolk's word, was sure to be deceived; yet I believe Suraj-
ool-Moolk had every wish to fulfil his promises if he could;
but there were literally no assets to work on, and no credit
to be had, and all waited for Lord Dalhousie's next move.

In November I received a private and confidential note
from the Ranee of Gudwall, a State smaller than Shorapoor, but occupying the same political position.

She knew of the prosperity at Shorapoor, and wished
me to take charge of Gudwall in the same manner.   The
offer, spontaneous as it was, gratified me much, but unless
I were placed in charge of the "Raichore Doab," in which
her State lay, I could do nothing for her, and in any case
I could not myself propose the measure.   The Ranee was
a woman of irreproachable character, and would, I felt
sure, be easy to deal with.

In December I received orders to go to Beejapoor to
meet the Commissioner of Sattara and the Collector of
Sholapoor, who, with myself, were to form a commission
for the investigation of lines of traffic and roads from all
sides, with reference to the opening of a new port on the
western coast at Viziadroog.   I had been suffering much
from fever and other ailments, and the change of air and
scene was delightful to think of.   I had never yet seen
Beejapoor, and had longed to visit it for years, on account
of its noble remains of Mussulman architecture.   We met,
and made out a report, which I had to write, and we were
a very pleasant little party; but my chief delight was in
sketching, in which I was unwearied, and found ever fresh
objects for my brush.   Had I had three months, instead
of three weeks, to spend, I could not have half exhausted
the subjects that presented themselves everywhere—
palaces, mosques, interiors, exteriors, combinations of

ruins and landscape, extended views, and choice "bits," all most picturesque and beautiful. I brought away as many drawings as I could; but I would willingly have lingered had I had leisure.

As the majority of the Rajah was fast approaching, I drew up, at the Resident's request, a report upon the results of my management of Shorapoor from the commencement; and this he transmitted to the Governor-General, with a letter requesting instructions as to the date on which the Rajah's minority should expire, and proposing, on his own part, that I should remain at Shorapoor after that event, in the capacity of political agent on the part of the Government of India, on a salary of 1500 Co. rupees per month, to be paid by the State of Shorapoor. I did not think it likely that the Rajah would desire the presence of any political agent, if he were allowed the option, much less that he would agree to maintaining one at the cost of 20,000 rupees of the local currency; but the Resident's letter had gone on to the Government, and I could only await the reply. When it came it was very satisfactory.

Extract from despatch from the Secretary in the Foreign Department to the Resident at Hyderabad.

"*15th January* 1853.

" SIR,—I am directed by the Most Noble the Governor-General to acknowledge the receipt of your letter, dated the 22d ult., No. 218, with its enclosures, and, in reply, to observe that the report upon the management of the affairs of Shorapoor exhibits results in the secured prosperity of the Prince, in the tranquillity of the State and contentment of the people, highly honourable to the industry, the perseverance, and the ability of Captain Meadows Taylor."

The period fixed for the majority of the Rajah was the

completion of his eighteenth year; but in relation to the political agency, his Lordship stated that " though it would be in the highest degree advisable, yet if, on attaining his full age, which the Rajah would then have reached, and finding his State orderly, and his means adequate to his expenditure, he should decline to comply with the suggestion, his Lordship does not know on what grounds the Government of India could insist upon it." The question, therefore, was to be referred to the Court of Directors.

A few days after the receipt of the foregoing, I had the pleasure to receive from F. Courtenay, Esq., private secretary to the Governor-General, a letter, written privately, by desire of Lord Dalhousie, which assured me his Lordship wished me to know that he had himself drafted the despatch before-quoted to General Fraser, and that he was glad of having had the opportunity of expressing his opinion of what I had done, and that, in regard to the blame he had attached to me on the proceedings of the Linsoogoor inquiry, he now completely exonerated me from it, being convinced, from the Ranee's dangerous and obnoxious intrigues and general ill-conduct in Mysore, that I had done no more than my duty in removing her from Shorapoor. Mr Courtenay added, in a postscript, " His Lordship has read this, and desires me to say that you may consider it as having been written by himself."

Could I have wished or hoped for more ? My friend, Major Johnston, was with me when the despatches arrived, and I sent for the Rajah to read them to him, and make over the executive authority in Shorapoor itself to him, as I had proposed to do that of several departments, informing him also at what period his minority would cease.

He took these communications in a very proper spirit— not greedily, but gratefully, and even sadly. " Till now," he said, " he had not felt his position or its reality ; but he would try and be worthy of the confidence of Government." He seemed most anxious about his mother, whose conduct was now horribly profligate ; and soon after his return to Shorapoor he tried to capture her chief favourite ; but the man escaped at night, and the Ranee, in a furious rage, shut herself up in a far wing of the palace.

" What will they do," he said, " when you leave them ? " Though he did not love his mother, yet she had power over him to tempt him into vicious courses, and this she did not neglect to exercise.

In June I received the Resident's reply to my general report for the financial year, 1851-52, which was probably the last I should make, as the Rajah would soon have the management of his own treasury. The cash balance in the preceding year had been 377,334 rupees, the highest figure it had yet reached : this year it was 309,442 ; but the extra expenditure on public works — such as the new palace and the irrigation works, three large embankments being in progress—fully accounted for the diminution of the balance. Indeed, I applied money as rapidly as I could to these useful undertakings, with a view to their future profit to the State. The great embankment and sluices at Kuchaknoor were now getting on fast ; and I had the satisfaction of hearing from Major Buckle that " my plans, surveys, and estimates were most creditable to me as an engineer."

The Resident's despatch ran thus :—

" Par. 37. As the time approaches when the Rajah will have attained his majority, and be intrusted, under the sanction of the Government of India, with the administration of his country, it becomes a matter of much interest to us to be assured that nothing has been wanting on our part to ameliorate the condition of the country and of its inhabitants during the time that it has been under our direction.

" Par. 38. On this subject, therefore, it is particularly gratifying to me to reflect that you have done honour to

R

the office you have held, and that you have discharged its
several important duties with the most marked ability,
and a devotedness of time and labour that has had no
intermission."

The Nizam's affairs continued in the same deplorable
condition. In June 1852 I had not received my pay
for December 1851. I had long ago warned the Resident
that he was being deceived, and he now began to acknowledge that I was right. What would be done? Would
the Government of India demand a cession of territory for
the pay of the Contingent only? or would the whole State
be placed for a time under British surveillance? all the
foreign mercenaries discharged, who were a perpetual
source of uneasiness and disquiet, if not of actual alarm,
and the establishment reduced so as to pay debts and leave
the State prosperous? This was the Resident's advice;
but at present no move was made in any direction.

I have not as yet alluded to my friend the Rev. Mr Kies,
whose occasional visits were a very great pleasure to me.
He was a member of a German mission emanating from
Basle, and supported by Germany.

He was so simple in his ways, and so learned at the
same time, that he won the respect and esteem of the
people wherever he went. He made no display, travelling
on his stout pony from village to village, trusting to
hospitality, which was never denied him, and meeting the
learned Shastrees on their own ground, being fully versed
in all their sacred books, and speaking Canarese perfectly.
He and I had many a talk on the subject of missions and
mission work, and his experience led him to believe that
there were great numbers in many parts who were really
dissatisfied with their own Hindooism, yet lacked courage
to break through the trammels of caste, and separate themselves from Brahminical influences. That eventually the
Christian faith would prevail, he did not doubt; but at
present there was but little to show for the patient,

1852.] A TRUE MISSIONARY. 259

humble teaching of many years of labour. In one note I had from Mr Kies, he told me that the priest of a village where he had previously preached the Gospel was dead, and with his last breath had laid injunctions on his people to receive him as their future Gooroo (spiritual teacher) ; and this they did, listening " simply and reverently."

Another letter I find, which is, I think, worthy of a place here.

" I am afraid, sadly afraid, that missionaries who go or who write home to Europe, make it appear as though they were securing more conversions, or hoped to do more, than they can effect. I think they have begun at the wrong end, by abusing Hindooism and idolatry, instead of meeting the natives on their own ground—the Shastras, their scriptures—and showing them how unreasonable, illogical, and void of all comfort they are compared with the belief of a Christian. The finest work they have, religious and philosophical, is the 'Bhagwat Gita,' an Episode of the Mahabarat ; but though there are fine thoughts in it, and fine doctrine, it rests upon no basis that the mind feels, and is intermixed with physical absurdities. You should, if you can, read Schlegel's Latin translation ; it is the best, as being nearest to the original Sanscrit. There is an English version ; but I do not know how to get hold of it. The missionaries are now, I believe, at last aware of the necessity of meeting natives on their own ground ; but for thirty years it was not so, and the mass of vituperation of Hindoos that has been printed is enormous—at least what they consider vituperation. Put it to yourself, as for instance in Italy, where there is much image-worship very like idolatry, would it answer any good purpose to call Saint this a rogue ? or Saint that a thief? or Saint t'other an impostor ? Krishna deserves all these names ; but it answers no good purpose to bestow them. I am often surprised at the supineness of the English chaplains of the Established Church. Missionaries take the trouble gene-

rally to learn at least one native language; but among
English clergymen I do not know of one who really makes
native languages his study, and many of them can hardly
speak intelligibly to their servants. Why is this? Is
there no field of work for them as well as for missionaries?
no good to be done to natives around them? no translations
to make? Of course there are. The work is plentiful;
but it is not done. Good classical scholars generally find
little difficulty in learning native languages; and why
should not a chaplain preach in a plain, simple fashion,
and be able to read the service to the natives at his station?
Much good, it strikes me, might be done were this subject
rightly considered."

Mr Kies was beloved and respected by all; and his
visits were eagerly looked for. He laboured on as long as
I continued in India; and I believe at last, owing to ill
health, returned to Basle, where he died—an honest, upright, humble follower of his Lord, and one who, by his
simple faith and kindly feelings, won many converts.

In September, all being perfectly quiet and prosperous
at Shorapoor, I went up to Hyderabad for medical advice.
The Rajah had married his third wife, according to the
custom of the family, and his first wife's half-sister had
also been married at the same time to the Rajah of Soonda.
She was one of my Shorapoor children, for whom I had
always felt a great affection; she was so clever, and yet so
gentle, and very handsome, and the Rajah of Soonda had
fallen in love with her at first sight, and would not be
refused. The expenses of these marriages, the ladies'
trousseaux and their jewels, were very heavy—hardly less
in all than a lakh of rupees; but the money was their
own, and devoted to their own purposes.

At Hyderabad I was very ill; the fever I had previously
suffered from returned with great violence, and my life
was almost despaired of. Under God's great mercy I again
recovered, and felt far better than I had done for several

months before I left. The Resident wished me to remain, pending the final instructions of the Governor-General regarding Hyderabad and the debts of the Nizam's Government, which were increasing every month. The Governor-General and the Resident were at issue in regard to the policy to be adopted with respect to the Nizam. The Resident proposed that the whole of his Highness's dominions should be placed under the management of the British Government, and all useless expenses reduced in order to pay the State debts, which were estimated at four millions and a half. Lord Dalhousie, on the other hand, protested very strongly against any interference with his Highness's affairs, which had been guaranteed by the British Government in the treaty of 1800; and he required only a partial cession of territory to provide for the payment of the Contingent and liquidation of the debt to the Company. These views, so essentially different, were irreconcilable; but I was not prepared for the result. The Resident came to me one evening and said abruptly, "Taylor, I have sent in my resignation ; I have just posted it myself, and I have told nobody—not even my wife; but I confide it to you. In a day or two it will be made public."

I was much grieved. I had worked under him and with him for more than nine years without a difference, and his kindness, both officially and privately, had been uniform and continued, nor can I ever forget his unwearied care of me and attention in my illness.

While I was still at Hyderabad his resignation was accepted, and he began his preparations for departure. I left Hyderabad on the 26th December, bidding him good-bye with extreme regret. Colonel Low, who on a former occasion had acted for General Fraser, was appointed his successor, and would, it was presumed, bring with him the final orders of the Governor-General in Council. He was expected early in March, so I should not be long in suspense.

I returned to my districts, and began my last revenue settlement. There was but little to do ; the period of five years had expired, and all that remained was a general revision and adjustment, with the remissions or other provision for outstanding balances. On the whole, we had been unlucky as regarded seasons, and had had three bad, through excess of unseasonable rain, against two good. I could therefore make no demand for an increase of rent, and the leases for waste lands taken up had been necessarily irregular. A regular system of returns of cultivation and revenue in all villages in correspondence with the treasury worked well, and the most ordinary supervision on the part of the Rajah would keep everything straight. I had not been long in camp when the Rajah came out to me, and remained for a few days' shooting. He appeared for the first time restless, and somewhat petulant, wondering how soon the orders would arrive regarding him. I could only assure him he could not be more anxious than I was on the subject ; but I could do nothing till they came. The Ranee had again been ill, and when her son visited her, had told him that unless he exerted himself he would never get the country out of my hands, and that he was now no child, "Why did he not act as a man?" No wonder, I thought, that he was petulant, and perhaps suspicious too. I had informed him of the probable political agency; and a draft of a letter was prepared from himself and others of the elder members of his family, declaring that no political agency was needed, and that the Rajah was fully able to manage his own concerns. Some signed these papers ; but others, especially the Beydurs, refused to do so, except a few, who sent me word they had done it under compulsion. The Ranee, to her credit, declared to her son that he would ruin himself if these papers were forwarded. I never heard of them till afterwards, so I suppose the Rajah was guided by her counsel.

On March 10th the Resident wrote to the Rajah that the Court of Directors and the Governor-General approved of his taking up the affairs of his State; but they desired that I should remain as political agent to advise him in State matters, and thus preclude the recurrence of former disorder and irregularity: to this the Resident requested a distinct reply, which would be forwarded for the orders of the Governor-General. On receipt of this letter the Rajah wrote to me asking the meaning of "political agent," which I explained, and he sent his reply to the Resident, which was at once forwarded; but the question of political agency was evaded under his assurance to Government that "his reliance in all matters was restricted to the favour of the Supreme Government."

Perhaps if the Rajah had been from the first assured that he would not have had to pay for the agency and its establishment, he would have consented to the step as a mark of distinction to his State, but the prospect of having to pay 20,000 rupees a-year was formidable. Lord Dalhousie had very distinctly given his opinion that the measure could not be forced upon the Rajah; and even if he consented, he ought not to be considered responsible for the heavy charges it would involve. I had always looked on the subject as extremely uncertain; for unless the Court of Directors sanctioned the expenditure, I did not see how the Governor-General could authorise it. Everything, however, must soon be finally settled.

The Rajah had come of age the previous October, and the delay in his public recognition by Government was only making him restless and suspicious. If the Rajah had agreed to the appointment of a political agent, I should of course have remained with him; but I had no wish to do so for many reasons, and I wrote privately to Colonel Low on the subject. The rumours of a transfer of territory by the Nizam became again rife in April, and as I felt sure my services would not be passed over, I waited patiently for the issue. I could not have remained at Shorapoor; but if I were given charge of the Raichore Doab, I could still look after it. The Rajah's vices were becoming notorious, and I cannot write of them; and his temper, to his own people, was growing like his mother's.

The Rajah's answer to the Resident not being considered satisfactory by the Governor-General, the Resident again wrote, detailing the exact sum to be paid to the agent, 1815 Shorapoor rupees per month—equivalent to 1500 Government rupees—and there would be additional sums for sepoys, &c. I was at Shorapoor, and the Rajah brought the letter to me, and asked me what he was to say.

"I cannot pay this large sum to any one," he said; "you know I cannot."

Indeed I was of the same opinion, and thought the expenses might well have been shared by the Company and by the Nizam's Government.

"But," continued the Rajah, "I suppose they will be angry with me if I refuse, and, indeed, I don't want you to go away. I know I shall do no good when you are gone; you don't know the people I have about me."

"Yes," I said, "I do, as well as you; and if you only act rightly, you will be able to control them far more easily than I did."

"O *appa!*" he cried, leaving his chair, and throwing himself at my feet—"O *appa!* if I were only a little boy again to lie in your arms, and for you to love me as you used! All that is gone for ever."

"No, no," I answered; "if I go—and I must go soon— I shall not be far away from you, and if you are in any trouble or difficulty, send for me and I will come. You can always write in English 'Come,' and I shall understand."

"I will," he said. "I know, whatever you may hear, you will not forsake your boy."

And I gave him my promise. That, except once more,

as I shall have to relate, was the last time I was ever alone with him. He wrote his answer to the Resident on the 1st May. It was clumsily worded, and Colonel Low did not like the style; but the Rajah did not intend it to be disrespectful or arrogant. He declined the political agency on the terms on which it was offered, owing to the great expense; and I thought him right.

Meanwhile events at Hyderabad were in full progress towards a settlement. The Resident had received his final orders, which were to demand that territory in payment of the Contingent might be ceded in perpetuity to British management, and the districts I had named in my minute of January 1851 were the basis of the transaction. The old Contingent was to be remodelled; all the local officers pensioned, and the force no longer called the "Nizam's Army," but, as the "Hyderabad Contingent," to be an auxiliary one to the Government of India. Should any reader desire to refer to these transactions, they are to be found in their entirety in the Blue-book of 1854, April 4th, and are in truth very interesting, as explaining measures on which Lord Dalhousie has often been arraigned. The Nizam objected to the "assignment in perpetuity," and the treaty was duly executed and signed without that condition, leaving him at liberty to redeem the provinces, if possible, at some future time.

I was still at Shorapoor. The Ranee intended to go on a pilgrimage to one of the great temples in the south of India, and took leave of me in apparently real grief.

"Do you remember, Taylor Sahib," she asked, "what I once told you about that boy? You have not forgotten it?"

"No, Ranee Sahib," I replied, "nor ever shall."

"Ah," she continued, "he is the last—the last of his race! He will lose all his ancestors ever gained; and all the pains you have taken with him, and all the money you have saved for him, will be poured like water into the sea; and you will be grieved—sorely, sorely grieved! But

I shall not see it, for I am dying, my friend, dying fast now. Will you forgive me all that I have done to you? I am a mean old woman. You are going one way, and I am going another; we shall never meet again."

I bent over her as she lay upon her bed, and touched her hand with my lips. She could not speak; but smiled, waved her hand gently, and I left her.

Next day she went to Linsoogoor, and being again seized with paralysis, died there on the 27th May. She was but forty years old; but when I last saw her she seemed seventy, haggard and wasted almost to a skeleton. The Rajah rode over to see her the day before her death, but she was insensible, and he disgusted all those present by his levity and the unruly crowd he had with him.

He returned to Shorapoor while she was yet living, and made no attempt to attend her funeral rites. I called upon him the day after her death, according to Shorapoor etiquette, but he hardly mentioned his mother at all, except as having " been very foolish."

So ended the Ranee Ishwarama.

If there were some good points in her character, generosity and charity to the poor, her profligacy and baneful influence over her son were terrible to think on, and continued to have effect on him to the last.

Suraj-ool-Moolk, the Nizam's Minister, was dead; and his nephew, Salar Jung, a most gentlemanly, well-educated young nobleman, had been appointed in his stead by the Nizam, with every prospect of success. He has since risen to the very highest eminence in India as a statesman, and by him the Nizam's State has been rescued from the decadence with which it was threatened.

I was now summoned to Hyderabad to receive instructions respecting the district that was to be given into my charge—which of the five that had been ceded was not made known to me. I arrived on the 11th June, and having reported myself, received a polite note from the

Resident, asking me to come to dinner, as he had much to say. He received me most kindly, and I was charmed with him, he was so frank, and clear-headed, and decided in all his expressions ; and I saw at once that I should work happily under him. Next day the districts were assigned. At first I was given Berar, the largest ; but an express arrived from the Bombay Government particularly requesting that I might be given that portion of the ceded territory which lay contiguous to the Bombay Presidency, and I was nominated to that instead.

The following extract from an official letter from the Resident to me was at once both explanatory and gratifying :—

" Para. 14. As I understand that you have felt surprised, and perhaps somewhat disappointed, at finding that districts of comparatively small extent are to be made over to your management, while larger districts are allotted to other Deputy-Commissioners of less experience in civil duties than yourself, I think it is due to you to assure you that the circumstance in question has not occurred from any want of confidence on my part in your qualifications or zeal for the public interests—indeed quite the reverse ; for my original reason in determining to send you to the western districts was my belief that many of the duties in that quarter will be of a peculiarly difficult and delicate nature, arising from the numerous Surf-i-Khas districts in that quarter, the revenue management of which remains, according to agreement with the individuals who enjoy them, with the Nizam's Government, while the police and judicial duties of those villages are to be conducted entirely under your orders.

" 15. I may also mention that long-pending and intricate disputes respecting boundaries and frontier taxes, &c. &c., must be inquired into and settled in communication with the collectors of Ahmednugger and Sholapoor of the Honble. Company's territories ; and I knew that I could rely on your tact and judgment, and general experience in civil duties, for the purpose of bringing these disputes to a satisfactory conclusion. Moreover, I may as well mention the fact, that it is within the last three days, and after the allotment of districts to the several Deputy-Commissioners had been arranged, that the western districts have been curtailed to their present extent at the particular request of the Nizam, who originally promised eight lakhs in that direction, making up the difference by adding lands to the southern portion of Berar. That fact, however, does not in any material degree alter the difficult duties above alluded to connected with the western districts, which I consider you so well qualified to overcome."

I had sent on all my tents and heavy baggage towards Berar by way of Beeder; but I now recalled it, as I was required to go first to Shorapoor, and then to my new district: it was, in fact, part of my old district of 1828–29, and a fine healthy climate, which to me Berar was not; and as one end bordered on Shorapoor, I should have no difficulty in getting there. The Raichore Doab, to which I had looked as my probable destination, was divided into two portions, and Berar into two, and mine appeared to be the largest in area, though not in revenue. "'You won't mind that,'" said the Resident, as I wrote to my father; "'your district requires a person of tact and experience of more than ordinary character, and therefore I send you'" —a flattering and gracious speech, for which I made due acknowledgment. It was curious that my destination should be so very suddenly changed.

The treaty, ratified by the Governor-General, had not as yet arrived from Calcutta; and as there was a great deal of detail to be arranged about the establishments and general management of the new districts, the Resident requested me to draw up a minute on the subject, which I did as rapidly as I could; and by the time the treaty had arrived, and the Nizam fixed the 18th July for a public

durbar to receive and sign it, my minute was ready.   On
the appointed day, the Resident, accompanied by a numerous staff, of which I was one, went to the *durbar*.   His
Highness was in excellent humour, chatted freely and gaily
with Colonel Low, and seemed highly pleased that the
differences between the two Governments had been so
speedily and so amicably arranged.   Next day, I and the
other new civil officers who were at Hyderabad received
our credentials, and there being no need for further delay,
I returned to Shorapoor to make my final arrangements,
and to give over my charge to the Rajah according to the
instructions I had received.   Lord Dalhousie had not been
particularly pleased with the tone of the Rajah's reply to
his despatch, which he characterised as "presumptuous;"
yet, as there was no pretext for compelling him to retain
the services of a political agent, he directed that the State
should be made over to him, at the same time warning him—

"That if he allowed his country to fall into disorder, the
Supreme Government would interfere and establish order,"
or perhaps set him aside altogether.

I had appointed the 30th June for the final ceremony,
and had written to tell the Rajah to be ready.   On my
way to Shorapoor I fell in with Captain Balmain, who had
been appointed to Western Raichore, and took him on
with me.   My future assistant, Lieutenant Cadell, awaited
me also at Shorapoor.   I will give the detail of the last
few days from my letter to my father, written at the time.

"I had prepared proclamations and other documents
directing all persons to obey the Rajah, and Cadell and I
went to the palace in the evening.   There were many
people present, and the letter from the Governor-General
was first read; then my proclamation; and I made a short
speech, saying I hoped that all present would be faithful
to the Rajah, and serve him as they had served me—that
I trusted they would do so, and take care of the State, and
not relapse into evil ways.

" Then, as I hung a garland of flowers about the Rajah's neck, and gave the State seals into his hand, a royal salute was fired, and the ceremony ended.

" The Rajah seemed to take it all very coolly, and as a matter of course, and said nothing; but he whispered to me that he could not say all he would in such a crowd ; but would send for me, or come up to me in a day or two.

" We remarked that there was no manifestation of satis-faction among the assembly, or among the crowds outside the palace ; on the contrary, many were weeping.

" The Rajah's first act was to seize his illegitimate half-sister, or rather take her away from her mother, and marry her by a left-handed ceremony, obliging the members of his family to be present, to their great disgust. For two days he was busy with the ceremony, offerings at temples and the like, and on the 3d July he wrote to me begging I would come to him in the evening.

" He asked me what he should write to the Governor-General, and I gave him verbally the outline of a plain, grateful letter. He then asked to be allowed to purchase my house, which was a great satisfaction to me, and he offered 20,000 rupees, an offer I gladly accepted, provided Government made no objection. He afterwards sent every one away, and spoke about his affairs more sensibly than I had ever heard him do before ; and as he gave me this opening I improved upon it, and showed him how, during the short time he had managed his affairs, he had already contrived to spend every rupee of ready money—how his servants and soldiers were even now in arrears of pay, as was the case in his father's time, and he himself obliged to borrow here and there in advance of the collections. I told him I did not see what it would all come to if he did not take pains to make things better, and much to the same purpose, when he began to sob, and cling about me, saying he had now no friends, and how he was to get on he did not know, but he would do his best. He said he

saw there was no use in soldiery, which his people told
him were necessary (this was in relation to the proposed
enlistment of Arabs and Rohillas, which I had heard was
intended), and that he would discharge many of them, and
reduce his extra expenses. He then told me there was
one thing which he wished me to know, and which had
long been on his mind—namely, that if he died without
legitimate issue he wished the British Government to
annex his State, and provide for his family and depend-
ants. I begged he would write this in a letter to the
Resident, which I undertook to forward ; but I represented
that he was very young, and that I hoped to hear of his
having a family and an heir.

" In such conversation our time passed, and I mentioned
everything I could think of in regard to the future management of the affairs. He said he did not know how to
thank me, or show his gratitude ; but that if he were permitted to settle on me an allowance for life, and a village
or two for my maintenance, as a proof of his regard, he
would be thankful.

" The next day he asked Cadell and me to dine with
him. The letters, including that about my estate, were all
ready, and were duly forwarded on the 7th July. The
village selected for me was an outlying one within the
British territory, and yielded 2500 Company's rupees, or
£250 a-year, and I shall be very lucky if I get it.

" The following day—Cadell having started in the morning—I went to the palace to bid the Rajah good-bye ; and
not only he, but all the members of the family, and the
chief people, male and female, in Shorapoor.

" It was a painful process ; there were crowds of people
all about me, clinging to my palankeen, as I went from
house to house. The Rajah had gone out to one of his
hunting retreats, leaving word that he could not bear to
see me go. As I proceeded, the people and the Beydurs,
men and women, gathered in the streets, and accompanied

me, and it was as much as I could do to get away at all. The Rajah's wives, whom I had known as children, clung about me.   Poor old Kesámá, now nearly ninety years old, blessed me : 'I cannot weep,' she said, 'my old eyes are dry ; but I bless you, you and all belonging to you.'

"It was a most exciting scene, and very painful.   Mine has been a long sojourn among a strange people, and whatever may have been their faults, there was no doubt of their warm attachment to myself."

The crowds followed me to the gates ; but as my bearers quickened their pace the numbers soon fell off.   At every village I was met by the people, and at the last one on the frontier a great concourse had assembled of all the headmen, *patells*, and *putwarries*, and principal farmers.   I do not think there was even one man who had a hope of the Rajah's maintaining his position; and as to themselves, they said—"We must escape oppression as best we can. It will be a hard struggle."

So ended my connection with Shorapoor for the present. It was hereafter renewed for a time under far different circumstances.   I had tried humbly and earnestly to do my duty to its people of all degrees ; and could I give *in extenso* my long letters to my father, they would show more of what my inner life and occupations were, and of my schemes and plans for the welfare of the State.   They are far too monotonous, however, and all I have been able to do is to note such events, and quote such extracts, as would give some notion of my endeavours and their results.

In one of his despatches General Fraser characterised the State of Shorapoor as "a wild and barbarous district, replete with disorder and irregularity of every conceivable kind."   And no doubt it was so when I took over charge. The Beydurs were the same, and their power was the same as in the time of Aurungzeeb, or indeed from the fifteenth century, and their feudal condition of service to their chief was the same. Sometimes, owing to their numbers and position, they had been able to dominate over all classes of the people; sometimes their power had exceeded that of their own chiefs, and had forced these to act as they pleased. Sometimes the Rajahs had in their turn brought them to submission; but they had never bent to any Mussulman or other foreign yoke, and none of the civilisation that such a process insured had ever reached them. As long as times were disturbed, they plundered at their will throughout the Deccan and Mysore, and it was only when stronger and more peaceful Governments had the rule that they were restrained. But if the old raids and forays could not be indulged in, there were at any rate cattle-lifting and *dacoity*, and other crimes, to fall back upon; and they looked upon these as most honourable achievements until the late interference with Shorapoor by the British Government.

This violence I had at least suppressed, and for years before I left there had not been one single complaint of any such doings beyond the frontier.

One of their systems, however, was not easy to eradicate. A man who had a quarrel with his village for any cause could always obtain the aid of Beydurs willing to take his part as a point of honour, and these proceeded to issue threatening notices, such as—

"To the authorities of ——. In the name of Mahadeo!

"The fire is on the hills! We are out on murder and violence because you have injured ——, and you had better settle with him."

If this notice were obeyed, all was well; if not, the people of the village were kept in perpetual alarm, their crops injured, and persons wounded, indeed often killed. This state of things was bad enough in the country itself, but when it extended to parties across the frontier it was far worse.

On one occasion a man of a small village near the river

S

Bheema quarrelled with his family, and went to the Beydurs of Adoor, which was fifteen miles distant, in the Nizam's country, where about a thousand of them were to be found. He returned with a party, who harried the Shorapoor village, burnt corn-stacks, and wounded the head-man desperately, besides seven others, also sending me an impudent message that the Shorapoor Beydurs were cowards and old women. My Beydurs were furious, and asked me to lead them on to avenge this insult; and I daresay they thought meanly of me because I did not. As the Nizam's local authorities would or could give no redress, I appealed to the Resident, who desired me not to stir, and sent down a detachment of infantry to march on the rebel village. It resisted, was stormed, and afterwards burnt; and some of my Beydurs were present, which was a satisfaction to them, though they would rather have gone under me. Not long after the offenders sent a deputation to me, praying for forgiveness, and they never transgressed again. They invited me to come and visit them, which I did, finding them on a fine level plateau—a much cooler climate than the plain.

As a body the Shorapoor Beydurs had been free from crime. They were not dishonest, and there was no petty thieving or roguery among them; they used to say they were too proud for that sort of thing. Though scarcely belonging to any caste, they were not given to intoxication, and rarely drank spirits; few even touched *sendhee*, which is the sap of the palm, fermented in a peculiar manner, and very exciting. In the years that I had been at Shorapoor there were, I think, only two murders among them. They never dreamt of resisting authority in such cases, but gave up the offenders to justice at once. In civil cases I never interfered with their usages, and they never complained of injustice. Their *bhâts*, or bards, and their elders, had a traditional knowledge of their laws and customs, and always attended the *punchayets;* but I do not think there was much difference between their law and that of the Hindoos.

The elders of the clans sat every day on their platform, under the great *neem* tree in the town, and attended to all complaints. They were grateful to me for respecting their former privileges, and elected me *goorekar*, or head executive over all the clans. They certainly never abused their claims, and by working well as rural police, saved me both labour and anxiety. I was very thankful that during my stay no blood had been shed, nor a single shot fired in anger among them.

All the members of the clans had had lands allotted for their original support, which had descended hereditarily. The minimum amount was one *cooroo*, or thirty *beegahs*, but some held as much as three hundred *beegahs* nominal. Ordinarily they farmed these lands themselves, and divided the produce, but never the land, among the family. When general security began to prevail, many took leases for waste lands, and were assisted by me with capital; but it often surprised me to see how much was cleared and planted by them without help. I opened out to them also a new occupation, that of carriers of cotton, and other Shorapoor products, *to* the coast; and of salt, spices, and English piece-goods *from* the coast,—and this business was proving very profitable. I introduced the best seed of cotton and other produce that I could get, and established a small manufacture of indigo, and tried by every means in my power to promote peaceful and civilised undertakings. I think, and hope, that I left these wild people better than I found them; they certainly were more prosperous. They were highly honourable, and once they had really solemnly sworn faith to me they never swerved. Not even their Rajah could tempt them when he tried; and they told him very sternly that they had pledged their faith to me, and till I made them over to him they would not break it—nor did they.

As a class these men were fine athletic fellows, constantly exercised in gymnastics and in the use of arms. They lived well, eating no meat except game; and they were comfortably housed, their habitations having solid mud, or mud and stone walls, and clay terraced roofs. There was no savagery among them, such as prevails among the Bheels and Gonds, and other tribes.

Their ordinary dress was a pair of loose trousers, of cotton cloth, descending to the calf of the leg; a turban, and waistband, with a chintz tunic for festal occasions. Their hunting or war costume was a brown leather cap, gathered in round the head; brown leather drawers over the cotton ones; and a leather jerkin or jacket without sleeves: they only carried swords. Their women were well made, strong and hardy, and very cleanly in their persons and in their homes, and were excellent housewives, making their husbands' clothes, spinning yarn for the weavers, and working in the fields, watering crops, and suchlike. It was rare to hear of a Beydur having more than one wife, and they were kind to their women as a rule.

The moral character of these people was very high, and such infidelities as did rarely occur were tried among themselves at their own *punchayets*. They were very illiterate, and considered it "low" to be able to read or write, or cast accounts. That was the work of Brahmins! They joined in some of the Brahminical observances of the State, and the *Dussera*, and the *Ooaydee* or *Bussunt*, were always attended by them. The *Dussera* I have before mentioned as a State pageant; the *Bussunt*, or Springtide, was very different. In the morning all the clans in Shorapoor assembled on the hills around, dressed in clothes dyed yellow, and, accompanied by their horn-blowers, drummers, flag-bearers, and pipers, marched to the open space before the great temple on the terrace where the Rajah and I used to sit. Games were then begun—wrestling, leaping, &c.; but that most appreciated was climbing the poles. Six of these, from twenty to thirty feet high, were put up, each with a small pavilion at the top, in which sat a man provided with jars of some slippery mixture. Large slices of pumpkin hung from the bottom of this cage, and the feat was to tear away one or more of these slices, and it was no easy task. Four, six, or eight stout fellows placed themselves round the base of the pole, others climbed on their shoulders, others again upon them, and so on, until one essayed to swarm from the last to the top, amidst clapping of hands and shouting. Meanwhile the man in the cage diligently emptied his jars of slippery stuff and water over them all, and often the whole structure would collapse, and the men fall in a heap. When any fellow, stronger and more fortunate than the rest, did succeed in snatching away the prize, the excitement was unbounded, and he was brought in triumph to the Rajah to receive his reward. These people also had a very popular game, which closely resembled prison-bars; and I taught them leap-frog, taking a back myself at first; and I have seen hundreds flying merrily over each other. I also introduced racing in sacks, which caused great amusement. Besides these sports, they had marbles, peg-tops, hop-scotch, and trap, as well as kite-flying, each in its season, as with us; and it was curious to find these games amongst a people who had never known the English; they were played, too, exactly in the same manner as with us, and are universal throughout India. Beydurs are keen sportsmen; with their sharp spears they attack panthers, wild hog, and often even tigers, fearlessly. They are skilled at hawking, both with large falcons and sparrow-hawks, training the latter to kill quail, larks, and snipe; and the former, partridges, wild duck, floriken, and hares. The last mentioned, however, were generally drawn into nets, and then knocked on the head with sticks. A sporting Beydur, "specially got up," was a very grand fellow indeed. He wore a large handkerchief tied round his head, of some showy pattern in brilliant colours. In the centre of his forehead was a large patch of crimson, which was brought down to the end of his nose, and across his eyes he had drawn his hand covered with dry ashes. Dabs of crimson ornamented his back, round which a delicate muslin scarf of some bright colour was brought and tied in a bow, the ends being finished with some gold tinsel ribbon, which hung down in front. Round his loins was wound a strong piece of cloth, with a knife stuck in at the waist. His trousers, tight round the body, looser to the knee, and after that very wide to the ankle, are generally white, or of pale salmon colour. His sandals are nicely oiled; and altogether, with his falcon or sparrow-hawk on his wrist, his two dogs at his heels, and a stout quarterstaff in his hand, he was an imposing, handsome-looking fellow, and was quite aware of the fact! Some wear gold ear-rings, silver rings above the elbow round the arm, and silver waist-chain. Sometimes a father took his little son out with him; and these juvenile "swells," dressed exactly to resemble their fathers, sparrow-hawk and all, were very amusing.

I need not attempt to describe the ordinary classes. They resembled most others of the Deccan, mixed Mussulman and Hindoo, but were ruder in manners than the corresponding classes in the British and Mussulman territories of the Nizam. They were industrious farmers, and the way in which they reared and cultivated American cotton-seed, and applied their capital to increase the produce of their country, was admirable. They were litigious and quarrelsome. In heavy criminal cases I employed courts, or *punchayets*, of the chief persons at Shorapoor, Lingayets, Hindoos, and Mussulmans, without exclusiveness as to their class, and including members of the Rajah's family; a President was then selected, and specific charges or indictments made against the prisoners. The evidence for prosecution and defence was recorded, and the court gave written judgment, which contained summing up and sentence. I found this plan very simple and efficacious, and the proceedings were always carried on with the greatest regularity. Where sentence of death was recorded, as in murders, the judgment was translated by me, with the evidence and defence, and forwarded, through the Resident, to the Governor-General for confirmation ; and I had not one instance of disapproval to record. Cases involving fine and imprisonment, with hard labour or without it, I used to try myself. No law had ever existed in Shorapoor, nor even the semblance of a court of justice, civil or criminal. Ordinary civil suits were tried by civil *punchayets* not limited to five members, and there were but few appeals to me from their decisions.

The population of the principality by census was about 500,000, or 130 to the square mile. The town itself and its suburbs 30,000.

The public dispensary and hospital at Shorapoor were very useful, and medicines were dispensed under the orders of the apothecary attached to the staff. In visitations of cholera, medicines were sent out into the districts, and competent persons despatched in charge of them. Vaccination made great progress at Shorapoor ; and in the country I myself was the chief operator, my tents being surrounded every morning by crowds of women and children so long as my supplies of lymph lasted or could be obtained.

My school at Shorapoor was well attended, and both Mahratta and Teloogoo, with Persian to Mussulman boys, were well taught. I had even a few English scholars, some of whom turned out well. In the districts there were plenty of schools, where Canarese and Mahratta were taught ; and to these I gave small grants in aid, and books which were used in the schools of the British provinces.

I have already spoken of what I had begun and done in public works. The lake at Bohnal was a complete success, and had repaid the money spent upon it several times over. The other irrigation works were incomplete, and there was but small hope that the Rajah would carry them on, although he promised very faithfully to do so. One grand scheme I formed—that of diverting the waters of the river Krishna from their bed, and bringing them through most part of the principality for irrigation purposes—had to be abandoned for want of funds, though perfectly practicable, as I had ascertained by levels.

I had made and cleared many roads, one of which extended to Linsoogoor, through a wild and rocky tract, for 36 miles, and opened up traffic between Shorapoor and the south.

I had planted many thousand mango and tamarind trees about the town and elsewhere, intended both for ornament and produce. When I left, the road to the Krishna, six miles in length, was bordered on each side by a double row of fine young trees, which gave ample promise of fruit. All these undertakings were gradually accomplished without distressing the revenue in any way; indeed there were ample funds for all such contingencies.

I have not the final returns of the revenue at hand to refer to, but I know that it was nearly if not quite doubled; and with the average liberal expenditure, there was a surplus of a lakh and a half. There were no debts whatever now, and I think, when I made over charge to the Rajah, that the State possessed every element of comfort and independence that could insure prosperity; but there was small hope of its continuance.

Even in the brief period that had already elapsed the Rajah had spent every anna he found in the treasury, had not paid the stipendiaries, and had only the usual year's

revenue to look to.   My warnings on this point had been
quite fruitless.

I need say little of myself.   Since my great sorrow I
had led a cheerless, lonely life ; no society, no one to speak
to from first to last, except the very rare visit of a friend
or traveller.   The palace children often came to see me,
and loved to hold their dolls' feasts among my flowers
with their playmates.   Native friends would come up in
the evenings, and a game of chess with one or other often
followed.   In the country, the village authorities would
gather round to hear of England and the world beyond
India, of which they had no conception whatever.   Sometimes travelling minstrels or singers, accredited from other
courts, such as Mysore, Baroda, Gwalior, or elsewhere,
arrived, and the State hospitality was exercised, and performances given and attended, and on these occasions I
gave my parties.

Neighbouring " lairds " had to be received and entertained, for Shorapoor had to maintain its character for
hospitality and kindly feeling to those adjoining it.

My books were my constant delight, and with these
and my telescope, a fine Dollond, I had always plenty of
occupation.   I read up Herschel, and other works on
astronomy, to enable me to understand something of what
I saw.   Night after night I have thus wandered about
those glorious fields of the heavens, ever new, ever re-
splendent, leading thought irresistibly into the Infinite.
I could not go on with literary work, as, at the day's close,
my brain was generally wearied out.   My work was
seldom less than twelve hours a-day, with little variation,
so to write was impossible ; but I felt I was gaining more
and more real knowledge of native life and character,
under circumstances that fall to the lot of very few
Englishmen, and that hereafter, if life were spared, I
might turn my experience to good account.   I kept up
voluminous private correspondence, particularly with my

father; and this, with my usual letters to the 'Times,' official reports and translations, and occasional articles for the Indian press, were all I could manage to get through in my busy life. I was very thankful for the many blessings given me, and tried to discourage the feeling of utter loneliness that would at times oppress me.

Ten years of my life were given to Shorapoor—a blank to me in many respects as regarded intellectual intercourse and literary progress; but yet, with all its drawbacks, more interesting than the dull routine of a small cantonment.

Now they had passed over, and a new phase of my life was opening before me in an enlarged and more important sphere of action. Through all danger, through all illnesses and weariness and trials, I had been mercifully preserved and tenderly protected, and was grateful to God for His great mercies—praying that in the future they might be continued unto me.

CHAPTER XIII.

1853-57.

ALTHOUGH suffering from a severe attack of acute rheumatism, I, with my assistant, Lieut. Cadell, pressed on to Sholapoor, where it was necessary that I should meet the Collector, who congratulated me very heartily on my appointment to the district, which joined his own, and we could work together with good accord, and looked forward to much pleasant intercourse from time to time.

My assistant had no knowledge whatever, or experience, in civil affairs; but I thought it best to place him at once in a prominent position, and to give him general directions which, as he was very clever and willing, I thought would suffice. I therefore made over to him part of the small establishment I had collected, and directed him to take possession of all the ceded districts which lay along the left bank of the Seenah river, between it and the range of hills that formed the "Bálá Ghât," or upper portion of the whole province; and with an escort of cavalry he set out to do what he could.

Fortunately the cession had been made at the close of the financial year, so there was no confusion of demand and account between the outgoing administration and the incoming one. I did not anticipate any opposition; but the British forces at Sholapoor and Ahmednugger had been warned to hold themselves ready to assist me in case any resistance might be made.

Nuldroog had been fixed upon as my headquarters, and I proceeded there without delay. I found a squadron of the Contingent cavalry encamped without the fort, which was in the possession of a large body of Arabs, who refused to allow the cavalry to enter, and whose temper appeared very doubtful.

At first, too, I was refused admittance. Their chief declared that he held a large mortgage on the fort and its dependencies, and that his men were in arrears of pay, and that until all his demands were settled, or I gave him a guarantee from the British Government that they would be settled, he would not give me up the fort. I, however, took no notice of his demands whatever. I told him the Nizam's Government was the only one with which he could have dealings, and that if he and his men did not at once march out, I had no resource but to summon the military force at Shorapoor, when I could not answer for the consequences. All the Arabs blustered a great deal, but finally retired inside to consider matters ; and a message was brought to me in the evening, to the effect that in the morning the fort would be given up. And so it was ; and as soon as they had bivouacked outside on the esplanade, I marched in at the head of my splendid cavalry escort, hoisted the English flag I had with me, and took possession forthwith. I should have regretted exceedingly if the obstinacy of these Arabs had brought about any collision, for their example was looked to by all the various parties of Arabs in the province ; and had they resisted my authority, all the rest would have done so too, and the Arab chiefs of Hyderabad were almost in possession of the whole tract.

They held it in assignment for their pay and debts ; and it was a convenient district for them, as fresh men could constantly reach them from Bombay and the coast without attracting observation, and be forwarded to Hyderabad to reinforce the main body. Also many private individuals

living at Hyderabad possessed estates and villages in the
province, and had mortgaged them to the Arabs—so that,
in point of fact, the whole area was under their control,
with very little exception; and the tenacity with which
they stuck to their possessions, whether for arrears of pay
or any other monetary consideration, had been too often
experienced to be doubted now. The Arabs in my fort of
Nuldroog could not have held it against any force, as the
guns were useless ; but had they continued their opposition, our occupation of the country would have assumed
a very different aspect, and might have caused a disturbance and collision with the Arabs at Hyderabad—a consequence which would have had, in all likelihood, serious
results.

Although I had often before been at Nuldroog, I had
never seen the interior of the fort, nor the English house
belonging to it, which had been built by the late Nawab,
who in old times had been a great friend of mine. The
ladies of his family had used it, and now it was to become
my residence. I found it a handsome building, although
not very commodious. In the centre was a large hall,
with two semicircular rooms on each side ; above the hall,
a bedroom of corresponding size, with bath-room attached,
from which there was a beautiful view all over the fort,
the town, and the adjacent country. In front there was
a broad veranda, supported upon pillars, and near at hand
the portion set apart for the zenana, and which was still
occupied by the ladies, who were to leave shortly. In the
fort itself were several massive buildings, terraced and
bomb-proof, which had been used in former days as
barracks, hospital, powder-magazine, and guard-houses.
There were also some other good native houses—all empty
now, but useful for my English clerks and escort, and for
conversion into treasury, jail, and public *cucherry*, or court,
until more commodious buildings could be erected, or
possibly another head station fixed upon.

The fort of Nuldroog was one of the most interesting places I had ever seen. It enclosed the surface of a knoll or plateau of basalt rock, which jutted out into the valley or ravine of the small river Boree from the main plateau of the country, and was almost level. The sides of this knoll were sheer precipices of basalt, here and there showing distinct columnar and prismatic formation, and varied from 50 to 200 feet in height; the edge of the plateau being more or less 200 feet above the river, which flowed at the base of the precipice on two sides of the fort. Along the crest of the cliff, on three sides, ran the fortifications, bastions, and curtains alternately, some of the former being very firmly built of cut and dressed basalt, and large enough to carry heavy guns, and the parapets of the machicolated curtains were everywhere loopholed for musketry. On the west side the promontory joined the main plateau by a somewhat contracted neck, also strongly fortified by a high rampart, with very roomy and massive bastions ; below it a *faussebraye*, with the same ; then a broad, deep, dry ditch, cut for the most part out of the basalt itself ; a counterscarp, about 20 or 25 feet high, with a covered-way ; and beyond it, a glacis and esplanade up to the limits of the town.

The entire circumference of the *enceinte* might have been about a mile and a half, and the garrison in former times must have been very large, for nearly the whole of the interior was covered by ruined walls, and had been laid out as a town with a wide street running up the centre. All the walls and bastions were in perfect repair, and the effect of the fort outside was not only grim and massive, but essentially picturesque.

Nuldroog held a memorable place in local history. Before the Mussulman invasion in the fourteenth century, it belonged to a local Rajah, who may have been a feudal vassal of the great Rajahs of the Chalukya dynasty, A.D. 250 to 1200, whose capital was Kullianee, about 40 miles

distant; but I never could trace its history with any
certainty, and during the Hindoo period it was only traditional. The Bahmany dynasty, A.D. 1351 to 1480, protected their dominions to the west by a line of massive
forts, of which Nuldroog was one; and it was believed
that the former defences, which were little more than mud
walls, were replaced by them with fortifications of stone.
Afterwards, on the division of the Bahmany kingdom, in
A.D. 1480, Nuldroog fell to the lot of the Adil Shahy kings
of Beejapoor; and they, in their turn, greatly increased
and strengthened its defences. It was often a point of
dissension between the Adil Shahy and the Nizam Shahy
potentates—lying, as it did, upon the nominal frontier
between Beejapoor and Ahmednugger—and was besieged
by both in turn, as the condition of the walls on the
southern face bore ample testimony, as well from the
marks of cannon-balls as from breaches which had afterwards been filled up. In 1558 Ali Adil Shah visited
Nuldroog, and again added to its fortifications, rebuilt the
western face, and constructed an enormous cavalier near
the eastern end, which was upwards of 90 feet high, with
several bastions on the edges of the cliff; but his greatest
work was the erection of a stone dam across the river
Boree, which, by retaining the water above it, afforded the
garrison an unlimited supply. I quote from a letter to
my father, written a few days after my arrival:—

"I was greatly delighted and surprised by the view
from the back of the house, where there is a balcony.
You look up and down a valley, in which there is a fine
brawling stream; and about a quarter of a mile below the
house a huge dam of solid masonry has been built across
the ravine, which holds the water back, and forms a
pretty little lake. Above this, on the south side, the
walls of the fort are built on the side of a precipice of
about 50 feet to the water's edge, and the tall grim bastions have a fine effect. The dam connects the main fort

with one opposite to it on a knoll on the north of the lake,
whose bastions and curtains extend down the north side
of the ravine; so on looking down you see the two forts,
one on each side of the valley, the lake between, and the
precipices beyond.   The dam is truly wonderful—it is
90 feet high, 300 yards long, and 100 feet broad at the
top.   The river at its ordinary height runs over the crest
of the dam in channels arched over, and the water falls
into the pool; but when there is a flood, the whole of the
water runs over the crest of the dam, forming a huge cataract, and is indeed a magnificent spectacle.   About the
centre of the dam there is a flight of steps by which you
descend into a small, beautifully-ornamented room, in the
Saracenic-Gothic style; and there is a very ingenious
contrivance by which, even when the river is in full flood
and the cataract falling in front of the balcony of the
room, the water which comes down the staircase is turned
off down a tunnel in another direction, and cannot enter
the room.   The look-out from this apartment is extremely
picturesque—the great pool below, the sides of the ravine
clothed with shrubs and creepers, and the brawling waters
as they run down the valley, forming altogether a striking
and very beautiful picture, of a character I had never
before seen."

It may easily be imagined that I was quite content
with my new quarters; and in a few days' time, when all
the rooms had been well washed out, and the broken
panes in the excellent English glass doors and windows
repaired, my pictures hung up, my precious books un-
packed, and some furniture and carpets I had brought
with me placed in the large room, the result was a very
comfortable apartment.   There was, too, a good garden
about the house, which was very soon cleaned up, and
eventually became one of my greatest pleasures—for no-
where that I had been in India did English flowers and
vegetables grow so well; and there were several fine

orange-trees and vines too, which, when properly looked after, gave abundant produce, as did the other fruit-trees, with which the garden was well stocked.

My first task was to take stock of my new province. Its boundaries had been ill defined at Hyderabad, and had to be rectified before the whole could be brought well together. To the west, the river Seenah, from a point nine miles from Ahmednugger to its junction with the Bheema, formed an excellent general line. Inside this lay portions of British territory belonging to the Collectorate of Sholapoor; but that did not signify. To the north a range of mountains, which bordered the valley of the Godavery, formed another distinct frontier. The river Manjera, which flowed eastwards, rising among these mountains, gave another distinctly-defined boundary to a certain point, where it diverged; and from this point to Afzulpoor on the Bheema, an arbitrary line had been drawn, which, as it included several large counties that were private estates belonging to one of the chief nobles of Hyderabad, could not be attached. Within the general boundary, too, many portions had either been wilfully concealed or improperly and dishonestly retained. However, the whole province, as defined in the treaty, would have been more than was really required; and in the end, after I had gone over the whole carefully, my boundaries became more definite, and it was satisfactory to think that all the country lying within them was under my own control.

As fast as I could get them, I despatched managers to the different head-centres of counties with my orders, and to convey my assurances of goodwill to the people. The Arabs were fast betaking themselves to Hyderabad, and neither my assistant nor I had experienced any except very temporary difficulties from them. In almost less than one month I was able to report that we had established the authority of the British Government of India

T

in every part of the province. My assistant's father, Mr
Cadell, was an eminent Writer to the Signet in Edinburgh; and I was much amused when he wrote to his
son that the proceedings of two men, with a small escort
of cavalry, taking possession coolly of a province half as
large as Scotland, with a strange population, were, to his
perception, the "most consummate piece of assurance" he
had ever heard of; and "pray, how were we going to
govern it?" Our district was rather more than 15,000
square miles in area; but though the shrewd old Scotch
lawyer saw, I daresay, a thousand difficulties, I saw none
which could not be overcome by patience, hard work, and
steady perseverance.

It was a fine climate, fortunately, and very healthy.
The tract lying between the Seenah river and the hills
was lower than the rest; but it was open, free from
jungle, and for the most part well cultivated. From it
the basalt plateau named the "Bálá Ghát" rose to a
height varying from 400 to 1000 feet, some of the
highest summits showing 2400 feet above the level
of the sea. This plateau, culturable from its very edge,
sloped gradually eastwards to the Manjera river, and
joined the northern mountain boundary, which extended
to Ahmednugger.

Nuldroog itself lay 2200 feet above the level of the sea;
and, compared with Shorapoor, the climate, even during
the hottest part of the year, was much less trying,
while in the cold season it was very cold indeed, and
not unfrequently frosty.

The "Bálá Ghát" was renowned all through the Deccan
for its luxuriant crops of wheat and barley, pulse and oil-
seed. Cotton did not thrive, and what was produced was
of very short fibre, harsh and unfit for export. Sugar-
cane grew well, and there was a good supply of hemp
and linseed; but the beautiful white millet of Shorapoor was
wanting, and that grown was coarse and hard in comparison.

I had known the people before when I was a boy, and
many still remembered me and my red trousers, and came
to see me. The population was almost entirely agricultural—thrifty, industrious, practical farmers and gentry,
who tilled their somewhat hard soil with singular perseverance and success; they were better farmers than
those at Shorapoor, and kept improving their fields till
they would have done credit to an English landowner.

I had liked the people in my early days because of their
sturdy, independent character. Mahratta was the only
language spoken, and this I had at my command—a circumstance which, I felt sure, would inspire confidence,
for everybody soon knew that they could come to me and
speak out their minds freely whenever they had occasion,
without any go-between, or interpretation, being necessary.
I knew, too, that the normal crime of the district, *dacoity*,
not only still existed, but was largely and desperately
practised—and this, which had defied me in former years,
must now be eradicated with a strong hand.

I believe that the people at large, with the exception
of the small portion forming the hereditary criminal
class, welcomed the new rule with sincere delight. They
knew it meant security of their land and possessions, as
well as justice and protection, and extension and protection of trade. Those who were unacquainted with the
working and ways of English rule in other districts were,
perhaps, somewhat disturbed at first at the idea, but they
were few, and the feeling soon wore off.

When I took possession of the province, there was no
court of law or justice whatever, civil or criminal, any
more than there had been at Shorapoor, and none such
had ever existed within the memory of any person. The
agents of the Nizam's Government, and the Arabs, used
to punish gross criminal offences, and, in some cases, petty
thefts; but in the great crime of *dacoity* all seemed to
have had a share, inasmuch as the agent always received

part, according to his share, of the property stolen! As for murder, no one ever noticed it, or thought of bringing the perpetrators to account.

After a great deal of very hard work—during almost night and day while it lasted—I had gained, partly from old accounts and partly from the details sent in from my new managers, a tolerably correct estimate of the resources of the province, which I submitted in a report to the Resident.

If I had taken the province according to the estimates and orders of transfer of the late minister and the *duftar-dars* of Hyderabad, I should have had a revenue of about *two and a half lakhs,* and a few scattered portions of territory, and there would have remained within my boundary-line large tracts of country not under my jurisdiction. This would have caused much confusion and vexatious embarrassment, and probably constant disputes would have arisen. Now, when I had got all together in a kind of ring-fence, as it were, I found, according to my rough estimate, that I should have about *eleven and a half lakhs* of Hyderabad rupees.

Colonel Low was just going away to Calcutta to be sworn in as a member of the Supreme Council; and before he went, he wrote me his very hearty approval of what I had been able to effect in so short a time, and particularly his great satisfaction at the complete and bloodless expulsion of the Arabs.

I must here, likewise, record my grateful thanks and remembrance of the very essential services rendered to me in respect to the latter by the native officers and men of the cavalry detachments sent for my assistance. The native officers were all gentlemen by birth, most intelligent, and highly respected by the people wherever they went. They proved excellent negotiators, and were fully trusted by all, even by the Arabs themselves.

At Owsa, a far stronger fort than Nuldroog, my

manager presented my letter to the Arab chief commanding the garrison, requesting him to evacuate the place.
The request was indignantly refused ; but on the appearance of a squadron of cavalry which I sent to my officer's
assistance, the Arabs received the native officers with
"honours," marched out at once, and gave up all the
large dependencies they had held in mortgage from the
Nizam's Government without any demur.   Owsa was the
last, indeed the only place, that caused me any anxiety ;
and I knew that the Resident had also been very anxious
about it, owing to its reputed great strength and the large
number of its garrison.   In Owsa, Purraindah, and Nuldroog, I now held the three strongest forts of the Deccan ;
yet all had submitted without using any violence, and no
further display of force than I have mentioned.

So ended my preliminary operations in my new province ; and I was about to leave Nuldroog, in order to
start on a tour through the district, when I received a
note from the Collector at Sholapoor asking me to come
to him and arrange many matters pending between us.
The prospect of a little holiday and society was very
pleasant, and I went.   His wife was an excellent musician
—both sang delightfully ; and it was a great treat to me to
hear once more the music of great composers skilfully executed, and to try my own voice in concerted pieces—a
pleasure to which I had for so long been a stranger.   They
were very kind and very patient with me; but I fear I
gave the ladies some trouble, I had grown so rusty.

Owing to my very unsettled life latterly, my letters to
the 'Times' had become irregular, and I could not keep
up the necessary communications for news which were required for fortnightly letters.

There were no posts through my district ; and letters
and newspapers would, of necessity, reach me very irregu-
larly, while the same objection applied to my despatch of
letters.   I reflected, also, that whereas hitherto my posi-

tion at Shorapoor had left me comparatively independent,
I was not so in my new appointment, and that I was not
justified in writing so unrestrainedly on political subjects
as I had been used to do. I therefore resigned my office
of " special correspondent " to the great paper, which, from
first to last, had uniformly treated my opinions and contributions with the greatest courtesy.

I could not, either, agree with the now confirmed
annexation policy of Lord Dalhousie, which began in
1853, and seemed likely to be continued ; and I knew
that among the people generally the annexations of Jhansi
and Nagpore, and the transactions in regard to the latter
especially, were spoken of with unmeasured mistrust and
suspicion. The proceedings in the Bombay Presidency in
regard to the inquiry into free lands, charitable grants,
and the like, had been, or was being, badly conducted,
and had excited much discontent. My very outspoken
Mahrattas took no pains to conceal their censure of the
conduct of Government as evincing a spirit of greed
and bad faith which was strange and painful to many of
them, and in these views people and gentry alike coincided.

During my period of connection with the ' Times,' however, I had enjoyed the privilege of discussing and explaining, as far as possible, all the great subjects which
pertained to the period : education and its results on the
people—for vernacular education had long since become a
declared policy—trade, railways and communication of all
kinds, cotton cultivation, irrigation in all its forms, along
with the general political events of the previous ten years,
momentous as they had been. I do not know whether
these humble efforts of mine had any effect in bringing
India and its people, its interests, and its increase of
civilisation, more directly under the notice of thinking
people in England. I hope so ; and I was vain enough
to think they might have some such effect, as they were

generally backed up by leading articles in the paper itself, and thus attained some importance.

Now, there were other correspondents in the field, newspaper articles were better written, and their number had increased largely, so that the exponents of India's condition and wants were manifold, and there was no use in my continuing to send communications which must necessarily be unconnected and desultory. My correspondence all these years with my faithful friend Reeve never slackened, and his letters were a great source of pleasure and encouragement to me in my work, and kept me informed of what was going on in the political and literary circles in London, so that I did not feel quite so much my exclusion from them.

On my return from my pleasant little stay at Sholapoor, I went out to my tents, which were pitched at Tooljapoor, my old favourite resort in 1825. How beautiful it was ! The hills were all clothed with verdure, and the view from my tent was lovely. On the north side of the promontory where I was, lay the town, built on both sides of a deep ravine, and at its head the celebrated shrine of Bhowanee or Kalee, which lay in the hollow beneath—not indeed, in itself, a remarkable edifice at all, but surrounded by picturesque cloisters and courts, always thronged by pilgrims, and which formed a curious combination of all kinds of Hindoo architecture.

Above the temple towered rugged cliffs on either side, and the ravine opened out into a large amphitheatre, bounded by precipitous hills that seemed like buttresses to the plateau above. To the south was a great undulating plain, stretching to the dim blue horizon, dotted by thriving villages, surrounded by luxuriant cultivation, and checkered by ever-varying masses of light and shade. The line of the hills and plateau extending towards the east or Nuldroog direction, was broken by headlands and ravines descending to the lower country. There was no wood, it is true; but the diversified outlines, now rugged, and again more regular, redeemed the landscape from any monotony.

The climate was delightful, like that of an English summer-day, in turn cloudy and sunshiny, with occasional light showers. On the day of my arrival, I had just breakfasted, and sat down to begin work in my *cucherry*, or office tent, when an old Brahmin came in, and for a time sat down quietly in a corner without speaking. Seeing that I was alone, he came up to my table, and peering closely into my face as he leant upon his staff, he said, " Are you the Taylor Sahib who came here many years ago ? "

When I answered that I was the same, he produced a bundle of old papers, and asked me whether I recollected them. As I looked over them, I saw that I had put my initials to each of them, but forgot at the moment why I had done so; for in any case of inquiry or settlement it was my habit to initial all the papers, and I thought these documents must relate to some old claim or suit to be revised. I was soon undeceived.

"Have you forgotten, sahib," said the old man, "that I once cast your horoscope, and told you that you would return here to govern us after many years ? And see! it was true!—you have come; and, indeed, there is little difference in the time I recorded—twenty-five years! I had not the exact data, if you remember, that I wanted— you could not give it to me."

It was all true enough ; there I was, the " ruler " over them, and I then recollected how strange it had appeared to me at the Residency when my destination was so suddenly altered from Berar to these western districts, on the requisition of the Government of Bombay. The prediction had certainly been a strange one, and was as strangely fulfilled, even to the very letter of time.

"And you have been a 'rajah,' too," continued my old

friend, " and have governed a country to the south for ten years; that I recorded—see, sahib!" and he pointed excitedly to the document.   " See, there is no mistake there either!"

" Not quite a ' rajah,'" I said, laughing, " only manager of the country while the rajah was a child."

" It was all the same," returned the old Brahmin; "you were all-powerful, and just like a rajah, and you governed the people.   And you have seen sorrow too, sahib; you were not married when you were here, and now you have lost wife and dear children, I hear?   I wrote that.   I saw it all plainly—it is here.   And you are not rich, they tell me?   Yet lakhs of rupees have passed through your hands. Did I not tell you that too?"

" No, indeed," I replied, " I am not rich; indeed much the reverse, and I have had heavy sorrows."

" It could not be avoided," he said; " no one could have mistaken what I discovered just twenty-five years ago.   You were born for work, not for the indulgence of wealthy idleness, and so you will continue.   If you want these papers I will give them to you; if not, let them remain with me," and so saying, he took his leave.   He soon afterwards went on a pilgrimage to Nassik, and there died.

I did not want the papers, and he kept them.   I cannot account for his prediction.   I only relate what happened.   I told my old Serishtadar, Baba Sahib, about my horoscope and its results; but he was not in the least surprised.

" We Brahmins," he said, " believe in astrology, and you English laugh at it; but when one who understands the art casts a horoscope and calculates it scientifically, the result is seldom wrong.   You were to have gone to Berar, and yet your fate has brought you here to Tooljapoor again, at the very time appointed, twenty-five years after, in spite of yourself and also of the Resident.   Can you doubt, after this? Is there not more in astrology than you believed?"

I made no comment. How could I, in the face of the simple facts that had occurred?

It was the rainy season, but there was so much to see after that could only be done on the spot in each division of my district, that my personal convenience must not be studied in any way; and I marched along the edge of the plateau from one division to another, halting at the head station of each for the purpose of investigating old accounts, records of cultivation and the like, and, above all, gaining as I went, knowledge of the people.

A settlement of the country for five years had been directed, and inquiries were necessary before any attempt could be made to carry out the measure. I did not even know what the revenue of the whole district might amount to; and the accounts received from Hyderabad, if not actually designed to mislead, were at all events most incorrect and incomprehensible, proving to be of no use whatever. I therefore began at the foundation—the village accounts—and was glad to see that they had been far better kept than those of Shorapoor, when I began a like inquiry there. The village accountant had proper lists of proprietors and occupants of land, according to the ancient Deccan system, which had never been altered, however much it might have been abused; and among the records of some of the chief towns and villages, were ancient settlements of the officers of the Bahmany kings of Gulburgah and Beeder, and the Adil Shahys of Beejapoor. The most regular and valuable records were the settlements by Mullik Umber, the great regent of the Ahmednugger State, which were more minute than those of the Emperor Akbar, and were founded upon an actual survey of the lands and their assessment, according to their productive quality. But these had only been preserved here and there, and it would be impossible to found any new settlement upon those that existed as a basis for all. The Nizam's Government had taken no record of cultivation; but the sums received from villages were entered in an account for every *talook*, or division, which was signed by the hereditary ministerial officers of each county, and which, up to the last financial year, had been regularly sent up to the head accountant's office at Hyderabad. From these documents, compared with the village accounts and registries, I could see my way to a new form of account which would embrace all particulars; and copies of these forms were made by the village accountants, to be filled up when the yearly period of settlement arrived.

It was very tedious work; but unless it were done, it would be impossible to submit to Government any clear or complete statement of the general revenue, or whence it was derived. My progress was necessarily very slow.

In the original instructions given to the Deputy-Commissioners, they had been directed to make use of the existing local courts of the Nizam's Government for the trial of all cases, civil and criminal: but as no local tribunal or judicial office of any kind was found by me, and none had existed for years, I determined to introduce a code of laws of my own, civil as well as criminal; and I took the regulations of Bombay as my guide, drawing up a short definition of crimes and their punishments—and in civil cases, of general procedure,—simple and intelligible to all classes. I assigned various powers to *patells*, or heads of villages, to *talook* officers, to my assistant, and to myself—mine being the highest court of appeal in the province from the decisions of subordinate courts, and the Resident being the final one to whom all appeals against me were to be referred.

This code and general plan of mine were approved of as a temporary measure at Calcutta, and I put it in force as soon as it was sanctioned. It lasted till Macaulay's penal code was sent for a practical trial in the assigned districts, but the civil procedure I had drawn up was, I think, retained. These, with instructions for the guidance of police, revenue proceedings and collections, and for the conduct of every department, occupied a great deal of my time : but all were as brief and concise as possible, though necessarily embracing every point for general direction.

After Colonel Low's departure from the post of Resident at Hyderabad, several distinguished officers were named as his probably successors. Sir Henry Lawrence, to whom I believe Lord Dalhousie offered the appointment, and my old friend James Outram, whom I would have gladly welcomed, were among those talked of ; but as the office of Resident now involved the head administration of the assigned districts, and as everything in regard to them was still in an incomplete state, a civilian of administrative experience was held to be the fittest person ; and Mr Bushby, once an assistant to the Resident at Hyderabad, was appointed to the office, which, until his arrival, was conducted with much ability by (then) Captain Davidson.

It was his wish, as it had been that of Colonel Low, that my district should have a well-defined frontier ; and all the boundaries, except those to the north, had been gradually adjusted. I had even been exempted from the vexatious task of administering justice and police affairs in the reserved portions which lay along the Bheema to the south-west, and they remained under the charge of their native proprietors. But to the north, on the borders of the Ahmednugger and Nizam's territory, there remained a small tract, hitherto undefined, and often much disturbed, the British and Nizam's villages lying confusedly together.

This was by far the prettiest and most picturesque portion of my province. The plateau of the "Bálá Ghát" continued to the hills forming the Ahmednugger range ; but at one point it lowered considerably, breaking into ravines, which ran south towards the Seenah, and north-east to the Godavery, a very rough tract, with a corresponding rough class of inhabitants, who required to be kept well under control.

While encamped at Patoda, the station of my native collector, I explored the whole of the crest of the plateau towards the north-west, and found the scenery very beautiful. There was no jungle, but the grassy hills afforded fine pasturage for cattle, and the views from the summits of the highest knolls were, in some instances, very grand.

In one place a small river, the Incherna, which received the drainage of a great portion of these hills, fell into the lower level of the western portion of my district with one leap of 398 feet, sheer perpendicular fall, and now, being well filled with water, formed one of the most graceful waterfalls I have ever seen. I did not expect to come upon anything so grand or picturesque as this fall and the basalt chasm into which it precipitated itself, and I was lost in admiration, remaining at the place for several days, in order to sketch the ravine and waterfall from every point of view. I have described it fully in my novel of 'Seeta,' to which I refer any curious reader who may wish to know more.

I descended by a well-known pass to the low country north of my district, and found, as I had anticipated from a copy of the trigonometrical survey map, exactly the frontier I desired. A considerable stream flowed from the west, almost in a direct line eastwards. Its name was the Suitana; while a smaller one, the Domeri, rising on the plateau, flowed due north, and fell into it. Within this line were sixteen scattered villages of the Nizam's mingled with British villages and my own; and after representing the difficulty of maintaining all three jurisdictions in a state of amity, they were transferred entirely to me, under the orders of the Nizam's Government. The whole tract had been in a state of chronic feud for years, and the

correspondence and other references, regarding all manner
of disputes, had been vexatious and endless. I found no
less than *seventy* boundary disputes had to be adjusted, of
which I settled the worst, leaving the tract for the final
supervision of my assistant, who now joined me. I determined to proceed to Ahmednugger, in order to confer with
Mr Bell, the Collector there, as I had already done with
Mr Loughman, the Collector of Sholapoor, upon all matters which required settlement.

Cadell had had a little adventure at Purraindah, by far
the strongest fort in the district, situated in his division.
He had not been able to visit it personally before, and
when he arrived the garrison shut-to the gates, mounted
the bastions, and declared they would not give it up. He
might do what he liked with the dependencies, but they were
the garrison, and they declared that until they received
orders from Hyderabad, they would not open the gates.
Finding remonstrance useless, Cadell wrote to me for help,
in the shape of a troop of cavalry, with which he could
watch the place to see that no malcontents got in to help
the garrison. I wrote to the *killadar*, or castellan, desiring
him to evacuate the fort, to which he demurred; and I
then wrote again, saying he *must* do so, or fight, for that
no orders could now come from Hyderabad, the country
having been entirely ceded to the British Government.
The troop of cavalry arriving almost immediately after
my letter reached him, the *killadar* saw that I was in
earnest, and thought " discretion the better part of valour;"
so he opened the gates, and as Cadell marched in and took
possession, the garrison laid down their arms, which he at
once returned to them. He described the place as the
strongest he had seen, and quite perfect in every way, and
there was a very respectable garrison of Rajpoots. I was
glad on every account that the affair had been tided over
so peaceably. I visited Purraindah myself afterwards, and
shall describe it later.

Having made all the arrangements I could in the newly acquired territory of Manoor, I went on to Ahmednugger. One of my villages lay within nine miles of the station, and, owing to its beauty, was a favourite resort for country parties and picnics. I met Mr Bell there, and he hospitably invited both Cadell and myself to his house, where we spent some days very pleasantly at the great station. I had not been there since the year 1826, and found it greatly improved and enlarged.

In my journey both to and from Ahmednugger, I had been much struck with the capabilities of the country for large irrigation works, and in particular for tanks. Streams, descending from the table-lands to the north, and tributaries to the Seenah, afforded ample supplies of water; and the ground, from its peculiar character, provided most convenient basins, which only required dams at certain places across their mouths to be converted into tanks.

In one instance a stream which had a catchment area of upwards of 200 square miles, after leaving the hills, ran through a nearly level plain of about four square miles in area, which ended in two bluffs about a quarter of a mile asunder. A dam of fifty feet high was perfectly practicable at a comparatively small outlay, and the water held back would form a lake twice the size of Bohnal. I determined, with as little delay as possible, to get up a report on the subject, and try to have some works of the kind begun for a country which was absolutely thirsting for water, and where every drop that could be procured from wells or from streams was used for the production of sugar-cane, ginger, turmeric, and other rich and valuable crops.

Mr Bell met us at a village which we had agreed upon, where there was good camping-ground, and which, though under his charge, was within our frontier, and there we passed some days in November very agreeably. As he

had brought his establishment with him, we compared
our work, and he was not a little surprised, I think, to
find mine quite as regular in all respects as his own, except in the revenue department, the particulars of which
we had still to unravel, whereas his had been decided by
survey. I was now settling three divisions in order to
enable my assistant to work for himself; and when these
were completed, I left him, to look after my eastern districts on the table-land, which I had not yet visited.

By the end of the year 1853 the whole was in fair
working order, and giving me no anxiety, except as to the
scarcity which seemed to threaten us owing to failure of
crops. There had been no rain since September, and comparatively little before that. Portions of the Bombay
Presidency were already suffering, and Shorapoor was also
in distress. The accounts from thence were very sad.
Neglect, riot, and crime prevailed; and I was indeed
grateful that, although I was worse paid as a Deputy-
Commissioner than I should have been as Political Agent
there, yet I was spared the pain of seeing all the fair
structure I had striven so long and so hard to raise
rapidly falling into ruin and decay.

All we Deputy-Commissioners had been placed on a
salary of 1200 rupees a-month, as a temporary rate of
payment, and, as yet, we received no " deputation " allowance, but were promised it, to provide for the expenses of
tents and moving about our districts.

When the local officers were pensioned, we hoped that
we, who had now become servants of the Company, might
be granted our Nizam's pensions apart from our pay, as
was at first arranged; but ultimately this was not allowed
—both were included in the pay of a Deputy-Commissioner, a proceeding which I have always considered unjust, for we were not serving the Nizam but the Company;
and if the Government of India had set us aside and sent
its own officers, it would have had to pay both charges

out of the revenue of the cession. When we were transferred to the new service, our rank was recognised in all
respects as those of " Company's officers " of corresponding length of service; but in this respect also were we
painfully deceived—we were placed in the category of
" Uncovenanted servants," by which we lost all our former
rank and privileges, and were reduced in status. One of
our number laid down his rank, and would never resume
it. However, hard as it was, we were grateful for employment at all, though I have never ceased to consider it an
ungenerous act of the great Government of India, to take
advantage, as it seemed, of our necessities, and to give us
lower pay than it gave to its own servants in like employment, and in charge of far smaller districts and with
less responsibilities than ours.

I will state the question clearly in figures. My pension
from the Nizam's Government was 300 rupees a-month, or
£360 a-year; my pay 1200 rupees a-month.

Had I received 1200 rupees a-month and my pension
as well, my receipts would have been 1500 rupees a-month.
Now I was to receive in all 1200 rupees—that is, 900
rupees pay and 300 rupees pension; so the 300 rupees
were saved, which we considered taking rather a mean
advantage of us. We were no more Nizam's servants,
but had been taken over into the Company's service, and,
as such, should have received salaries on the same scale as
those already in their employ.

By the close of the year I had already made considerable progress in the suppression of the terrible normal
crime of dacoity. Several old dacoits had turned approvers, and had given details of robberies and murders, which
had been shockingly numerous. Through them stolen
property was traced, and recovered too, to a very large
amount; and out of one dacoit's house at Owsa, articles
of various kinds, to the value of 1200 rupees, were taken,
which had been his share of the plunder secured on that

U

occasion. I was blamed at first by the Resident for raking up old cases; but I held my ground, for those I had tried were all comparatively recent, though the crimes had been committed before the cession. I was determined to eradicate the pest if I could, and I thought the only chance lay in attacking the old gangs and in bringing their crimes home to them. This had been done in Thuggee, why not in Dacoity? The question was referred to Calcutta, and soon decided as regarded the assigned districts. All criminal offences, such as dacoity and murder, were deemed open to trial within a period of ten years from the date of their perpetration; and according to this rule I was at liberty to work, and I did so vigorously. Already I had achieved something, and more would follow.

By Lord Dalhousie's request I kept up my correspondence with Mr Courtenay; I think his lordship liked to know unofficially what I was about, and I wrote free and unreservedly. A report I had sent in upon my system of administration had interested him a good deal, and I heard he took it away to study in private, and that he desired I might be told this. He had also entirely acquiesced in my plan of revenue settlement to precede a survey; and to hear that what I had done was approved of, was very cheering.

I found the eastern portion of my district in a far worse condition than the western, and I find myself writing thus to my father in March 1854:—

"While at Nelingah I was more oppressed with work than I had been anywhere. I found the district in shocking order: no proper accounts, and no confidence among the people; a ruined, impoverished set of pauper cultivators, who have been so long oppressed and neglected under the Arab management, that they are, I imagine, blunted to all good perceptions. Murder, robbery, attacks on villages, plunder of cattle, and destruction of crops, had got to such a height last year, that civil war could not have had a worse effect upon the people or on the revenue; and all agreed that if British rule had not come in this year, the whole district would have been utterly ruined and wasted. I never saw anything like it. I thought Shorapoor bad, but this is infinitely worse, and the labour it is to get anything put right has been excessive. I can only say that I have been obliged to work frequently from 4 A.M. to 8 P.M., with only respite for dressing and break-fast; but there is no help for it. I have been giving five years' settlements to such villages as are ready to take them, but there are many which are so disorganised that they require to be specially nursed."

I had likewise introduced a regular system of village accounts with the rent-payers and the treasurers, which I will briefly detail.

Each village accountant kept a day-book and ledger, in which the sum he was to pay was entered to his debit, and his payments successively at stated times to his credit. His account was entered in the village ledger in the same manner. If he paid an instalment, it was entered to his credit in his book as a receipt; and this payment was entered into the day-book, and afterwards posted to his account in the ledger. Peculation was therefore almost impossible, or any undue exactions, and the people now began to understand the protection that the system im-plied. The district treasury had a similar account with villages, and the particulars of each village instalment were forwarded to the head treasury with the general re-mittances. Any error or any exaction by any individual could thus be traced up to its author at once, and the check and counter-check were quite efficient in practice. The village accountants were at first rather clumsy about their books, but they soon grew accustomed to the sys-tem; and before the season of collections was over, I had the satisfaction of finding that the plan was working easily and well in every portion of my province.

Before I returned to my headquarters, Nuldroog, I had
the satisfaction of beginning two new irrigation reservoirs
near Tooljapoor, on plans and surveys which I had previously submitted. I intended that these should form the
commencement of a system of tank-irrigation from Tooljapoor to Ahmednugger, a question in which the Governor-General seemed much interested, and in which he
encouraged me heartily to persevere.

The Resident also, Mr Bushby, began to see the necessity of it; and I was the more rejoiced at obtaining sanction for this, because great distress was prevalent, though
it scarcely amounted to famine yet, and three new works
would enable me to employ a great number of persons. I
was glad, too, to find that both my neighbours, the collectors of Ahmednugger and Sholapoor, had become strong
advocates for irrigation-works, and had sent in urgent
representations to Government on the subject. In these
undertakings I had to make the surveys, plans, and calculations entirely myself; but I always managed to find
time to do these before my daily work began, so that other
business was never interfered with or postponed. It
seemed strange to me that though irrigation-works were
progressing in the North-West Provinces with great
energy, in the Bombay Presidency no one seemed to take
the least interest in them, and, had it not been for these
gentlemen, would probably ever have given a thought to
the subject; and indeed, to this day, I believe but little
progress has been made in these most useful works.

I had great difficulties to encounter in the treasury department for the first year or two. Rents had been paid
in all sorts of local currencies, and I was required to account for them in Company's rupees. Now I had as many
as fourteen different kinds of rupees current in my province, each with its separate value, and the market value
was often fluctuating; the assay rates did not correspond
at all with the market value, and, in short, the whole was

a system of inextricable confusion; and I was obliged in
the end to notify that none except Company's rupees
would be taken in payments to the State, and this relieved
us of all difficulty.

For a long time the proposed revenue survey caused
much trouble and vexation. A small manual had been
sent us from the Punjaub of the system in use there,
which was by plane-tables,—and plane-tables were sent
afterwards. Every Deputy-Commissioner was to have
a school of instruction, and to teach the *putwarries*, or
village accountants, to survey their own lands ; and the
work was to begin at once. This was all easy enough
to write about; but the carrying such orders into effect
was a very different matter. I believe I happened to be
the only Deputy-Commissioner who knew how to survey,
and the rest looked to me to begin operations.

Extensive correspondence on the subject took place, and
cost me much additional time and trouble ; but I could
not use the Punjaub instruments and the compasses with
which the work was to be done—it was impossible ; and
after much writing and loss of time in useless endeavours
at explanation, I introduced a plan of my own. I had
some better plane-tables made, and worked them by back-
sight, like a theodolite, and my plan succeeded very well.
I also established a school of young men, instead of the
putwarries, who proved apt scholars, and did good work,
and I sent in my report with some specimens of surveyed
lands. My plan was approved, and I was simply desired
" to go on."

I found distress very great at Nuldroog—not so much
among the people of my own district, as among starving
wretches who came there from all quarters so emaciated,
and so shrivelled and weak, that all, men, women, and
children, were fearful to look upon. Often, during my
morning rides, I came upon dead bodies lying by the roadside, creatures who had sunk down to die before they

could reach the town; and many crawled in who were too far gone to be recovered. Except at Hingolee I had never seen famine in its worst form before, and this was horrible to witness. I did what I could myself, and every one at Nuldroog did the same: my own share amounted to several thousand rupees, which I could very ill afford; and it was not for a comparatively long time that I could get any answer to my earnest request to be allowed to use what money I needed, to give employment to those able to work. At length, however, I got a favourable reply, and about four thousand miserable wretches were set to work to cut down the scrubby jungle in the fort, and to clear out the old ruined works. Gradually, as rain fell and prospects brightened, the people began to return to their various homes. What would have become of us at Nuldroog if the famine had been universal, I can hardly conceive; for its results from which we suffered were fearful enough.

The monsoon was heavy, and all the month of September proved very unhealthy at Nuldroog. My establishment and nearly all the clerks, both English and native, suffered from fever, dysentery, and other complaints; so that to get through the needful work was very trying. We had no other convenient shelter, and so were obliged to remain; but I thought it doubtful whether the place could be retained as a head-station. However, a further trial of it was directed before it was given up.

The year 1854 had been a truly laborious one to me, and except during the very short period of the late rains, I had been under canvas since July 1853. The work accomplished had been enormous. In English, Persian, and Mahratta, the references and letters had been 34,474, upwards of 9000 of which had passed between my assistant and myself, many being on very intricate and tedious subjects. We corresponded officially always in Mahratta.

For my own share I had had 272 criminal cases to dispose of, thirteen of which were indictments for murder ; of civil cases and appeals I find no record among my letters, but no doubt they may have been mislaid or lost.

My revenue for the financial year was all collected— except about 3000 rupees, which still had to be remitted —and amounted to 10 lakhs and 66,000 rupees of all sorts ; which, allowing for large deductions, exchanges, &c., became Rs. 886,565 13 3.

The revenue for the previous year had been, according to the local accounts, Rs. 699,305 11 8, so that there had been an increase of Rs. 187,260 1 7. The amount of land previously under cultivation had been 1,192,395 *beegahs ;* that for the present year 1,221,947 *beegahs*, or an increase of 29,552.

Further particulars are unnecessary, and would scarcely interest the general reader.

In spite of a little fever, from which I suffered at Nuldroog, I was in rude health. I enjoyed the climate of the district, and along the edge of the table-land it was generally cool in the hottest weather.

I was always able to work at least twelve hours every day, and often more, except on Sundays, when I always read the service in my tents to my English clerks.

Every department of the district was now in fair working order, and I was quite prepared to show the Resident, if he came to see it, as it was hinted he would, all my interior economy, and wished it to be compared with other districts of the same class.

I was directed by the Resident to meet the Collector of Sholapoor on the frontier, in order to settle a boundary dispute which had arisen between the Rajah of Akulkote's territory and the Nizam's, and in regard to which there had been some serious fighting and bloodshed ; so I made for the spot early in November, expecting that everything would be satisfactorily arranged in a few days.

It proved, however, that I had to survey 26 miles of

disputed boundary, and to make a map of it, before the question could even be understood at all; documents on both sides had to be examined, and evidence taken.   Finally, after recording our opinion in separate minutes, part of the boundary was laid down; but the Akulkote men came in the night, pulled up the stones which had been placed as landmarks and threw them away.

As I could wait no longer, and the Collector had no authority to enforce our decision, I left the place on the 18th December, heartily regretting that my detention had been so long and so unprofitable; and I moved to a village on the eastern frontier to begin the revenue settlement for the year.   I should then be close to the Resident's line of march from Hyderabad to Nuldroog, and could easily join him at the nearest point.

I was glad to find the people on the eastern and western frontiers taking heart; and I had the pleasure of letting nearly all the uncultivated lands, which had become covered with low mimosa jungle.   There was a better spirit abroad in the country, and the local bankers were ready to make advances for the cultivation of these waste lands on low rates of interest to any extent.   The fact was, that agents from some of the great mercantile houses in Bombay had acted upon a circular which I had sent them some months before, pointing out to them the capabilities of my province for the production of oil-seeds and other staple commodities of trade; and they had sent agents with bills of exchange to a very large amount to invest in these purchases.   One of these agents had bills to the extent of three lakhs (£30,000); and in all I traced more than £60,000, which was a very welcome addition to former capital.   No such influx of money had ever been known before, and I recommended the agents to deal directly with the farmers, without the intervention of any third party; and they took my advice, and ultimately all were quite satisfied.

The Resident and his staff left Hyderabad on the 20th
December, and I met him at Kullianee, in the Nizam's
territory, on the 1st January 1855.   He received me very
kindly.   As I rode into camp, he was just starting on his
elephant, and he asked me to come with him, which I did,
and we were soon deep in friendly talk about all sorts of
things.   We travelled together to Nuldroog, where I had
plenty to show him—all the treasury books and accounts,
the jail, &c. &c.; and I had collected the *putwarries* of a
number of villages and their books, and explained my
system to him.   He was pleased to say "he could hardly
believe that so perfect a system could have been organised;" and he was more and more satisfied as we proceeded further, and the books of other groups of villages
were shown to him.   He did not like Nuldroog at all, and
said there must be another head-station—and in this view
I quite coincided; but there could be no change made for
the present.

I was very anxious to lay my projects for irrigation-
works before him, and he marched with me to Tooljapoor,
where the largest tank had been marked out, and this
seemed to decide him in regard to the more extended
system which I had advocated.   He said he was very
anxious to show that the "assigned districts could do as
much for their size as the Punjaub," and promised to send
on to Government all the plans and estimates that could
be prepared.

He could propose no change in judicial matters, as my
small code was working very satisfactorily; and he confided to me that I was the only Deputy-Commissioner
who had attempted to introduce anything of the kind.

The Resident had not very much time to spare; we
therefore went on from Tooljapoor to Owsa, but I regretted
his being unable to see the prettiest part of the district,
which lay along the edge of the table-land.

He was immensely struck, however, with the regularity

and beauty of the fine old fort of Owsa; and indeed, if the Arabs who formed the garrison when I first took possession of it had chosen to resist, the place could only have been taken by a regular siege. I left the Resident at Bhalkee, a point on the Hyderabad road; and we had, when we parted, settled everything as far as we could. I showed him the survey work, which pleased him. No other Deputy-Commissioner had as yet even attempted a commencement, and it gratified him that I had done so, in spite of my refusal to make use of the Punjaub system. We parted very good friends; and as I fancied, on his first coming, that he had acquired rather a prejudice against me, I was the more pleased at the result of our meeting. I knew my district was in a much more orderly and regular condition than any other ceded at the same time, and I was anxious it should be inspected.

At the request of the people, I chose the site of a new market-town near Nelingah. There were more than a hundred applications for sites, so I designed a market-place and a hall of assembly; and the Resident having given his sanction, we began to build at once. Nelingah was now a place of trade and a resort of merchants, yet how it was reduced! The old accounts showed its revenue to have been 12,000 rupees a-year; now it did not reach above 3000.

After much tedious and lengthy correspondence respecting the difference in value of currencies collected during the first year, which I had cut short by accepting only Company's rupees in payments during the present year, I was able to submit my accounts of revenue and collections at an early period; and the following copy of a memorandum I sent to my father in July will show what progress had been made:—

" *Cultivation.*—Contrasting the returns of 1852-53 with those of 1854-55, and after adjustment of all transfers of villages attached to proprietors, lands released, &c., there

is a clear increase of new cultivation of *beegahs* 139,190.
A *beegah*, by the average of local measurement, is here upwards of an acre—about 1.30.

 "*Revenue.*—The gross and net revenue of 1851-52, including all estates resumed by us, customs duties, &c.,
was :—

Gross revenue, Hyderabad rupees, . . .	856,263	7 5
Village expenses, ...	164,882	13 5
Balance, net revenue, Hyderabad rupees, .	691,380	10 0
Gross revenue for 1854-55 in Company's rupees, .	922,666	8 0
Deduct village expenses, ...	97,993	8 9
Balance, net revenue, in Company's rupees, .	824,672	15 3

Result.

Net revenue, 1854-55, Company's rupees, . .	824,672	15 3
Net revenue, 1851-52, Hyderabad rupees, . .	691,380	10 0
Increase in tale, . . .	Rs. 133,292	5 3

 "The value of the different rupees is not here given ;
and either the Hyderabad rupees may be turned into
Company's at 21 per cent, or the Company's into Hyderabad, and here is the result :—

Company's rupees, 824,672, at 121 for 100 Hydera- bad rupees, ...	997,853	1 11
Net revenue of 1851-52, as above, . . .	691,380	10 0
Net increase, value, Hyderabad rupees, .	306,472	7 11

Or, if the Nizam's Government's share only of 1851-52 for
the whole province is reckoned, the amount will stand as
follows :—

Net revenue of 1854-55, as above, Company's rupees, 824,672, at 121 per 100, ...	=997,853	1 11
Realised by the Nizam's Government in 1851-52, according to account, ...	562,457	14 9
Given to the Nizam's Government by cession on the result of 1854-55, in Hyderabad rupees, .	435,395	3 2

"Even this is not all, for the Rs. 562,457 14 9 contained the customs duties abolished in 1854-55. These amounted to Rs. 35,000; and there is a further profit in decrease of village charges, which were 19.41 per cent on the gross revenue in 1851-52—and in 1854-55, 10.84 per cent.

"The average rate of assessment per *beegah*, or acre, is nine annas and two pies (about one shilling and three halfpence); and there is no other tax or cess whatever.

"In reference to the gross revenue of 1854-55, the total remission from unrealised balances is Rs. 620 5 6: or 922,666 8 Company's rupees have been realised, all but Rs. 620 5 6; or £92,266, all except £62."

There remained, therefore, no doubt whatever that the cession of this province had been highly profitable to the Nizam's Government. The actual receipts had very nearly doubled, and the revenue was secured in Company's rupees instead of in fluctuating currencies. The local profits of the Nizam's *talookdars*, or collectors, had been enormous. They had collected all the revenue, for the most part, in a local currency, which was little short in value in the market of the Company's rupee; but instead of giving their Government the benefit of the exchange into Hydera bad rupees, they had paid Hyderabad rupees only by bills on Hyderabad, which were cashed in the local debased currency of the city itself.

If this were a specimen of one province, what must have been the result from them all? Berar, like Nuldroog, showed a similar difference of value and increase in favour of the cession.

In August of this year the distress seemed almost greater than the year before. There had been no rain since June, and the poorer classes, who were accustomed to gain their living by weeding fields and other agricultural work, were now starving, and flocking in crowds to Nuldroog. We all did what we could, as we had done

the year before, and it was a heavy drain on private individuals. I urged the Resident to allow me to begin the
roads to Sholapoor and Hyderabad, which he had promised, and which would have greatly relieved the local
strain upon me and others, but I had to wait a weary time
for an answer.

During this month, too, I lost the valuable services of
my assistant Cadell. He had gone to Hyderabad on leave
for a month, and when there, Bullock, who was Commissioner in Berar, applied for furlough to England on medical certificate ; the Raichore Commissioner was ordered to
act in Berar, and Cadell was sent to Raichore. I was very
sorry to lose my friend. He had managed four out of my
ten divisions admirably from the first ; he was always kind,
courteous, and considerate to natives of every degree, and
had won golden opinions from all. We had worked well
together, and he was thoroughly acquainted with his
duties in every respect. Personally, I was very much
attached to him, and shall never forget, while I live, our
pleasant days together.

No assistant was appointed in his stead, and the whole
work of the province fell upon me, without any additional
pay ; but I was grateful for excellent health, though I
hardly hoped it would long hold out under the terrible
strain now put upon me.

We had no rain till September ; but the new roads, to
the commencement of which a tardy sanction had at length
been given, provided labour for upwards of 4000 men,
women, and children, and saved them from starvation. I
also cleared out the fort altogether, and thus employed
1500 more persons : every old wall was levelled, and the
stones were thrown into hollows and covered with earth.
In October heavy rain fell all over the district, and we
thanked God that all dread of famine was at an end. The
very early crops had withered, but now every acre of land
was being re-ploughed and sown, and the prospects were

very cheering. Another road to Tooljapoor was sanctioned, and put in hand; and I had completed thirty
miles of one and fifteen of another, having being obliged
to do all the surveying and laying out myself. They
were only cleared and levelled to begin with, and would
be metalled afterwards.

My brother-in-law, William Palmer, was at last appointed as my assistant. He had served in a similar
capacity in North and South Berar. In the latter province no system whatever had been introduced, neither
revenue, account, nor judicial, and the Resident had
gone, there on a tour of inspection. Cadell, too, wrote
from Raichore to say that he had everything to originate
there, and he did not like it at all; but I hoped he was
in a fair way for promotion. The work at the large tank
at Tooljapoor had been stopped, pending formal sanction
by Government—but this had been granted; and after
testing all my old levelling by a new instrument which
my father sent to me from England, the embankment was
begun in earnest. In December all looked well—crops
were luxuriant, work progressing, and people happy and
contented; and for this peaceful close to a very trying
year, I felt most grateful. I again received orders to
meet the Resident on his return from South Berar to
Hyderabad, at any point nearest to my boundary. I
therefore, while waiting for him, carried on the survey of
the road from Tooljapoor to Kullianee, and contrived to
get through from seven to nine miles per day, laying
down marks for the contractors and workmen. I finally
met the Resident at his camp at Bundapoor on the 14th
January 1856. He was exceedingly kind and friendly
towards me. He expressed himself dissatisfied with the
condition of South Berar, and was pleased to say many
flattering things about the order and regularity in all departments which he had found at Nuldroog. As still
further improvement had continued since his visit, I

would have liked to have taken him through part of my district; but time did not permit of it, and he could not delay longer his return to Hyderabad. There was no difference of opinion between us except in regard to the survey, as to which I consistently maintained my first position, that unless it had a scientific basis, and the surveyors had a practical education and knowledge of their work, they could not deal with village lands like those of Nuldroog, some of the areas of which were from 20,000 to 30,000 acres in extent; and that to persevere in the Punjaub scheme would not only entail loss of time, but of money also.

We had several hot arguments about this; but at last the Resident confided to me that the Punjaub work had been an utter failure when scientifically tested, and he showed me some of the correspondence, which was convincing.

I was therefore allowed now to work out my own tables in my own way. I had a number of clever pupils, who were ready to set to work at once, and I promised to show results in a very short time, which I hoped would be considered satisfactory. All official clouds and differences were dispersed, and we were of one accord in all matters. In private Mr Bushby was one of the pleasantest of companions; and we sat up each night into the small hours of the morning, engaged in pleasant talk, and schemes for the further improvement of my district. He had sent on all my plans for roads and irrigation-works; and estimates, exceeding a lakh of rupees, had been passed by Government. All this made me very hopeful.

I thought very earnestly at this time of taking furlough to England, and seeing my father once more, and of bringing out my children to India, if it were practicable. My heart yearned to see them and all the dear ones at home, yet there were many difficulties. I had no society, and no means of continuing their education; and Nuldroog, or life in tents, was quite unfit for them. I could not, either, go home on medical certificate, for, thank God! my health was first-rate ; and no doctor in Bombay, seeing my ruddy cheeks and strong frame, would have ventured to give me one. So I had no alternative but to wait patiently the tide of events.

I was not without a hope, that as a head-commissioner was to be appointed to superintend the whole of the districts, I might be nominated to the post. This would have involved residence at Hyderabad, where I could have had home and friends for my children ; but in this I was disappointed. Alas! I was not a regular Company's servant, only an outsider, "uncovenanted," and the Company's rules could not be infringed! Already, I heard from Mr Courtenay, there existed much jealousy in regard to the offices held by "local officers ;" and much as Lord Dalhousie wished personally to serve me, he dared not provoke further dissatisfaction.

On the 6th March, Lord Dalhousie departed from Calcutta for England, leaving behind him a minute, which has its place in history, in which he detailed what he had done during his vice-royalty. His last annexation had been Oudh ; but that had not been his own work. It had been for some time imminent, and was finally decided upon by the Court of Directors and the Government of England. It is only in future histories of India, and from his own papers, should they ever be published, that the character and acts of Lord Dalhousie as Governor-General can be properly estimated; as yet, he has had his eulogists, and his bitter opponents, almost, indeed, amounting to defamers.

To my humble perception he was the most practically useful and single-minded ruler that India had ever possessed. His great mind took in every question with a singular clearness, whether it were large or small, momentous or unimportant, and he improved everything he touched. To him India owes electric telegraphs, railways, extension of practical education, large irrigation projects, roads, and the removal of many disabilities under which natives suffered. No one who ever worked under Lord Dalhousie could for a moment question his unerring detection of any weak point, and the great power of mind and application which distinguished him, and at no period of Indian history had the administration of India been so admirably conducted.

To receive a word of praise from him was the desire which lay nearest every heart; and when given, it was never in a cold or niggardly spirit, but warmly and most encouragingly. To myself personally, though I knew him not, he had been, both privately and officially, kind and considerate from first to last ; and I only regret that I cannot find among my papers the last expression of his lordship's sentiments towards me, in transmitting a copy of the last despatch of the Court of Directors in reference to the affairs of Shorapoor.

I have spoken of my own work, and have called it hard, lasting from twelve to sixteen hours daily ; but this was made up of the petty details of one province. Lord Dalhousie did as much each day, with the direction of all India on his mind. " No one can record," wrote the ' Times,' " for few knew, of his daily toil, or how, with a delicate frame, he overcame it, but which overworked and destroyed his physical powers, and in 1860 sent him to his grave."

When he left her, India seemed secure and peaceful, and he retired with a very sincere conviction that so she would long remain !

I was desired in February to meet a native commissioner from Hyderabad, to settle the boundary of jurisdiction, which had been under dispute, and we were to act in concert. I waited wearily for a month, losing the best period of my season ; and when at length the commissioner arrived, he had received no instructions, and further delay ensued. At length, after he had made references to his Government on various points, we arranged affairs amicably.

I was principally engaged in trying criminal cases, which were both numerous and heavy; but there were no dacoities now, and these cases belonged chiefly to the period before the cession. As a proof of what I had to do in judicial affairs, I may here mention that Mr Compton, who was judge of Sholapoor, sent me a memorandum of the result of his work within a certain period. He had tried 72 cases, whereas my file showed 172 for the same!

My police system was working well. Every *patell*, or head of a village, was made a local magistrate, with certain powers, and a small allowance; and as a mark of distinction, the post was much esteemed. It gratified me also to find that my rules for the police were ordered for adoption in every province of the cession.

My accounts were made out, and sent up to Hyderabad with the administration report in July. The increase of cultivation in three years had been 184,000 acres. In 1855-56, 72,000 acres of new land had been taken up, but 34,000 were abandoned in the famine, which would not have been the case had rain fallen, and we should have had, with that, 218,000 acres of increase. As the revenue augmented, petty taxes would be remitted, as I had arranged from the first. This year 40,000 rupees would be struck off, yet the whole revenue would not be seriously affected. I need not give again all the details, as those of the previous year will suffice.

In August Mr T. N. Maltby, of the Madras Civil Service, was appointed head-commissioner, and Mr Bushby was relieved from the extra duties which had been imposed upon him, and which were very onerous. We looked out now for changes and amendments, which would form part of a more regular system than we had yet experienced.

It was very evident to our commissioner, in the first place, that without increased establishments, the demands for regular reports, constantly increasing, could not be complied with, nor could the strain on any one who could and would do the work be borne much longer. As some relief to me, my head ministerial officer, " Baba Sahib," a very shrewd and excellent revenue officer, whom I had brought with me from Shorapoor, was promoted to the rank of extra-assistant; and he, with my assistant Mr Palmer, relieved me of much of the petty detail which had distressed me before. Cadell had been appointed Deputy-Commissioner in South Berar, and Eastern Raichore had been added to the western portion as part of the new arrangements. He was now, I was glad to see, on the highroad to promotion, and he had truly well earned his advance. My work never slackened in amount; and in reply to my father's query as to how my day was spent, I wrote as follows: "Up at 5 A.M., and go out about the survey of the roads. In by eight o'clock and answer letters, English and Mahratta, till ten; bathe, and breakfast over at eleven. Then to *cucherry* work, trials, &c., till 6 P.M., without stirring—often, indeed, till seven. Dine and sit an hour or so with Palmer, if he is there, or with some native friend, by way of a rest, which brings up the time to half-past eight or nine. Then to my room, and work at translations or other business till eleven or twelve. Count up all this and you will see there is no time for anything except hard work; yet, I am very thankful to say, I have neither pain nor ache."

The public works did not slacken either. Every road I had surveyed and marked out was in active progress, and there were now six long distances under the labourers' hands.

Our new Commissioner had written to me to say that he proposed taking my district the first in his projected tour of inspection. He was to leave Hyderabad on the 20th November; and as I had a little leisure time and needed rest, I went into Sholapoor on a visit to my kind friends, Mr and Mrs Compton. What a treat this was to me! She was a highly-accomplished and exquisite musician, and it was delightful to listen to her. I had heard so little music since I had been in England, and had nearly forgotten all I knew; but it came back to me, and I had the great delight of singing all my favourite duets, Italian and English; and they were so kind and sympathetic, these dear friends, that my heart warmed to them both, nor did our friendship ever lessen. My pleasant stay ended abruptly, as I had to return to Nuldroog sooner than I expected. Another assistant was added to my staff, Lieutenant Temple of the Madras Army, who, having passed an examination as civil engineer, and having been employed in the survey, and as superintendent of roads and tanks, would be of the greatest use to me. He arrived at Nuldroog on the 30th November, and was followed by a second native assistant, Jewanjee Rustomjee, a Parsee, so that now I had two English and two native assistants. Mr Maltby had seen at a glance that it was no use over-working his Deputy-Commissioners. He unfortunately met with a severe accident, which prevented his leaving Hyderabad; and I was much concerned at this, for I had looked forward to his coming with sincere pleasure, and I knew that he was one to appreciate all I had done and was striving further to accomplish.

During my little visit to Sholapoor I made the acquaintance of the surveyor-in-chief for the railway, and I asked him to come with me to see my embankment works, roads, &c., and, above all, to test my survey with the theodolite. He came to Nuldroog, tested the surveys of three considerable village lands, and gave me a certificate that he could find "no appreciable error whatever." Here was a grand triumph for me! Government had refused me a theodolite, and I had been working in my own fashion, and somewhat in the dark.

My system with the plane-tables was quite new to my friend, and he did me the honour to ask me for one of my instruments, which I considered a high compliment. The certificate he had given me was too valuable to retain, as it entered into full details of his tests, and I forwarded it to the Commissioner.

Although he had not seen them in actual working, Mr Maltby ordered at once the adoption of my system of accounts in all departments, and directed it to be put in force in all districts of the Commission. My police regulations had already been adopted, and, at length, what I had been working for so hard seemed to be appreciated; and I received, by a minute of the Supreme Council, the "special thanks of the Governor-General in Council for my valuable services." And so ended the year 1856, with many thanks to God for all His merciful protection. Everything around me was peaceful and prosperous; there was good hope of a fine season; my roads were opening out lines of traffic all through the country; and trade was brisk and profitable.

I had held many criminal trials during the year; but the last one in 1856 was more than usually extraordinary. A farmer and shepherd, the possessor of some wealth, had two wives—one old, the other young. The elder wife had no family, and he had married a younger one in the hope of having an heir born to him. Much jealousy existed between the women, though they did not live in the same house, or even in the same village. One morning, early, the shepherd was found dead in his sugar-cane field, which he had gone to watch alone during the night. His head was literally knocked to pieces with large stones, but the body could be perfectly identified. There had been a feast in his house the evening before, and a kid had been killed by his nephew, and many of the neighbours had partaken of the dinner, at which the shepherd and his elder wife had appeared to be on the best terms. At the inquest and local investigation, many suspicious circumstances were brought forward against the elder wife and the nephew, and both were committed by me for trial. One of these was, that the wife of the nephew declared her husband had been absent most part of that night; and when he returned home he threw a thick sheet over her, which he had with him, saying she must be cold, and that he was going to her village, and she must follow. On this sheet were large patches of blood, which she had not observed at night; but she had given it to the police when they came in the morning. I had sent the sheet to Hyderabad in order that the blood-stains might be analysed; but it could not be proved that the blood was human, and the male prisoner swore that it was that of the kid which he himself had killed for the feast.

There was a great deal of circumstantial evidence in the case; but it was impossible to convict the prisoners upon this only, and they were very ably defended by a native advocate. When the defence was closed, I was on the point of recording an acquittal, although I was inwardly sure the prisoners had done the murder; and I had taken my pen in hand to write, when the woman, a tall masculine figure, began to beat her breast, and cried out with a loud voice—

"Stop, Sahib! do not write! You do not know the truth; you would write what is wrong. All that my advocate and the witnesses have said to you is false. Lies! lies! lies! *I* did the murder, and" (pointing to the nephew) "*he* helped me! He knocked him down with a big stone, and then we killed him between us."

It was quite in vain that I cautioned her that this confession must be made use of against her if she persisted in it. She only said the more—

"Lies! lies!—we did it, he and I, and he will tell you so himself. Is it not all true?" she said, turning to the other prisoner. "Don't be ashamed of it. Speak the truth before God and the Sahib."

"It is all true," said the young man, quite calmly—"quite true; and I will tell how we did it. Was I not his heir? and he had always denied me my share because he said he would have children by his new wife. Could I bear that, Sahib?"

"Could I bear his leaving me for a wooden-faced girl?" cried the woman, beating her breast violently. "No, no! I did it! I did it! I and he; and if he were alive now, and we two were free, we could not let him live. Take down all I say!" she shrieked—"take it all down, and hang me afterwards, for my heart is burning! burning! burning!"

I recorded their confessions, which were long and very circumstantial, not only corroborating the evidence in every material point, but explaining how the murder had been long planned,—how the woman had engaged five men of a village in the British territory to do it, and had given them two rupees each as earnest-money; but their courage failed them, and they had given the money back to her: then, as she said, there remained no one to do it but her husband's nephew and herself. After all was recorded, I passed sentence of death upon both. The proceedings were sent on to the Sudder Adalut or Supreme Court of Calcutta, the sentence confirmed, and the horrible pair hanged together. I shall never forget the look and action of that woman as she cried out to me "not to write," and poured forth a torrent of confession which she could not repress.

In another case of dacoity which followed, the clear evidence of the widow of the owner of the house attacked, who was a young and very beautiful Brahmin girl, affected me very deeply; and the subject of that trial forms the opening of my romance of 'Seeta.' The deposition of Seeta given at the first inquiry is that of the Brahmin widow, with very slight alteration.

Indeed my operations against the dacoits of my district were beginning to tell heavily upon them. One large gang, very notorious in 1827-29, were at length brought to justice, and stolen property to a very large amount was recovered from them and recognised. A zemindar of the adjacent British province, a great man in his way, was also tried and convicted on many charges of dacoity, and was sentenced to fourteen years' penal servitude; and these instances of conviction, and many more, purged my province of dacoits.

New-Year's Day of 1857 found me at Nelingah, where I had been for two days. All was now very prosperous, and the crops were splendid. Every one was in good heart, and applications for waste lands were very numerous; in a comparatively short time none would remain to be taken up. My new assistant, Temple, had gone to work steadily, and was studying Mahratta with every prospect of becoming a proficient. He liked the people, and they liked him; and, as I had before done with Cadell, I made several yearly settlements to show him how the work was done, and he was a very patient and good - tempered scholar. He had been with me on the Hyderabad road so far as it extended, and he completed the survey of two branch lines to Nelingah and Sowárá to Latoor—all of these I left to him to look after, as he could afford the time; but the works were making rapid progress everywhere. From Nelingah I went to Kharósa, half-way to Owsa, as I was very anxious to see some Hindoo cave-temples of which I had heard a good deal, and none of the archæologists of Bombay seemed to know anything about them. I found them well worthy a visit—excavated in a cliff of laterite or coarse stone; but some of the pillars left were richly decorated with carving, and several of the halls of the temples were large and airy. The whole were a miniature, apparently, of the caves of Ellora, but very humble copies of these noble temples; and though there did not exist even a tradition of their origin, I concluded they must have been the work of the Rajahs of Kullianee—either the Chalukyas, or their successors the Yádávás of Deoghur or Dowlatabad. I could discover no inscription to copy and send to the Asiatic Society of Bombay, but I measured the temples and sent plans of them, as I did also those of the fine Buddhist excavations near Daraseo, which in many respects were very remarkable, and had been previously unknown.

The day I arrived at Kharósa I received the melancholy intelligence of the death of the Resident, Mr Bushby. He had over-fatigued himself when out on a country excursion, and brought on an illness from which he never rallied. I regretted him very much; for although we had had some differences of opinion on various local questions, yet to me individually he had been kind and encouraging. We corresponded constantly, and he was ever urging me on to attempt and begin further public works, and expressing satisfaction at the result of those already completed. It was impossible to conjecture who might be his successor.

After staying a few days at Owsa, for the trial of the prisoners confined in the jail there, I went by the new line of road to Sowárá and Nuldroog. This latter portion was quite finished, and measured 24 feet in width, looking like a good gravel-walk the whole way. This had before only been a rough track for carts, indeed sometimes merely a path winding among the great basalt boulders. At Nuldroog, the first building I had used as a jail was now too small, and I began enclosing the large magazine with a wall 21 feet high and plastering it inside. There were now 400 prisoners in the jail, and I had established a school of industry, which was going on well. Some of the prisoners were making rope and tape, others weaving, and more manufacturing carpets of strong cotton—some of these were very pretty, and showed much skill. Nor did I allow the women to be idle; they made various articles in a kind of knitting which was taught them, and other kinds of work. The prisoners were likewise set to build the new jail wall, and were useful in a multitude of ways.

After a good look round Nuldroog, just to see that all was right, and testing all the surveys of villages within reach, I went on to Sholapoor for a few days' rest, and to indulge myself in a little music; and I promised to go there for a long visit during the rains, when I could not move about my district. My friend the surveyor-in-chief was not at Sholapoor, but Lieut. T. of the Artillery, who had belonged to the Trigonometrical Survey of Scinde, accompanied me to Tooljapoor, bringing his theodolite with him. He was curious to see what I was doing, and he remained long enough to test my surveys of several large villages—all of which, I am glad to say, he found correct.

I asked him to make a report to me on the subject, which he did, explaining in detail the tests he had made, and their results, which I sent on to Mr Maltby—and if the Commissioner had any doubt about our work, I knew this report would remove it; but he wrote word that he was sure we were fully able to carry it on correctly; and I was rejoiced to find that my plan of using the plane-tables was turning out so thoroughly successful.

I had now leisure to make measurements for the completion of the noble embankment at Bhâtoree, which was one of my principal projects. The high-water level showed an area of upwards of two square miles; the water would have an average depth of 25 feet, and the irrigation channels on the right bank of the stream would carry water to Ahmednugger itself, which needed it sorely. This great work had been begun, according to tradition, by Salabut Khan, the great Minister of Ahmednugger, who died in

1588, and whose mausoleum overlooks the admirable site for the lake which he had selected. As each would benefit alike by the work, the Nizam's and the British Governments were to share its expenses; and I was so anxious to see it put in hand, that I worked very hard at all the plans, sections, and surveys. Bhâtoree was one of the most delightful of all my villages, and I had constant visitors from the cantonment. Lieut. Cotgrave of the Engineers, with an assistant, was sent to help me.

Between us all, we finished what we had to do; and the cross-levels of this basin gave a result of upwards of sixty millions of cubic yards of water-storage, while the expenses of the work would be comparatively moderate. Mr Cotgrave had not had experience of tank-engineering, but he very soon took in the project, and entered into its details with great spirit and zeal; and on looking into the particulars of the former portion which had been completed, we were both exceedingly struck by the profound science which had been evinced by the ancient Mussulman engineers.

A survey of the high watershed lying between my district and the great valley of the Godavery river was necessary in order to calculate the amount of rainfall for storage in the large tanks I had proposed; and I began this from Bhâtoree, and finished about 100 square miles of it, which all fell into the basin I had tested when I came first to the district.

I had now gained the amplest data for irrigation projects both here and at Bhâtoree; and when I should find leisure to do so, would submit them with my administrative report. How anxious the people were for water!— not only for cultivation, but for their cattle; and what noble memorials would these works be of our rule in the province! I had discovered among the hills a refuge in hot weather—a village 2470 feet above the sea-level by barometer and boiling-point of water. I did not leave it till the end of March, and then it was quite cold at night and very agreeable during the day. The scenery was beautiful all along the mountains to Ahmednugger westwards, and over my own district eastwards; while to the north lay the wide plain of the Godavery. and Aurungabad and its hills beyond. Even with the naked eye I could see the glitter of the marble dome of the great tomb of Aurungzeeb's daughter in the far distance, and of other domes and minarets in the city; but my time was up—I had to meet my assistant Palmer, and to lay out a new piece of road south to Daraseo and north towards the city of Beer. After all was done, the rainy season would begin, and we should assemble at Nuldroog.

My plans were changed by a note received from Colonel Davidson, from Baroda, where, after leaving Hyderabad, he had been appointed Resident. Now, it appeared, he was promoted to the vacancy at Hyderabad, and sent me word that he should be at Nuldroog on the 12th April. I received his note while at Manoor on the 6th, and I had 120 miles to travel over as best I could in order to meet our new chief, who was an old friend of mine. By relays of horses, and a palankeen from Tooljapoor, I managed to reach Nuldroog on the morning of the 10th, as the sun was rising, and I found everything looking very nice. Next day at 4 A.M. the Resident arrived, and I was very glad to welcome him, and to congratulate him on his new appointment. He had been overworked at Baroda, and looked ill; but the offer of the Hyderabad Residentship was too tempting, and he had abandoned his previous idea of going on furlough to England for a few months' leave, until he should have established himself in his new position.

As soon as it was light, he asked to be shown all over the fort, expressed his approval of the new jail, and heard all about my schemes for roads, and all the irrigation projects, to which he promised his help and countenance, declaring that one of his first undertakings at Hyderabad would be to complete the road to a junction with my frontier. I explained the progress of the survey, and, in short, everything connected with my work in all departments, and he had not one single objection to offer to any of my plans. He stayed with us till the evening, Temple having ridden in from Owsa during the day; and we then sent him on, with our hearty good wishes for a safe journey, and after this relapsed into our usual monotonous routine of daily work.

I returned to my camp, and made surveys and plans for the last large tank I had to prepare for execution in the ensuing year. It would collect the drainage of $57\frac{1}{2}$ square miles; would have an average depth of 24 feet, and an area of $13\frac{1}{4}$ square miles; and would, when completed, be a truly noble work.

I had much anxiety at this time about many things, and one especially was the very severe illness of my father-in-law Mr Palmer, who throughout my life had been so steady, loving, and truly helpful a friend to me in all my doings. He recovered, however, very slowly; but his son, my assistant, was obliged to leave me and go to Hyderabad for advice about his eyes, which began to fail him terribly. He could now scarcely see to write his name, and was unfit for duty. I took charge of his subdivision myself; and the travelling season being over, returned to Nuldroog by the close of May.

On my way to Nuldroog, my assistant Baba Sahib had met me at Daraseo, and in course of a conversation which we held privately, he told me that very disagreeable rumours had been flying about that disaffection prevailed in the British territory, and that it was reported an attempt would soon be made to turn the British out of India altogether.

I had heard this myself, but it had made no impression upon me. Who could or would think it could be true, while the whole of India lay apparently in profound peace? Who could dream of any rising?

"Do you remember," said Baba Sahib, "the anonymous letter sent to you by the Bombay Government some time ago? I think it was in February; that was a warning, and kindly meant, though it sounded rude and insolent. Now the almanac for this year 1914 is most alarming; it goes back to the 'hundred years' of the battle of Plassey, and declares that the rule of the Company must come to an end in bloodshed and tumult. This is what is disturbing men's minds, and we must be very careful. When I saw the almanac for the year, I had almost determined to write to you to have it stopped, and prevent the public reading of it if possible; but I knew that you would say such a step would give it too much importance. Do you not hear ugly rumours yourself?"

I scarcely liked to confess that I had; but since February I had been receiving several anonymous letters sent through the ordinary post, with various post-marks, all warning me, as a friend to natives, to take furlough to England and join my family, and leave the district to its fate. They were worded mostly in this way:—

"Although you have many friends, and the people worship you, you have still enemies who will approach you when the time comes, and you will never know who strikes you down."

All these letters were marked "private," or "to be read by himself," and, like other anonymous productions, which were common enough, I had read them and then torn them up. I had not the smallest fear of the people in my district; but these letters, taken in connection with those which had been sent confidentially to Lord Elphinstone, had more effect upon me than I cared to acknowledge.

The advent of 1914 had been preceded by frightful cholera and floods in Bengal, discontent about the greased

cartridges, and the mutiny of the 19th Bengal Native
Infantry; but such events seemed to have no possible
connection with the general uprising of the people; and
even if, in Bengal, they were suspicious of infringements
of caste, what could that possibly have to do with the
peaceful and apparently loyal farmers of the Deccan?

In Bengal, however, there now appeared to be real
alarm.   Lord Canning's proclamation of May 16th proved
that there was, as there seemed to me to be, direct sympathy between what the people of Bengal were warned of
by Lord Canning and what I knew was being felt all
round me.   I could only infer that the evil prophecy of
the curious almanac, the same in purport everywhere, had
in reality disturbed the minds of the unthinking and superstitious.   What could be done?   I heard the same apprehensive reports from Hyderabad.   The Resident and
others wrote to me about them; and from Ahmednugger,
Sholapoor, Berar, and other localities, came the same
tidings: and out of all the letters which reached me and
Temple, there was scarcely one which did not make some
reference to the subject.

I confess I was considerably relieved when I received
an order to remit all the money I had in the treasury to
Bombay for the Persian war.   I felt, in any case, it was
better to be without it.

I well remember the receipt of the " Extra" from Meerut
of the 11th May.   Who that was in India at that time
can forget it?   One could not but shudder at the awful
news; but there arose a hope that it might only be a local
mutiny which could be checked without spreading further,
and that peace would soon follow; and yet, if common precaution had been taken at every station as early as February or March, before the evil wind of 1914 began to blow,
many and many a valuable life would have been spared.
Now it was too late, for throughout the Bengal army disaffection was widely prevalent, and was beginning to bear

fruit almost day by day everywhere. Warnings had not
been wanting. Friendly natives had endeavoured by many
means to put Englishmen on their guard; but no hints
were taken, no precautions used, and the blow fell at last.

The following letters were written home to my friends,
though with no view to publication at the time; but for
the convenience of my family and others interested in the
subject, they were printed and circulated privately without
my knowledge :—

NULDROOG (WESTERN CEDED DISTRICTS, DECCAN),
June 21, 1857.

No Government despatch that ever left India will be looked
for with such anxiety as the mail which takes this. The
close of the Affghan war was a period of intense excitement;
but then it was for an army retiring, and one which could,
united as it was, have borne down everything before it. Now
the fear arises from the army itself. To say that a Bengal
army exists, is, I fear, hopeless. The list of regiments that
have broken into open mutiny, or have been disbanded because
of disaffection, has extended to more than half the regular regiments already, and who shall say how far it may not extend?
How will it be possible to trust any after this? Happily, as
yet, no disaffection has been manifested in the Bombay or
Madras armies, and the native States are one and all faithful.
There has been excitement at Hyderabad, of course, and one
night a standard was planted, around which some rabble
assembled; but the Minister sent a party of Arabs to keep
order, and those assembled fled, nor has any attempt at sedition
been renewed. Davidson has a small detachment and a few
guns at the Residency, more to assure the people of the Residency Bazaar than aught else; and all is quiet. There had
been suspicion of communication between disaffected parties in
the native regiments and the city rabble, but no trace could be
found; and such reports have been common at all times, for
the last twenty years, in any periods of general excitement.
The Minister and Nizam are steadily with us; and it seems
they have the Arabs *in hand*, which perhaps some doubted. Of

course the general interest is now centred in Delhi ; and I think and hope that you will hear of its fall by this mail. News, by electric telegraph, to Davidson, of the 2d, from Delhi, said that a breach had been made; but the most material was, that the king had thrown himself on our protection, and that the mutineers were divided among themselves. They had been defeated with great slaughter outside the walls, by our troops, under General Barnard ; and the results of their two attacks on the outpost of the Meerut post on the Hindun, were also slaughter and defeat. That the whole will be quelled, and speedily too, I have not the least doubt ; but, meantime, it is a period of intense anxiety and excitement, as you may believe. It is most satisfactory to see the *people* of our newest provinces —the Punjaub and Oudh—as yet unmoved by what is going on. Those of the North-West have not been loyal, and more plundering has been carried on by the rural population about the large stations than by the mutineers. Here we are all perfectly quiet, and I trust in God may remain so. With a purely agricultural population there are no elements of excitement; and unless it be among any of the chiefs in the Southern Mahratta country, no chance of disaffection exists on this side India.

One naturally asks what has been the cause of all this—of a whole army becoming at once disaffected, and officers and men, Hindoo and Mohammedan, abandoning allegiance, pay, and pensions, — risking all in this wild attempt to subvert the Government, for no one can doubt that that is the end aimed at. It is not only that present advantages have been risked, or considerations of them thrown away ; future considerations are involved as well. All sepoys, or most of the Bengal army, are connected with land,—there was hardly a farmer or proprietor of any kind who had not a son or relative in the army ; many were themselves landed proprietors : all are known, and, as traitors, have forfeited their estates. It would seem also, by the wanton butchery of officers, and by the measures at once pursued, that it was desired to leave no chance of accommodation or retreat. I suppose all this will come out some day. It is impossible but that a commission must be appointed to sift

Y

the whole to the bottom, and devise a remedy. The authorities, blindly confident, or timid, or conceited as they may have been, must open their eyes now, and not only look danger in the face, but provide against its recurrence. Some people talk of Russia; but I cannot think what she can have to do with it, or how secret means could have been devised for the corruption of the army. That a general conspiracy was made, who can doubt?— the fact of the circulation of those mysterious cakes of bread last year showed this, though no one suspected the sepoys, or at least declared that they did.

But observant men have done so for many years. I have never met an officer who had seen Bengal troops, who was not amazed at their lax discipline. Colonel Jacob, long ago, said that the "normal condition of the Bengal army was *mutiny*," for which he was nearly losing his commission; but it was fact. At Mooltan, and through the whole of the Punjaub war, the men were hardly to be trusted; and after it, Sir Charles Napier had to quell one mutiny, which had not the appearance of being an isolated ebullition of feeling, though it did not spread. Caste has been the bane of that army, and it has been most strange to me always to hear caste spoken of as an advantage. Brahmin sepoys are, no doubt, a fine race; physically, no finer men exist; temperate and well-behaved always, and they are liked by officers; but they have viewed with dread the gradually extending territory of the British beyond seas, which to them are dreadful, and yet where they might sooner or later have to go—nay, *would* have to go. Enlistment is only made for general service now; and while it has been made by young hands, to get the only service possible, the old hands had not taken the oath, and it must have been an object of the lower and younger grades to free themselves from theirs. There are many reasons why mutiny has broken out, which I see are prominently given in the newspapers— foreign service, suspicion about the Enfield cartridges, general lax discipline, absence of European troops, and the like; but there are others which I do not see noticed at all, but which strike me as having had some effect. These are: 1st, The way in which the Commission in Oudh has been working, and its result as regards the landholders. This class—petty Rajahs, Thakoors, and landholders of all degrees—are powerful under the native governors, and lawless to a degree. They had as much land as they liked, and paid only what they chose. The Government was at perpetual feud with them; and they had the best of it, I suspect. Now that is all changed, and there can be no distinction of persons. 2dly, It is said that the appointments in the Commission, as regards the heads of it, were not good—too many regulation men—and that the revenue screw was not spared at all. I do not know how this is, but suspect that all combined has had more to do with the Mutiny than any other cause—or if not more, that it has had the effect of arousing to action all other subjects of real or fancied discontent. 3dly, I doubt also whether the revenue system of the North-West Provinces is sound—Thomason's system, so belauded by its supporters. It has *not* secured property to the middle classes; and the yeomen, who are our sepoys, have lost lands, which are swallowed up by moneyed men. The Santhal rebellion was of this kind; but there, interest and exorbitant charges on money transactions had driven *savages* to despair. The middle classes of tenants in the North-West are not savages, and watch and have watched with jealousy the operation of laws and courts which have sold up old properties and encumbered new ones. I cannot dilate on these subjects; but keep them in mind, and I think you will see hereafter that they have had effect banefully to weaken attachment which might have been secured by other means.

I am confident in your English resources. It will be seen that a very large force of European troops is needed for India, and that henceforth they must be *en masse*, as Sir Charles Napier most truly observed and urged. Isolated parties are of no use, and, as in case of the assembly at Delhi, can only be got together after long delays, and then inefficiently. I have no doubt the Government will send from 10,000 to 20,000 men directly, and meantime what there are will hold their own *at least;* but I hope the Delhi matter will have been settled by this time, and, after that, the rest is rather of detail only. Without money, without leaders, without guns, resources, or

ammunition, what can a rabble of sepoys do? Social mischief
only; and that, horrible as it has been and may be, is the
price at which we are purchasing experience. Perhaps, in the
end, all will be better than before. Illusions will be dispelled,
and there will be no trifling with danger. There must be a
native army, but that of Bengal will not be what it has been.
There will be more European cavalry and infantry, and more
artillery; more irregular levies or armed police; in short, we
shall be wiser and sadder, and shall not trust, as we seem to
have been doing for many years, to our good fortune or *prestige*.
This, too, may have been one of those solemn warnings, given
in God's providence, resulting from struggles in men's minds
between forms of belief—the *fact* between heathenism and
Christianity. What the Saxons were to Charlemagne, the
Hindoos, *mutatis mutandis*, may be to us. A great struggle
between light and darkness, civilisation and savages, is no
doubt progressing, and, like others before it, will have its
phases of excitement and misery. Lord Canning is doing well
now, but was not decisive enough perhaps at first. Yet who
shall say it?

MEADOWS TAYLOR.

NULDROOG, July 6, 1857.

You will read with horror in England the accounts from the
Bengal stations, where regiments have mutinied. I will not
dwell upon them. Mutiny, and a declaration for the sepoy's
cause, whatever it is, might have been expected in an organised
rising of this kind; but it is clear now that the extermination
of officers, with their wives and families, was one main object—
and, alas! it has been accomplished with fiendish barbarity in
many instances. I cannot think otherwise than that England
will be stirred as she has rarely been stirred before; and that it
has needed but the perusal of the accounts of the last month,
and even of the last fortnight, to arouse a spirit of vengeance
against these miscreant sepoys, such as has been rarely, if ever,
displayed among you, and that troops will be sent out instantly
in large numbers. We have not yet heard of the fall of Delhi
—that is the point on which all interest centres at present;

and the operations there are not known, except that General
Barnard had repulsed three sorties from the place, with great
loss to the mutineers.   By the last accounts—that is, up to the
16th—the General was waiting for some reinforcements from
the Punjaub, which had reached Umballa on their way down
to him.   I daresay the place is strong; and as all in it are
fighting with halters in prospect if taken, they are doubtless
desperate; and it is clear nothing can be risked.   Reports have
come down country to Bombay that the place has been taken,
but they are not officially confirmed as yet; so we must wait in
patience.   They are strong in Calcutta, and I daresay by this
time have some of the Chinese troops there; if so, they will be
pushed up the country with all speed.   The Punjaub is quiet
—no rising or disturbance—which speaks well for the local
administration.   All through the Deccan and south of India
there is entire tranquillity.   Hyderabad is well in hand by
Davidson, who will get credit for what he has done.   The
Nizam and the Minister are stanch, and the Arabs well in hand
also; they have no sympathy with the Bengal movement, or
with a king of Delhi, and will be faithful to us.   Here we are
all quiet and peaceable as any one could wish, and also in all
the adjoining districts, British and Nizam's.   We were rather
apprehensive a week ago, that a regiment of Nizam's Contingent cavalry, which had mutinied at Aurungabad, and was at
first stated to be in full march on its station, Mominabad,
about sixty miles from this, might make a dash at us for the
sake of the treasury; but that report was false.   No men
moved from Aurungabad till General Woodburn's force arrived
there by a forced march of seventy miles from Ahmednugger.
The General went straight to the cavalry lines, surrounded the
regiment, when the greatest number of the men submitted at
once—in fact, joined him; but some remained till a charge or
two of grape was sent among them, when they fled for the most
part, sixty-four being taken prisoners.   Of these, several have
been hanged, and some transported; and the example will have
a good effect, no doubt—indeed has had, for no one has stirred
elsewhere.   I have about eighty of the men of this corps on
duty in the district, but all have behaved well, and seem right

glad to be out of the mess.   There was an ugly sort of conspiracy at Sattara, when the matter first broke out; but Rose,
the Collector there, who is a good officer, has nipped it in the
bud, and all is square again.

You will see that the ex-king of Oudh has been confined,
and that Government have a clue to his participation in the
matter.   I have from the first thought that Oudh was the
cause of this.   Our Bengal army are Oudh men for the most
part; and, as I may have said before, the check on habitual
lawlessness in Oudh, and no less lawlessness in the ranks of
the army, was hardly to be endured.   No doubt the conspiracy
has been long matured.   It has been no cartridge question, or
any other question, but a struggle to break bonds, which were
getting tighter every day.   If this outbreak had not occurred,
the crisis would have come in some other form, and might possibly have been worse.   As it is, it is only a question of time.
The Ganges is rising fast, and steamers can get up with troops
easily and quickly.   5000 men from China will hold everything
till you can send us more; but for some years to come India
will require many more European troops than she has had.   In
this Lord Dalhousie failed, that he trusted the native army
when it was clear they were not in hand as soldiers should be.
With a new annexation at one end in the Punjaub, and one in
the middle—and considering the character of Oudh, which was
far more lawless than the Punjaub ever was—there should have
been a heavy European force there and at Delhi.   All this is
too late now: we have only to retrieve the losses, and our
power will be stronger than ever, and the attachment of all
well-disposed classes greater; for it is clear to all, when any
disorganisation ensues, what will be the result to property.
Government will be sadder but wiser; and the administration
of India for the next hundred years more civilised than it has
been since Plassey.   The savagery of the worst State in India
has had its burst—a fearful one it has been—but the retribution will be as fearful.   All these men are landed proprietors in
Oudh.   Dare they return there to be hunted down?   Every man's
name is known, and his place of residence; and when our turn
begins again, woe to them!   Small mercy will be shown to the

violators and murderers of English women and helpless children.
As it is, there appears a lull. About half the Bengal army has
not stirred. Many of the corps are doing good service, and
will perhaps wait to see the issue of Delhi. By-and-by, as
corps move up from Calcutta, the rebels will be between two
fires. We know they have no ammunition or material in shot
and shell but what may have been got at Delhi, and no ammunition but what was found there. Where are they to get caps
for their muskets, which are all percussion? We see at Benares
that they threw away 1400 stand of arms. Now, if they kept
their arms and discipline, they might be formidable; but without either, they are no more than the rabble, which has never
yet stood—and never can—regular armies. So I see good hope
in prospect; and as we must have had it *out* one day, the worst
is over, I think. Every one will blame Lord Dalhousie, I
daresay. I only see that he was wrong in not covering his
annexations with sufficient European troops, and this the
Russian war prevented his doing. We ought to hear by the
mail coming in what you say at home to the beginning of the
Mutiny. But we cannot hear what you know of the worst for
another fortnight, or month perhaps. This mutiny will give us
an electric telegraph to you, no doubt, when you can hear daily
news from India. But we should be thankful that we have at
least steam to carry over distress to you in a month, and perhaps gain help. You will see that men are equal to the emergency. Lawrence at Lucknow has done wonders. Colonel
Neil and his Madras Fusiliers are renowned already—a gallant-
spirited man as any we have. In the Punjaub, too, they have
determined men and troops enough, as they have got rid of all
the Bengal men. We only want troops for the North-Western
Provinces and Central India, and we shall be all right in a
few months. Meanwhile, the more anxious England is the
better.

You will see what Lord Canning has done about the press.
I think it was needed now; but it may be relaxed, except
to native prints, hereafter. And I hope these murders and
massacres will ease Exeter Hall and its party of some of its
cant in regard to "sympathy with natives."

STORY OF MY LIFE. [CHAP. XIII.

I am quite well—and here, but that we read newspapers, should have no anxiety whatever. Tell this to all who ask after me. God bless you! and believe me ever yours faithfully,

MEADOWS TAYLOR.

[In the month of August Captain Taylor was promoted to the Deputy-Commissionership in North Berar, and proceeded to his new station at Booldana.]

JAULNAH, *September 7, 1857.*

I have got so far on my journey to my new country,—that is, about three-fourths of the distance. We cannot travel luxuriously as you do, but I have come about 180 miles in nine days, with my tents and servants well up, which is not bad work. I give all a rest here, and hope that Bullock will come in from Booldana to-day, till when I shall occupy myself with writing, and first to you. I had intended to have done so on the road; but the double marches, evening and morning, though they are not over ten or twelve miles at the most, interrupt every attempt to settle to anything. My journey has been a very pleasant one; there was no rain to speak of: and through the Nizam's country, in which I could not possibly have been treated with greater civility and distinction had I been the Resident himself, deputations met me from all the large towns and stations, and I was helped on in every way I could desire. The country is perfectly peaceful and loyal to us. But it is sad to see so much of it waste, and to hear the people complaining, not so much of active oppression, as of no one taking the least interest in them, except to screw what can be got out of them. I see, however, changes for the better in the system of district management, and there seems to be a system at last; but it must be, even with Salar Jung, that he has little assistance, much opposition, and in all cases very lukewarm co-operation. I trust, however, that a man so thoroughly in earnest and single in purpose will succeed as he deserves to do. His conduct through the trying crisis of June and July has been very admirable; and as it has passed the ordeal of the Mohurrum safely, Hyderabad may be considered thoroughly safe, I think, as its people throughout the country are entirely well affected.

You ask me in your last what the effect of this mutiny upon the princes of India seems to be. It is not an easy question to answer, but I will give you my opinions ; and, unless we sustain very unlooked-for and serious reverses, I do not think they will alter. At present, then, I think all is in a satisfactory state. Certainly there is no sympathy with the mutineer sepoys, neither politically nor as far as creed is concerned. The papers will give you details, but not one of the large States has moved or openly displayed sympathy with the sepoy movement. Wherever these Poorbia sepoys, whether Hindoos or Mussulmans, have had service, they have mutinied and gone towards Delhi, as they did from our service. Contingents of native princes, which at first appeared loyal to us, but which consisted of the *same classes* of soldiers as our men, broke away as well from us as from their nominal masters and joined the general confederacy. You see this exemplified in the events at Indore and Gwalior, and the cases of the Kotah contingent, Bhopal people, &c. ; but as soon as Holkar was rid of his mutinous soldiery, who marched to Delhi, and his own Mahrattas rallied round him, he welcomed the Resident back, and matters now are much safer and quieter than before. The princes of Rajpootana have been loyal and stanch, I believe, to a man, helping with their men as far as was needed. I can, however, readily understand their not sending large bodies into the field, with an infectious spirit abroad, and without any apparent head, knowing that there is amongst them as strong a love for plunder and anarchy as existed in the time of the Pindharees, nay worse. Native States have therefore kept quiet, sending only what they themselves could entirely depend on ; and in this they have been right.

That there is any combination among native States against us, I have no suspicion ; and a combination to set up a head, as an Emperor of Delhi, would, I should think, be the last thing that any one of them wanted. If it were possible that such a result followed, even for a while, the impossibility of cohesion is most transparent to all ; while the certainty of exaction, extortion, plunder, and insecurity of property, is alike clear to every one. Better, therefore, as it is, to them; and they are accordingly quiet, if not active and sympathising friends. At a first glance you might think that the Nizam State would sympathise with a " Delhi Raj." But the Nizams were faithless to Delhi, utterly so, and would have to pay a heavy reckoning, nay, be utterly extinguished, if possible. The Mahratta princes, what remain of them, hold territories wrested from Delhi. Would they be spared? The Rajpoot princes, the oldest feudatories of Delhi, have, as I have said, displayed active sympathy with us, retaining and protecting the political agents with them, and helping with supplies, and in other ways of which the papers give details. I have from the first looked anxiously to see whether any grand political movement or confederation could be detected, but as yet there appears none, and I think the Government will have the same intelligence from the Governor-General. No; as yet the movement appears confined to the Bengal army, and to that portion of it which is called Poorbia or Hindoostanee. The Sikhs will have none of it : Goorkhas are stanch ; but wherever these Poorbias are, there are disaffection and open savagery of the worst description. The reason of this is as yet a profound mystery. That the whole of the Bengal army was prepared to rise about the 15th May, there can be no doubt now ; and that its rising was not simultaneous, has been providential. Even now, regiments that have been disarmed break away occasionally. Corps of irregular cavalry that have been considered stanch, mutiny and make off to plunder, and join, if they can, the Delhi or Rohilkund parties, even without arms, or pay, or plunder. To doubt, therefore, a preconcerted plan in this mutiny would be absurd. It has existed, and exists ; and out of the whole Bengal army I do not think there are at present more than half-a-dozen Poorbia regiments who are stanch, or who have proved loyalty by action. It will be long before the origin of the movement is known. Whether, as has been supposed, it is in reality a plot of the Delhi princes to attempt to regain sovereignty,—whether it is owing to intrigues in Oudh,—whether an attempt among a powerful body, bound

together as the Hindoo Poorbias are by one bond of religious
belief, to establish a dominion of military priests as existed in
the ancient days of Hindooism,—or whether it is one of these
outbreaks of savagery against civilisation, of which we have
instances innumerable in the history of civilisation, remains to
be seen.   My own impressions lead me much to the latter belief.   Civilisation is pressing hard on Hindooism, perhaps also
on Mohammedanism : I do not say Christianity, for that as yet
is far off; but that amount of civilisation which has proved
progression of knowledge to be incompatible with Hindooism,
and to be sapping its very existence.   This may have led to
conspiracy among Brahmins, and by them the Rajpoots or
Kshettriya classes have been aroused to action.   These classes
compose the Bengal army.   There are no others.   Hindoostanee Mussulmans are much Hindooised, and were originally
part of the Hindoo people.   Hence, when it became necessary,
there has been for the time a complete identification of the
interests of all.   Again, for the last fifty years we have been
breeding up a race of stalwart priests for our army.   In the
most deplorable manner we have strengthened every prejudice
by enlisting none but them.   The magnificent *men* of that
army were the admiration of all, they were accordingly pam-
pered and indulged by all ; they *would not allow* intermixture
of other classes ; they recruited themselves ; and each corps,
from the officers down to the lowest private, were not only
classmen, but fellow-priests as Brahmins, or holy warriors as
Kshettriyas.   Can anything more pregnant with mischief be
imagined ?   Yet so vain were Bengal officers of their men, and
of their men's *caste*, which was the strangest thing, that mention or thought of anything low-caste was ridiculed,—and the
Madras and Bombay armies held as things of nought.   So it
went from bad to worse, as regards discipline ; and while the
sepoys strengthened themselves in their regiments, civilisation
was treading hard on their heels outside.   Sepoys were not
educated men, except in ceremonials as Brahmins.   Education
was spreading over Bengal and the North-West Provinces very
fast.   It would have followed into Oudh, and as yet Oudh was
a stronghold of dark Hindoo fanaticism.   The Oudh Brahmins

are known by other Brahmins for their attachment to, and study of, the mystic rites of Bhowanee or Kali.   These rites are held in abhorrence by Deccan Brahmins ; they call them fearful and unholy, and those among them who have knowledge of them are held in dread by the rest.   Of such are the Bengal sepoys, the Brahmins and Rajpoots of Oudh and as far south as Benares.   And since they have broken forth and shown themselves in their true colours, it has not surprised me to see that the mask completely thrown off has displayed in savagery that spirit which in those districts produced Thuggee, which had its most noted leaders from among these very classes.   I have given you these reasons to explain why I think this more a movement of savagery against civilisation than aught else, and I still adhere to my opinion that the annexation of Oudh was the incentive to this outbreak.   Perhaps the way in which Oudh was managed at first, and till Lawrence got it, made it more immediate than it otherwise would have been.   Outram took Oudh, but has always eschewed details of management. The first managing man under him was a thorough-bred Bengal civilian, as the phrase goes,—haughty, quarrelsome, imperious, and a red-tapist of the worst school.   So I have heard him described.   He did much mischief, no doubt ; and *then* must have begun the organisation, or the idea of it.   Strange to say, Lord Dalhousie could not see danger in trusting a new country to the military occupation of a people whose freedom (lawlessness is a better word) his measures were curtailing every day.   He, too, believed in the Bengal sepoy as others did.   Yet he was bringing that sepoy's father and brothers into subjection, looking after and taxing their lands, preventing them from indulging in outrages and dacoity.   For years and years we have recruited from Oudh ; and for years and years we have known the Oudh population to be the most lawless in India.   Was it expected that it would like civilisation, or a strong Government, or restraint of any kind?   And were not the very men we enlisted as lawless in their way as their brethren at home,—refusing foreign service, refusing discipline, refusing intermixture of other castes?   All this was : some saw it, and some wrote about it.   Those who did write

about it, either to the public or to Government, were marked
and ruined men ; they were never advanced.　Many people are
getting courage to speak out *now*, but it is too late.　It was a
pleasant delusion, that Bengal army, while it lasted ; and so
were all other Bengal delusions pleasant—nothing was like
them.　The men who held them were inflated ; they were, in
fact, Bengal civilians, and who should gainsay them ?　——
wrote to me only the other day that he knew every one, for
years past, who had striven publicly or privately to expose
these delusions, had been a marked man.　So it went on.　One
would have thought that when last year the cakes of bread flew
through the North-West Provinces, it would have aroused suspicion of some intrigue, or would have been traced.　What
notice was taken of it ?　None, that I know of ; or if any suspicion was entertained it was shut up.　If Government knew
of suspected disaffection—or if at any time what Napier wrote,
what others hinted, what even broke out in occasional mutiny,
was known,—and I am impressed with a conviction that it was
known, and feared too,—why was India left so defenceless in
regard to European troops ?　But this is another part of the
subject, now, alas ! causing waste of life and treasure, which
will keep India back for years.

There is another matter, or cause of disaffection, which I will
briefly mention, because it affects the *people* of the country.　I
have doubted the revenue system of the North-West Provinces
very much ever since I knew it.　It has made village communities throw off attachment to Government, I think, by
weakening the bond between them ; and it has reduced the
bond of the landholders, whether great or small, to a simple
question of money-payment, the most easily broken.　It has
also given headmen too much influence, and reduced village
communities to a state of vassalage to them, rather than retaining them in a direct communication with Government authorities.　This system is the far-famed " Thomason " system ; one
which, no doubt, got in most money with least cost—but otherwise, *I* think, and have always thought, was regardless of the
people, and regardless of the bond which should have been
maintained, rather than broken.　You see the result now in

some shape. Leaders of villages have abused authority, petty chiefs have leagued with them, both parties have taken to plundering property not belonging to their own classes. Here and there, there are symptoms of revulsion, and the *people*, tired of being plundered, have risen on their headmen, and invited back the European magistrates ; and this will progress, I think and trust, as if to show, without doubt, the utter inability of these people to rule themselves without plunder and massacre, and the utter insecurity of property in whatever shape it may exist. This may have its effect in time in restoring order ; but the operation of reducing to order a country which has become disorganised is necessarily slow at any time, and one can hardly see or think whom to trust when Government has crushed, as it will crush, the originators of the Mutiny. It is sad to think, too, that all the promotion of natives to offices of trust and confidence has in most instances proved futile to check disorder or maintain authority. There have been, it is true, some faithful men, some bright instances of personal exertion to aid our authority, but they are lamentably few ; and it must be almost more bitter to those who have selected these authorities to see them supine or faithless, than to encounter the mad savagery of the native army. It is too soon now to speculate upon final results as to the civil government of the country. It may, it is true, be comparatively easy when order is once more established ; but the shock to all has been a rude and violent one. The civilisation of mind, which most of us thought had made progress, proves to be only skin-deep, and not to have affected the masses of the people at all, and will have to be commenced again, I hope in a more earnest and practical spirit than before. I adhere to my opinion that a government on the part of the Crown will be the best policy to pursue, and there can be no doubt that a double Government will not answer. Whether it is understood by the people, that the Company has been, as it were, abandoned by the Crown— that it only occupies the place of " farmers " of the country, or is in the position of a weak interloper, and can be thrown off— I do not know ; but there is much in the discussions on the renewal of the charter, and the comparative absence of European troops, to favour the supposition in minds which cannot understand European politics or the constitution of our own country. I see that Sir Erskine Perry has already made a motion on the subject; but the extent of the calamity must be fully known before a remedy can be applied, and I think the result will be a Government into which no division of authority can enter. No one will be hardy enough now to support the doctrine that India can be governed by opinion. It must be by European troops well distributed that Government can be maintained. I shall be anxious to see what turn your counsels take on this subject, one on which all in India are well assured that England is doing her best, and that the past will be retrieved in time.

I have nothing particular to say of myself. I was very sorry to leave the Nuldroog district; the people were quiet and attached, the country was fast improving, and improvements as to roads and other matters were in active progress. I do not know on what principles Berar has been managed, and have to get acquainted with the people,—a long matter, with a district of its size. I will write you more from Booldana by-and-by, and when I see my way into what is before me. God bless you.— With my dear love to all kindred, believe me ever yours faithfully,

MEADOWS TAYLOR.

BOOLDANA, NORTH BERAR, September 26, 1857.

I arrived here on the 14th, and took charge of the district, and your letter of the 6th of August reached me a few days after. I wrote to you from Jaulnah, when staying there to wait for Bullock, and I hope that letter has come safe to hand. I do not think I have missed any mail since this war began; for such as my opinions are, and means of observation, I am anxious you should have the result of them for yourself, apart from all public discussions which reach you from India and are made in England. You have done my first letter much honour, —more than it deserves, I fear, for it was written in a hurry, and in some alarm perhaps, and more than there need have been; and yet I cannot say I have ever felt alarm for anything south of the Nerbudda since the Mutiny broke out, and as yet, you see, we are safe. So long as Hyderabad remains quiet and attached, there is no apprehension, I think, for Southern India ; and I sincerely believe that it is both. The Mohurrum passed off quietly, and there is no excitement at present. On one point they appear obliged to temporise, which is, the trial of Torra Borg Khan, the Rohilla zemindar, who led the attack on the Residency. He has not been hanged, as he ought to have been, nor given up, nor will the head of the Adalut in Hyderabad condemn him for taking part in a *holy war;* it would be against Mohammedan laws, and the Minister appears helpless in respect of bringing him to punishment for the present. He is, how- ever, still in confinement, and it is safe policy not to press any- thing at the present. I have no apprehension of any Mahratta league. In the Deccan the old Mahratta families are weak, and I do not think there is any one who would have sympathy with Sindia after the long break there has been in the connec- tion. The Brahmin influence was never liked by the true Mahratta families, and *he* would not join Nana Sahib, the representative of the Peshwah, nor would the Sattara family. There have been reports that Sindia was deposed by his troops, and Delhi proclaimed. But this wants confirmation, and is not believed. Holkar, the Guicowar, and the Kolapore chief, the Jagheerdars in the South Mahratta country, are all stanch and quiet, and, whether singly or collectively, are too weak to attempt coalition ; such at least is my impression, and I imagine Lord Elphinstone says the same. The Mahratta people of the Deccan, too, are well off as to employment and landed settle- ments; they appear to me to have ceased to be warlike in every way, and, under a good system of government and easy taxa- tion, have fairly abandoned old ways and settled down into active farmers. No doubt there were some intrigues at Sattara which were put down with a strong hand by Rose, the Col- lector, who behaved admirably. There were some plots also at Poona and Belgaum, got up by low adventurers, without leaders or means, but having a bad *animus.* These also were promptly discovered and the conspirators executed. The reported mutiny of one Bombay regiment at Kolapore caused some alarm for the

time lest it should spread; but it was an attempt by the Hindoostanees of the regiment, which was, beyond anything we
have seen yet, insane and futile; and these men were disposed
of very gallantly by the Mahratta Horse and the true men of
their own corps.   In this matter the Kolapore Rajah was well
affected, and gave what help he could; and you know he is one
of the representatives of Sivajee, and many of the old Mahratta
families hold by him and his little court.   The Brahmins of
the Deccan are not military people in any way, and they are
well represented and provided for in Government employ.   I
do not think there is discontent among them, and if there were,
they have no sympathy among the Mahratta people, who do
not like them.   Under all these points of view, I do not think
there is ground for apprehension of any Mahratta rising or
combination, and I hope my views may be ultimately correct.

Now the more I look back to what I wrote to you first, the
more I am inclined to adhere to the opinions I then expressed,
and have since repeated.   The Mohammedan sympathy in
the movement has been secondary as far as the people are concerned, even in the North-West Provinces, but the share of the
King of Delhi and his large family of *soi-disant* Shahzadahs
in the original plot, while it remains to be investigated, is
meantime borne out by facts.   I have long considered the Bengal army utterly unsafe.   It had become impossible to control
the priestly faction of which it was composed, and to which all
others were subordinate; for the Mohammedan portion of it
was just as arrogant in respect to caste prejudices as the Hindoo, and followed the Hindoo lead.   It was impossible to con-
vince Bengal officers of the mischief attending any caste as an
element of military service under us.   No attempt was made,
or could have been made (except by taking the bull by the
horns, which no one dared to do), to break down the caste
influence, except by the very partial effort of the enlistment of
sepoys on oath for general service—which of course, and as
might have been foreseen, was useless in contact with the old
and very powerful element of the former system.   I daresay
this was admitted by those who chose to think—and I will
venture to say there were few who did not; still the old pre-

Z

judice in favour of high-caste Brahmins, arising no doubt out
of the comparative ease by which they were managed as soldiers
in garrison, the fine appearance of the men, and the bravery
occasionally displayed in recent times, with the *prestige* of old
victories, all combined to perpetuate the illusion; and while
the soldiery were led to look up to the service as an hereditary
right, they became the less disposed to brook any interference
with it. You see how these men were spreading fast into the
Bombay Army. As Hindoostanee men rose to rank as *suba-
dars* and native officers in general, and returned to their native
villages, they were employed to bring down batches of recruits,
fine stalwart young fellows, who enlisted readily, and no doubt
served well. Mahrattas, as their country has been settled, and
become, as it is, one expanse of cultivation, needed no employment for their young men, and, except the very lowest classes,
did not enlist in the army. Those regiments into which a Hindoostanee element has been once infused, became more and
more Hindoostanee from year to year; and the 16,000 men
said now to be in the Bombay army would have been doubled
in a few years more, with the same kind of contrivance, the
same views, and no doubt eventually the same conduct as the
Bengal army itself. Happily, most happily, this has been
broken up. The design of enlisting any more of these people,
and the danger of even allowing what there are to remain, is
too imminent to be overlooked, and it will be averted. In
the Madras army I believe there are a few Hindoostanees here
and there, but very few, and they will, I trust, be got rid of.
But in the Madras army there is another influence not unlike
what prevailed in Bengal, which needs to be checked in time;
this is the Mohammedan, and you will do good service by bringing it to notice in those quarters where it can be remedied.
The military portion of the Mohammedans of the Madras
Presidency lie about Arcot, Seringapatam, Vellore, and other
places, and are exclusively military, looking, as the Bengal and
Oudh Brahmins did, to hereditary services. They are known
to be bigoted, and even natives mistrust the Thull Ghat Mussulman as turbulent and unfaithful. They have their old ideas
of rule under the Mysore dominion of Hyder and Tippoo, brief

but brilliant ; possibly have no sympathy with Delhi, but true
sympathy with the cause of Islam. They are not cultivators,
like the Sikhs and Mahrattas, but look to service as sepoys—in
short, to a military life, rather than to any other, and have found
it in the Madras army to a great extent. It is only necessary
that this combination, which provides all the cavalry and
many of the infantry regiments, should not be allowed to proceed as it has done in Bengal ; and there is plenty of time to
avert it. I have known many men who thought that the more
a regiment was connected by family ties the better; but we
now see the danger of it as regards the Bengal army, and,
under the constitution of the native mind, everywhere the
same ; and the danger attending combination induced by a
sense of power, I think should be prevented. I am not writing or thinking any wrong of the Madras army, which as yet
has proved wonderfully stanch and obedient in many trying
times and foreign wars : I only wish to prevent the possibility
of its becoming other than it is and has been—the possibility
of its gaining that conviction of power, which has destroyed
the Bengal army, as it will assuredly any other army which is
infected by it. By what means this can be best effected is not
in my power to state. It must be done silently, gradually, and
without exciting suspicion. I have often thought a partial
admission of half-castes, as also enlistment of negroes, or some
of the martial Cape tribes, would be good, and negroes best of
all ; and often and often, in old letters, have I dwelt on this
subject, and alluded to the increasing predominance of *caste
power* in the native armies, particularly in that of Bengal ; but
who attended then ? Another idea is, that part of every native regiment should be European,—say one flank company or
both flank companies, with more English non-commissioned
officers. The French mixed natives and Europeans together in
this manner with good effect, both as to work in the field and
discipline in garrison, and it prevented combination. It has
long been the opinion of able men that artillery should be exclusively European, and natives used only as assistants, as I
may say, under them ; and in this I entirely coincide. It is
the artillery only of the mutinous Bengal army which does any

execution, and costs us men to recover; and yet the guns have not in general been well fought, and are taken by comparative handfuls of our troops. But I am wearying you, I daresay, with these disquisitions.

The siege-train has reached Delhi, and the final result there cannot be delayed. Every one knows by this time of the munificent aid you are giving us, and the rest is but a work of time. The cold weather is before us, the British army will have the best of the year for field operations, and it is little to say, I think, will perhaps, in the end, be disappointed that there is so little left to do. I myself think there will be comparatively few left in Delhi when it is assaulted, and that our final operations will be in Oudh, where most of the mutineers will fight *pro aris et focis*, and not for the King of Oudh, or any potentate whatever. It will be satisfactory to you to see how few persons of rank are concerned in this movement, and how few of the people in general, when the millions of which the population of Hindoostan is composed are reckoned. Idle savagery exists everywhere, and the country has never been disarmed. Plunder and violence might be expected from such classes, and it has no doubt abounded, to the misery and disgust of those better classes who were secure under us. I cannot but think that this has had a great effect in our favour throughout the country, and must, too, in the worst districts about Delhi and in Oudh. I trust the complete disarming of the Bengal Presidency will be the first work of the *new* Government. It has worked well in the Punjaub; and indeed for all India a "licence to carry arms bill" would be very advisable. Oudh must be disarmed, of course. They did not hesitate to disarm the Punjaub almost as the first measure, and we see the benefit of it now; but they dared not attempt to disarm Oudh, because it would have affected the Bengal army, and so it remained as before, strong in itself as having perpetually resisted the Oudh Government, and stronger as being part of ourselves, with which we dare not interfere. It will be broken now and reduced, and with it will be broken all military *prestige*, and I hope combination, not only of the Brahmins and Rajpoots, but of the petty rajahs and zemindars who abound. In our next revenue settlements, too, we might break up combinations in regard to land, and by seeing that every one gets what he requires for cultivation, make him dependent more upon Government than on his feudal chief. I mistrust those North-West settlements, I assure you, very deeply, and think that had the Government made grants to the people instead of to the middlemen, they would have had more content, more real attachment than in the other course. That course, however, got most money at least cost of collection, and so was persevered in.

I do not go into details of events; those the newspapers chronicle steadily. A few Bengal regiments remain stanch, and do good work, as the 31st at Saugor, &c.; but the rest are gone, and happily, I think, sparing our Government any chance of sympathising with them afterwards. You will know the sad, sad particulars of Cawnpore in time; and I beg you to read the deposition of a soubadar of the Bombay army, who for his faithful conduct has been promoted, with 1000 rupees, and the military order of merit. I dare say, and hope, that there will be many such examples come to light by-and-by. You may hear by this mail that Delhi has been stormed, and Lucknow relieved by Havelock and Outram. If they do not kill the King of Delhi, I hope he will be transported to England with all his family. The King of Oudh should go too, and be kept there, as Dhuleep Singh is, in honour and respect. There should be no flinching in this, I think.

I would not have you think, from anything I have said, that I am against the annexation policy of Lord Dalhousie. The fault was, not guarding it sufficiently; and if, as I believe, it has been the direct means of showing the true temper and worth of the Bengal army, it has been the more welcome now that we are free to remedy it. We should have been hard pressed if this outbreak had occurred when we had the Russian war on our hands. I am delighted to see the question of the Queen's Government openly canvassed; and it should be carried steadily through till Queen Victoria's proclamations are in every village of India belonging to her.

This is a nice little station. Myself, Captain Grant, and his wife, are the only tenants of it. Bullock's house, which he lets

me live in, is very comfortable. The situation is on the table-
land just above the Ghât, on the south side of the Berar valley,
six miles east of a place called Dewul Ghât, which I daresay
you will find in any good map. The climate is very good—
just now most delightful; and I am quite hearty, and well as
ever I was in my life, I am thankful to say. Now good-bye,
and God bless you all!—My most affectionate regards and remembrance to all, and believe me ever yours most faithfully,

MEADOWS TAYLOR.

I cannot find my usual statement of revenue and cultivation for this official year, 1856-57, which would have given
the details of each department. I only find in a letter to
my father, dated June 4, that the net amount of revenue
was 919,000 rupees in round numbers, and that the 40,000
rupees lost by abolition of customs duties had been nearly
made up.

The increase in cultivation had been very nearly 35,000
acres in the year, which, together with the previous increase, made a total of 219,000 since the cession. 237
miles of road had been completed, and much more had
been surveyed, marked out, and was in progress.

The survey showed a result of 260,000 acres completed;
and the surveyors, who could not do field-work in the
rains, were now occupied in making fair copies of village
maps and registries. These maps were most creditably
executed, and some of my pupils evinced decided talent
as draughtsmen.

I was in daily expectation of a reply in regard to the
principles and working of the survey which I had drawn
up, and submitted in November 1856; but eight months'
work had shown decided and continuous improvement in
every respect; and as the tenures of land had not entered
into the first propositions, and I had to make many ex-
planations in regard to future contingencies, my final
report was delayed. My readers would scarcely under-

stand the minutiæ of village and landed tenures, and I
will not inflict them upon them here ; but I may mention
that I found a great proportion of the occupants of land
to be *mirasdars*—that is, persons who hold their portions
of land in hereditary occupancy, and had so held it for
generations, on a fixed rent. Most of these had suffered
from local exactions, and but too many had thrown up
their ancestral lands, and had emigrated to the British
provinces. Of these great numbers had now returned,
and had taken up their former estates where they were in
possession of yearly tenants. Others, in cases where the
land had been improved, had paid the occupant a sum of
money for reoccupancy ; but all *miras* rights were re-
claimable within a period of forty years of absence. To
preserve the local rights of these *miras* proprietors, the
tenants of *miras* lands had only been recognised as yearly
tenants; but they were not disturbed so long as they paid
their rent regularly.

The third was a fluctuating class, who took up lands
which generally belonged to the village area, on yearly
tenure only. These were constantly changing, and passing
from village to village, for the most part unthrifty people,
with neither capital nor credit, and but few cattle.

I could see plainly the advantage of settled classes, and
of giving them security of tenure, in order to induce the
employment of capital and the improvement of their
estates ; and I proposed that all holders of land should be
made proprietors, and that the land should be not only
actual property to all, but that it should be allowed to be
bought and sold or mortgaged like any other marketable
commodity. Also, as the lands in all surveyed villages
had now been defined, that the owners and occupants
should have the option of taking out title-deeds for them,
on stamped paper, which at the head should have a map
of the land or estate, whatever it might be, great or small;
and that in the body of the deed the boundaries and

general description of every field or division should be detailed, the estate to become the hereditary property of the holder, subject only to a lien on the part of Government.

I fixed the term of thirty years for the first settlement of revenue, at the expiration of which period a revision should be made, and the rent fixed as a permanent settlement in perpetuity.

The Bombay survey was admirable, as far as it went, and the occupants of land were secured by registry; but I thought that possession required more security than registry, and that actual title-deeds would provide this, enable the land to be bought and sold, and satisfy the proprietors. I saw, too, that by the plan I proposed the real marketable capital of the country would be enormously increased, and the intrinsic value of the land would become a source of wealth to every individual holder. I also, at the same time as the land survey, carried on a survey of village sites. Every house was numbered, and its boundaries defined and measured, and title-deeds for this description of property were to be given separately.

When all my rules were drawn up and completed, I made a translation of them into Mahratta; and having assembled the chief men of villages, the officers and *miras-dars*, as well as other landholders and occupants, as many as would attend, I laid before them the paper I had drawn up, telling them what I proposed to do if permitted by Government.

At first anything so definite and so valuable was doubted, and I believe the people, who had all through their lives been under a system of exaction and oppression, thought there was some dark sinister plan lying below the surface; but when they came fully to comprehend the projects laid down, and received my assurance that title-deeds would be given for all lands, even the smallest holdings, the delight (for I can call it nothing else), the enthusiasm, and the gratitude of the people knew no bounds. It seemed to all as if a new life were opening before them—peace for themselves, and their descendants after them.

Two years previous to this, I had saved the people from a measure proposed on the system of the North-West Provinces, by the Supreme Government. This was, to make a settlement of my district, and all the others were placed in the same category, with zemindars. Now there were no zemindars, in the Bengal sense of the term, in the ceded districts, with whom any settlement could be made. The officials who went by that name were the ancient hereditary officers of counties, not necessarily landed proprietors, except in payment of their local services. It was impossible to elevate such persons into landholders, or to give them the rank and position of such, or to transfer to them properties which belonged to other people. Such a course would have interfered seriously with those landed proprietors in villages who were very sturdy in maintaining their hereditary rights; and the settlement in this manner seemed to my perception utterly impossible, and any attempt to force it on the people would have produced not only universal discontent and anger, but in all likelihood a serious insurrection. I wrote, as I was obliged, a great deal on the subject, and I believe I was considered "most impracticable and obstinate," and incurred, I have little doubt, much ill-will; but for that I cared absolutely nothing. I could not uphold what I believed would be an injury and a wrong to my people, or become a party to any course which I considered was not only unjust and unpopular to the last degree, but which would abolish all those ancient hereditary tenures to which the people had clung with devoted pertinacity through all revolutions and vicissitudes for many centuries, and which the old Mussulman kings and rulers of the Deccan had continuously respected.

My view of this question was very strenuously supported by my friend Bullock, Commissioner in Berar;
and, in the end, I rejoice to say that we so far prevailed
as to enlist the sympathies of our Chief Commissioner on
our side, who earnestly protested against the system proposed from Bengal, and was successful in his opposition,
inasmuch as the question was deferred for " future consideration." In his Administrative Report of 1870, Mr
Saunders, Resident at Hyderabad, and *ex-officio* Chief
Commissioner, states, p. 14:—

"Orders were actually issued by the Government of
India for a settlement of rights on the basis of the village
community system, and were suspended only in deference
to the earnest protest of Mr Maltby, the then Commissioner of the Hyderabad Assigned Districts, some of whose
assistants, such as Mr Bullock and Captain Meadows
Taylor, had passed their working lives in the Deccan, and
perfectly understood the nature and meaning of the facts
they had to deal with in their newly-acquired provinces."

Again, after the final territorial arrangements with his
Highness the Nizam in 1860 were completed, the question
was revived by the Government of India, and orders were
again issued in the most stringent terms. All honour
is due to Mr Saunders, who, although himself a Bengal
civilian, possessed ample means of studying the question
from previous reports and local observation, and had the
firmness to resist and maintain the existing system; and,
as he states, "when the report was drawn up, the final
orders of Government were passed, and the system of
field assessment and recognised recognition of cultivating
occupancy was formally sanctioned."

The people of Berar had also obtained a zealous advocate in Mr Lyall, Commissioner of the province, also a
Bengal civilian, whose report, after study of all previous
correspondence, formed, perhaps, the basis of those by Mr
Saunders, and rescued the rights of the hereditary and all

other classes of occupants from transfer to a class of
persons who had never possessed them, and who, indeed,
made no pretence whatever to them in any way. I had
the subject much at heart, and must apologise for this
long story about it; yet I cannot refrain from quoting Mr
Lyall's own words, which explain the system on which
the new settlement was made in 1869 :—

"The English Government has now placed the tenure
of land in Berar on a stable foundation. After some
hesitation, for a settlement on the North-West Provinces
model was first actually ordered, the Bombay system of
survey and settlement according to fields has been adopted.
The whole country is being marked off into plots, and as-
sessed at rates which hold good for thirty years. Subject
to certain restrictions, the occupant is absolute proprietor
of his holding; may sell, let, or mortgage any part of it,
cultivate it, or leave it waste, so long as he pays its assessment, which is fixed for the term of thirty years, and may
then be raised only on general principles; that is, the
assessment of an entire district or village may be raised
or lowered as may be expedient; but the impost may not
be altered to the detriment of any one occupant on account
of his improvements. . . . When the registered holder
alienates his estate, he does it by surrender and admittance, like in English copyholding. Indeed the Berar
occupancy has many features resembling the copyhold
estate in the reservation of manorial rights. Thus, in
fifteen years, the Berar cultivator has passed from all
evils of rack-renting, personal insecurity, and uncertain
ownership of land, to a safe property and a fixed assessment."

All this is in exact accordance with the plans laid down
by me in 1856 as the principle of my own survey of the
province of Nuldroog ; but in my humble opinion it does
not go far enough. It neither gives title-deeds for the
land, nor does it assure the landholder that after the

expiration of the thirty years' assessment any further
adjustment of rates shall be final and unchangeable in
perpetuity. Possibly the grant of title-deeds may be
deferred only till the present term of thirty years has
expired; but I rejoice to see that a perpetual settlement
with all *bonâ fide* proprietors of land throughout India is
now publicly advocated, if not publicly notified; and I
trust the bill to be passed on the subject will include the
issue of title-deeds. I cannot imagine a more beneficial
or more popular measure, or one more calculated to secure
the gratitude of the agricultural classes of India. These
deeds would be issued by millions, and the property in
land would be an enormous addition to the national
wealth of India.

I feel that this digression may have been wearisome to
some of my readers, but in writing the ' Story of my Life '
I cannot pass this over without notice, as it was a point
on which, firmly believing myself to be in the right, I deliberately risked not only the goodwill of the Government
of India at that time, but my own employment as Deputy-
Commissioner. I would never have agreed to carry out
the unjust measure proposed in ignorance of local tenures
by the Government of India, and my friend Bullock and
myself were prepared to have resigned our appointments
in case stringent orders were issued on the subject; and
there is no act of my public life which, to this day, gives
me more sincere pleasure and satisfaction than my successful resistance to the orders of Government to the settlement being made according to the North-West system.

It was hoped the Mutiny would be confined to Bengal;
but very early in June the regiment of cavalry stationed
at Aurungabad, or a portion of it, was decidedly in a
mutinous condition, and was, perhaps, only checked by
the attitude of the infantry and artillery who were loyal.
Application had been made to Ahmednugger for assistance,
and the General marched at once upon Aurungabad with

part of a dragoon regiment and some horse - artillery. Hearing of their approach, some of the native cavalry broke away at once, and proceeded to Hyderabad and Hominabad, exciting much alarm throughout the country. The dread was great lest the whole Contingent might be infected with the spirit of the army of Bengal, for most of the Contingent infantry were from Oudh, and thus their example might have spread to the Madras army; happily, however—most happily and providentially—the Contingent remained otherwise firm.

The re-establishment of a new empire at Delhi would not at all have suited the Nizam; for his ancestors had declared themselves independent when the empire had fallen into decadence. And this consideration alone, had others been wanting, would have preserved his loyalty.

It was impossible not to feel great anxiety at Nuldroog. After the mutiny among the cavalry was known abroad, and, I think, when the mutineers arrived at Hominabad, they must have had some communication with those who were with me. They seemed uneasy for several days, and the native officer who was in command seemed uneasy too; but the men professed entire loyalty when I went among them; and as they were quartered in the town, they could not do much harm to any one. They were watched carefully by the police. Eventually three of the troopers broke away at night and went towards Hominabad—the rest remained at their post. I had no means of pursuing the fugitives, indeed my doing so would not have answered any good purpose; and even supposing the cavalry had come to Nuldroog, on account of its treasury, and attacked it, as it was reported they intended to do, I had ample garrison inside the fort, in police and infantry, to have repelled them. The great gate was the only mode of communication with the interior, and the approaches on all other sides were defended by inaccessible precipices.

Sholapoor, too, where the troops were quite loyal, lay within twenty-six miles of us, and a reinforcement could be obtained in twenty-four hours at any time if needed; but the stout old fort no doubt induced a feeling of security which might not have been felt in less well-defended quarters.

On the 23d July, I was very agreeably surprised by a letter from the Chief Commissioner, Mr Maltby, informing me that I had been nominated " settlement officer " and " surveyor-in-chief " to all four districts of the cession, on a salary of 1500 rupees a-month for the present, and 300 rupees travelling allowance. All my maps and proposed plans of settlement had been approved and confirmed, and I was to set about collecting an establishment as soon as possible, so as to begin my work directly the monsoon admitted of my so doing. This was indeed good news; and I looked anxiously to the time when I could surrender all revenue affairs to a successor, who I hoped would be Cadell, as he knew the district and the people so well, and all were attached to him. My new duties would be infinitely more congenial and agreeable ones to me, I felt; and to get rid of the interminable details of revenue business would be a very great relief. I was in high spirits at the prospect opening before me, and at the thought that all my labour at the commencement of the survey would now bear good fruit for the people and save me much trouble. Mine was, however, "the only district in which any attempt had been made to carry out the orders of Government, and my proceedings, from first to last, had been eminently successful, and reflected the highest credit upon me." So wrote Mr Maltby; and I was very much gratified at his kind expressions.

I was quite easy about my district in every respect. The revenue would increase up to two lakhs, which would be its maximum, till the conclusion of the survey; and in all other respects everything was progressing steadily and well. There had not been a single case of dacoity for upwards of a year now !

But I was doomed to disappointment, and all my pleasant dreams rudely dispelled, at least for the present, by the receipt of an express from the Chief Commissioner, on the 24th August, informing me that I had been appointed Deputy-Commissioner of Berar, *vice* Bullock, who was transferred to my district ; and I was to proceed there with all possible speed.

With this public notification came private letters from the Resident and Mr Maltby, both to say that my immediate transfer was a necessity—but why, they did not tell me. Their letters urged me to make no delay whatever, and the Resident's note was characteristic :—

" Go to Berar directly, and *hold on by your eyelids.* I have no troops to give you, and you must do the best you can. I know I can depend upon you, and I am sure you will not fail me."

I would have started that very day, but my camels were out grazing in the country, and Temple was absent, to whom I must make over the treasury and all current business. What would come of the survey now I knew not, nor of my appointment as " settlement officer." I saw the call was very urgent. It was not a time to waste words or thought in idle speculations. My duty was clear before me, and the times were too exciting to venture to ask any questions. I was, however, assured that I should be promoted to be a Deputy-Commissioner of the first class on a salary of 1500 rupees a-month.

It became known later that the survey operations had been suspended till more peaceful times, and all public works as well — till the present threatening aspect of affairs was at an end.

On the day appointed for me to leave — the 27th August—I was presented with a public address from all the official and principal persons of the province. This ultimately received 1622 signatures, and I append a translation of it here. I had not the least conception that such a proceeding had ever been intended. The address was beautifully written in Mahratta, and presented to me on a very handsome silver salver, which I now use constantly.

True Translation of a Mahratta Address to Captain Meadows Taylor, Deputy-Commissioner, Daraseo District, August 27, 1857.

(After the usual preliminary compliments.)

"Since your arrival in this country we have all been happy and prosperous. Now an order has come from Government that you are to go to Berar, and Government has no doubt directed this because of your qualifications, and fitness, and ability for that duty. As it is a higher office than this, it will be a source of pleasure to you; and we all pray to God that He will be pleased to protect so kind and merciful an officer, and we shall be very grateful, so God will hear our prayers.

"But now we are to be separated from you, and are thereby fallen into a sea of grief. We shall never be able to give sufficient praise to you for the manner in which you have protected the people hitherto—how you have created means of prosperity—and for your various good qualities. Still we have it in our hearts to address you in some sort, and you are to be pleased to accept it in order to gratify all.

"In the year 1853 you came to this district as Deputy-Commissioner; and, considering its circumstances then and now, there is a very great difference in its condition, of which you are the sole cause. When you came, there were no good roads in Nuldroog; all the village streets and paths were filthy and useless, and even men travelled with difficulty. But you, with much personal exertion, have made proper arrangements for the good comfort of

all. We all know this, and it has all come of your kindness.

"There was an immense quantity of waste land in the
district. This has been cultivated since you came, and is
now inhabited; and by provision of water and other circumstances in the country, hamlets, villages, and market-
towns have been founded and built, and trade has very
greatly increased, by which all obtain a livelihood, and
there is no distress of any kind.

" Before, in this district, dacoits and gang-robbers and
plunderers who openly committed murder, used to go
about in force, and the inhabitants were much afflicted by
them. But you established police, and settled everything,
and so entirely extirpated these people, that not even a
trace of them remains. From this protection of life and
property, one of the principal benefits which result from
the British Government was secured to this district.

"In the year 1855 there was a very heavy famine in
this land, and it was difficult even for rich people to support themselves. In that hard time many poor people
were at the point of death; many could get no food, and
in their straits even abandoned their children. We all
saw this. Then you made great exertions to save these
poor people, and began with large establishments to clear
the fort, and to make roads—as well to the advantage of
Government as to the people; and thus you maintained
the poor, who had no other means of subsistence. Of
those who were not able to labour, you, from your own
private funds, supported thousands. So if we seek foɪ
benevolent and useful people like you, we find few of
them.

" From the tanks which you strove to get constructed,
this district will be greatly benefited, and from this youɪ
name will be sung with praise when our women grind at
their mills. But if we now say all we have to say it would
only fatigue you, and take up much time; therefore we

2 A

will be concise, and close this with what is due to your
good qualities.

"But what shall we say? You were as father and
mother to the ryots. You heard the complaints of the
poor and protected them. In your *durbar*, as flies to
honey, all classes and degrees of persons gathered and
mingled together without apprehension; but we never
saw yet that you ever used harsh expressions to any one.
Your perfect knowledge of our language assured com-
plainants, for they knew they were understood, and were
contented; and never, on any occasion, have we seen that
any one was treated with indignity or affronted in your
durbar.

"We, who are the servants of Government in this district, as also all the ryots, well know what your conduct
has been, and know also that your kindness to us has
never decreased. You have taken care of us as of our
children. Were we to relate how you have exerted yourself for us, we should never make an end of it. It will be
difficult for us to obtain another superior like you, and
we considered it good fortune when we obtained service
with you. Now you are going from us, and our misfortune is apparent to us. Be it so. Wherever you go, may
God prosper you, and may our country be prosperous
through you. So we entreat God. Our hearts are full,
and we can say no more. So also, before you came here
you were at Shorapoor, and there, too, you made all
happy, and made that district prosperous. Such praise
have we heard from many persons who came from
thence.

"Now our last request is this, that as you have bestowed
on us so many obligations and so much love upon us, we,
to show our gratitude to you, have signed this address,
which all assembled have agreed on, and we pray you
will be pleased to accept it. This is our unanimous

representation, which you are to be pleased to accede
to.

(Signed)　　　" JEWUNJEE RUTTONJEE,

SHUNKUR RAO RUGGONATH,

Extra-Assistant Commissioners ;

" And 1123 *zemindars, patells,* and other respectable
inhabitants."

(Dated Nuldroog, *Aug.* 27, 1857.)

I can never forget the scene in the public *cucherry* when
this was read to me. My old friend Shunkur Rao Baba
Sahib, read it with the tears running down his cheeks,
and there were few dry eyes among the vast crowd that
had collected. The old cry, " Mahadeo Baba Ke Jey ! "
was raised outside and taken up by thousands. It was
the first time I had heard it at Nuldroog. I was much
moved. Nothing, I thought, could exceed this simple
but earnest expression of the feelings of the people towards
me, and their manifestation of regard and affection was
very grateful to my heart ; and if I had stood between
the people and wrong in the matter of land—if I had
governed them justly to the best of my ability—if I had
insured for them peace, and laid the foundation of prosperity, this was indeed a grateful reward—all I could
have hoped or wished for on earth.

That night as I left the fort and town, I found all the
road and street lined with the people, cheering me with
the old shout, " Mahadeo Baba Ke Jey ! " and many were
weeping, and pressing round to bid farewell ; and I was
followed for more than two miles out of the town with
the same cheer, by a crowd from which it seemed difficult
to get away.

At every village I passed through that night, and till
my frontier was reached, the village authorities, elders,

and people came with their farewells and best wishes, in crowds, from all points within their reach, praying for my speedy and safe return. My departure from Shorapoor had been affecting and painful to me, but the demeanour of the people here was, if possible, more touching and affectionate.

CHAPTER XIV.

1857–58.

I ARRIVED at Jaulnah on the ninth day. I had intended to travel faster, but a feverish cold I caught on leaving Nuldroog, when my palankeen doors were open and a chill night wind blowing through them, confined me to my bed for one whole day and night, and retarded my progress, so that I could not make double marches. The warm greetings and farewells did not cease till I reached the city of Beer in the Nizam's dominions,—everywhere the same reception, most hearty and affectionate.

The native district officer at Beer, on behalf of the Nizam's Government, came out to meet me with a large retinue, a distance of six miles; and I found my tents pitched in a very pleasant garden close to the city, and a most ample breakfast cooked at the officer's house, and ready to place upon my table. He pressed me very much to stay as long as I could, but I dared not linger; and in the afternoon I pushed on again to a village on the Hyderabad road, where there was a good bungalow.

Next day I had to cross the Godavery at Shahgurh; fortunately it was not in high flood, but it was not fordable. Here I found all my camels, baggage-ponies, and servants, clustered together on the bank of the river—the ferrymen would not permit them to pass; and as soon as I came up there were some very ominous cries of *Deen!*

Deen! * while the ferrymen, who had taken their boat
to some distance, waved me off. I had no escort—only
four men out of twenty-four who had been sent with me
from Beer; the rest had already crossed the river. I
had not brought my own cavalry escort from Nuldroog;
some of them still appeared very restless, and I thought
it was safer to leave them where they were. As I and
my servants were parleying with the boatmen, an old
Byragee whom I had never seen before, raised the old cry
loudly : " Mahadeo Baba Ke Jey ! " he shouted—and many
joined, drowning the *Deen! Deen!* most completely ;
while on the opposite side of the river, near the town of
Shahgurh, a large body of cavalry came in view, making
it very doubtful to my mind what would be the next
move. This, however, was soon decided by one of the
horsemen, the officer in command of the party, tying a
white scarf to his spear, and at the same time despatching
two other boats with a few dismounted men to my assistance. On seeing this, the party who had set up the cry of
Deen! Deen! bolted up the bank, looking sulky enough,
and I saw them no more ; while the three boats took me,
my bearers, servants, baggage, and camels, across the river
in safety.

The horsemen had been sent by an old friend of mine,
the Talookdar of Umber, with orders to see me safe over
the river. He did not expect me so soon, or he would
have sent them before. He had heard that the Mussulmans of Shahgurh had betrayed a very fanatical spirit,
and had said I was not to be allowed to proceed ; and he
feared for my safety.

This escort would not permit me to halt at Shahgurh,
but carried me on to a village eight miles further, where
they had ordered a small tent to be pitched for me, and
there I slept. Next morning we all went on to Umber.
My old friend was ill and could not leave his house ; but

---

* " For the Faith ! " the Mohammedan call to arms.

he sent his son with a large cavalcade to meet me, and entertained me most hospitably all day.

My friend, who was able to visit me in the evening, told me that he feared several mutineers of the Aurungabad cavalry were concealed at Shahgurh, and that a Mussulman priest had been preaching rebellious addresses ; but that he should send fifty men to the crossing place for the protection of travellers.   I left the escort here that had accompanied me from Beer.   The men were sadly vexed at the scene at the river, and that they had not been with me ; but as we could not all have crossed together, I, anticipating no difficulty, had desired them to precede me.   I now dismissed them with a letter to the Talookdar of Beer, thanking him for their services.

Next day I marched twenty miles, and arrived at Jaulnah.   I was rather amused at the "cloud of cavalry" sent to attend me by my old friend, whose only regret was that he was not well enough to accompany me himself.   Orders had been forwarded to a Parsee merchant at Jaulnah to see that a house was ready for me ; and as the cantonment was nearly emptied of troops, there were plenty at my disposal, and I found myself located in a very comfortable well-furnished bungalow belonging to the Colonel of the 6th Cavalry.   Here Major Gill, who had been for some years employed by Government in copying the Buddhist frescoes in the caves of Ajunta, came to see me, and gave me a letter from Bullock, which had come in by express, begging me to wait for him at Jaulnah, which I was glad to do, especially as a heavy fall of rain set in, and marching would have been next to impracticable.   Two days afterwards my friend joined me, and told me what had occurred.   On the outbreak of the Mutiny several of his cavalry escort had broken away, very much as mine had done, and the whole district was reported to be unsound.   He had asked for troops, which it was impossible to send him ; and after a very sharp correspondence on both sides, our sudden exchange of districts was peremptorily ordered. I had been told nothing of this, but had simply acted according to the short urgent letter I had received; but the prospect of having to keep Berar quiet after what I now heard, was not encouraging by any means.

I was likewise told that I must be prepared to find the internal economy of the district very irregular. When Bullock had gone on furlough to England, his successor had not carried out the general instructions promptly, and I should find the progress made slow, but he hoped I would soon set things all right; he had begun to work hard on his return, and thought he had put matters in training. I told him he would not have much trouble with my district, as it was in capital working order; and so we parted. This was no time to show vacillation or uneasiness, and I was determined to go through the country and among the people exactly as I should have done had I heard no unpleasant rumours. There were no troops to be had, so there was no use thinking about them. As much of the Contingent as could be spared, and several half-mutinous regiments of cavalry and infantry, were collected at Edlabad, near Boorhanpoor, and prepared for service with (then) Sir Hugh Rose's force; and for the time, no bolder course could have been adopted. Nevertheless, the Resident was assailed fiercely by the press; accused of shifting the responsibility of managing mutinous troops on others, and of ruining the chances of Sir Hugh Rose's success by placing in his rear a large brigade of the best troops in India, who could not possibly be depended on. But Colonel Davidson knew his men. He issued a spirited address to them, appealing to their loyalty, and encouraging them to go forward and win fame under Sir Hugh Rose. The men obeyed; and after the brigade joined Sir Hugh, it shared in the whole of the Central India campaign with him, and behaved well to the very last. Colonel Davidson had in view a much higher aim than merely keeping the troops employed in the field. His object was to show that the Nizam had no sympathy with the re-establishment of the monarchy of Delhi; and that his own troops were assisting the English to quell the Mutiny, and crush the authors of it; and in this point the Resident's bold measure was successful beyond his hopes.

On the 19th July, the Residency at Hyderabad was attacked by a concourse of Rohillas and other city fanatics, who were easily repulsed; but the Resident was at issue with the Commander of the Hyderabad Subsidiary Force, who not only differed from him on the question of retaining the Residency at all as a fortified post, but advised its total abandonment, and the location of all belonging to it within the cantonment. Happily the Resident took his own way, and he saw clearly that his desertion of the Residency would have the effect of weakening the Minister (now Sir Salar Jung, G.C.S.I.), and also the Nizam himself, both of whose lives had been threatened by fanatics. It was when it was determined that the Contingent Force should take the field, that my friend had applied for troops, and the utter impracticability of the request was resented. " Berar," wrote the Resident to me, "which contains more than two millions of people, *must* be kept quiet by 'moral strength, for no physical force is at my disposal."

Delhi, attacked first in June, and before which a position only was maintained till the siege began on the 1st September, was taken by storm on the 14th, but resistance continued inside until the 20th. Every native in India who could think at all, had watched the progress of the siege from June to September with the greatest anxiety as to which would win the victory—England or the Moghul; and many doubted whether the small force of English in India could make any impression on the immense power of the native army of Bengal. And the long delay, to which they were so little accustomed in English operations generally, strengthened this feeling considerably.

As I approached the head station of Berar, Booldana, I received deputations from the principal landholders, merchants, and bankers of the chief towns, who were all eager for authentic news ; but I could discover no symptom whatever of disaffection. The great Mussulman colony below the plateau of Booldana had been one of the chief points of anxiety to my predecessor; and, as soon as I could, I marched there, sending down a light tent before me. I gave no other warning, and was quite unexpected by the native officials and my English assistant, whom I found in charge. Though my sudden appearance at the head town of their country, when I had as yet visited no other, at first excited some surprise, and perhaps suspicion, we soon became excellent friends. At first I felt rather doubtful, as nobody came near me, and my servants heard very disagreeable rumours; but at length one leading man came forward, then another, and another, I suppose, to take my measure; and then all the people came, many hundreds, and raising the old cry, " Bolo Mahadeo Baba Ke Jey !" which some one set up, the whole assembly joined in heartily, and proffered service whenever and however I needed them. "They would watch the frontier," they said ; "they would not let in Scindia's disaffected people ; they would follow me to Delhi if I would only take them there; they wanted no pay—only food, and ammunition for their matchlocks ; they would be true and faithful to the English,"—and many more promises were made, and faithfully kept.

From that day they never gave me the least uneasiness ; and, if I had had occasion to call them out, would, I firmly believe, have done their duty nobly.

I wrote what had occurred, privately, to the Resident, by express, and I believe my despatch was a very considerable relief to him, as he was under great anxiety about Berar.

I need say nothing upon the condition of the internal economy of Berar at this time. Cultivation and revenue alike seemed to have declined, and did not exhibit the elasticity of Nuldroog. I had to set things to rights as much as I could, and the Commissioner wrote that he would come to me in January. Very hard work fell on me, as my assistants were new to the duties, and had not been trained to a regular system, which, had it been adopted from the first, would have rendered matters easy now to all. There was, too, a heavy arrear of appeals and civil suits ; but every allowance was to be made, for the territory had undergone so many changes from one hand to another; and my friend Bullock's health having failed, and his being obliged to take furlough just after his appointment, had not given the district a fair chance. The climate was very enervating, and the district so extensive, that I felt very thankful my first appointment to it had been altered for Nuldroog, as I am quite sure my health would never have held out under its relaxing influence. Indeed I felt anxious now as to whether I should be able to stand it ; but this only experience would prove.

Booldana was a pleasant place on the south table-land, above the valley of Berar, and had been fixed upon as the head station on account of its fine climate ; for there was the greatest possible difference in the air up there and that in the valley below. The views were beautiful down the wooded ravines, and my early morning rides were far more picturesque than any about Nuldroog. But I had no time to stay there long, and, after a few days' rest, I took my establishment into the valley, and began work in earnest. It was not by any means pleasant, as I was obliged to find much fault with the managers of divisions, who, being provided with ample instructions, had neglected to carry them out, and had neither kept their own accounts in order, nor those of the villages under them. Neither were the village books nor the records properly kept. These were matters of detail, as to which I need not perplex my readers, for, except at great length, they could not be explained intelligibly; and if they were, it would not answer any purpose.

I confess I thought I had been badly paid at Nuldroog, having received 300 rupees a-month less than had been granted to the Deputy-Commissioner in Berar, solely because the latter had a higher revenue and population: the area of both were nearly similar. However, it was no use grumbling now. I had done the work at Nuldroog to the best of my ability, and now I was going to try to set things straight here, and I hoped to get the district rapidly into order. As yet I had received no additional pay. I, as second-class Deputy-Commissioner, was holding a first-class district; Bullock, as first-class Deputy-Commissioner, holding a second-class district. But we supposed some arrangement would be come to in time.

Although both Delhi and Lucknow had been taken, yet the pacification of the country was far from complete; and rebellion in the Central Provinces, close to my own northern frontier, had made, and was making, rapid progress.

There was now much more alarm and uneasiness than before the taking of Delhi, which was far too distant from us to excite more than passing interest.

I received many anonymous letters, apparently from friends, warning me of contemplated assassination, and stating that when I was disposed of, the native troops at Ellichpoor were prepared to rise, and, aided by the military and predatory classes of the district, would plunder the chief towns, and join the rebel forces beyond the Sâtpoora range which constituted my whole northern frontier. At Nimawa, Captain Keatinge had been obliged to conceal himself in the jungle, having his wife and children with him; and they escaped almost by a miracle.

At Jubbulpore and Saugor, rebellion was at its height, not only in the mutiny of native regiments, but by the risings of petty rajahs and nawabs, and of the people of the district, always noted for their turbulent and predatory habits.

There was hardly one spot where loyalty prevailed; for as the regiments broke away from their several stations, with or without violence and murder, as it might be, all restraint was removed from the lawless classes of the people at large, and these were every day growing stronger under the evil spirit and licence which could not be checked.

On the eastern portion of Berar lay Nagpore, by no means to be trusted; and it was owing to the large force of faithful Madras troops who were stationed there that no serious outbreak occurred in favour of the deposed family, on whose behalf, it was reported, intrigue was busy throughout the whole country. On my western frontier lay Khandeish, not secure either. Nana Sahib had active agents there, as he aspired to be Peshwah; and all the northern frontier of that province was in contact with Scindia's and Holkar's territories, where rebellion was rife.

Berar was the centre of these three great provinces, which stretched across the whole of India, and formed, as it were, the barriers that were to prevent the rebellion from spreading southwards; and of the three, Berar was the most important perhaps, as, if the rebels had broken through the passes of the Sâtpoora range—a very easy proceeding—and had been joined by the military classes and indigenous marauders of the province, it is impossible to say how far disaffection might have extended to the Nizam's dominions.

From October, therefore, as the circle of war and mutiny grew wider, reaching my northern frontier, the danger increased almost daily; and it was only the thorough attachment and loyalty of the people to the English rule which saved Berar, under God's blessing, from insurrection.

I have already mentioned the goodwill and proffered devotion of the Mussulmans of the western portions of my district; and as I travelled up the valley slowly to Akola, I was equally gratified by the conduct of the Rajpoots, who resided there in large numbers. There had been fierce and bloody feuds between these two great classes from time to time, on occasions of religious festivals; and this seemed a good opportunity for them to break out again; for I had literally no troops on whom I could rely, and those at Ellichpoor were more a source of uneasiness to me than anything else, as, although they were as yet orderly and quiet, it was felt that any excitement might cause them to break off and join their rebel brethren at Jubbulpore or in Central India. Their officers were very mistrustful of them, for many were from Oudh; and who could rely on them after the mutiny of Scindia's troops and their march to join the main body of the rebel forces?

I was grateful for the attachment evinced by the Rajpoots of the Akola district, who also proffered service wherever and whenever it might be of use. All I could do was to ask their aid in watching the passes, and in apprehending parties from the north who might seek to sow rebellion among us. This they promised to do; and in two instances they actually did so, succeeding in arresting and bringing to justice a number of delegates from Scindia's mutinous troops at Boorhanpoor, whom I tried and sentenced to transportation and penal servitude. And these events prevented any further attempt of the like nature.

There were several petty rajahs of the mountain tribes of Gonds who received hereditary allowances or stipends from the Berar administrators, and who were responsible for the several passes which led from the north. All these came to me and tendered their services, nor did any one case occur of disloyalty or neglect.

The northern frontier was thus made as secure as I could under these circumstances make it; but, in Colonel Davidson's expressive phrase, I was literally " holding on by my eyelids."

I will not deny that it was a period of fearful anxiety. No aid could be expected from without, and the anonymous warnings were more frequent than ever, while evil reports flew daily through the country. My servants kept a horse saddled for me every night in case of necessity for escape.

I had no guards except a few police, and I was carrying on my duties in my tents as usual: making the yearly settlement; examining village books, district books, and accounts; trying appeal and civil cases; holding criminal trials, and the like. One great benefit to me was my being able to speak the vernacular language, Mahratta, fluently. The people felt that I understood them, and came to me freely with petitions as to any real or imaginary grievance.

There had been some corruption at work among my *chuprassies* or office attendants, which seemed to be of long standing; and I one night overheard a conversation between two of them who lay outside my tent walls, when they thought I was asleep, about division of the proceeds of their gains, upon the receipt of petitions, which would have been amusing enough but for the mischief that such extortion for presenting petitions to me occasioned. I at once adopted my Nuldroog plan, which was to have a large box fitted with hinges and a padlock: a slit was cut in the lid, and notification made that all petitions henceforth were to be dropped into it, and that petitioners were to attend every afternoon, when the box would be opened before me, and the papers publicly read. The box was placed in an open space before my tent, and was pres-

ently filled with petitions; the two men, whose confidential talk I had overheard, were then called up. I took
my usual seat outside my tent, and after addressing the
crowd, I had the men's badges removed, and they were
turned out of camp in disgrace.

I think, nay, I am positive, that if every Deputy-Commissioner, situated as I was, had such a box, they would
find it an admirable plan. It had an excellent effect in my
district, and inspired great confidence among the people.
Any frivolous complaint was at once dismissed ; but many
corrupt practices and grievances were brought to light ;
and as each petition was taken out of the box, the name
of the petitioner was called out, and every applicant knew
that his paper was considered, and heard it read before me.
A memorandum was then written on the back, referring it
to the district native officer for report if necessary.

I was now fairly among the people ; and though so often
cautioned and advised of danger, I felt that reliance on
them was the safest course. Once, in a Bombay paper,
it was stated that I had been attacked and murdered ; but
I wrote to contradict the report before the departure of the
mail for England, and the dear ones at home knew nothing of it ; nor did I, as I see by my letters home, mention
any current reports, and, indeed, I alluded very little to
the condition of affairs at all, or my own cares. I lived,
however, in a state of perpetual alarm, and every day
added to the anxiety I endured. Every detail of deeds of
violence in Central India—of which, almost daily, fresh
rumours reached me, sometimes very much exaggerated—
the arrival of every " express," night or day, in camp—
caused unavoidable excitement. Who could say what news
it might not bring? At that time all Deputy-Commissioners of provinces and political officers used to send such
expresses, when and how they could, to each other, giving
local news, and with a request that the express might be
forwarded to the next authority. Many a man in India

was " holding on," never flinching from his post, dying
there bravely in many a terrible instance, or, when hope
was gone, escaping with bare life, often through hosts of
enemies, and thankful for that mercy. " What if Berar
should go ?" I often thought ; and how could I hope to
escape ? How thankful I was that I was alone — that
I had only myself to think of ! Had I had wife and
children with me, as many had, my anxiety would have
been increased a thousandfold.

True, my people appeared steady and trustworthy, and
business proceeded as usual, as I moved my camp from
village to village ; but Berar was 250 miles long, with an
average breadth of 60 miles or more, and the population
was two millions. Who could answer for all ? And from
day to day for some months, one felt as if in the morning
one might be murdered before night, or at night be dead
before the morning.

The Resident's anxiety on my account seemed to increase ; but I assured him in my letters, which were rare,
that so far I could not trace any disaffection, and that a
good spirit seemed to prevail among the people, even where
I had felt most uneasiness myself. Still I often longed to
be in the roughest scenes in Central India rather than
bear the load of responsibility on my mind day and night :
it was a terrible strain upon me.

I was at Ellichpoor on the 9th December, and I stayed
there till the 13th. It was very cold, the thermometer
showing 36° and 40° in the mornings. It was the head
civil station of a subdivision of my district, and I was
greatly indebted to Captain Hamilton, who superintended
it, for his watchful supervision of the frontier. The people
were deeply attached to him, and gave him information
freely. How welcome were the large baskets of delicious
peaches grown in his garden at Chiculdah, the sanitarium
of Ellichpoor ! and I wished I could go up there again and
revisit the old scenes.

2 B

The native officers of the cavalry and infantry both visited me, and I congratulated them on the honours which their regiments were winning in Central India. They appeared to be intensely gratified at the news which reached them from time to time, both in newspapers and private letters, and at the prospect which was opening for further good service under Sir Hugh Rose, whose forces were now advancing into the disturbed districts.

Many of the men also came to me "for a talk," and raised the old cry of my regiment, which was known to all. So I hoped the disaffection of the cavalry at Ellich-poor was a groundless rumour.

When the glorious news came from the Northern Provinces, the victory over the Gwalior troops at Cawnpore, and the second relief of Lucknow, with many other successful engagements in Central India, the year 1858 opened very brightly, and with good hope that the general campaign against the rebel forces would be brought to a brilliant conclusion in a few months. Already the various combinations of the rebel army and the various rebel chiefs had been much broken; now they were growing dispirited, and had nothing to fall back upon. When the constant arrival of troops from home made it manifest to all that England was fully roused, and was putting forth her strength and her enormous resources to save and help her sons, the hopes of the rebel leaders fell, and they felt their inability to war against her.

I am not, however, writing a history of the time,—that is in far abler hands than mine. I can only relate what affected me personally.

My own position was decided by the Governor-General, who decreed, as I thought he would, that my friend was to be reinstated in Berar, and I to return to my old quarters—Nuldroog. The Commissioner, Mr Maltby, had been at Nuldroog, had seen all my work, and approved of it, and had been much struck by the independent, though thoroughly respectful, demeanour of my Mahratta farmers. They had visited him freely, and assured him of their prosperity and loyalty, and he wrote me a very flattering letter on the condition of the district generally. In Berar I had done my utmost to redeem irregularities and reconcile conflicting accounts ; but three months had been too short a time to do all I wished, or to leave things as straight as I should have liked.

Bullock was to leave Nuldroog at once, and wished me to meet him in the eastern portion of the district as soon as I could ; and I too was anxious to get back to my old work before the very hot weather began. Berar was beginning to tell upon me ; the old fever had returned in periodical attacks, and I was tormented with severe neuralgia, from which I could obtain no relief whatever. I had used the hot springs at Salbudlee with some good effect, but it was not lasting, and I greatly dreaded the hot season. All the accounts had been sent in, and I found that one lakh out of two, set down for remission, was recoverable : the village books were now in order, and only careful supervision was needed.

While in the eastern portion of the district, I had been able to perform an essential service to Government, which had great effect on the war in Central India. One day I received an express from Colonel Hill, Assistant Quartermaster-General of the Madras army, attached to General Whitlock's force at Nagpore, which had not marched, and was not able to do so, for want of draught and carriage bullocks. He requested I would, if possible, purchase and send to him 600 at once, leaving 400 more to follow ; and added, if I could not manage this, there would be no hope of getting any except from Mysore. The Nagpore province either would not, or could not, supply them. I set to work directly. The province of Berar contains the finest draught cattle in India, and plenty were to be had at moderate prices. No sooner were my wants known than my camp was crowded with noble beasts. In two days I had got half the number, which were sent on under an escort of police, and day after day other herds were despatched; and this enabled the siege-train and heavy stores to be sent on without delay, so that eventually the whole force was set in motion, with an ample supply of trained cattle.

I received not only the thanks of the generals commanding for this assistance, but of the Governor of Madras in Council; and it was very clear that, if these cattle had not been sent up from the south, Whitlock's force could not have accomplished what it did in marching upon Jubbulpore, and, by a lucky stroke, capturing the Kirwee treasures. I thought myself fairly entitled to a share of the Kirwee booty for the service I had rendered; but it was decreed afterwards by Sir J. Phillimore, that as I did not belong to the force, "my chance, *though just in equity*, was not admissible."

In my letters home at this period I wrote very earnestly on the question of pressing the direct rule of the Crown in the future government of India, and that the time had arrived for a change to be made with advantage.

There was a very general impression that the great Company was only a farmer of the revenues; and while royal houses would acknowledge and respect the Crown, they would have, especially after late events, no such feeling for the Company.

I suggested many other material changes as to high courts of justice and tenures of land, several of which have been carried out; and I had the honour done me of some of my letters being read in the " House."

The letters written to my cousin Reeve, and already given, embody most of my opinions and suggestions.

Strange indeed was the weird prophecy of Plassey in 1757-58 !

The Company's rule was to last for a hundred years. In

1857-58 it had virtually expired, and 1859 witnessed its total extinction!

It was my intention, after leaving my friend, to go direct *viâ* Aurungabad to Beer. Mr Maltby was now on his way to Berar, and Bullock and I moved on to meet him early in February, when he asked me to accompany him through the district, and to visit with him the caves of Ajunta and Ellora. This would have been a very pleasant holiday for me; but again I was to be disappointed. We met the Commissioner near Oomrawuttee, on his way to Ellichpoor, and the very next day came an " express " from the Resident, directing me to lose not a moment in proceeding to Hyderabad on business relating to Shorapoor.

I had seen by the papers a short time before, that the Rajah had been suspected of treason, and that troops had been sent to watch the eastern and western frontiers of his district. Now I learned that he had attacked a small force which had been ordered to Captain Campbell's assistance—this officer having been sent to Shorapoor on a special mission; and the Rajah being defeated, had fled to Hyderabad, where he had been arrested.

Mr Maltby spoke very kindly to me of all he had noted in the Nuldroog district, and hoped I should soon be again at liberty to continue my work there, especially the survey operations. I ventured to ask whether I might be allowed anything for my labours in Berar; but he could not say—and my travelling expenses had been a very serious pull upon my resources. I was to receive plenty of thanks; but although these were very gratifying, they did not pay me for the very hard work and terrible anxiety I had gone through: but—there was one comfort—I had " held on by my eyelids!"

I pushed on now by double marches to Hingolee, and thence to Hyderabad, where I arrived on the 18th March, after having travelled 300 miles in sixteen days—not very fast perhaps; but my continued travelling had blistered my people's feet, and I could not get on quicker.

I went of course to Mr Palmer's house, and found him well and cheerful; but the Resident would not hear of my being with any one but himself, and sent for me directly. I was very kindly received. He at once increased my pay, appointed me now Commissioner of Shorapoor, on 1800 rupees a-month, or, at the least, 1500, and said his wish was to keep me altogether in the political department.

He told me all the high officials, and chiefly the Governor-General, were more than satisfied with what I had done in Berar.

CHAPTER XV.

1858.

THE Rajah of Shorapoor was a prisoner in the main-guard
of the " Royals " at Secunderabad, and I went three times
to see him. He had deliberately rebelled against the
British Government, and was to be tried for his life by a
military commission, which would shortly assemble. As
may be imagined, he was deeply affected on first seeing
me, and he threw himself into my arms, quite unable to
speak for some time. Even the honest fellows of the
guard were moved, and much surprised that my appearance should have so sudden and extraordinary an effect
upon their prisoner. In appearance he was much improved
—he had grown stouter, fairer, and more manly; but
though handsome, his features bore unmistakable signs of
dissipation and excess, which I was sorry to see. Now,
his face was so distorted with his emotions that it was
difficult to judge what it would be in repose.

" O *appa, appa !* " was all he could cry, or rather moan,
as he sat at my feet, his face buried in my lap, and his
arms clasped tightly around me; " O *appa*, I dare not
look on your face ! I have been so wicked—oh, so wicked !
I have done every crime—I have even committed murder!
Oh, if the earth had opened, and swallowed me up, it would
only have been just. I cannot tell you all now, *appa*. My
throat is parched, words will not come; but to-morrow, *appa*,
you will come again—do come, and then I will tell you all."

It was useless to remain then, and only painful to us both. So I promised to return on the morrow, and went away.

It was a sad case, and I feared there was no hope for him—none whatever. His unwarrantable disaffection began with that of the Southern Mahratta country, where some of its chiefs had, as was proved afterwards, laid their plans for a general insurrection, in connection, no doubt, with Nana Sahib, and the general mutiny in the Bengal army; and the vigorous conduct of General Jacob alone prevented this rebellious movement.

The Rajah of Shorapoor had been early inveigled into these intrigues, and was an active promoter of them. He was invited specially, as an ancient feudatory of the Peshwahs, to join again the Mahratta standard; and owing to his reputed wealth and the numbers of his clan, was not a chief to be overlooked by those disaffected.

If he could be induced to take the field with ten thousand men, the Beydurs of the Raichore Doab, of Bellary, Dharwar, and Belgaum, as well as those also of Mysore, would rise and follow him as their leader, and could plunder as they listed. His vanity and cupidity were excited, and he fell an easy prey to these representations.

Even after the Beydurs of the Southern Mahratta country had received some very severe checks, the attitude of the Shorapoor Rajah was considered threatening and suspicious. He had collected Arabs and Rohilla mercenaries in addition to calling his own clan together, while he was more than suspected to hold communication with foreign mercenaries at Hyderabad. Those were anxious times, and it was impossible to allow any known conspiracy to exist, without watching it very narrowly. A strong force was sent, under Colonel Malcolm, and placed about equidistant between the Beydurs of Shorapoor and those of the Southern Mahratta country; Colonel

Hughes, with a Madras force, watched the eastern frontier of Shorapoor; and the Contingent troops at Linsoogoor lay, as it were, between, ready to act in concert with either force, according to necessity.

The Resident, however, was very anxious to save the Rajah, and to rescue him from his evil counsellors, feeling a peculiar interest in the boy who had for so long been a ward of the British Government; and early in January 1858 he despatched his assistant, Captain Rose Campbell, to Shorapoor, to remonstrate with the Rajah, and endeavour to bring him to a sense of his danger, and his promised allegiance to the British Government.

This considerate kindness was, unfortunately, thrown away. The Rajah was in the hands of the worst fanatics of the country, on all sides—even from Mysore and Arcot —and would listen to neither warning nor advice; and at length, when Captain Campbell received an intimation from the Rajah's own servants and relatives that his life was in serious danger, the force from Linsoogoor was ordered to support him, and arrived at Shorapoor on the 7th February, encamping near the town. A narrow valley, surrounded on all sides by lofty hills and rocks, was pointed out as the camping-ground; but Captain Arthur Wyndham, who commanded the force, was too wary to be misled, and moved on to an open plain, where he was comparatively safe from any danger of surprise.

At night he was attacked by the Rajah's whole force of Beydurs and foreign mercenaries; but he held his position bravely, and early in the morning Colonel Hughes, who was at Deodroog, twelve miles distant, and to whom a special messenger had been despatched, arrived with all his troops. It was very plain that had Captain Wyndham remained on the ground first pointed out to him, he would have endured very heavy loss, if not total defeat. As it was, his force suffered but little, but he had inflicted serious damage on the Shorapoor rebels.

Colonel Hughes arrived early on the morning of the 8th, and he and Captain Wyndham, with their united troops, drove the Beydurs and others from the hills into the town with severe loss. Unfortunately Captain Newberry, Madras cavalry, was killed in a charge against a body of Rohillas, and his subaltern, Lieut. Stewart, badly wounded. As the city of Shorapoor was very strong, the approaches difficult of access, and the walls and bastions crowded with defenders, they did not attack it at once, but waited for Colonel Malcolm's force, which had moved close to the western frontier of Shorapoor, and who had been requested to come on with all possible speed.

When this reached the ears of the Rajah, and he heard also that Colonel Malcolm's force had with it a large proportion of English troops, who, together with two companies of the 74th Highlanders under Colonel Hughes, made a sufficiently imposing array — he saw that there was no chance of escape except by flight ; and, in the evening, accompanied by a few horsemen, he left Shorapoor, and proceeded direct to Hyderabad.

He believed me to be at Nuldroog, and intended to have given himself up to me there ; but hearing on his northern frontier that I had been removed te Berar, he changed his route, and made for Hyderabad, where he arrived with but two followers left. There, having made a fruitless attempt to gain the protection of the Arabs, he was found wandering about the bazaar, was apprehended, and taken to the Minister, Salar Jung, who at once sent him on to the Resident.

As soon as the Rajah's flight became known, all the Beydurs and mercenaries left Shorapoor during the night, and dispersed, whereupon the English forces marched into the city unopposed, and found it almost deserted.

Such is an outline of the occurrences that took place, and I hoped that when I next visited the Rajah, he would disclose to me all the particulars of his rebellion and the causes that led to it. I found him much calmer during our second interview, but very reserved on many points.

" Do you remember, *appa*," he said, " that the day before you left me, you warned me of the evil people who were about me; and you said, if I did not dismiss them, and lead a steady life, I should not hold Shorapoor five years; and I promised you I would send them all away, and look after my own affairs ? "

" I remember it well," I replied, " and how you wrote to me and told me that you were in trouble, and would come to me ; and I sent you word to do so at once, for that I should now be near your border. But you never came, though I was there nearly a month, and I expected you."

" No," he said, " they would not let me go to you, *appa ;* and if I had gone it would have been no use ; you could have done nothing. What was to be has come to pass, and I must bear my fate now, whatever it may be. When that evil wind blew, the people came and said it was the time to rise. The English had lost everything in the nortl., and were beaten everywhere; they could not keep the country, they said, and were flying to England as fast as they could get to their ships. This was told me, *appa,* by Brahmins and others from the south, from Poona, from everywhere.

" They promised, by their incantations, to raise me to be Rajah of all the country—from Shorapoor to Rainéshwar —and if I marched at the head of my twelve thousand, they said, all the country would rise, and we should be conquerors. Then Mahrattas from Poona, from Sâttara, from Kolapoor, from Mungoond, from Bheem Rao, who had secured all the disaffected people of Raichore, per-suaded me to join them, and offered me what I pleased if I did so ; but still I did not go. I was still true to the English and to you. I knew I was right. I did not move a man ; nor did I allow one of my people even to go to the assistance of the Beydurs of Hulgully, their brethren, many of whom were slain. And then my people rebelled against me, and called me a 'coward and a fool,' because I would not let them go. Arabs and Rohillas now came around me, and one man, worse than all the rest, swore to me on the Korán that the Arabs and Rohillas of Hyderabad, and all the Mussulmans, had declared a crusade against the English; that the Madras troops would not fight, and they would all come and join me if I would rise. And these men and my own evil companions gave me brandy, and made me drunk, and they took my seal and used it, and led me into evil which I could not help, and did not know.

" When Captain Campbell came to me with the letter from the Resident, ask him whether I did not receive him with all honour and respect. But the people about me and the Hyderabad men said he was a Kafir and a Feringhee, and that he must die. Had not all true men put to death any English they could find? And they told me about Cawnpore and Jhansi, and Delhi, and how all the English had been slain—even women and little children; and I thought of you—and of your children—girls too,— and I was grieved; but they made me drunk again, and they determined to murder Captain Campbell the next time he came; but I sent him private warnings, and this I could prove to you. Ask my uncles; ask ——, and ——, and others; they will tell you. Ask Captain Campbell if they did not warn him. I speak no lie, why should I? my life is not worth saving now. I have done too much crime to live; I dare not tell you all; you would not touch me or let me come near to you. O *appa, appa!* why did you leave me? If you had stayed with me, all would have been well! I tell you, if Captain Campbell had come to me again, no one, not I myself, could have saved his life; the men who were to cut him down were standing ready: but he attended to my warnings, and was saved.

" Then the troops came, and when I heard the first gun fire'd at night, I knew all was gone. I had no faith in my people's courage, although I had not been able to stop their madness, and I went up to a bastion and stood there all night. They told me—what a lie it was !—that the Linsoogoor troops had lost their officers and fled ! but when I saw, as day broke, the whole force and the English soldiers driving all my people before them into the city, and a shell burst close to the bastion where I was, killing some, and wounding more—ah ! why did it not kill me ?—when I saw this, I say, I knew there was no hope left, and I thought to myself, ' I will go to *appa*, and give him up the *Sumusthan* to do with as he pleases.'

" I told Rungama (the eldest wife) to hide herself, and to tell the others all to hide for the night, and get on as well as they could to Nuldroog to you. When I got to Narribole, I heard you had gone to Berar, and I turned through the hills and across the jungle to Hyderabad, riding the horse you bought for me. This is all my story, *appa ;* it is true, all of it. If I can remember any more you ought to know, I will tell you. I wish you to know everything."

Hours had passed while he poured out this tale ; hours of intense suffering to him, and bitter self - reproach. Sometimes he would stop, and throw his arms round me passionately ; sometimes kneel beside me, moaning piteously ; again he would burst into loud hysterical sobs which shook his frame. I did my best to soothe him, and gradually he gave me the details narrated above. I have given only the heads, which I took down for the Resident's information. It would be impossible to remember his wild incoherent exclamations, his sudden recurrence to old scenes when he had played as a child about me, with his sisters ; of the enjoyment they had had in the magic lantern I showed ; of the little vessel on Bohnal Lake, and the happy expeditions there : and all those recollections of his innocent early life, made the scenes through which he had lately passed the more grievous and full of reproach.

I asked him if he would like to see the Resident, who had promised to accompany me on my last visit to him if the Rajah wished it. To my surprise, he drew himself up very proudly, and replied, haughtily—

"No, *appa ;* he would expect me to ask my life of him, and I won't do that. Tell him, if you like, that if the great English people grant me my life, I and mine will be ever true to them; but I deserve to die for what I did, and I will not ask to live like a coward, nor will I betray my people."

I think this speech, which I reported word for word, pleased the Resident better than anything he had heard of the Rajah before.

"The poor lad has spirit in him," he said; "and I will not forget all you have told me of him."

I went once more to see the Rajah, the day before I left for Shorapoor. I should soon see his wife and his other relations, and I wished to know whether he had any instructions or messages for them. He was calm, though he could not repress his old loving ways to me—but very quiet. I told him I was going by *dâk* to Shorapoor. "What could I do for him there?"

"*Appa,*" he said, "you remember once I said to you, that the British Government should have Shorapoor if I left no heir; and I have none. I only wish now I had written this down; but at that time I had hope still: and I wish now to say, that I want you to have it yourself; the people love you, and you must never leave it. I will write this with my own hand, if they will give me pen and ink and some paper."

"No," I said, "it could not be as you wish; and besides, the Government may pardon you when all is known."

"And spare my life? No—I will never ask it."

" That would not save it," I answered. " If Government is merciful, they will give you your life freely, without your asking it."

" What do you think, *appa ?*   Shall I have to die ? " he asked.

" I think so," I said. " It would be wrong in me to give you any false hope, or to raise the slightest shadow of one in your mind. Many have been false who should have remained true, and you were a child of the English."

" Why do you reproach me ? " he asked, sadly.   " You know all ; it was not of my own will, when I was in my senses, *appa.*"

" I do not reproach you," I said, " for I do know all ; but those who will try you do not.   Speak the truth before them boldly, and exactly as you have done to me, and send for me if you think I can help you."

" I will surely tell all," he answered calmly ; " but if they press me to disclose the names of those who excited me, I shall be silent.   Government is powerful enough to crush them if they rise.   But what can they do ?   Was I not the strongest among them?   And yet, where am I now ?   Shall I, who have to face death, be faithless to those who trusted me months ago? Never, *appa !* I would rather die than be sent over the black water, or shut up in a fortress always.   Suppose they sentence me to that, I could not bear it.   No ; the meanest Beydur could not live if he were imprisoned—and shall I, a Rajah ? "

" If you have to die," said I, a good deal moved, for there was much nobility in his speech, " die like a brave man."

" I shall not tremble when they tie me up to a gun," he answered, gravely.   " If you could be near me to the last, I should be happier.   Only one thing, *appa*—do not let them hang me.   I have done nothing to be hanged for, like a robber.   Tell the Resident that is all the favour I ask.   Promise me to tell him."   And I promised.

"I have nothing now to give you, *appa*," he continued. "They have taken away all I had, even my amulets; but take what you will at Shorapoor, in remembrance of me. As to all my people in the palace, they are yours; and you will care for them, I know. I shall never see them again, now. I ask nothing more."

Then, throwing himself into my arms, he clung to me for a long time, silently; then kissing me gently on the forehead, he said—

"Go, *appa*—go now. I shall never look upon your face or hear your voice again; but I am thankful to have seen you. Tell them all that you have been with me, and that I was not a coward."

And so I left him, among the men of the guard, who looked on with kindly, wondering eyes.

"He was very fond of you, sir," said one of the sergeants, as I passed out, "and before you came was asking for you constantly. You must have been as a father to him."

"He was like a child to me," I said, "till evil people came between us, and temptation proved too strong for him. Now, I fear, it is too late to help him."

I told the Resident all that had taken place, on my return, and all the Rajah had said, especially about his not wishing to make any disclosures that would implicate his associates; and he respected the poor boy's reticence on these points.

"We will save him if we can, Taylor, when the time comes," he said. "Just now, things must take their course. But I am sure there is good stuff in the lad; and if we can save his life, he will be all the better for this experience."

My bearers to Shorapoor were laid; my servants and baggage had preceded me by some days—and they would, I hoped, have all ready on my arrival.

Mr Palmer had no hope of the Rajah's life being spared,

but he took a great interest in him, and only feared that
his death might be considered necessary as a warning to
all the plotters in the South, of whom, no doubt, there
were many, though there had been no actual rising except
the unimportant one at Hyderabad, and the intrigues in
the Southern Mahratta country before mentioned.

I bade all Hyderabad friends farewell on the 30th
March in the evening, and went on by stages to Shorapoor, putting up in the villages during the day, for it was
too hot to expose myself to the sun. The nights were,
fortunately, cool and pleasant still, and I hoped to arrive
at my long journey's end by the 3d April, when I should
have travelled over 500 miles.

I reached the Bheema river on the morning of 3d April,
long before it was light, indeed not long after midnight,
hoping to get into Shorapoor soon after daylight; but it
was quite impossible. I found the river-bank crowded
with people, from all the villages round, come to welcome
me back again to my old scenes, and I had to wait to exchange greetings. Very warm and affectionate they were.
"Now," they said, "they would have no more fears; all
would take up their lands and go to work quietly, so long
as I remained with them:" and I assured them I should
remain. All the head-men, *patells*, and *putwarries*, all the
principal farmers and traders, assembled to give me the
first greetings; and they told me the road was lined with
crowds from all the country side. Many had been waiting for days, as it was reported I should arrive sooner
than I did. When I could get away from these, I passed
on in the same manner from that village to the next,
always with crowds running beside my palankeen, and a
blaze of lights carried by the village torch-bearers. Now I
had to stop while some old friend dismounted from his
horse or pony to embrace me or kiss my feet; and again,
when village authorities came out to meet me with their
simple offerings and libations of water. I could, in truth,

2 C

have dispensed with the crowds, for the dust rose heavily in the air, and there was no wind to scatter it, and the torches increased the heat perceptibly, while to sleep was out of the question. When day broke, the throng seemed greater and greater—men, women, and children pressing on my palankeen to touch my feet, or even my clothes—and, as I neared Shorapoor, vast numbers, apparently thousands, came out to meet me, and my bearers could only advance at a slow walk, often being obliged to halt altogether. So through the first suburb and up the steep road to the city, amidst shouts of the old cry of "Mahadeo Baba," the scream of pipes and Beydurs' horns, and thumping of big and little drums, I was conducted into the first street, where further progress was clearly impossible.

I had never before seen even this excitable people so frantic; women weeping passionately, grasping my hands, kissing my clothes, or touching my feet—crying, "Oh, you are come again; we see you; we shall suffer no more!" They raised their children above their heads and showed me to them, showering blessings on me the while.

The terraced house-tops were full likewise, and the shouts and cries quite indescribable. It was now eleven o'clock, and my slow progress through the town occupied almost an hour more. The sun was blazing hot, and I was faint and wearied out; still the showers of garlands, the handfuls of sweet powder and dyed rice, thrown on and over me, continued till I was close to the palace guard, when my bearers turned in, and I was free.

Captain Wyndham and all the officers had been most anxious, especially when the shouts were heard as I entered the streets; and my delay was so unaccountable that they feared I had met with opposition, till they were assured I was only "being welcomed," and therefore abandoned their idea of sending a troop of cavalry, which they had ready, to my assistance.

I had never dreamed of such a welcome. It was intensely gratifying, and I was deeply affected by the feeling displayed by all, which could not be mistaken. Captain Wyndham and others had seen something of my
reception from the roof of the palace, and had wondered
not a little, as I had myself. It proved, at any rate, that
I was not forgotten ; and I thanked God for this from my
heart very gratefully. The English officers congratulated
me very warmly.

I was very glad of a refreshing bath and a substantial
breakfast, which had been got ready for me ; and then I
lay down to have a sleep, which I needed much after the
night's work. When I awoke, several old native friends
were waiting for me. We were located in the new palace
I had built for the Rajah, which afforded good airy shelter
for us all. The large upper room was the "mess" and
public room, and soon all the male members of the Rajah's
family and State officers assembled there—Pid Naik's sons,
their uncles, and great-uncle.

All were as much concerned as I was at the unexpected
events which had led to my second arrival at Shorapoor ;
but they told me that for more than a year past they had
lived in perpetual alarm at the conduct of the Rajah, who
seemed to have become quite deranged by constant intoxication.

In the evening I went to see the Ranees, who had
assembled at the house of the father of the eldest Ranee,
close to the palace. As may be imagined, it was a sad
and trying scene for us all. I could not either console
them or hold out any hope that the Rajah's life would be
spared. They had, too, lost all they possessed, except the
few ornaments they wore. When the Rajah had desired
them to escape the night he fled, they had gone out by
the northern gate on foot, and made the best of their way
to villages, where they were sheltered by the people.
Some few women-servants followed them ; but when they

heard the Rajah had gone to Hyderabad, and was a prisoner, they took advantage of a proclamation issued by Captain Campbell, and ventured back to Shorapoor—not to the palace, as that was occupied by troops and soldiers, but to the house where I found them. Some of their clothes had been sent to them, but everything valuable was declared prize property, and was confiscated.

When the ladies grew more calm, I told them about my interviews with the Rajah, and the various messages he had sent them. They had almost expected to have heard before now of his public execution,

"I could not save him, *appa,*" cried Rungama, the chief Ranee, whom I had petted as a child—"I could not save him; he was quite mad of late, drinking brandy those horrible men gave him constantly, which made him furious. Then, when he was quiet, he used to lay his head in my lap, and call for you, and tell me he knew he should lose the *Sumusthan,* but that he would die like a soldier at the gates if the city were attacked. Again and again we all implored him to go to you, but we did not know you were so far away; and he always said if he left, the Rohillas and Arabs would plunder the city, because he owed them so much—and so he stayed."

According to an arrangement made with the Resident, I issued a general amnesty to all except certain persons who had been leaders and exciters of this most miserable rebellion. The people of the city and of the suburbs were still in the villages to which they had fled; but now they returned. All the shops were opened; and in a few days the markets were full, and firewood, fruit, and vegetables were as plentiful as ever. Captain Wyndham's company occupied the palace, and were ordered to secure all valuables as "prize." My house was tenanted by a company of the 74th Highlanders. The troops of all arms had entered the city; but though property of every kind had

been summarily looted, the people had remained un-
molested.

In the treasury there remained nothing except a few
State jewels ; others had been hurriedly secreted, but
were returned by those who had them in charge. I do
not think a single article was missing, and any coin found
had become prize-money.

I deeply regretted that all the old records had been
either burnt or destroyed,—letters from former kings of
Beejapoor and Beeder, Rajahs of Beejanugger; of the
Emperor Aurungzeeb, with the impress of his large hand
dipped in sandal - wood ; of the Peshwahs, and others.
Great portions of these I had already translated, and had
intended to continue when I should have leisure, hoping
to complete a very interesting historical State paper ; but
all were gone now.

The Resident allowed me to draw on the Residency
treasury for as much as I required, and I got bills cashed
as they were wanted for current expenditure. Many of
the *patells* and heads of villages came in during the first
week and assured me as to the cultivation of the country,
and that such of the newly-cleared land as could be managed would be taken up at once ; so altogether there
seemed a fair prospect of revenue.

The investigation upon the occurrences which led to the
rebellion was cut short as much as possible. There was
no good in raking up old scores, especially as the Rajah, as
chief of all, had been the one responsible, and he was on
his trial at Hyderabad. There was one man, a Mussulman of Hyderabad, who had preached a holy war at
Shorapoor, and had been the instigator-in-chief of much
trouble, and who, in concert with a wicked Brahmin
whom I remembered, Krishna Shastree, pretended to
miraculous power and divination. These two had, by
their false prophecies and mischievous counsels, deluded
the Rajah more than any others ; and, as dangerous

characters, were worthy of death, or at least transportation for life.

The Brahmin eluded all pursuit, and disappeared. The
Mussulman, however, was apprehended after some time at
Hyderabad, and sent to me for trial, when evidence was
produced conclusive as to the projected murder of Captain
Campbell, in which he was to have taken an active part;
and his own treasonable conspiracies being distinctly
proved, he was condemned to death. The sentence was
confirmed by the Resident, and he was publicly hanged at
Shorapoor.

The great interest of the time was centred in the Rajah's
fate. There was no doubt, had he been taken in arms
during the attack by Wyndham's force, that he would
have been at once tried and summarily executed—and
even now there seemed but small chance of his life; but
the Resident wrote to me saying he thought, if I asked it,
the Rajah's life might be granted, especially if I explained
with what ruffians he had been surrounded, and how
misled.

I sent an "express" at once with an earnest appeal for
mercy.

A few hours after my arrival in Shorapoor the old
Brahmin priest came to me privately.

"Do you remember, Sahib," he asked, "what I once
told you, and what the Ranee said when we were with
her at her bedside?"

"Perfectly," I answered; "you said the Rajah would
not live to complete his twenty-fourth year, and that he
would lose his country."

"Yes, Sahib," he went on; "part of the prediction is
already fulfilled, and the rest will surely follow—it is
quite inevitable."

"Do you think the Rajah knew of the prediction?" I
inquired. "If he did, it may have made him reckless."

"I do not think he knew it," replied the old priest;

"for the last time I saw the box it was in the treasury, with the seals unbroken, as you left it."

(Captain Wyndham had secured the box, and kept the horoscope with the rolls of calculations as a curiosity, not knowing their purport.)

"We cannot say," I continued, "what may yet happen; the proceedings are not over, and the Resident and I are both determined to save the Rajah's life if we can."

"It's no use, Sahib," returned the Shastree, shaking his head mournfully; "your intentions are merciful, but you are helpless before his fate. He will die—how, we may not see; but he must die—he cannot live. You, Sahib, and I, are the only two living that possess this secret, and you must be so good as to tell me directly you know his sentence. I cannot believe that the Government will spare him. I firmly expect that he will be blown away from a gun."

When the Resident's letter came, I sent for the old Shastree and read it to him, and also my own strong appeal in reply. "I hope the Rajah's life is now safe," I said. "Listen to what I have written. The Governor-General, who is kind and merciful, will scarcely refuse this request, supported by the Resident."

The old man shook his head sadly. "Till the last day has passed to which the calculation extends, I have no hope," he said; "it cannot be wrong, and but little time remains. It grieves me, Sahib, to go over the figures again, but the present aspect of the planets is very calamitous to the Rajah, and all through next month the combinations show extreme danger. We cannot help him, and you have done all you could; you can do no more—only wait." So we did, anxiously.

From the time I had quitted Shorapoor, no regular accounts appeared to have been made up; but I had been joined by my old head accountant, Seeta Ram Rao, now Assistant Deputy-Commissioner, to whom I could offer better pay, and who was rejoiced to serve again under me. He knew all about the revenues of Shorapoor, and could help materially. A schedule of the whole period of the Rajah's administration was drawn out, and the result was that three and a half lakhs, or £35,000, of new debt had been contracted, while every rupee of the former surplus had altogether disappeared.

We had much to do in revising district accounts; but all was progressing well, and my life was a very pleasant one. I had charming companions in Wyndham and his wife, who became my very dear friends, and our love and friendship will continue while life lasts. They were interested in all my doings, and it used to be a great delight to me to show them all my roads and the improvements I had made during my residence at Shorapoor. The roads were sadly out of repair, but we scrambled over them on horseback, and I soon had them put to rights again.

I could not get back my house while the 74th remained; but I held my *cucherry* in the hospital, and was constructing a large, airy, thatched barrack for the soldiers.

At last the news came.

The Rajah of Shorapoor had been sentenced to death; but the Resident had commuted his sentence to transportation for life, which was the most his power admitted of. This sentence had, however, been still further commuted by the Governor-General to four years' imprisonment in a fortress near Madras (I think Chingleput). In addition, the Rajah was to be allowed to have such of his wives as he pleased with him, and his own servants. If he showed evidence of reform and steadiness, his principality was to be restored to him.

I sent off at once for the Shastree.

"Listen," said I, "to the gracious and merciful determination of the Governor-General. The Rajah's life is safe; and if he is quiet and steady for four short years, he will regain his State! What could be more considerate

or more lenient ?   What becomes now of the prophecy ?
This letter proves it is false."

"I wish I could think so, Sahib," he sighed, "and that
my poor young master were really safe; but, alas! he is
in the greatest danger. Nay, it seems closer than ever
now; but we shall see, Sahib. Sometimes a merciful God
puts away the evil omens just as the fulfilment of them is
imminent. I will go and tell the Ranee this good news.
I only wish the time were past, and that I could be happy
in it too."

The Ranee would hardly believe the message I sent
her. She and the other Ranees were to join the Rajah
almost directly, and were to make their preparations at
once.

The head Ranee, Rungama, asked me to come to her;
and when I entered, quite regardless of etiquette, she
threw herself into my arms, and danced about in the
wildest glee. She had expected the news of her husband's
death when she saw the old Shastree come into her rooms,
and the revulsion of feeling was almost too much for her.
She and one other Ranee were to go. The third was no
favourite with the Rajah.

A few days after, the Resident's order finally came that
the ladies were to be sent off on a certain day to meet the
Rajah at Kurnool. Everything had been already prepared ;
there need be no delay ; and I intended them to start
that very afternoon. I took leave of them both in the
morning, and had settled down to my work after breakfast
was over. It chanced to be a day set apart for the arrangement of yearly allowances and gifts to Brahmins, and all
the chief Brahmins were present, and the old Shastree
among them. Several were seated at the table with me,
assisting me, when suddenly I heard the clash of the
express-runner's bells coming up the street. I thought it
might be some message from Linsoogoor, or some new
arrangement for the Ranees' departure. The runner entered

the palace court, and his packet was soon in my hands. It contained a few lines only, from the Resident :—

"The Rajah of Shorapoor shot himself this morning dead, as he arrived at his first encampment. I will write particulars when I know them."

My countenance naturally changed; and the old Shastree, who was beside me, and had been reading over Sanscrit deeds and grants to me, caught hold of my arm, and, peering into my face, cried, almost with a shriek—

"He's dead! he's dead! I know it by your face—it tells me, Sahib, he's dead!"

"Yes," I said, sorrowfully. "Yes, he is dead; he shot himself at the first stage out of Secunderabad, and died instantly."

Then ensued a sad scene of weeping and wailing; and one of my friends in the adjoining room, hearing the tumult, rushed in, crying, "Thank God, you are safe! I feared something terrible had happened. Why are these people so agitated?"

"It is terrible enough," I answered. "The Rajah has shot himself, and the news has just come by express."

"Ah!" said the old priest, as soon as he could speak, "he could not escape his fate, and the prophecy is fulfilled."

It was, indeed, a strange accomplishment of the prediction. In a few days more the Rajah would have completed his twenty-fourth year; and now he had died by his own hand! I sent for the Ranee's father, and bade him break the news gently to his daughter. I could not bear to see the poor girl's misery, and I should have to visit her later; so he and an old friend of his departed to perform their sad task.

The day after, I heard by another express the particulars. The Rajah had been told of the Governor-General's commutation of his sentence, and was very deeply grateful for the mercy shown to him. He had promised earnestly to try and deserve the consideration which had been extended him, and was particularly pleased that he was to be allowed the society of his two Ranees, speaking joyously of the prospect of meeting them at Kurnool.

He had travelled in a palankeen, with the officer commanding his escort near him, all the way to their camp.

When they arrived, the officer took off his belt, in which was a loaded revolver, hung it over a chair, and went outside the tent. While washing his face a moment afterwards, he heard a shot, and, running back, found the Rajah lying on the ground quite dead. The ball had entered his stomach and passed through the spine.

Was the act intentional? I think not. He had a trick always of taking up and examining everything lying near him, more especially if it were new to him; and he had had this habit from childhood, and I had often checked him for it. I do not think he could ever have seen a revolver—and such a weapon would be too tempting to escape notice; he would be sure to snap it, or meddle with the lock, and the pistol may have exploded without his intending it at all. No one was with him—no one saw him,—so that only conjectures could be raised about the event; but I, who knew him well, do not believe it was suicide.

Whether accidental or intentional, the result was the same. The Rajah was dead, and his kingdom was lost, ere he completed his twenty-fourth year; and the grim old prophecy deduced from the horoscope was literally fulfilled!

CHAPTER XVI.

1858-59.

TOWARDS the end of May, Lord Elphinstone and the Resident had both been extremely anxious in regard to Shorapoor and its Beydur population.

It had transpired at the Rajah's trial, and had previously been suspected, that certain chiefs of the Southern Mahratta country had formed a plan for insurrection; but as the Rajah had refused to give any names, or to implicate others in any way, no action could be taken: and the Rajah simply pleaded in his defence that he had refused to join the rebellion when invited and pressed to do so. General Jacob had taken the precaution, very wisely, of disarming Meeraj, a very strong fort; and his admirable check of formidable rebellion at Kolapoor, and the active measures he used, effectually crushed the hopes of the insurrectionists. I have little doubt that had the Rajah gone to the assistance of the Beydurs of Hulgully when they asked his aid, the whole of the Southern Mahratta country and Raichore would have joined him in far greater force than they afterwards displayed when they rose at last on the 29th May 1858, under the chief of Mirgoona, and openly murdered Mr Thomson, a Bombay civilian, who had ventured to remonstrate with them.

The force was afterwards attacked by Colonel Malcolm and utterly routed on the 2d June: their chief was captured, tried, and executed.

Another rising was planned by one Bheem Rao, formerly a Government collector at Bellary, who with 250 men took up his position in the fort of Kopaldroog, but was pursued and killed by Major Hughes and a detachment from Linsoogoor. The remainder of the rebels were taken prisoners, and either hanged or shot.

There were many such parties in the Deccan: and I confess that, when I heard of these troubles, I wondered what my Beydurs would do: but they had received sufficient warning in the fate of their Rajah and in the prompt discomfiture of their rebellious neighbours, and not a man stirred or showed the slightest sign of insubordination. They even assisted me materially in guarding the frontier, and the ferries across the Bheema, against the insurgents who tried to pass through Shorapoor. The Arabs of Hyderabad employed by the late Rajah were satisfied that the Beydurs would soon join them if they could only enter the country, and were not a little discomfited to find these very people guarding their country against their entrance. So, finding they could get no sympathy, all disturbance ceased, and we were once more at peace; and I could assure Lord Elphinstone, with whom I had been in private correspondence, that no apprehension of the Beydurs being induced to join the rebel party need be entertained.

The victories won by Sir Hugh Rose, that of Gwalior, and the death of the Ranee of Jhansi, the capture of the Nawab of Banda and his treasure, Sir Hope Grant's proceedings in Oudh, and the seizure of Tantia Topee—all these went to prove that the power of the Mutiny was broken, and that India would soon be at peace in all its borders.

How earnestly I had looked forward to this year as the one in which I should again see all my dear ones in England! but now leave was impossible to obtain, and indeed no one would have asked it, except it were urgently needed for health's sake. Fortunately I was in too good condition to ask for a medical certificate, though at times I had much suffering. My father proposed to bring my children to me; but in my present position I felt it would hardly do. I had no home for them; my work was of a very unsettled nature, and the country was still very much disturbed. I consulted the Resident; but he earnestly begged me not to risk such a step, adding that he knew I sorely needed change, and it was better to wait another year, when leave could be obtained without difficulty. I felt he was right, and a very serious fit of illness in September warned me that I should soon need rest from work; but I recovered, and went on as usual again.

Authentic ghost-stories are comparatively rare; but a circumstance occurred at Shorapoor which made a great impression on men's minds, and may be accepted as one.

There were two companies of the 74th Highlanders at Shorapoor with Colonel Hughes's force. After the place was taken, one company was located, as I have before stated, in my house on the hill, the other remaining in camp below the town, till they should return to Bellary. One afternoon—I have forgotten the date—Capt. ——, the senior officer, was sitting in his tent writing letters for England, as the mail letters had to be forwarded by that evening's post, and had had the side wall of his tent opened for light and air, when a young man of his company appeared suddenly before him in his hospital dress, without his cap, and, without saluting him, said, " I wish, sir, you would kindly have my arrears of pay sent to my mother, who lives at ——; please take down the address." Capt. —— took down the address mechanically, and said, " All right, my man, that will do;" and, again making no salute, the man went away. A moment after, Capt. —— remembered that the dress and appearance of the soldier, and his manner of coming in, were highly irregular, and desired his orderly to send the sergeant to him directly.

"Why did you allow —— to come to me in that irregular manner?" he asked, as soon as the sergeant came.

The man was thunderstruck. "Sir," he exclaimed, "do you not remember he died yesterday in hospital, and was buried this morning? Are you sure, sir, you saw him?"

"Quite sure," was the reply; "and here is a memorandum I took down from him of his mother's address, to whom he wished his pay should be sent."

"That is strange, sir," said the sergeant; "his things were sold by auction to-day, and I could not find where the money should be sent in the company's registry, but it may be in the general registry with the regiment."

The books were searched; the address taken down was proved to be correct, and the circumstance made a profound impression upon all who knew the facts.

These Highlanders were capital fellows—very steady in a town where there were all sorts of temptations to excess. As the weather grew cooler, they got up a play —a melodrama—called, I think, "The Maniac Lover," and acted it well in the *cucherry*. Many of the Shorapoor "gentry" and their wives being invited, the latter sat ensconced behind bamboo screens; and although no word could be understood, the natives applauded very vigorously. I wrote a ballad, entitled the "Battle of Shorapoor," with a very long string of verses, which became exceedingly popular, and detailed the march of the troops, the fight, with various incidents, and the final discomfiture of the rebels; and this was constantly sung with great spirit, all joining in the chorus. The men had also games of cricket, skittles, &c., to amuse them, and some were even fond of chess.

The officers were pleasant companions, and we generally dined together. They were succeeded by a company of H.M.'s 56th Regiment in June.

I laid out a new road into the town, which was about 24 feet wide and about a mile long, leading from the alley

up to the north gate. Its deepest gradient was 1' in 25',
and along it carts and pack-bullocks could travel easily.
My plantations of mango and tamarind trees were generally thriving, and the oldest ones were now bearing fruit.
Bohnal tank required no repairs, and was quite complete
in all respects; but as to the others, nothing had been
done, except a little at Kuchaknoor. No outlay upon
public works had been permitted since I left.

By June all the arrangements of estates and pensions
were reported as finished. There were objections to the
Ranees receiving their estates back again, for the present
at any rate; but an allowance of £1000 a-year was settled
on Rungama, and pensions on the other ladies in proportion. Rungama was very grateful; she did not expect
half so much. I often paid her a visit, and she was
gradually growing more cheerful and resigned.

The year closed pleasantly to me, though I could not
get leave to England; but as soon as ever the prohibitions
were withdrawn, I was prepared to ask for it. The survey
in Nuldroog was to be carried on according to my plan, as
an experiment, although my present duties did not admit
my taking up the surveyorship.

The Governor-General was pleased to record of me that
'Captain Meadows Taylor has been deputed to Shorapoor,
where his past experience and local knowledge make his
presence most invaluable."

It was not yet decided who should take my place at
Nuldroog. Mr Maltby had been obliged to go to England; and my friend Bullock was acting for him—without any hope, however, of obtaining the appointment
permanently, as it was far too good for an "uncovenanted
servant" to aspire to! We had all hoped that the gracious
proclamation issued on her Majesty's assumption of the
Government of India, which I had the pleasure of reading
in Oordoo and Mahratta to the people of Shorapoor, would
have extended to us, and done away with the invidious

distinctions "covenanted" and "uncovenanted;" but it was not to be so.

At the close of the year I had a visit from the executive engineer in the Raichore district, who came to look at my contemplated works, and checked the levels and surveys of the great Kuchaknoor tank. There was a slight error of fourteen-hundredths of a foot detected in the outward bench-marks of the embankment; but in all other respects my work, even with the imperfect instruments I had used, was entirely correct. I proposed to go on and complete the tank; but until some decision was come to about the principality, no public work of magnitude could be attempted. The Resident had gone up to Calcutta to confer with Lord Canning, and perhaps the fate of Shorapoor would be decided by them. However, in the end, it was left uncertain.

A very unpleasant affair had taken place at Hyderabad. At a reception which the Nizam had held, and at which the Minister and the Resident had both been present, a man had fired a loaded pistol either at the Resident or the Minister, who were coming out together. It could not be determined for whom the shot was intended. Fortunately the ball missed both, but wounded the Minister's foster-brother. The ruffian then drew his sword and made a cut at the Minister, which an attendant received upon his arm, and the villain was immediately cut down by Captain Hastings Fraser and others standing by. The scene had been exciting and disagreeable, and showed plainly that the germs of treason were not yet destroyed. There was, however, no further disturbance.

I could get no satisfactory answer to my application for furlough to England, being answered that, as soon as the question of the Shorapoor State was decided, I should know my fate; and meanwhile, if it were at all possible, I was to hold on.

At the beginning of May 1859 I had finished my tour

of the district, and made a settlement for the current year. The country was in a wretched condition. A great mass of the cultivation had been thrown up the year before. The farmers had been deprived of their best lands by the Rajah, who had given them to his favourites. There were no proper accounts, and the whole was in worse confusion than when I had first taken over charge. Numbers of families had emigrated in disgust. I could give very little assurance to any, as to future settlements; and, indeed, I was forbidden to do so, for Government was still silent as to the destiny of the State.

I did what I could, but it amounted to very little. The people would not invest their capital unless the country were to remain under British rule, and I could not conscientiously counsel them to do so. "Directly you went away the last time," they said, "the men about the Rajah chose the best of our newly-cleared lands, and they were taken from us and given to them. True, you have now given them back to us; but can you assure us that the same won't happen again if your back is turned? Let us wait and see what will happen."

No change occurred in my position until August, when, in addition to Shorapoor, the whole of the Raichore Doab was put under my charge; and as Raichore had been deeply disaffected, I was desired to report upon its condition specially. I did not relish this employment; and I began to fear, too, that this accession to my duties would prevent my going to England, as I had hoped to do, the year following. I was now by no means strong, and I looked to the future with grave anxiety. With Raichore and Shorapoor combined, I should have a country quite 20,000 square miles in area under my jurisdiction, and a population hardly under, perhaps exceeding, two millions. There was but one English assistant, with four native assistants, in Raichore; but my assistant in Shorapoor, Seeta Ram Rao, was a host in himself, and

I could trust that province to him with every confidence.

It appeared, too, that I was to receive no additional pay
for my extra work ; but there was no help for it. The
order came, and was obeyed with the best grace I could
command.

I went to Linsoogoor for a few days, and there performed the sad and painful task of reading the burial
service over a dear friend's wife, who had died suddenly,
and who expressed a wish that I should be the one to
perform this last sad office for her. I could not stay
long, but simply took charge of the province, returning
again to Shorapoor to investigate a trial for murder—a
very difficult and complicated case, which no one but
myself could dispose of. Captain and Mrs Wyndham
accompanied me, and remained till October, when we
moved out to Bohnal, to begin my tour.

It was a delightful time, cool and pleasant. There had
been a good monsoon, and the lake was full and running
over. We had charming rides every morning over the
roads, both old and new, and which were now as smooth
as gravel-walks.

After a fortnight spent at Bohnal, where the schooner
was in capital order and in constant use, we set out for
the western frontier, so as to visit the great falls of the
Krishna, which I wanted to show my friends. I took
them also to the cairns and cromlechs I had discovered,
and we all enjoyed our holiday at the falls most thoroughly.

Here the great river Krishna leaves the table-land of
the Deccan, and falls, by a descent of 408 feet in about
three miles, into the lower level of Shorapoor. The fall
itself is not perpendicular, but becomes a roaring cataract
half a mile broad when the river is in flood. The scene
then is indescribably grand, an enormous broken volume
of water rushing down an incline of granite with a roar

that can be easily heard at a distance of thirty miles, and
a cloud of spray dashing up high into the air; while the
irregularity of the incline, its huge rocks, and the deep
holes which the waters have excavated, increase the wonderful effect of the cataract, and brilliant rainbows flash
through the spray, changing with every breath of wind.
Finally, the water falls into a deep pool, which becomes a
whirling mass covered with billows that, rushing in every
direction, clash and break against each other, sending up
great piles of foam. As a Beydur standing beside me said,
"It is like all the white horses in the world fighting together, and tossing their manes into the air." Nor was
the simple fellow's illustration without point.

I had never seen such a sight during my life, and perhaps few cataracts in the world can surpass it, when in
flood, for sublimity and beauty.

I believe few English people have visited this spot. I,
at least, have never met any traveller who had heard of
it. When we were there, the water was lower than on
my first visit; but the effect of the fall, the rocky gorge
below clothed with wood, and the grand old fort at the
end, partly Hindoo and partly Mussulman, was very
beautiful.

Our route lay across the ford, which was a memorable
spot in history, when the Mussulman army crossed to
engage that of Beejanugger in the battle which was
fought on the south bank of the Krishna in 1565. The
ford had been carried by a bold stratagem. The Mussulman leaders marched slowly up the left bank of the river
for two days, watched by the Hindoo troops, who left the
ford almost unguarded. The Mussulmans then doubled
back, carried the defences of the ford by storm, and the
whole army followed. By this utter defeat of their opponents, the Mussulmans gained possession of the city of
Beejanugger and the whole of the northern portion of the
kingdom.

We found the remains of the defences still quite traceable at the ford, and corresponding in all respects with
the description given by Ferishta. From hence to Linsoogoor was only an easy march, and we returned into
cantonments.

At the end of October I started on my first march to
Moodgul. I dared not loiter longer, and felt I must see
with my own eyes, and hear with my own ears, before I
could report specially upon the district.

I found a good road to Moodgul, and the canter in the
fresh morning air was delicious. Moodgul is a fine old
fort, built upon a group of granite rocks rising perhaps
100 feet above the plain. It had been a bone of conten-
tion from the earliest times of the Bahmany dynasty, and
alternately fell into the possession of the Hindoos or the
Mussulmans, whichever chanced to be, for the time, the
strongest party. Now it was considerably ruined, but
most picturesque, and I explored it thoroughly.

I could only stay two days, and these were mostly occupied in inquiring into a dispute relating to a Christian
settlement there, which, as it involved religious jurisdiction between his Holiness the Pope and the Archbishop of
Goa, I was incompetent to decide. The congregation were
all weavers of blankets, and shepherds, originally converted by one of St Francis Xavier's missionaries from
Goa. It had been somewhat richly endowed by the several kings of the Adil Shahy dynasty of Beejapoor, and it
still retained these grants through all revolutions. There
were two other congregations in the Doab, one being composed of potters at Raichore ; the name of the place of the
other I forget. The church at Moodgul was a humble but
respectable edifice, and service was performed by a deacon,
the Mass in full being celebrated when a priest came from
Goa on his rounds.

On my arrival some time after in England, I wrote to
his Eminence Cardinal Wiseman about this congregation,

furnishing him with all particulars respecting them, and received a courteous reply, to the effect that my communication was both valuable and extremely interesting, and would be duly forwarded to Rome.

I hoped next to visit the grand old city of Beejanugger, and to add some sketches to my collection. At the town of Kanakgherry the Rajah came out to welcome me, and entertained me most hospitably. Here I saw the finest Hindoo temple I had yet visited. The interior was supported by huge pillars of granite, in the form of horses, on which female figures were mounted; the frieze and ceiling were richly ornamented in carving. I do not think it is much known, but it well repays a visit. After breakfast the Rajah came to me, and Shorapoor and its affairs were the subject of discussion. "Could I give any hope," he asked, " of its being restored to the family? would the British keep it? or would the Nizam have it?"

I could say nothing, for nothing had been determined upon. My friend, whom I had often before seen at Shorapoor, deprecated the idea of the Nizam having Shorapoor.

"Why should the people suffer more oppression?" he said. " Of course I would wish to see it given back to the family—my relatives; but if that may not be, why should the Nizam get it? The 12,000 Beydurs would far prefer the just rule of the English, and would not revert to their evil ways under you."

Such was the old gentleman's opinion, and I agreed with him perfectly; but I had no hope of the restoration of the family being allowed. Pid Naik's eldest son, who was the next heir, was steady, sensible, and thoroughly loyal, having opposed his cousin, the late Rajah, in all his insurrectionary movements; still, I thought the British Government would eventually annex the State as an example and a warning to all others.

From Kanakgherry I went on to Anagoondy, where the lineal descendant of the great Rajahs of Beejanugger re-

sided. He had sent me a very pressing invitation to come
and visit him, and volunteered to show all the marvels of
Beejanugger to me on my arrival. Anagoondy, "The
Elephant's Corner," had once been a suburb of Beejanugger, and proved to be one of the most curious places I had
ever visited. To the north was a perfectly inaccessible
range of bare granite hills, surmounted by piles of fantastic
rocks, along the tops of which ran high walls, with bastions at intervals, in the Hindoo style. The only entrance
to this labyrinth of rocks was through a very narrow gorge
on the eastern side, also strongly fortified by double walls
and large bastions. Passing round the corners of these
walls, the ground opened out to some degree, and was
cultivated, affording a lovely view of the rugged hills on
the south side of the Tungabuddhra, a rough brawling
river rushing through the valley.

The Rajah had made a good road through his estate, and
showed me many points which afforded exquisite views of
wood, rock, and water, with the mountains in the background ; and he always stopped the carriage at these places,
to show me the prospect, with evident enjoyment. He
was driving a handsome light phaeton, and met me at the
barrier. He was a fine active young man, with a very
pleasing and intelligent countenance, and we were soon
good friends. He had prepared the porch of a temple on
the bank of the river for me, and I found an ample breakfast provided, and his own servants in attendance.

The situation of the town among these most picturesque
piles of rock was very curious. I went to return the
Rajah's visit in the afternoon, when he proposed to take
me to his island in the evening. I willingly agreed. I
found his reception-room nicely furnished in the English
style ; and we sat chatting pleasantly for a long time.
He seemed pleased to find me acquainted with his family
history—their wars with the Mussulmans, and their final
gallant struggle with the crusade against them in 1565.

" Ah!" he said, " my ancestor, Ram Raj, alone would have beaten them back; but the coalition of four kingdoms of the Deccan proved too strong for him. They are all gone now, and have left no trace except these cities—not a soul to pray for their manes, or light a lamp in their name; while I still am here, and represent my great ancestors as their lineal descendant. I have only the ' Elephant Corner' of the great city to live in, it is true; but I am quite content, and the Nizam allows me this corner and its dependencies, while the English have granted me some lands on the south bank of the river, and a pension."

In the evening he came quite alone, poling a small basket-boat.

" I always go down to the island by myself," he said; " it is such good fun shooting the rapid; but I have men there to paddle me up again in a bigger boat."

I got into the little craft, and he pushed off into the stream, striking as directly across it as the current would allow. We were soon drawn into the rapid, and dashed on for a quarter of a mile at great speed—the Rajah with his long bamboo pole fending the boat from rocks on either side very skilfully, and evidently intensely enjoying the excitement.

At the end of the shoot, we entered the still water, where the island was situated—a richly-wooded spot, laid out as a garden in the English style, well stocked with fruit-trees and a profusion of roses and gardenias, whose scent filled the evening air with perfume. In the centre was a pretty pavilion, also in the English style; and this was, the Rajah told me, his favourite resort. There were numbers of tame pea-fowl; and at his peculiar call some cranes and flamingoes, with geese and ducks, all came flocking round us to be fed—a motley and curious collection. "These are my pets," said the Rajah, " and my children's too."

When it was growing dark, his gardeners brought a

large basket‑boat to the landing‑place, and six stout
fellows paddled us up the rapid to my resting-place. I
had spent a very interesting day, and my host pressed me
much to remain some time; but this was impossible—my
tents had already gone on to Humpee on the south bank
of the river, where the old city commenced, and I had
much to see there. " If you really must go," said the
Rajah, " I will take you there myself in my large boat,
and you will then see the views from the river, which are
very striking, and, more interesting than those on the
road; but I wish you could stay—you are the only Englishman with whom I ever felt on easy terms of friendship; and none of your people seem to know or to
remember who I am."

The Rajah was punctual to the time appointed next
morning, and brought a stout crew with him, as we
should have to paddle up several rapids; and before sunrise we were off.

It was a lovely voyage of several miles. At each bend
of the beautiful river new prospects opened, and new piles
of granite rocks, some of them 500 feet in height, came in
view, fringed with trees and brushwood, which softened
their grim outlines, and rendered the effects of light and
shade most charming. I took many sketches from the
water, while the Rajah looked on wonderingly, and
longed to be able to do so likewise. At last the " Gate of
the River," as it is called, came in sight, where the stream
lessens to a very narrow pass, bounded by piles of rock of
the most fantastic forms imaginable; and leaving our
boat at the landing-place, we walked up to the courtyard
of the great temple, in the cloisters of which I found my
servants had taken up a comfortable position, instead of
pitching my tents.

" If I can, I will come to-morrow," said the Rajah;
" but in any case, you must not go till I return. I must
be with you when you go over the great temple."

I promised I would stay, and he took his leave.

After breakfast I ordered my palankeen, and wandered over the western portions of the city. I saw that the barriers of rocks extended to the south, forming a strong line of defence, the only aperture being a pass between them and the spurs of the Raman Mullay Mountain. This was the pass by which the Bahmany king, Mujahid Shah, entered the lines of defence in 1378, and endeavoured to take the city; but owing to the neglect of one of his generals, who had been directed to occupy an eminence to the west of the city, which was the real key to the place, and who failed in his duty, the king could only penetrate the first line of defence, where a huge image of Hunooman, the monkey-god, stands alone, carved out of a great granite boulder.

The king, on seeing it surrounded by Brahmins, charged and dispersed them; then dismounting, he struck the image with his steel mace, breaking off a portion of the right leg.

"For this act," cried a dying Brahmin, "thou shalt die before thou reach the city"—a prophecy strictly fulfilled; for King Mujahid was assassinated on his march to Gulburgah. In Ferishta, a vivid description is given of this battle; and the positions occupied by the contending parties are so exactly mentioned, that they are, to this day, easily traceable.

I spent all the day sketching. The Rajah's sleeping-palace was a curious conception of Mussulman-Gothic architecture, the upper rooms of which would make a delightful residence if purged from the bats, swallows, and wild-pigeons' nests. The fine tower, with a Gothic pavilion at the top, from whence there is a glorious view; the elephant stables and treasury, still perfect; and the ruins of the Rajah's palaces, and their courtyards, which are very extensive—with a host of other picturesque scenes, and masses of ruins,—gave me more than enough to do

with my pencil and my brush.   Beejanugger is well described by the Nawab Abd-ul Buzzak, a Persian merchant, who visited the city in 1443, and resided there.
His account of the population and general aspect of the
city, the religious ceremonials, and the splendour of the
king's court, are very graphic and eminently truthful.
The journal has been translated for the Hakluyt Society,
and well repays perusal.   I have described the temple in
a volume published by Mr Murray on the ' Temples of
Western India,' and I endeavoured to extract my information from the most authentic sources.

CHAPTER XVII.

1859-60.

AFTER breakfast, the Rajah arrived in his chair, which he insisted upon my using, while he took my palankeen instead; and we set off for the temple which had been built by his ancestor, Achoot Rao, in 1534-36. Anything more exquisitely beautiful, or so wondrously finished, could hardly be conceived—except, perhaps, the temple of Nundidroog, which even excels this in some particulars; but that of Kanakgherry, which I had considered very marvellous, sinks into insignificance before this.

Lofty pillars of granite support the roof, carved out of solid blocks of stone; some of these are fashioned like horses or lions; on the horses' backs ride female figures: others have rows of slender figures round them, cut away from the main stem, giving a graceful airy effect, which is very charming. Every portion of the interior is covered with rich, minute carving, and some parts were polished like glass.

Outside, the basement consists of rows of elephants; above these run several courses of different ornaments of elegant patterns. The projecting eaves of the cornices are likewise elaborately carved; and the whole presented an appearance of extreme lightness and grace, which I had not before noticed in any Hindoo edifice. Tippoo Sultan, when encamped near Beejanugger, had had a mine sprung in the roof, in the hope of destroying the building; but it had only made a small hole, and Tippoo then said he had been warned in a dream not to attempt to destroy the holy temple. The deity to whom it was dedicated was "Withul" or Krishna, and it had been the intention of one of the Rajah's ancestors to have removed the holy image from Pundharpoor to it, as being a more appropriate dwelling-place; the god, however, refused to stir, and, in consequence, the building has never been fully consecrated.

Close to the exterior of the temple there is what appeared to me to be a richly-ornamented triumphal car, to be used on festivals; but this proved to be also of granite —a great boulder having been wrought as it stood into the perfect resemblance of a car, the wheels of which seemed only to require a push to make them turn, so well was the carving executed.

I had felt ill all day, and at last, in the middle of my drawing, such violent fever and ague came on as obliged me to give it up very unwillingly; and as the attack lasted some hours, my sketching came to an untimely end, and I was unable to see the remainder of the temple or the east side of the city.

However, before the fever began, I had managed to ascend the "Matun Purwut," a stupendous pile of rocks, by the stone steps which had been cut in them; my bearers easily carried my chair, and from the top—an elevation probably of five hundred feet—I had enjoyed a magnificent view. The whole area of the old city lay spread out before me—the noble temples, and their lines of building—the ranges of fantastic rocks piled on all sides—the course of the river, for miles above and below the "Gate"—and the blue Raman Mullay Mountains, and their varied spurs, stretching away to the south.

The Rajah pointed out to me all the objects of interest —the battle-fields of Mujahid Shah, and the Lake of Cumlapoor, glittering in the bright sunlight. It was indeed a magnificent panorama, and one never to be forgotten.

I was very sorry to say farewell to the Rajah, whose genuine and most courteous hospitality and agreeable manners had made a great impression upon me. I had been told I should find him haughty and repellent : on the contrary, he was entirely free from presumption, full of information and intelligence, active and manly in his habits, and of very prepossessing appearance—in every respect a "gentleman,"—and I was glad I had gone out of my way to visit him.

I stayed a day longer to recruit after my fit of fever, and went again to the great temple, and to the avenue of pilgrim's cloisters, and so round to the palace of the kings and its surroundings, all of the highest interest. The palaces could never have equalled those of Beejapoor : there were no arches, and the roof had evidently been made of wood, covered with concrete, and supported on wooden pillars. These had either been destroyed on the spot or carried away, as no vestige of them remained. There was nothing to compare with the fort at Beejapoor. The defences of Beejanugger were mean and weak in comparison ; and the ancient Rajahs, who had built the city, had evidently trusted more to the natural strength of the position than to the work raised by men's hands.

One Cesar Federicke, a Venetian merchant, gives a very interesting description of the city in 1565, after the residence there of the victorious Mussulman kings for six months. He says :—

"The city was not altogether destroyed, but houses still stand empty, and there are dwelling in them nothing but tigers and other wild beasts. The *enceinte* of the city is about four-and-twenty miles, and within the walls are several mountains. The houses stand walled with earth, and no place, saving the palaces of the three tyrants and the pagodas, other than made with earth."

Evidently, therefore, the city was exactly the same as the Hindoo habitations of the present day,—the walls of

houses being of mud, or clay and stone, and the roofs of
clay beaten down—very substantial as long as the roof is
good, but which crumbles away on the percolation of water.

In the large volume which illustrates the 'Temples of
Western India,' which I have before alluded to, many fine
photographic illustrations of Beejanugger will be found,
and the views of the temple of Withul or Wittoba are
especially worthy of examination.

From Beejanugger I ascended the pass through the
Raman Mullay Mountain by a beautiful road constructed
by the Madras engineers, at an easy gradient the whole
way up. I was well enough now to ride, and enjoyed the
lovely scenery to the full. At the top I found a nearly
level plain, and a total change of climate from India to
Europe. Ramandroog is, I believe, about 4000 feet above
the sea-level, and its climate is delicious throughout the
year. Even during the hottest season the sea-breeze
makes its way up, and there is no oppressive heat. Here
there is a sanitarium, and I had sent word to the medical
officer in charge that I was coming up for advice. I well
remember we had to have a fire lighted that evening as it
was so chilly, and that we sat over it till a late hour most
thoroughly enjoying it. How I slept that night! All the
evil demons that had been tormenting me — neuralgia,
rheumatism, and all their doleful train—vanished as if by
magic with the change of air. The doctor said I had been
too long without a thorough change and rest from work,
and that there was nothing for it but to take furlough and
go home to England as soon as I could. He would not
answer for my life, he said, if I remained at Shorapoor
through another hot season. I enjoyed some days at
Ramandroog very much; my strength and appetite returned; I felt fresh vigour and renewed health, and could
take a good long walk without fatigue. However, I might
not stay; time was precious, and I set off again to my
work.

I went to Koorgah, where my tents were pitched, and where there was a fine ancient weir for irrigation, which required repair on my side, the authorities of Bellary having already restored their portion. The old Rajahs of Beejanugger had been great constructors of irrigation works from time to time, had thrown several dams across the Tungabhudra river, and had diverted the various streams so as to employ them extensively for the cultivation of rice, sugar-cane and cocoa-nut, ginger, turmeric, and other produce. At Koorgah the constructor had been Achoot Rao, and the inscription bore date 1537. This dam consisted for the most part of large loose blocks of granite, placed together on a broad base in a triangular form, and which had gradually become consolidated by silt. Many noble tanks, too, had been constructed by the Beejanugger dynasty, the largest being nearly three square miles in area.

My district work now fairly began, and was fearfully heavy, while the petitions against one grievance or another became almost too numerous to attend to or settle at all as I could wish. Here the fever returned, and I could only do my work lying on my bed, for I was too weak to sit up much, and I began to fear I should soon fail utterly.

For change I went further north to Kopaldroog, a marvellous fort indeed, being entirely impregnable. It consists of two fortifications, one, encircling the town, which had been remodelled by the French engineers in Tippoo's service, and all the bastions and cavaliers fitted with embrasures, and ramparts for heavy guns; the other fortification being of the great granite rock within the *enceinte*, the batteries of which command every portion of the land below on all sides to a great distance.

This hill-fort must be upwards of 500 feet high, and is inaccessible except by a flight of very rude rough steps which wind in and out among the rocks, and are in some places extremely narrow and unsafe. How many guns were ever carried up, it is impossible to say, but there were several old ones in the upper batteries. I went up this rock once, my bearers having contrived a light conveyance out of an arm-chair, and I travelled along easily. Had the insurgent Bheem Rao confined himself to operations against villages, he would have done much mischief, and roused the people, who seemed ripe for insurrection ; but he got possession of Kopaldroog by a stratagem, and found himself there in a trap. He could not hold so large a place, and his party betook themselves to the steps of the fort, where many, including the Rajah himself, were slain, and the rest were forced to surrender at discretion, for they had no food. I found the summit of this rock was composed of a large circular battery, and below it some deep cisterns in the naked rock contained beautiful clear water. About three miles south of Kopaldroog lay another rock-fort, if possible even stronger and more difficult of access, but not so high, and equally well provided with water in the same manner.

At Kookanoor, near the border of the Dharwar Collectorate, I found a very beautiful Hindoo temple dedicated to Siva. The pillars of the porch and hall were of polished greenstone, and seemed almost as if they had been turned in a lathe, the different circles of ornamentation were so exact ; and the designs were cut out as sharply in this tough, hard stone, as if they had been chased in metal. Near the town was a curious monolith of sandstone thirty-five feet in height, richly decorated, and having a figure of a cock on the top. There was a long inscription on the pillar, apparently in ancient Canarese, and I regretted very much that no one was able to decipher it. A little further on I found another superb temple; the ornamentation of its pillars was truly exquisite, and the designs so delicate that the various patterns were copied by the goldsmiths of the country for gold and silver ornaments.

This was the limit of my district, which contained, in addition to the foregoing, many illustrations of the Jain and Hindoo architecture, dating from A.D. 76 to the 13th century. Many of their works are represented in the volumes before alluded to, but very many more certainly remain comparatively unknown. Had I been originally appointed to the Raichore District, I should have delighted in making myself acquainted with all these wonderful and very curious and beautiful buildings; but as I have recorded, my lines fell in other places, and now I had not the time to devote to them as I wished. The archæological features of Raichore would have supplied a noble field for research. It had been the battle-ground of the ancient western Hindoo and Jain dynasties, as well as the Mussulman and Hindoo, and each in succession had left their distinctive marks of occupation.

I pushed on to Gulburgah and Humam Ságor, once a great city, as was apparent from its ruins, which spread over a large area. There was nothing, however, remarkable in them. Here my friend, the Rev. Mr Keis, of whom I have before made mention, paid me a visit, as he happened to be in the neighbourhood on one of his tours, and we had a pleasant talk over old times. He had succeeded well in his work since our last meeting, and one whole village community had become Christians; they were weavers by trade. He was travelling about in his old fashion, a true missionary, going from village to village ministering to and teaching the people as he found occasion—everywhere welcome, and everywhere respected; for the people saw his earnestness, and his pure, humble, godly life, and loved him for his simplicity and his benevolence.

I visited the fort of Gujundergurh, which belonged with its dependencies to a Southern Mahratta chief, and also a remarkable place of pilgrimage near it on the side of the mountain, which proved exceedingly picturesque.

Almost half-way up the hill, and at the foot of its precipitous sandstone top, is a cavern in which an image of
Siva is placed.   This is approached by steps, wide at foot
and narrowing to the last gallery.   The cavern is a natural
aperture between two enormous blocks of granite; and on
further examination of the hill, I found that the whole of
the flat upper portion, which was upwards of 300 feet in
height, with precipitous sides, rested upon granite, which
had been raised from the plain around by some subter-
ranean upheaval.   The fort was built on a portion of this
elevation, and as its chief had been implicated in the late
insurrectionary movements, and his loyalty was still very
doubtful, part of the walls and gates had recently been
blown up, and the fort thereby rendered untenable.

I had now done what I could in the Raichore Doab,
and I have not described my work minutely, as it was of
the same character as that I had previously been employed upon, and there would be no use in multiplying
details.   The fever had again returned, with neuralgia
and other trying accompaniments, and I felt that something must soon be done.   I could not hold on much
longer.   It was no use attempting anything more in
Raichore, because it now transpired that the province was
to be restored to the Nizam, and Nuldroog also; and that,
as the revenues had largely increased, and were more than
sufficient for the purpose for which the original cession
had been made, the assignment would now be restricted
to Berar, the whole of which, without any reservation,
was to be retained, along with some portions to the south
and east, which had not been included in the previous
agreement.

Evidently the time had come when the Commission
would be remodelled, but how it might affect me, it was
impossible to tell.   Had my health continued good, I
should never have dreamed of leaving India, for I loved
the country, and I loved the people; but I felt I could no

longer stay now. I had no wish to retire from active
work, and hoped to return to live and die, if God willed
it, among the people. And I thought in any case I could
take leave and go as far as Malta, where my father would
meet me, and I could bring back my children with me,
and by that time the new arrangements would be completed, and I should know what position I would occupy
when the new treaty with H.H. the Nizam was concluded.

I was obliged to admit now, that work was growing
very difficult to me. Medicine seemed powerless to check
the perpetual ague and fever, and a debility and want of
energy came over me which I could not struggle against.
The doctor at Linsoogoor told me very plainly that I had
no chance of recovery in India, and that if I stayed, my
illness must go on from bad to worse. I sent up his
report upon my case to the Resident, at the earnest
entreaty of my friends, who thought me very ill, and
made an application for two years' leave of absence, which
was all I could hope to get under the rules.

I gave over charge of the Raichore Doab to Mr Ricketts,
my only Assistant, and, taking a sad farewell of my
friends, whom I never then thought I should see again,
I went to Shorapoor to try and close my work there.

The Treasury was in a prosperous condition, and I was
allowed to take from it the price of my house, for which
I fortunately held the late Rajah's note of hand. I was
very thankful for this piece of good fortune, although I
had of course to put up with the loss of interest on my
money.

At Shorapoor the utmost anxiety prevailed as to the
ultimate destiny of the State, but I could give no opinion
whatever; and its fate remained yet uncertain. There
was much dread that it would be made over to the Mussulmans, their old hereditary enemies; and I found this
fear was disturbing the people very much.

"We shall no longer be true Hindoos," was the general
cry.   "Cows will be killed in our precincts, and the flesh
will be sold in our streets.   Hundreds of years have passed
since this indignity has been offered us, and now we dare
not resist it."

What could I say? or what assurance could I give
them that such would not be the case?

I grew better at Shorapoor.   I went out to Bohnal, and
had a last sail on the beautiful lake.   I left instructions
for the completion of Kuchaknoor, in case it should ever
be found practicable to go on with it.   I looked round all
the roads and plantations, and saw them in a satisfactory
condition.   I settled all estates belonging to individuals
on a more permanent basis, and recommended that the
Ranees should have theirs restored to them.

My last farewells to all the people were very trying.
They saw I could not stay, and had little hope they should
ever see me again.   On the 25th February they asked me
to preside at a last *durbar*, and presented me with the
following address, which is literally translated:—

*Translation of a Mahratta Address, presented to Captain
Meadows Taylor, Deputy-Commissioner of Shorapoor,
by the Inhabitants of Shorapoor Territory, February
26, 1860.*

(After compliments.)

"We, the undersigned Pundits, Alims, Rajah's relatives, Government servants, merchants, Wuttundars or
hereditary State servants, Jagheerdars, soldiers, ryots, and
others, residents in and belonging to Shorapoor principality, respectfully beg to subscribe the following Address
to you, in the sanguine hope that you will accept it as a
token of our respect and esteem towards you:—

"1. We unanimously beg to state that, on account of
your being in readiness to return to England, we are

plunged into much grief; but your health having declined, from your residence in this country for the long
period of thirty-six years, engaged in the arduous service
of Government, protecting and benefiting thousands of
people with much care and benevolence, you are disabled
by over-exertion from continuing any longer to perform
your very laborious duties for the benefit of the country
and its people, without some relaxation; therefore, you
have necessarily determined to go home, and remain there,
among your relatives and friends, and thus return with
renewed vigour to support thousands of people in this
country. But this, we hope, temporary, separation has
overpowered our minds with sincere anxiety, and we have
only one alternative to allay it—in the hope of expecting
your happy and safe return amongst us soon, and humbly
to pray to the ever-blessing Almighty to restore happiness
upon you, your beloved father, and daughters, kindred
and friends.

" 2. Since your arrival in this country, you have done
great things to secure happiness to the people; and though
they are too numerous to be enumerated here, yet, by re-
capitulating some of them, as far as our abilities will allow
us, we trust they will enable us to pass our time in joy,
by frequently refreshing our hearts with their recitation
until you return to this country. With this desire, we
have ventured to intrude upon your precious time, in the
hope that you will kindly pardon us, and permit us to say
what we feel on this occasion.

" 3. The cause of your first coming to this district was
this: certain unsatisfactory circumstances having occurred,
which threatened the welfare of the State and its Prince,
in reference to their relations with the State of Hyderabad, the considerate British Government became a medi-
ator between the two States, and appointed you Political Agent in this principality, in the year 1842. From
that period until 1852, you administered the country

very judiciously, and according to its requirements; and
brought it into a very prosperous condition, both as regards the public revenue and the improvement of the
morals of the people. All this is not only known to us
who have this day assembled here, but it is patent to the
world.

"4. In this district certain crime-thirsty wretches used,
before your arrival, to commit atrocities to the injury and
suffering of the people. But you, with the weapons of
your judgment and discretion, extirpated their vices, and
led them to pursue virtuous paths of life, thereby affording true security to life, honour, and property; and the
country prospered day by day. In any country where
courts of justice are established, and justice is properly
administered, that country does not acquire a bad reputation. So the misrule which prevailed in this district
before 1842 was speedily annihilated by the awe of your
prompt and impartial justice, just as darkness vanishes
on the appearance of the sun.

"5. By introducing wise measures into the revenue
affairs of the State from 1842 to 1852 the people fearlessly cultivated waste lands, and thereby the revenue
doubled in ten years. This advantage was not only
secured to Government, but to the people; because during
their former administration the people did not know the
value of continuously holding any lands from which they
could derive profit for their labour, whereas they now
cultivated considerable quantities of land in excess of
their former means, thus contributing to the public
revenue, as well as adding to their profits. Hence in
1852 about one and a half lakhs of *beegahs* [150,000 acres]
of lease expired, and cleared fields were ready to yield full
assessment in the following year, in addition to the ordinary cultivation of the State.

"6. From the increase thus obtained, works of public
utility and remuneration — viz., roads, State buildings,

tanks, wells, &c., were constructed, and avenues, gardens, groves, &c., were planted. This is one of the reasons by which your name and fame have become popular, and everlasting in this district.

"7. At this healthy state of affairs, the late Rajah of Shorapoor having attained majority, you considered it advisable that the management of the country should be intrusted to him, and Government having, on your recommendation, sanctioned the measure, you made over the principality to him, giving him your friendly and full advice in regard to his future conduct in his responsible and dignified position, and as to governing his people; and then you proceeded to join your new appointment of Deputy-Commissioner at Nuldroog. There, too, by your amiable disposition, generosity, benevolence, ingenuity, and zeal, you created abundant security and happiness to the people of that country, and profit to Government. You built there new tanks, constructed roads, and other works of public utility, and thus became entitled to the respect and gratitude of the people. Convinced of your abilities, the Government sent you as Deputy-Commissioner to the district of Berar.

"8. Here, in this principality, for two or three years after the Rajah's assumption of independent management of his country, he conducted his affairs tolerably well; but, at this period, he was unfortunately surrounded by a band of designing and capricious men, who took advantage of his youth, imbued him with bad notions, and, misusing his name, committed atrocities with impunity. This becoming known to the Resident at Hyderabad, he deputed his second Assistant to Shorapoor for the purpose of ascertaining the true state of affairs, and dispersion of all ill-advisers.

"But while things were in this state, the Rajah's intriguing band unauthorisedly fired at the Government troops who were encamped below the town; then the

young Rajah became alarmed for the consequences, and
fled to Hyderabad, to seek refuge with the Government
itself.   The inhabitants of the town, beholding these
things, fled for their lives, accompanied by their wives
and children, abandoning their homes and property, lest
worse things might happen to them.   Immediately after
the Rajah's flight, the British troops took possession of the
town, and plundered it for three days, thereby making it
desolate and deserted.   At this unhappy period we, of
this place, were praying to God to send His messenger in
your form for our relief; but as you were in a higher
appointment, and in a distant country, we had not much
hope of your coming at all.   But lo! when God pleases
and blesses, the very impossibilities become possibilities
at once.   So, according to the heartfelt desires of the
people of this country, the Resident, by God's will and
influence, suddenly thought of sending you here, and took
the necessary measures accordingly.   With what joy and
thankfulness the population, old and young, great and
small, received the intelligence of your nomination to this
place (because we had our long-cherished hopes and confidence in your magnanimity and justice) is beyond all
description.   And our anticipations of good from you
were greatly strengthened when we knew of your true
feelings for the Rajah when you saw him at Hyderabad.
Your feelings were so affected and plunged into grief at
the sight of that unfortunate Rajah, that it was hardly
possible, even for his own parents, to grieve at his misfortune more bitterly than you.   Thus have you continuously manifested great interest and kindness towards this
principality and its rulers; and this being universally
known to the people, even before your arrival at Shorapoor, those who had abandoned their homes in despair
and anxiety, speedily returned without apprehension.
All this, of course, depended upon your kind and humane
disposition and goodwill towards the people.

"9. On your arrival here you caused all the anarchy and misrule that had taken place to disappear. You introduced new regulations, and secured a proper and correct system of management. From this much good and advantage have accrued to the people. By your constructing good roads around the town, much comfort and convenience have been enjoyed by the traders and people in general; and the praises which are merrily sung to your name by the travellers, old and young, on these roads, are indeed gratifying and pleasing to the hearers.

"10. The thousands of mango-trees, planted by you in and about the town during your former administration of this country, are now bearing abundant fruit; and, as you are now again planting thousands of trees, with great pains, for our benefit, we humbly pray to God that He will likewise ordain you shall be present here when these infant trees shall similarly bear fruit.

"11. You have used your full powers in securing and continuing various rights, perquisites, *meeras* or hereditary lands, and allowances, &c., which were enjoyed by the people; and if, in spite of your generous endeavours, any unfortunate person's expectations were not realised, it is no fault of yours, but his own misfortune. Consequently, we are all content with what you have done for us, and are under great obligations to you.

"12. When sedition and rebellion occurred here in 1858, certain senseless persons were concerned in them, and they were liable to heavy penalties; and if you had punished them, notwithstanding the proclamation of amnesty, you would not have exceeded the requirements of the law, nor their deserts; but, not considering their past violent and intriguing acts, you have saved their lives and honour from destruction. For this singular kindness, these people should be grateful and thankful to you for ever; and this assembly ardently believes they will be so.

"13. Another, the principal request and prayer of this

assembly, is, that this principality should be restored to
the family of the late Rajah, in compassion for their misfortune, and the maintenance of charitable and other
ancient institutions which have existed and have been
enjoyed for centuries. To attain this end, we trust you
will accord your support; but we are aware it depends
mainly upon the future good conduct and loyalty, as also
destiny, of the expectants of this dignity. It is the duty,
nevertheless, of this assembly to pray constantly to the
Almighty that Government will, in their exalted generosity, pardon all past misdemeanours, and indulgently
protect the remnants of the late chief's family.

" 14. That your project for constructing a series of new
roads and a market-place, and for lighting the town, as
well as for erecting travellers' and strangers' homes, sink-
ing wells, building tanks, &c., for the use and benefit of
the people, as well as for improving the public revenue,
should be carried out after your return, in renewed health,
is the heartfelt prayer of this assembly.

" 15. All your acts being of benevolence and for the
good of the people, there is very little time to recount
them all here; and it is likewise hardly possible to give
preference to any one of them. We, therefore, most respectfully beg to entreat that you will kindly accept what
we have briefly stated above, as a sincere expression of
our feelings towards you, and we crave that you will
pardon us for our rather long intrusion upon your time.

" 16. It may only be known to the light of the world,
the Sun, if there were any persons like you on the face of
the earth; but, as far as our experience goes, we know
not a more kind-hearted, equitable, painstaking, skilful,
and benevolent gentleman than you; and we are con-
strained to think that your qualities have no parallel save
in you.

" 17. We are afraid that you may have tired of our
loquacity; but, our hearts being full with heavy anxiety

at the thought of our approaching temporary separation, and being unable to bear it without giving utterance to our feelings, we have ventured to occupy a good deal of your time, for doing which we have already craved your pardon.

"18. In conclusion, we most ardently hope that, by the blessing of the Almighty Protector, you will happily and safely reach your country, and meet your most beloved and endeared father, daughters, brothers, and all who for a series of years have been intensely longing for your return, and cause them to rejoice. And we further heartily and sincerely pray to the Lord of the Universe to bestow upon you abundant longevity, renewed health, greater grandeur, and higher powers, and safely and happily bring you again to this country, in order that thousands of people may find a ready asylum in you for their protection, and so your fame and glory may be greatly aggrandised; and, by the grace of God, we confidently hope to realise these our desires and expectations.

"Again tendering out warmest, sincere, and affectionate but respectful thanks to you for the cordial support and courtesy you have usually evinced towards us, according to our respective positions in society, during your former and present career in this principality, we are proud that you carry with you our heartfelt gratitude and good wishes. May God bless you and yours for ever!

"We beg to remain, with the utmost respect, dear sir, your most obedient, faithful, obliged, and humble servants and well-wishers,

(Signed) " RAJAH VENKETAPPA NAIK, sen.,
RAJAH VENKETAPPA NAIK JELLEEPALLEE,
RAJAH KRISHNAPPA NAIK,

and 987 others of the Rajah's relations, Pundits, Jagheerdars, and other principal inhabitants of Shorapoor.

(*True Translation.*)
" J. SEETA RAM RAO,
Extra Assist. Commissr."

I cannot describe the scene; but its passionate character can be imagined from the purport of what is recorded above in the quaint, simple words of the people. None of them had been strangers to me; many had grown up from children under my sight, and had now children of their own about their knees; others were old and grey-headed; and many whom I had known had gone to their rest. It was not an easy task to leave them all; but I had to go, and I do not think I am forgotten there even now. I intended to depart quietly in the night; but I found the chiefs of the Beydur clans assembled in the streets, and it was as difficult now to reach the north gate of the city as it had been to enter it two years before—only, instead of a clamour of joyous welcome, there was now sad wailing of women, while the men walked by me in utter silence. Now and then some one would exclaim, " We have no one now to care for us; but our women will sing of you as they grind corn in the morning, and will light their lamps in your name at night. Come back to us; oh, come back!"

It was very sad and very solemn, and can never be forgotten. At every village the people came about me, the mothers holding up their children for me to put my hands upon their heads and bless them; and it was all so simple, so earnest, and so heartfelt, one could not but feel its sincerity. People ask me what I found in the natives to like so much. Could I help loving them when they loved me so? Why should I not love them? I had never courted popularity. I had but tried to be just to all, and to secure to the meanest applicant consideration of his complaint, by allowing unrestricted communication with myself.

Thousands wished to have signed the address had time permitted it; but there are quite enough signatures to show the attachment of the people to the only Englishman whom most of them had ever seen, and certainly the first

who had exercised any authority over them. At Nuldroog
the sincere love of the people was shown in the address
before given; in Berar I accepted the loyal and peaceful
demeanour of the population as a marked proof of their
attachment to me in the most trying crisis of the great
rebellion.

In all I had ruled over 36,000 square miles of area, and
a population of upwards of five millions of a most industrious and intelligent people, not only without a single
complaint against my rule, but, as I think and hope, with
a place in their affections and respect, gained by no other
means than by exercising simple courtesy and justice to
all. I was often told by various friends, "You do too
much for people who will never thank you." I do not
think so: I did not do half enough, and I could have
done more had I had more help. God is my witness, I
tried to do as much as I could, and heartily regretted
being obliged, through physical inability, to leave undone
many a measure of progress and advancement which I
hoped to accomplish.

I travelled slowly to Hyderabad, for I could not bear
long marches now, and stayed at the Residency, where
there was still much to do before I could leave. Even
now furlough to England was very difficult to obtain, and,
but for the Resident's private intercession with the Governor-General, I should not have got it at all.

I was very glad to be able at this time to render my
friend, Colonel Davidson, the Resident, an essential service in writing a series of letters to the 'Friend of India'
in justification of his conduct in remaining at the Residency after the officers commanding at Secunderabad had
thought it desirable to leave it, and also in sending away
the Contingent troops to act under Sir Hugh Rose. Both
these acts of the Resident were severely censured, and
deemed "worse than rash;" but I considered that the
complaints made were totally unfounded. Had the Resi-

dent gone into Secunderabad, the desertion of the Residency would have been looked upon as a sign of fear, and
the loyal minister, Salar Jung, would have been left to
his fate. What might have happened had he not been
able to control the fanatical element of Hyderabad, or
had the British all entrenched themselves at Secunderabad, who can say? By remaining firm, the Resident
showed the minister that he had every confidence in him
—a confidence which has been fully merited, and never
abused by Sir Salar Jung.

I regarded the march of the Contingent, too, as a triumph
of will over disaffection. No one denied that many of its
members had trembled on the verge of mutiny, and no
doubt, in their cantonment, they were sorely tempted and
chafed by inaction. The effect, however, of the Nizam's
troops having joined the English cause, while Scindia's
soldiers coalesced with the rebels, soon became known
and apparent to all, as the Hyderabad Contingent fought,
as Lord Strathnairn himself has told me, more like
Englishmen than natives. The honours they gained in
the field kept them quiet, and as their loyalty was now
beyond question, the whole of the Nizam's territory kept
quiet also; nor, with the one exception of the insurrection at Hyderabad, was there a single instance of
treason to the English during the whole of that most
trying period.

My letters were upheld and supported by the 'Friend
of India,' and I believe produced a good effect in England,
although the opposition party was a very strong one. I
pressed Colonel Davidson very earnestly to come home
with me, for he was very ill; but he would not leave his
post, and died there the year following.

I left Hyderabad at length, and as the road *viâ* Hominabad and Nuldroog was now finished, I went by it as far
as Sholapoor; then there was the railway. At Nuldroog
I had left my plate and various articles in the treasury;

but, alas! some one had, during those troublous times, broken open the plate-chest, and several articles had been abstracted, most of which, however, I afterwards recovered; but I was much grieved at the loss of a small bag containing all the autograph letters I valued most, and a few little ornaments which my wife had always worn. They were of no value to any one intrinsically, and must have been taken for the sake of the bag, which was prettily embroidered in gold thread.

On the road I reached one of the stage bungalows for travellers, and, being very weak, was being lifted from my palankeen by one of my servants, when two gentlemen came forward to help me. "Was I Captain Meadows Taylor," they asked, "who was anxiously expected at Malta?" "Yes, I was;" and they told me they had been fellow passengers with my dear ones, who were awaiting me there, and gave me many particulars of them. Going home seemed at last to be growing a reality!

I passed a day and a night at Sholapoor with my dear friend Abingdon Compton, and he urged me, if I missed the steamer, which seemed very probable, as I was too weak to travel very quickly, to go up to stay with his wife at the Mahabuleshwar; and indeed, he said, I had better not go to England till the next steamer, as he knew Lord Elphinstone was at the Hills, and wanted to see me, and, in any case, it was no use my waiting a fortnight in the heat at Bombay. I promised to go if I missed the steamer; but I was in time, having just two days to spare before it sailed. How strangely events happen! Had I missed that mail, I should have gone to Mahabuleshwar, and should, as I afterwards found, have been offered by Lord Elphinstone the "Directorship of Jails," an appointment which I could have held, worth £2500 a-year! He had kept it for me; but finding I had gone home on sick leave, was obliged to bestow it elsewhere. I should have stayed in India, and have taken up my appointment, telling my

father to come on at once. I could have remained at the
Hills, would have entered a new department of the service
where there was no press of work, and where I could travel
as I pleased. But luck was against me! Yet, why should
I say this? I might not have been able to stand the
Indian climate longer, even at the Hills, and with lighter
work. At all events, God willed it otherwise. I heard
before I left, that Nuldroog and Raichore were to be restored to the Nizam, and that Shorapoor was to be given
to him as a token of the appreciation of the British Government of his faithfulness and loyalty in the Mutiny.
So, what would have become of me without Lord Elphinstone's kind offer was not apparent, and I should have at
once accepted it had I remained in India.

I had a pleasant party of fellow-passengers; one poor
fellow, who had been badly wounded by a bullet in the
lungs, was specially consigned to my care, although, as his
father said at parting, "You do indeed look fearfully ill
yourself." And so I was; the relaxing heat of Bombay,
and all my final journey and preparations, had exhausted
me terribly, and I had grown so fat and unwieldy that to
move about was a trouble to me. I asked one lady on
board, whose husband had been Political Agent in Minia-
war, why they had not come to me when obliged to fly?
" We dared not," she said, " go to Berar. We were told
you were a marked man, and dangerously popular. There
would be no hope for us—nay, we heard you were already
murdered!"

Yes, we had almost all in that ship been through trying
scenes and many dangers, and a merciful God had brought
us out safely from the land.

We arrived at Malta in due course, very late, after midnight, and no passengers could land till morning. I was
sitting with the poor fellow who had been my constant
care, and who was so ill that night we thought him dying,
when a gentleman came up to me.   " The P. and O. agent

has come on board," he said, " and tells me he will take
you and me ashore if we like, to-night. I know how anxious
you are to go."   I put my night things in a small bag,
and went. I could not stay behind. It was as much as
I could do to get up the long flight of steps into Valetta,
and I had to sit down often; but at length the hotel was
reached. All was quiet, every one in bed ; but this was
no time for ceremony, and in a few minutes I held my
darlings to my heart.

. . . .

CHAPTER XVIII.

1 8 6 0 – 7 4.

I NEED not dwell upon that time. Any one who has followed me through the latter years of my life in India, so
lonely and so utterly cut off from all society of any kind,
will appreciate what it was to me to find myself again
with those dearest to me on earth, to learn to know them
and be known by them. And the days flew by, I feeling
stronger, and my face losing the deep-drawn lines of pain
about my forehead and mouth, which my children said
they "ironed" out; and so they did, no doubt. I was,
however, very far from well, although the excitement and
delight of my first arrival had kept me up wonderfully.
But Malta was growing hot, and we started for Naples,
where we spent some delightful days, taking a fresh excursion every day—one to Pompeii and Herculaneum, the
former presenting exactly the appearance of a Deccan
town unroofed ; one to Baia, and another to Vesuvius,
which we partly ascended, but my strength was not equal
to much yet. My old Indian helmet, with a scarlet *pugeree* tied round it, with gold ends, attracted much attention, and hats were raised as we drove along ; and on passing the main guard, there rose a cry, " Il Generale ! " and
the guard fell in and saluted, to our very great amusement.
There was a sudden exodus from Naples, owing to a rumour
of cholera, and an apprehended attack by Garibaldi, and
we decamped with the rest. We landed at Civita Vecchia,

a very motley crowd, and a general scramble began for luggage and places in the train. My red *pugeree* stood me in good stead, however, and the officials came forward at once. Everything was at the service of " Il Generale " or " Eccellenza."

"Air you a Ingine general, sir ? " asked an American, as I was entering the carriage.

" No, sir; an Indian officer, but not a general," I replied.

" Wal, sir, you air very fair for Ingy, you air. If you was to come to our country, they wouldn't know you for a Ingine ; no, sir, they would not, I tell you, sir."

We stayed a fortnight in Rome. We saw all the pictures and the statues and the palaces. We made excursions to Tivoli and to Hadrian's villa. We saw St Peter's, too, under decoration for a great ceremony; and above all, I was introduced in the strangest manner to his Holiness the Pope. We had no tickets for the reserved seats for the occasion, not having secured them in time, and our old guide Stefano was sorely distressed at this. He, however, told us not to despair, " he had a great friend, a priest, who was to take part in the ceremony ; " and motioning me to follow, he marched straight to the door of the sacristy, and beckoned to his friend, explaining to him who I was, and how I had arrived too late to get tickets. I was bidden to enter, and was presented to a very benevolent-looking old gentleman as " Il Generale Inglese." I had hardly time to realise that it was the Pope himself, when he put out his hand to me, while I bent low and kissed it. He told me I was welcome, and desired the priest to see that we had good seats. We were conducted to a little door in one of the great pillars, where, ascending a spiral staircase, we found ourselves in a cosy little box, just large enough for four people, from which we saw and heard everything most perfectly.

" Did I not manage that well ? " cried old Stefano, rubbing his hands.

What a world of new thought and beauty was opened
to me! I revelled in the pictures and in the galleries at
Rome; but even more, I believe, in those of Florence,
where we literally lived in the Pitti Palace and the Uffizi.
I think, however, I was most interested in the ancient
remains—the statues and the busts—not only those of
emperors, kings, and statesmen, but of the citizens and
their wives, recalling the features of the age to which they
belonged, the head-dresses and graceful draperies as worn
at the period. Many of the women's faces struck me as
being truly noble, and their figures too, and as more intellectual and handsomer in type than those of the men.
We could have lingered in Florence, in Bologna, in Milan,
in Venice so dreamy and so exquisite, for weeks, nay,
months; but time was passing, and we left beautiful
Italy—its pictures, statues, noble ancient remains, its
churches, and its lakes behind us—and crossed over the
Splügen Pass into Bavaria. Surely the world can contain
no fairer spot than those lakes of Italy, and it is quite
impossible to decide whether Maggiore, or Lugano, with
its wild grand beauty, or fair Como, lying sparkling in
the sun, carries off the palm, all are so lovely and all so
different. I do not know, and have not seen, the other
Passes over the Alps, but I should think none can exceed
the Splügen and the Via Mala in grandeur and in beauty;
nor could I, an old road-maker, cease to marvel at the
great science and daring displayed in the engineering
work. From Chur—after a *détour* made to visit dear
relations in Bavaria, and stay some days with them in
their beautiful old *schloss*—to Paris, by way of Basle and
Strasbourg, a weary railway journey in very hot weather.
Paris was almost unbearable from the heat, and we only
waited long enough to get a few clothes, and then on to
London, and back to home-life once more. My health,
which at first had seemed almost re-established, now again
broke down, showing that the evil still existed; the fever

returned perpetually; and the best physicians, both in London and Dublin, shook their heads. The news from India was not reassuring. The treaty of 1860 was now accomplished; the Raichore Doab and Nuldroog were transferred to the Nizam, and the principality of Shorapoor conferred upon him as a free gift in return for his loyal conduct during the Mutiny. It was clear to me that except my Deputy-Commissionership, I had no hope of promotion, unless I should be made Settlement Officer.

My eighteen months' leave expired in November 1861, and I obtained an extension for six months more; and as I was in London on this business, I had the honour of being summoned by the then Secretary of State for India, who was anxious for information in regard to Berar and its revenue settlement. He seemed to approve of the system I had introduced in Nuldroog during 1856-57, and listened earnestly while I described its details; he requested me to write him an official letter on the subject, and hinted that, although the Head - Commissionership might not be given to an " uncovenanted servant," the appointment of Settlement Officer was one which I could hold.

Time passed. I confess I have no distinct memory of events. Constant illness, and, worse than all, a sort of debility of the brain, seemed to possess me, and were most distressing. I had not only lost my energy, but my memory also in great measure, and I was obliged to have every note looked over before it was posted, lest the sense should not be clear, or a strange jumble and repetition of words should be found. Indeed I grew worse and worse, and the thought that I should, if this continued, be obliged to give up India altogether, made me miserable. My doctors apprehended, I have since heard, paralysis of the brain, and entreated my family to oppose my return to active work. As the expiration of my leave drew near, I made desperate efforts to have it renewed still further, offering to do without pay altogether if my place might be kept open for me. Sir Ranald Martin told me six months more would perhaps recruit my health, and promised to back my petition: I had friends too at the India House to help me. But it was of no avail; the rules of the "uncovenanted service" could not be broken, and my request was refused; so no alternative remained for me except to go out as I was, ill and weak, or to resign the service altogether. It was a hard battle. My heart was in my work, and I ardently longed to go back and try to carry on what I had been planning for the benefit of the people among whom I had lived my life, and whom I loved; but it seemed as if God, in His wisdom, had taken from me the power and strength I needed. "If you go back," said Sir Ranald Martin, "to the climate of Berar, you must die: you are totally unfit for duty, and the fever and ague are as bad as ever. Think of your life, and think of your children, and may God help you to a right decision. I never had a more painful case to deal with."

I thought over all this earnestly, and asked for help and guidance, and I saw clearly that it would not be right to run into the jaws of death as it were; so I gave up the struggle, and sent in my resignation with a very heavy heart. No one knows, even now, what a bitter grief it was to me to do this; but I trust I did what was right. I returned to Dublin very much cast down. I was not able to do anything except paint, and I took refuge in this, and in music; any attempt at writing set my head throbbing; and neither words nor thoughts would come. I looked sadly at the commencement of a story I had begun years before in India, and wondered whether I should ever be able to complete it.

A friend, finding me one day sitting on a door-step in Dublin, faint and sick, and shivering with ague, took me home and told me how his brother, who had suffered terribly from Australian bush-fever, had derived much bene-

fit from homœopathy. I had tried everything else, and
every physician of note without avail, and I promised my
friend to consult the doctor he told me of, and to give the
system a fair trial.

I told my story to the kind physician he recommended,
and also honestly confessed my want of faith in the system.

" I don't mind that," said the good man ; " but it is
rather hard to ask me to cure a malady of thirty years'
standing, when so many great men have failed.   However, I will try to alleviate—I cannot cure it ; and I trust,
under God's blessing, to give you some help.   But you
were right not to return to India."

I followed the prescriptions he gave me faithfully, and
I amused myself by fishing, painting, and reading very
light literature, and tried not to think about anything.
The effect was really marvellous.   I grew stronger and
more energetic, and I felt some of my old power returning
to me ; and after a few months I went to my friend and
asked his leave to begin to write.

" Do you feel able now ? " he asked.   " If you do,
begin ; but you must be very cautious, and do not fatigue
your brain.   If you feel the least tired or confused, stop."

I took his advice, and I began my novel of ' Tara.'   The
incidents and actions of the story had been planned for
nearly twenty years ; and I knew all the scenes and
localities described, as I had the story in my mind during
my visit to Beejapoor, and had noted the details accu-
rately ; while my long residence in an entirely native State,
and my intimate acquaintance with the people, their
manners, habits, and social organisation, gave me oppor-
tunities, which I think few Englishmen have ever enjoyed, of thoroughly understanding native life.   One day,
when talking of my projected book with my dear friend
Mrs Cashel Hoey, whom I have known since she was a
child, and whose career I have always watched with ever-

increasing interest and affection, she said suddenly, " Now you have the plot so clearly defined in your brain, come and write it out chapter by chapter ; I will set it down exactly as you dictate to me." We went together to my study, and locked the door, and there for six hours we worked at it, she writing in total silence, and a perfect sketch of the whole tale was made, the details of which were filled up afterwards. I never remember feeling so utterly exhausted in my life; but the relief when it was finished was intense, and we both were glad that we had resisted the entreaties to us to stop our work, and rest, which my children, fearing for me in my state of health, made more than once in vain. After this, I felt sure of my subject, and wrote confidently, but very slowly, for my brain had not regained its full strength yet; but the occupation interested me, and was a source of infinite de-light. When my book was partly finished, I wrote to Messrs Blackwood, offering it to them, and telling them how it had been promised twenty years before, for ' Black-wood's Magazine,' when I had written the ' Confessions of a Thug.'

My book was accepted, and, still writing very slowly, I finished and published it in 1863. It was most favourably received. All the leading papers—the ' Times,' ' Morning Post,' ' Athenæum,' ' Saturday Review,' and the Quarter-lies—were loud in its praise ; and I only mention this at length, because I had been very anxious as to my recep-tion in the literary world, after a silence of so many years ; and I was not a little gratified to find myself welcomed once more so warmly.

' Tara ' was the first of the series of three historical romances which I had proposed to write on the three great modern periods of Indian history, which occurred at an interval of exactly a hundred years. ' Tara ' illustrated the rise of the Mahrattas, and their first blow against the Mussulman power in 1657.

'Ralph Darnell,' my second work, was to illustrate the rise of the English political power in the victory of Plassey in June 1757.

'Seeta,' which was to be the third, was to illustrate the attempts of all classes alike to rid themselves of the English by the Mutiny of 1857.

'Ralph Darnell,' which appeared in 1865, was also well received, and I had every encouragement to persevere.

I read a paper upon my discoveries of cairns, cromlechs, &c., in Shorapoor, before the Royal Irish Academy, with illustrations and sketches of what I found, which, I believe completely established the identity of those remains in India and in Europe, and, I have reason to think, was valuable archæologically. It was published in vol. xxiv. of the Society's 'Transactions,' and illustrated with sixty-eight engravings. This had been a subject which, since I had made the first identification in relation to the cromlechs and cairns of Rajun Koloor, I had followed up with the greatest interest, until I obtained ample confirmation of my views in the cairns on Twizell Moor, Northumberland, in the autumn of 1864.

I was placed in charge of the Indian Department of the Dublin Exhibition of 1865 by my friend Dr Forbes Watson ; and on the occasion of the visit of H.R.H. the Prince of Wales to the Exhibition, was called on to attend and explain various matters to him. He was especially struck by the large raised map of the eastern coast of India, constructed to scale by the late Mr Montgomery Martin, which I had painted afresh, and of which the Prince showed a very intimate knowledge. He had evidently studied Indian subjects deeply, and appeared gratified by the information I was able to give in regard both to the natural productions and the articles of manufacture displayed.

My next task was to write the historical and descriptive portions of two superb volumes of Photographs of the

City of Beejapoor and the Hindoo Temples of the Southern Mahratta country. These volumes were published by Mr John Murray, the architectural portions being contributed by my friend Mr James Fergusson.

This led to my undertaking the descriptive letterpress of a work entitled 'The People of India,' which consisted of a series of photographs of the different races, tribes, and orders of the people all over India, and involved much labour and research. The descriptions were necessarily very short, and as much information as possible had to be compressed into a few meagre lines. The work was brought out by the India Office, and no limit was affixed to it. Up to the present year (1874) six volumes have been completed.

I also began a series of Indian articles for Messrs Cassell, Petter, and Galpin's Biographical Dictionary, which, as far as I know, are the only contributions to Indian biography which exist. Of course the space here was also very circumscribed, and all I could do was to make the notices intelligible and useful for reference.

Thus I worked on, and employed myself as busily as I could, painting during my leisure hours. In 1868 we went abroad, and remained away for a year, wintering at that loveliest of places, Mentone—one of the sweetest spots, I think, the world contains. How we all enjoyed it, and what glorious walks, donkey-rides, and excursions we made! and the flowers—but they are too beautiful for description. We used to bring home basket-loads of crimson and scarlet anemones, violets, tulips, and a thousand more, less gay, perhaps, but none the less beautiful. I worked on at the biographies and descriptions all the winter, steadily refusing to be tempted out until the afternoon. A project for a 'Child's History of India' was also growing in my brain, originated by a dear friend, a lady, coming to me one day with an armful of most stupendous-looking volumes, and saying, as she threw them down wearily, "Oh, Colonel Taylor, do tell me what I am to do. How can I teach the children the history of India out of those?" And indeed it seemed a truly formidable task. I was not able to set about a history of India just then, but later I confided the scheme to Messrs Longman, who begged I would make mine a 'Student's Manual of the History of India;' and this I eventually wrote some time later. The work was very laborious, and involved much minute study, occupying me in all about two years.

I had not long returned from Mentone when I was solicited by the Institute of Civil Engineers of Ireland to deliver a lecture upon the method of constructing large earthen embankments and sluices for irrigation tanks in India; and as I was much interested in the subject, I made the lecture as comprehensive as I could, and described the system adopted so as to retain the rainfall as much as possible. I had all my own plans, elevations, surveys, and sections, and some details of ancient native work. My lecture was printed in the 'Transactions' of the Society; and to my gratification, I was not only elected a member, but received a diploma as civil engineer, with liberty to practise as such within the United Kingdom.

My hard work over, my History was delightfully interrupted during 1869 by an announcement from the Secretary of State for India that Her Most Gracious Majesty the Queen had been pleased, on the 2d of June, to appoint me a "Companion of the Most Exalted Order of the Star of India." The honour and gratification of the gift were enhanced by a communication from his Grace the Duke of Argyll, as he presented me with the Order, that the selection of my name had been made by her Majesty herself.

I felt very grateful for this honour—which had been entirely unsolicited by me—not only as a recognition of any public service I had been able to perform during my Indian life, but as an assurance that I had not been forgotten though so long absent. Her Majesty had indeed recognised me at the first levee I attended after my return ; and her words, " I am glad to see you back again," will always be treasured by me, as a very gratifying proof of her kind interest in so humble a servant as myself.

In 1871 my History appeared, as complete as I could make it in the limited space necessarily at my disposal, and I trusted that, having now a compendium, as it were, at their command, Principals of colleges and schools would bring the History of India more into their educational course. I inquired in many directions, but I could not discover that Indian history was taught anywhere. Why, I know not ; for surely there can scarcely be any subject of greater importance to Englishmen than the history of the noble dependencies won by their ancestors, which, one would think, would be both more useful, and perhaps more interesting, than many subjects which seem to form part of the essential education of our boys.

I had to take a long rest now. The labour of the History had very much exhausted me, and I spent the interval in travelling and painting, and was elected honorary member of the Royal Hibernian Academy. In 1872 I began 'Seeta,' finishing it in June the same year ; and up to the time I write, I have not begun any more works of fiction. After this ' Story of my Life ' is finished, I hope, if I am spared, to revert to the romantic and medieval period of Deccan history, and write an illustration of it, the plot of which is growing in my brain.

From time to time I contributed articles to the 'Edinburgh Review,' on various subjects connected with India: every year one or more of these appeared. And I enjoyed this kind of literary labour very much, and am grateful it was given to me to do.

Also, from time to time, I gave public lectures on subjects connected with India, both in Dublin, Birmingham, Whitehaven, and other places. I wanted to bring India nearer to England—to bring its people nearer our people ;

and if, by my simple descriptions of life among the natives, any have felt more interest in their Indian brothers and sisters, or have been led to read and study more, my object has been attained. The following were the subjects of some of my lectures :—

" Ancient Literature of India."

" Village Communities."

" India Past and Present."

" Some Great Men of India."

" Some Great Women of India."

And others, of which I have only notes.

I always found my audiences interested and amused ; and I believe it only needs such illustrations to arouse an interest in, and bring India home to, the minds of English people.

I heard frequently from friends in India who did not forget to tell me about my old people and districts whenever they could hear of them. How Nuldroog and the Raichore Doab are now administered I know not, or whether the revenue remains as it was under English management. Of Berar there is at least no question. I have already stated that a portion of the Bombay survey was introduced in 1860, and its benefit and progress have been wonderful. Not only do the people possess their holdings, instead of being merely "tenants at will," liable to be dispossessed by any outbidder ; but the cultivation has extended, as it was plain to see would be the case, with insured possession. All that is now wanting, to my perception, to complete the land settlement—which is exactly in principle what I proposed for Nuldroog in 1855—is the grant of title-deeds for estates and area of house occupation ; and I hope these may be eventually issued. The increase of revenue has been enormous, and has accompanied the increase of cultivation. According to the Administrative Report of 1870-71, a final total of £905,467 was reached, which showed an increase of

£504,985 in ten years; and as a large portion of the district is still unsurveyed, the revenue will, in the end, there is little doubt, exceed a million sterling. I trust this magnificent practical result may induce Government to undertake a perpetual settlement on the sound basis of proprietary right, instead of the many shifty measures which have hitherto been in operation.

I have little more to add. I went to India with only one friend there on whom I could rely, and upon him I had no claim except a slight relationship. I have had no education so to speak. What I know I have taught myself. I have gained my position, such as it is now, by steady hard work and perseverance; and that my humble services have been acknowledged by my Queen and my country in giving me the Star of India, is a recompense for which I am very grateful.

My literary work has been a great pleasure to me; but I can only write about the people among whom I lived, and whom I love and shall always love to the last. Had I known how to write about modern society, fast young ladies, *roué* young gentlemen, fair murderesses with golden hair, and all the "sensation" tribe, I doubt not I should have filled my pockets better; but it was no use,—I was too old and stiff to change my ways. The old Tooljapoor Brahmin spoke truly, "Much, very much money, passed through my hands," and yet I continue poor. But I am thankful,—thankful for having sufficient to live on, though not riches; for loving and beloved children; for many, many dear friends, who make me welcome always in the North, and in Yorkshire, and in Norfolk (is not the hot corner kept for me at Didlington when I am able to shoot?)—in London, where I sometimes go for a few weeks to have a glimpse of the great world and its doings —in Dublin, where, in my dear old home, I have a large circle of kind and loving friends. And is not this enough to make me happy and contented with my lot?

One word, one last reflection in regard to India, may not be out of place. It is to advise all who go there in whatever capacity, or whatever position they may hold,— use true courtesy to natives of all degrees. My experience has taught me that large masses of men are more easily led than driven, and that courtesy and kindness and firmness will gain many a point which, under a hard and haughty bearing, would prove unattainable. By courtesy I do not mean undue familiarity—far from it; self-respect must always be preserved. But there is a middle course which, if rightly pursued in a gentlemanly fashion, not only exacts respect from natives of all classes, but gratitude and affection likewise.

Grateful to God for all the mercies of my life, for His sustaining power, and the ability to do what I have been able to accomplish through all my life, all that I hope for, in my humble sphere, is that my efforts may be accepted by Him ; and that, in Sir Henry Lawrence's words, " I may be thought of as one who strove to do his duty."

                              MEADOWS TAYLOR.

OLD COURT, HAROLD'S CROSS, DUBLIN,
      June 1874.

CHAPTER XIX.

CONCLUSION.

1874-76.

DURING the autumn and winter of 1874-75, my dear father suffered much from bronchitis and general debility ; but in the quiet of his own study, to which his health almost entirely confined him, he wrote his last novel, 'A Noble Queen,' which appeared in chapters in 'The Overland Mail,' and also in 'The Week's News,' and was published by Messrs H. King & Co. His friends earnestly hope that the story may be published shortly in volume form, and thus become known more widely than at present in England. In India it has been much appreciated, and eagerly looked for on the arrival of each mail ; and, to quote the 'Times of India,' " apart from its historic and literary interest, it abounds with attractive and excellent descriptions of Indian scenery." The story relates to the Mussulman kingdoms of Beejapoor and Ahmednugger; and its historic heroine is Chand Beebee, the dowager queen of Ali Adil Shah—its ideal heroine being Zora, the young granddaughter of an exiled dervish. My father also completed during these winter months the seventh and eighth volumes of the 'People of India.' Whether this great work will be continued by the order of the Secretary of State for India is not yet apparent; but the

2 G

materials are almost inexhaustible, and it deserves to be
made as complete as possible.

In May 1875 my father's eyesight suddenly failed him,
and he wrote the concluding pages of 'A Noble Queen'
with considerable difficulty. It was hoped earnestly that
this dimness of vision was only temporary, and that, with
renewed health, the precious sight might be regained.
He visited London in order to obtain the best medical
advice, and was told by the physicians that his best and
only hope of recovery lay in passing the following winter
in some warm, dry climate.

"I should like to go to India again, if you think the
climate would suit me," he said. And after a long and
deliberate consultation, leave was given ; and he was told
he might revisit the old scenes, now made yet more
attractive by the residence at Hyderabad of his married
daughter.

When the news of his determination to spend the
winter in India reached Hyderabad, His Excellency Sir
Salar Jung wrote in the kindest possible terms, expressing a hope that, if my father fulfilled his present intention, he would consider himself as his guest during his
stay, and allow him to make all the arrangements he
could for his comfort.

This invitation was gratefully accepted, and on the
12th of September 1875, he and I, with our faithful
servant John, sailed from Liverpool in the s.s. Guy
Mannering for Bombay. The change of air and the sea
voyage seemed to benefit my father's general health,
though there was scarcely any improvement in his sight.
His memory was so wonderfully clear, and his recollection
of places and scenes so accurate, that our captain was
astonished, and declared he was led to look for and find
out many points of interest that he had, in previous
voyages, overlooked. We arrived at Bombay on the
15th of October, and, after a rest of two days, started for

Hyderabad. The long railway journey, of twenty-seven
hours, was borne without much fatigue, and my father
seemed to rally wonderfully under the delight and excitement of meeting those so dear to him once more. His
loss of sight was a sad drawback, but his patience under
this terrible affliction was very touching. He could see
a little, but not enough to read or write himself, or employ
himself in any way; and this to one of his indefatigably
industrious habits was a trial which only those who knew
him could appreciate. When not writing or reading he
used to draw, or knit, or crochet, and his delight was to
surprise his friends with some specimen of his work. His
interest in all that went on around him was as keen as
ever; and the numerous visits he received from his native
friends afforded him great pleasure. Some came from
long distances, only to see him, to touch his feet, or bring
their simple offerings of fruit, sugar-candy, and garlands
of sweet jessamine; and it was very touching to see the
love and reverence the people bore for him. One, a native
of Shorapoor, told him how the people yet bewailed his
loss, and how the women sang ballads to his honour as
they ground their corn, and related stories of him to their
children. He seemed to be so essentially the *people's*
friend; and that his memory and his deeds lived still in
their hearts, was evident to all who saw the manner of
their coming.

Owing to the prolonged absence of H.E. Sir Salar Jung,
both at Bombay and Calcutta, on the occasions of the visit
of H.R.H. the Prince of Wales, my father did not see so
much of the Minister as he otherwise would have done;
and this was a source of much mutual regret. But everything that princely hospitality could suggest, in the providing of house, servants, horses and carriages, and every
comfort, was done by Sir Salar Jung to render my father's
stay as pleasant and as comfortable as possible. He was
able to partake of the hospitalities of the palace, too, on

several occasions, especially that of the grand *fête* given on the arrival of Sir Richard Meade as Resident at Hyderabad ; and he was able also to accept and enjoy invitations to the Residency, and among other friends. One great regret to him was that his health did not admit of his taking the long journey to Calcutta, in order to be present at the great gathering of the members of the "Order of the Star of India." He wrote his apologies to Sir Bartle Frere, begging him, if he would, to make known to H.R.H. the reason of his non-attendance, and received in reply a note which gratified him exceedingly. Not only was Sir Bartle Frere desired by the Prince of Wales to assure Colonel Taylor how much he regretted being deprived of the opportunity of making his personal acquaintance, but he added that he wished Colonel Taylor especially to know what pleasure he had derived from the perusal of his works on the voyage out to India. This gracious message and recognition of his literary labours were very pleasant to him, and afforded another instance, among so many at that time, of the graceful thoughtfulness and kindly feeling of his Royal Highness. In January 1876 my father was once more attacked by his old enemy, the jungle fever, and for many days and nights it seemed doubtful whether he would be spared to us yet a while. On the advice of his medical attendants, we took him back to Bombay, the climate there being considered better for his complaint, as it was more relaxing, and had not the excessive irritating dryness of Hyderabad. He remained at Bombay for a month. During this time he received many visits from persons acquainted with his Indian career and literary works, and enjoyed, on several occasions, long and earnest conversations with them, especially on subjects connected with native education and literature.

On this latter point he was exceedingly anxious, and it was his purpose, had his life been spared, to have contributed a series of letters to 'The Times of India' on the subject. In one letter, to a native gentleman friend, which has been largely quoted, after thanking him for his criticisms on 'Seeta,' and admitting that it is impossible for a writer, not a Hindoo, to describe Brahminical observances and caste customs with absolute correctness, he thus proceeds :—

"Now, why do not you, or some one of your friends, take up the subject of novels or tales, and instruct *us* on the subject of your people? If you wrote in Marathi, or Gujerati, you would have a vast audience. If in English, we—if the work were simply and truthfully written—would welcome the author warmly. Think of the still existing popularity of Goldsmith's 'Vicar of Wakefield,' which is undying; and how simple and pathetic the tale is. You have matter, too, for a hundred romances in Grant Duff's History, if you follow history ; but that is not needed for general interest so much as writing that will move the hearts of the people, and become the foundation of a national literature of fiction, healthy, pure, and instructive to future generations. Why should we know only the dark side of Hindooism, and see none of the bright and light side, from the pens of its sons, now so rapidly advancing and advanced in modern science and thought? Any one of your people who might attempt this department of literature would, if he wrote simply, naturally, and without pedantry, secure for himself not only present reputation, but undying fame. I cannot believe the ability is wanting; all that is required is to be stimulated to healthy exertion on a pure model to achieve a decided success."

And on another occasion he writes :—

"I am glad to hear that my works have been read, if it be only to prove to those who read them that my interest in the people of India, of all classes, is as strong as ever, and increases with time. I would fain see the educated portion striving to strike out new lines of occupation for

themselves ; and I do not despair of yet seeing illustrations of native life, native legends, and native history
written by yourselves. Such as I am, though we strive
never so much, cannot penetrate beyond the surface of
that we see ; and as for myself, in regard to ' Tara,' ' Seeta,'
and my other books, where I have tried to work out phases
of native character, male and female, I only hope I have
produced pictures something like reality, and not carica-
tures. I think portions of ' Tara' and ' Seeta' would translate easily into Marathi; and I should like to hear that
extracts of these books were done into Marathi to serve as
reading-books for the new generation. Until Marathi and
other native languages have a homely literature of their
own, I confess there is the want of a principle which
would encourage many to better things."

On the 15th March we embarked on board the s.s.
Australia, belonging to the Rubattino Company, who had
with great kindness reserved two cabins for my father's
and my own use, without extra charge, in spite of an over-
full complement of passengers. We were bound for Genoa,
as we intended passing a little time in the south of France
until the spring should be far enough advanced to permit
of our return home. On the voyage my father became far
more ill, and the loss of all power in his lower limbs was
a great additional trial. He could no longer walk at all,
and was carried up and down from his berth to his chair
on deck. We reached Genoa, however, in safety on the
6th April, after a very calm voyage of twenty-one days,
and travelled on next day to Mentone, where becoming
gradually worse, and more and more helpless, he sank to
rest peacefully and painlessly on the 13th of May 1876.

To the last my dear father retained all the brightness
of his intellect, and his interest in all that passed. The
night before his death he heard read with great pleasure
the account of the arrival of H.R.H. the Prince of Wales

in England, and spoke long and earnestly of the royal visit to India; of the good it was likely to produce there; of the courtesy which distinguished the Prince's behaviour to all natives of whatever degree, and his wish that such an example might be largely followed.

The papers both of England and India were filled with notices, all speaking of the varied and great talents my dear father possessed as soldier, administrator, man of science and of letters; but we, whose privilege it was to be with him in his home, knew him best as the tenderest and most loving of parents, the wise friend, the true-hearted, humble Christian gentleman, ever casting his cares upon Him who cared for him in his strange neglected boyhood and early manhood, and who helped him to become what he was in private life, and to attain the public distinctions which were awarded to him.

He rests at Mentone, in that spot so sacred to many English families and homes, amid the lovely scenes he delighted in, and among the sweet flowers he loved so well.

A simple cross of white marble marks his grave, on which are inscribed the last words he uttered on earth:—

"The Eternal God is thy Refuge, and underneath are the everlasting arms."

ALICE M. TAYLOR.

Hunmanby Vicarage, 15th Sept. 1877.

THE END.